Essay Index

CARLYLE'S FRIENDSHIPS
AND OTHER STUDIES

Frontispiece. Line drawing of Carlyle made by the Bloomsbury artist Duncan Grant in 1970 from a photograph of 1867 by Julia Margaret Cameron.

For Professor Saunders.
Thomas Carlyle after Mrs Cameron by D.G.

CARLYLE'S FRIENDSHIPS
AND OTHER STUDIES

CHARLES RICHARD SANDERS

DUKE UNIVERSITY PRESS

DURHAM, N. C.

1977

DEDICATION

To my wife, Virginia Hightower Sanders, who was the first to help me with Carlyle studies and who has contributed much to all that I have done, and to those faithful friends who through many years could always be depended upon for encouragement and assistance, particularly George and Renée Armour, David DeLaura, Kenneth J. Fielding, Duncan Grant, Gordon S. Haight, the late Frederick W. Hilles, Walter Leuba, Carlisle Moore, Gordon N. Ray, James S. Ritchie, Norman H. Strouse, and Frank Taylor.

CONTENTS

PREFACE

Until recently the social side of Carlyle's nature has been far too much neglected. Although his letters contain many passages in which, weary of the city and the crowd, he expresses a deep-felt yearning for the country and solitude, they also contain passages of equal sincerity and strength in which he expresses his desire for companionship and conversation with other human beings. Dominant in him was a conviction that a man does not fulfill himself as either an individual or a writer without the stimulus, approval, and disapproval which only close association with other men and women can provide.

This volume deals with only a few of the many friendships which enriched Carlyle's life. Those which are studied here are highly various, however, and demonstrate the remarkable talent which Carlyle had for receiving pleasure and profit from friends who were strikingly different among themselves. There were both discrimination and catholicity in Carlyle's choice of his friends. The wide range of his friendships included Thomas Murray, Robert Mitchell, Edward Irving, Francis Jeffrey, John Sterling, Robert Browning, John Stuart Mill, Charles Dickens, John Forster, W. E. Forster, John Ruskin, Ralph Waldo Emerson, Charles Gavan Duffy, Henry Parkes, Charles Eliot Norton, James Anthony Froude, Thomas and James Spedding, Richard Monckton Milnes, Arthur Helps, the Marshalls of Leeds, the Stanleys of Alderley, Lord Monteagle and members of his family, Charles Buller and other members of his family, Lord and Lady Ashburton and other members of their circle, Basil Montagu, Mrs. Montagu, and their family, and various members of the Strachey family. Some of these friendships have been studied; others are being studied; and still others need very much to be studied. The more we know about his relation to his friends, the better will we understand him.

The "other studies" included here are articles first published in widely scattered places and therefore not easily available to the reader. I hope that they will prove worthy of inclusion in this volume.

ABBREVIATED REFERENCES

Carlyle, *Works*. Thomas Carlyle, *Works*. Centenary Edition. 30 vols. London: Chapman and Hall, 1896–99.

Carlyle and His Contemporaries. *Carlyle and His Contemporaries*, ed. John Clubbe. Durham, N.C.: Duke University Press, 1976.

Collected Letters. *The Collected Letters of Thomas and Jane Welsh Carlyle*, ed. C. R. Sanders, K. J. Fielding, Ian Campbell, John Clubbe, and Aileen Christianson. 7 vols. Durham, N.C.: Duke University Press, 1970, 1977.

Froude, *Carlyle*. James Anthony Froude. *Thomas Carlyle: A History of the First Forty Years of His Life, 1795–1835; A History of His Life in London, 1834–81.* 4 vols. London: Longmans, Green, 1882; 1884.

Harrold, *Sartor*. Charles F. Harrold, ed. *Sartor Resartus*, by Thomas Carlyle. New York: Odyssey Press, 1937.

NLS. The National Library of Scotland, Edinburgh.

Wilson, *Carlyle*. David Alec Wilson. *Carlyle*. 6 vols. London: Kegan Paul, Trench, Trubner and Co., Ltd.; New York: E.P. Dutton and Co., 1923–34.

CARLYLE'S FRIENDSHIPS
AND OTHER STUDIES

THE VICTORIAN REMBRANDT:
CARLYLE'S PORTRAITS OF
HIS CONTEMPORARIES

"I care very little about the stars. I look round upon my fellow-creatures," William Allingham heard the old Carlyle say.[1] The statement is significant in many ways, coming as it does from one who in his youth had achieved proficiency in mathematics at the University of Edinburgh and who at one time was a serious candidate for a position as an astronomical observer. This marked interest in people was lifelong with Carlyle. It appeared quite as early as his interest in mathematics and various other subjects. In his old age he wrote about the fascination that certain faces in the village kirk had for him in his childhood: "Strangely vivid are some twelve or twenty of those old faces I used to see every Sunday, whose names, employments or precise dwelling places I never knew, but whose portraits are yet clear to me as in a mirror."[2] It was not, moreover, people in mass who gripped his imagination but people in their separate identities, people as individuals. A. H. Upham has expressed this well: "Carlyle's real interest lay in depicting not peoples but *people* that were unusual to the point of fantasy, from Richard Arkwright, the 'bag-cheeked, pot-bellied, much-enduring, much-inventing barber' of Chartism to sea-green Robespierre and the rest of the Procession of Deputies."[3] Yet Carlyle early became aware of a conflict in his nature between this interest and his strongly antisocial tendencies, a conflict that also proved to be lifelong. From first to last, there were

1. *Diary*, ed. H. Allingham and D. Radford (London, 1907), p. 270. For other studies of Carlyle's skill in portraiture, see R. Brimley Johnson, *Pen Portraits by Thomas Carlyle* (London, 1906); Benjamin D. Chamberlin, "Carlyle as a Portrait Painter," *Sewanee Review*, XXXVI (July 1928), 329–41; and Logan Pearsall Smith, "The Rembrandt of English Prose," in *Reperusals and Re-collections* (New York, 1937), pp. 202–21. The range and importance of the portraits imbedded in Carlyle's letters is discussed in my article "Carlyle's Letters," *Bulletin of the John Rylands University Library of Manchester*, XXXVIII (Sept. 1955), 199–224.
2. Froude, *Carlyle*, I, 10.
3. "Rabelaisianism in Carlyle," *Modern Language Notes*, XXXIII (Nov. 1918), 413.

many times in his life when he wished to shut himself off from other
people with their clamorous noises and furious, meaningless activities. The conflict is reflected very clearly in some good advice he
gave to Jane Welsh in a letter dated 8 January 1824: "My dearest
Jane! if you would avoid being wretched, never estrange yourself
from the beaten ways of men: mix in their concerns, participate in
their interests, imitate their common habits, however poor and mean.
No one knows more bitterly than I the consequence of neglecting
this."[4] The conflict also was in his mind when he made the important
decision to leave the lonely farmhouse of Craigenputtoch and to live
in London. Soon after the Carlyles had established themselves in
Chelsea, Carlyle wrote a letter to his brother, Dr. John Carlyle, which
suggests that he sensed at last some possibility of victory over the
antisocial side of himself: "Never (as I have long felt) till a man get
into practical contact with the men round him, and learn to take and
give influence there, does he enjoy the free consciousness of his existence. Alas, I have long felt this, and felt it in vain. Nevertheless
there is a kind of inextinguishable hope in me that it *shall not* always
be so; that once, for some short season, I shall live before I die."[5]
With the excellent example of one of his heroes, Dr. Samuel Johnson,
before his eyes in Boswell's great book, he valiantly fought this battle
for the rest of his life and achieved, not complete victory, but magnificent results. One result was the tremendous affection that his
generation as a whole came to have for him. "I may say," he wrote
truthfully from Mentone a few months after his wife's death, "I have
been well loved by my contemporaries—taken as a body corporate—
thank God!"[6] Another extremely important result was the hundreds
of inimitable portraits of his contemporaries that he left for posterity
to enjoy.

To draw these portraits, Carlyle had to conquer not only his re-
curring desire to escape from people but a strong desire, also recur-
ring, to escape from the present age into the past. At times his antipathy for his own time was intense. "Mingle with the bright spirits of
former ages . . . ," he wrote in a letter to William Graham in 1821; "the

4. *The Love Letters of Thomas Carlyle and Jane Welsh*, ed. Alexander Carlyle (London and New York, 1909), I, 321.

5. Dated 28 Oct. 1834. In *Letters of Thomas Carlyle, 1826–1836*, ed. C. E. Norton
(London and New York, 1889), p. 459.

6. Froude, *Carlyle*, IV, 339.

concentrated essence of the past will entice you from the weary insipidity of the present."[7] In the England of 1830 there was very little
to admire: "Alas, poor England, stupid, purblind, pudding-eating
England! Bentham with his Mills grinding thee out Morality; and
some Macaulay, also be-aproned and a grinder, testing it and decry-
ing it, because it is not his own Whig-established *Quern*-morality!"[8]
Past and Present (1843) was born out of Carlyle's efforts to persuade
the present to profit from the lessons that the past could teach. It
badly needed such lessons. It was, moreover, a time which placed
many difficulties in the way of a writer attempting to deal adequately
with a great historic subject, as Carlyle felt that he was doing in his
work on Cromwell's age. "No history of it *can* be written," he wrote
to Emerson in 1845, almost in despair, "to this wretched, fleering,
sneering, canting, twaddling, God-forgetting generation. How can
you explain men to Apes by the Dead Sea?"[9]

Fortunately, in other moods Carlyle spoke of his own age as one
full of interest and of his intense desire to understand it. In 1828 he
wrote in his notebook: "Above all things, I should like to *know England*, the essence of social life in this same little Island of ours. But
how? No one that I speak to can throw light on it; not he that has
worked and lived in the midst of it for half a century. The blind following the blind! Yet each cries out: What glorious sunshine we
have!"[10] The here and now, if rightly observed and understood, could
reveal its own grandeur and could be a noble subject for thought and
writing. *Sartor Resartus* emphasizes this idea. The following passage
was entered in his notebook about the time he was completing *Sartor*:
"Nevertheless, *God is in it*: here, even here, is the Revelation of the
Infinite in the Finite; a majestic Poem (tragic, comic or epic), couldst
thou but read it and recite it! Watch it then; study it, catch the secret
of it, and proclaim the same in such accent as is given thee.—Alas!
the spirit is willing, but the flesh is weak."[11] His belief that a thinking
man should not turn his back on his own age had become a strong

7. *Letters of Thomas Carlyle to William Graham*, ed. John Graham, Jr. (Princeton,
1950), pp. 23–24.
8. *Two Note Books of Thomas Carlyle from 23 March 1822 to 16 May 1832*, ed.
C. E. Norton (New York, 1898), p. 172.
9. Dated 16 Feb. In *The Correspondence of Thomas Carlyle and Ralph Waldo
Emerson, 1834–1872*, ed. C. E. Norton (Boston and New York, 1894), II, 92–93.
10. *Two Note Books*, p. 132.
11. *Ibid.*, p. 211.

conviction with him by 1842 and was the basis of his criticism of the New England *Dial* as he expressed it in a letter to Emerson:

One of my grand difficulties [in working on *Cromwell*] I suspect to be that I cannot write *two Books at once*; cannot be in the seventeenth century and in the nineteenth at one and the same moment; a feat which excels even that of the Irishman's *bird*: "Nobody but a bird can be in two places at once!" For my heart is sick and sore in behalf of my own poor generation. . . .

I love your *Dial*, and yet it is with a kind of shudder. You seem to me in danger of dividing yourselves from the Fact of this present Universe, in which alone, ugly as it is, can I find any anchorage, and soaring away after Ideas, Beliefs, Revelations, and such like,—into perilous altitudes, as I think; beyond the curve of perpetual frost, for one thing! . . . . Surely I could wish you *returned* into your own poor nineteenth century, its follies and maladies, its blind or half-blind, but gigantic toilings, its laughter and its tears, and trying to evolve in some measure the hidden Godlike that lies in *it*;—that seems to me the kind of feat for literary men. . . . Well, I do believe, for one thing, a man has no right to say to his own generation, turning quite away from it, "Be damned!" It is the whole Past and the whole Future, this same cotton-spinning, dollar-hunting, canting and shrieking, very wretched generation of ours. Come back into it, I tell you.[12]

We know that Carlyle never gave up his own interest in history and the past. *Past and Present, Cromwell*, and *Frederick the Great* were all to be written after 1842. The danger was not, as he knew, in studying the past; the danger was in forgetting or rejecting the present in his study of the past. More and more he came to appreciate the role of the thinking, observant man who kept his eyes open wide to the world around him and who served his own and later generations as the abstract and brief chronicle of the time. "A man with eyes," he wrote to Varnhagen von Ense, "with soul and heart, to tell me in candid clearness what he saw passing round him in this universe—is and remains for ever a welcome man."[13] There can be no doubt that Carlyle consciously and conscientiously took this role on himself as he watched his Victorian world with mingled fascination, antipathy, and delight.

To the task of observing and portraying his contemporaries he brought the same high gifts that served him as he drew his memorable

---

12. *Correspondence of Carlyle and Emerson*, II, 10–12.
13. Of 19 Dec. 1842. In "Letters from Carlyle to Varnhagen von Ense," *New Review*, VI (April 1892), 416–18.

historic portraits. These gifts were duly recognized and appreciated in his own day and have been acknowledged in later times. Froude placed Carlyle at the head of literary portrait painters.[14] John Burroughs, Logan Pearsall Smith, and others have compared him to Albert Dürer or to Rembrandt.[15] The historian Lecky spoke of "his unrivalled power of etching out a subject by a few words so as to make it stand out in prominent relief," and called him "the very greatest of word-painters."[16] Even Lytton Strachey spoke of him, not quite accurately, as "a psalm-singing Scotchman with a power of observation and description which knocks you flat."[17]

Certainly he was served well by a pair of remarkable eyes. Emerson spoke of them as "thirsty eyes," "devouring eyes," "portrait-eating, portrait-painting eyes." He found, even in a photograph of Carlyle, "the organism of the eye full of England, the valid eye."[18] Froude said: "Of all the men whom I have ever known, he had the greatest power of taking in and remembering the minute particulars of what he saw, and of then reproducing them in language."[19] One of Carlyle's first biographers, W. H. Wylie, was impressed by the contrast between his bright blue eyes, "the chief charm of this strange, rugged countenance," and the rest of his face. The other features were hard, stern, cold, and forbidding, but the eyes were remarkably quick, yet sad, wistful, and infinitely tender.[20] After William Allingham had gazed for a few moments at the corpse of Thomas Carlyle, whom he had known well, he went home and made the following entry in his diary: "The large beautiful eyelids were closed forever on a pair of eyes that, whether for carrying messages inwards or outwards, had scarce met their equals on earth or left such behind."[21]

Carlyle's gift of language was equal to his power of observation. It was a gift, he believed, that he had inherited from his father: "None of us will ever forget that bold glowing style of his, flowing free from the untutored soul, full of metaphor, though he knew not what met-

14. *Carlyle*, II, 284.
15. Burroughs' *Fresh Fields* (1885) is quoted to this effect by Wilson, *Carlyle*, V, 577. For Smith, see n. 1 above.
16. For Lecky's praise of Carlyle as "the very greatest of word-painters," see Wilson, *Carlyle*, VI, 311–12.
17. In an unpublished letter formerly in the possession of the late James Strachey, his brother.
18. *Correspondence of Carlyle and Emerson*, I, 268, 334; II, 126.
19. *Carlyle*, III, 259.
20. *Thomas Carlyle* (London, 1881), p. 327. See also p. 71.
21. *Diary*, p. 309.

aphor was, with all manner of potent words which he appropriated and applied with surprising accuracy—brief, energetic, conveying the most perfect picture, definite, clear, not in ambitious colors, but in full white sunlight. Emphatic I have heard him beyond all men. In anger he had no need of oaths."[22] He had highest praise for his father's "clearest brief portraits" of Annandale notabilities and compared his father's skill here with that of Wordsworth. But he added that even Wordsworth was inferior.[23]

We may note that he spoke of his father as an untutored soul who used metaphor but did not know what metaphor was and who painted in black and white rather than in ambitious colors. The question arises as to whether Carlyle himself was a conscious artist deliberately using definite methods. His writings, we know, contain many scornful references to the fine arts and what he called, rather loosely, dilettantism. Froude reports that he "often ferociously insisted that he knew nothing about the fine arts, and wished to know nothing."[24] Certainly he would have nothing to do with art as applied to portrait painting if it violated the principle of realism and produced anything other than a likeness of its subject: "A portrait, an actual *likeness*, were it done only with a burnt stick on the board of a pair of bellows,—how infinitely preferable to the finest brain work when it is a *no-likeness* of anything in heaven or earth."[25] In his historical writing he felt greatly handicapped until he had been able to find portraits that he took to be reasonably faithful likenesses of the subjects involved. He told his friend Duffy that he had formed the habit of pasting engraved portraits on a screen in his workroom when he could find no better ones of the people he was writing about.[26] A leader in the movement to establish National Portrait Galleries in England and Scotland in 1853 and 1854, a movement which he suggested that the Prince Consort might worthily promote, he insisted in letters to Lord Ashburton and David Laing that the pictures selected should be those which gave definite evidence of being real likenesses. To Laing he wrote: "In all my poor Historical investigations, it has been, and always is,

22. Froude, *Carlyle*, I, 16.
23. *Letters and Memorials of Jane Welsh Carlyle*, ed. J. A. Froude (New York, 1907), I, 3. See also Wilson, *Carlyle*, V, 491.
24. *Carlyle*, III, 265, 421.
25. Unpublished letter of 22 Jan. 1858 in the John Rylands Library.
26. Sir Charles Gavan Duffy, *Conversations with Carlyle* (New York, 1892), pp. 92–93.

one of the most primary wants to procure a bodily likeness of the personage inquired after; a good *Portrait* if such exists; failing that, even an indifferent if sincere one. In short, *any* representation, made by a faithful human creature, of that Face and Figure, which *he* saw with his eyes, and which I can never see with mine, is now valuable to me, and much better than none at all. This, which is my own deep experience, I believe to be, in a deeper or less deep degree, the universal one." [27] In writing to Lord Ashburton, he declared: "My experience is, there lies more elucidation of the hero's real character in such a Portrait than in half the written Lives you will read about him"; he deplored the difficulty he had had in Berlin in an effort to find an authentic picture of Frederick II; and he expressed an intense desire to see "an exact likeness of the Man Jesus." [28] Once in talking to Richard Monckton Milnes he said, "I would rather have one real glimpse of the young Jew face of Christ than see all the Raphaels in the world." [29] He repeatedly insisted that the artist should actually see the person whom he was portraying: even an Erasmus by a Vandyke was not wanted. [30]

Carlyle believed, furthermore, that a good likeness always placed the emphasis upon the face and eyes. Whistler, he declared with some irritation in a letter to C. E. Norton, had failed precisely here in painting Carlyle himself:

Whistler has vanished from my eyes and from everybody's that I hear of for a long while, laboring and lounging somewhere about Liverpool in some Armidas Castle there, who knows? Besides which the full-length portrait you had put your hopes in seemed to me little other than a fatuity; was considered to be unfinished after many weary sittings, and to be a portrait not of my poor features, but of the clothes I had on; which, and not the face, seemed to occupy the strenuous attention and vigorous activity of my singular Artist all the while. He made a solemn enough "Exhibition"

27. See Wilson, *Carlyle*, V, 100–102. The Library of the University of Edinburgh has the original letter in complete form.

28. *Ibid.*, pp. 39 ff.

29. Wilson, *Carlyle*, III, 45. Joseph Neuberg, after accompanying Carlyle through a Berlin picture gallery in 1852, wrote: "Carlyle made all kinds of side-thrusts at the painters, with their pictures of Christ and their Madonnas; and Cornelius several times called him 'a godless man.'" Thomas Sadler, "Carlyle and Neuberg," *Macmillan's Magazine*, L (Aug. 1884), 289.

30. Wilson, *Carlyle*, V, 337. Carlyle told Allingham: "People set about writing history in an entirely wrong manner. They ought to try and *see* the people and events, and set them forth in due order and all possible clearness." *Diary*, p. 262. See also the *Correspondence of Carlyle and Emerson*, I, 272–73.

of this and other paintings and etchings; of all which the etchings only seemed to me to have any real excellence.[31]

When in 1869, three years after the death of Mrs. Carlyle, an artist was attempting to use a photograph as the basis of an acceptable portrait of her, Carlyle gave him this advice: "The eyes, in every face, are the chief feature; but in this face they were in it *infinitely* so,— bright hazel, radiant with many meanings."[32]

Actually, Carlyle as a portrait painter was a very great artist whose conscious methods are always interesting and often highly effective. Not merely the principle of emphasis and fidelity of vision concerned him; he was fully aware of the importance of shadows in portraits. One of his favorite books was Boswell's *Life of Johnson*, and he did not fail to note the judicious balance of light and shadow deliberately employed there. Carlyle regretted that Lockhart failed at times to use such a balance in his *Life of Scott*. His comment here has often been quoted: "How delicate, decent, is English biography, bless its mealy mouth!"[33] Allingham reports once hearing Carlyle praise, certainly with some exaggeration, Samuel Cooper, the seventeenth-century miniature painter, as "the best portrait-painter who ever lived," because he was faithful to his subject in every respect; when Cromwell told him to paint the wart into his portrait, he did.[34] In Carlyle's own portraits, however, as in Rembrandt's, the use of shadow serves an artistic purpose that goes far beyond mere truthfulness or what Carlyle liked to call "veracity." It produces an effect of depth, solidity, and richness that corresponds to the use of bass chords in music. His pictures are never flat or shallow; however boldly certain details in them may project themselves forward, others that are fully as significant flow back into the darkness and unite themselves with mysterious entities of the dark. As the various details of the portrait are bathed in this harmony of light and shadow, they find their right proportions, receive their proper emphasis, and fall into their natural relationships. The Victorians quite appropriately compared Carlyle's descriptive power with the stereoscope on their

31. Dated 1 April 1875. From the autograph letter in the Harvard Library.
32. From a letter dated 23 April 1869. In R. H. Shepherd, *Thomas Carlyle* (London, 1881), II, 236.
33. Froude, *Carlyle*, I, Preface, ix–xi.
34. *Diary*, p. 271.

parlor tables. G. S. Venables said that Carlyle had "a stereoscopic imagination" and that he "put everything before you in a solid shape."[35] After reading the first two volumes of Carlyle's *Frederick the Great*, Emerson wrote in his *Diary*: "I do not so much read a stereotype page, as I see the eyes of the writer looking into my eyes, with winks and long-commanding glances, and stereoscoping every figure that passes, and every hill, river, wood, hummock, and pebble in the long perspective."[36]

In observing and representing the physical details of his subjects in their right proportions and proper perspective, furthermore, Carlyle rarely treats these details as ends in themselves, however interesting or even picturesque they may be. Rather, he wishes to discover and suggest what the persons with whom he deals really *were*, where their points of strength or weakness lay, and what they might be worth in quality of spirit and fiber of character. Like Chaucer, Rembrandt, and in our time William Butler Yeats, he produces appraisal portraits—pictures that are also judgments. Hence, he selects with greatest care, as they do, the details to be painted into the portrait. The extremely important question arises as to what principles he follows in interpreting and evaluating these details.

Certainly the principles upon which he worked have nothing to do with phrenology, which was in its heyday in the first third of the nineteenth century. This was the time when the writings of Spurzheim were in great demand in England, when the great doctor himself visited Edinburgh and was received with acclaim there, and when, for a while, his disciple George Combe also flourished in Edinburgh. Carlyle was never once tempted to yield to the doctrines of the phrenologists. As a thinker, his own head was much too hard for that, and one guesses that they would have had considerable difficulty in reading the meaning of the various bulges and the absence of bulges that went to make up the shaggy contours of his skull. We know that in the winter of 1832–33 he heard with great delight a paper read by Sir William Hamilton in Edinburgh, which Carlyle declared, "completely demolished" George Combe.[37] Perhaps the nearest Carlyle ever came to using the methods of phrenology was

35. Wilson, *Carlyle*, V, 538.
36. *Ibid.*, p. 313.
37. Wylie, p. 152.

in his judgment on John Henry Newman. In 1879, soon after Newman had been made a cardinal, the old Carlyle in talking with William Darwin, son of Charles, is reported to have said of Newman:
"He is a kind, affectionate man, who hopes to creep into Heaven under the Pope's petticoats"; and then to have added: "but he has no
occiput." Young Darwin investigated and discovered that Woolner's
bust of Newman actually showed that he had no back to his head.[38]
When we place beside Carlyle's comment here the remark that
Froude said he once made to him, namely, that Cardinal Newman
did not have "the intellect of a moderate-sized rabbit,"[39] we may
conclude that Carlyle still had a long way to go before he achieved
the nicely phrased and delicately delineated interpretations of scientific phrenology. Furthermore, it was not on the basis of the peculiar
shape of Newman's head in the back that Carlyle judged him; rather,
it was because of what went on in the front of it.

His methods have much of intuitive judgment in them and something of the reading of character through the old-fashioned study of
physiognomy. We are told that when G. F. Watts was painting Carlyle's portrait he found it impossible, even after he had summoned
his strongest arguments, to get his subject to agree with him on two
points: first, that art was worth something beyond the historical
record it could give; and second, that physiognomy was not always
to be trusted—that a high forehead or a long upper lip was not necessarily a sign of intellect, or gray eyes of a contemplative temperament.
D. A. Wilson, in commenting on this incident, says that Watts could
never in this world have persuaded Carlyle that his Jane's long upper
lip, which her adored father also had, was not an indication of intellectual strength.[40] When Carlyle was seeking the most authentic
likeness of John Knox and first gazed with delight upon the Somerville portrait, his comments were characteristic; "I never saw him
before—now I understand the man. See how firm and upright he is.
I like that mouth. He was one of the salt of the earth."[41] Yet it was
not merely a person's face but the appearance and motions of the
whole body that gave Carlyle hints as to that individual's character.
Coleridge's wobbling from one side of the path to the other as he

38. Wilson, *Carlyle*, VI, 448.
39. *Ibid.*, V, 450–51. See also Duffy, pp. 220–21.
40. *Carlyle*, VI, 130–31.
41. *Ibid.*, p. 329. See also p. 316.

walked filled him with disgust. The *St. James Gazette* for 5 February 1881 relates an incident concerning the way Carlyle judged a man that is so amusing we can only hope it is true:

> His shrewdness, especially in judging of character from small indications, was extraordinary. He once denounced, as a scoundrel, a man of business, who, at the time, was in the best repute, and who, shortly afterwards, turned out to deserve all that he had said against him. "How," he was asked, "did you find him out, Mr. Carlyle?" "Oh," said he, "I saw rogue in the twist of the false hip of him as he went out at the door."[42]

The gift of metaphor that Carlyle believed he had inherited from his father served him very well indeed in his portraits. It often enabled him to suggest a single unifying effect through a few words and to throw the emphasis skillfully upon the one important detail or quality. It also helps to explain why his portraits are almost never stereotyped. The following words, taken from a letter to his mother, 11 June 1837, leave us with a somewhat different impression of King William IV from that which we usually encounter in history: "The King is by many said to be dying here; dropsy in the heart. Poor old fellow, I saw him about a fortnight ago, coming in from Windsor through Hyde Park: he looked fresh and decent; clean as from spring water. The little boys cried: 'Ha, old Billy, how d'you do?' "[43] The simile of the fresh spring water combined with the delightfully humanizing greeting of the little boys works a kind of magic in this picture. Louis Napoleon is treated just as skillfully but does not fare so well intrinsically in the following portrait, in which, after a series of interesting details, one bold metaphor takes over and dominates the picture:

> Met him at dinner—he made up to me rather, understanding me to be a writer, who might perhaps be of help to him somehow. His talk was a puddle of revolutionary nonsense. He was internally a mass of darkness. I used to meet him often in the street, mostly about Sloane Square, driving a cab, with a little tiger behind; his face had a melancholy look that was rather affecting at first, but I soon recognized that it was the sadness of an Opera Singer who cannot get an engagement. When I heard of him afterwards as Emperor, I said to myself, "Gad, sir, you've got an opera engagement such as no one could possibly have expected!"[44]

42. Quoted by Wylie, p. 218.
43. *New Letters of Thomas Carlyle*, ed. Alexander Carlyle (London and New York, 1904), I, 79–80.
44. Allingham's *Diary*, p. 261.

We are left with the impression that substantially the French Emperor from first to last was nothing and that he could appear otherwise only through acting a role. Carlyle refuses to be impressed by the mere size of Shelley's friend, Edward Trelawney, as suggested by the metaphor in the following passage: "The Buller rout had Trelawney for lion, a huge black-whiskered, beetle-browed column of a man (carrying nothing that I valued)."[45] Likewise, he uses a single fundamental image to annihilate George Sand and her followers: "The French literature of G. Sand and Co., which many people told me was a new-birth, I found to be a detestable putrifaction, —new-life of nothing but maggots and blue-bottles."[46] The same device is used in the condemnation of Heine as a "filthy, foetid sausage of spoiled vituals."[47] A single image also dominates Carlyle's description of Southey as being all leanness and long legs, looking when he rose from his chair like a lean pair of tongs.[48] Many of these metaphors suggest the fireside, the barnyard, and the surrounding hill country of Carlyle's boyhood. A surprising number of them refer, like those in *King Lear,* to animals and birds. They are used, for instance, to intensify the unfavorable impression that Carlyle had received of Charles Babbage, the mechanical genius and mathematician: "Babbage continues eminently unpleasant to me, with his frog mouth and viper eyes, with his hide-bound, wooden irony, and the acridest egotism looking through it."[49] Jeremy Bentham is "a rhinoceros—strong and clumsy."[50] Benjamin Jowett is "a poor little good-humored owlet of a body,—'Oxford Liberal,' and very conscious of being so; not knowing right hand from left otherwise."[51] Two leading Oxford High Churchmen fare even worse than Jowett: "Your two Oxford 'Dignitaries' are interesting scarecrows; hard to say which is uglier,— Pusey with his praying[?] suffering contracted weazel countenance,

45. Letter to Dr. John Carlyle, 14 July 1836, *New Letters,* I, 14.
46. Undated letter to John Forster, written about 1844, in the collection of autograph letters in the Victoria and Albert Museum.
47. Wilson, *Carlyle,* VI, 23. Wilson also says that Carlyle, in talk with Sir M. E. Grant Duff, "tore up" Matthew Arnold for speaking of Heine as the "continuator" of Goethe.
48. Letter to Dr. John Carlyle, 23 March 1835, in Norton, *Letters of Carlyle, 1826–1836,* pp. 504–505; letter to Alexander Carlyle, 27 Feb. 1835, *ibid.,* p. 496.
49. Froude, *Carlyle,* I, 171.
50. Letter to Matthew Allen, 7 June 1820. Original in the John Rylands Library. Published in Richard Garnett's "Eight Unpublished Letters of Thomas Carlyle," *Archiv für das Studium der Neueren Sprachen und Litteraturen,* N.S. II (1899), 317 ff.
51. Letter to Dr. John Carlyle, 22 Aug. 1859, in *New Letters,* II, 200.

Sewel[l] with his small triumphant ferret one."[52] Emerson's face was
that of a cock; Wordsworth had the "immense head and great jaws"
of a crocodile; the historian Lecky, with his long neck, was a giraffe;
and Herbert Spencer was dismissed as "an immeasurable ass."[53] G. H.
Lewes, to Carlyle another extremely ugly man, is "*Ape* Lewes" or
"hairy Lewes," rather ludicrous in his role of gallant, Adonis, and
conqueror of hearts in George Eliot's life drama.[54] Although Carlyle
had some praise for Walt Whitman after reading *Democratic Vistas*,
in general he could not like him: "If you could endow the parish bull
with the faculty of human utterance and holding a pen between the
halves of his hoof, *this*, I imagine, is much the thing he would write,"
he wrote to Charles Eliot Norton of Whitman's poetry.[55] When he
visited Connop Thirlwall in 1843, he was greatly but not altogether
favorably impressed by Thirlwall's chaplain, whom he describes as
follows: "Turned of forty; lean and yellow; has boiled big eyes; a
neck head and nose giving you a notion of a gigantic human Snipe.
Is not that a beauty? . . . We are alone all but this Sucker-Chaplain or
Snipe."[56] Although these comparisons with animals and birds often
bring out unfavorable or unpleasant features and characteristics of
Carlyle's subjects, Monckton Milnes' cheerful good nature, liveliness,
and smallness of stature are all suggested by Carlyle's delightful description of him as "a pretty little robin-redbreast of a man."[57] Sometimes the metaphor may be involved in dramatic action, as in the fol-

52. Letter of 23 Sept. 1841 in the Henry W. and Albert A. Berg Collection of the
New York Public Library. Quoted with permission.

53. See, respectively, the letters to Jane W. Carlyle, 10 April 1841, Trinity College,
Cambridge; to Lady Ashburton, 3 Nov. 1847, collection of the Marquess of Northampton, Duffy, *Conversations with Carlyle*, p. 55; to John A. Carlyle, 4 Jan. 1873, NLS,
527.80; and Wilson, *Carlyle*, IV, 385.

54. Duffy, *Conversations with Carlyle*, pp. 222–23; Letter to Dr. John Carlyle, 2
Nov. 1854, from the unpublished original in the NLS. In a letter to his sister Mrs.
Aitken, 25 April 1850, Carlyle spoke of "a certain *dramatic* G. H. Lewes, an airy loose-
tongued merry-hearted being, with more sail than ballast" (*New Letters*, II, 93–94).
Yet Francis Espinasse says that Carlyle spoke of Lewes as "the Prince of Journalists."
Literary Recollections (London, 1893), p. 282.

55. Letter dated 2 Dec. 1875. Original in the Houghton Library at Harvard. See
also Moncure D. Conway, *Thomas Carlyle* (New York, 1881), p. 100; and Allingham's
Diary, 3 Oct. 1872, p. 212.

56. Letter to his wife, 19 July 1843, in Trudy Bliss's *Thomas Carlyle: Letters to
His Wife* (Cambridge, Mass., 1953), p. 173. Carlyle says further that this "portentous
human snipe" reminds him of C. H. Terrot, Bishop of Edinburgh. See Bliss, p. 115.

57. Letter to Emerson, 1 April 1840, in *Correspondence of Carlyle and Emerson*,
I, 302. Carlyle spoke of Milnes as "one of the idlest, cheeriest most gifted of fat little
men" in a letter to Emerson of 30 Dec. 1847 (*ibid.*, II, 188).

lowing account of Carlyle's clash with the well-known Radical, J. A. Roebuck:

> He is practicing as Advocate now, that little Roebuck, as lean, acrid, contentious and loquacious as ever. He flew at me, do what I would, some three or four times, like a kind of cockatrice,—had to be swept back again; far more to the *general* entertainment than to mine. He does not fly into a shriek like Maurice, that is his quality; but he is a very impertinent little unproductive gentleman; and I suppose has *made* many a man incline to shriek. We parted good friends,—with small wish on my part or his to meet again.[58]

Closely related to the use of a dominating image is Carlyle's fondness for epithets that, having once attached themselves to their subjects, are repeated again and again in the same or varied forms. "Seagreen Robespierre," "Mirabeau the Lion's whelp," "Ol' Clo' Disraeli," and the "People's William Gladstone" are familiar examples of this device. How remarkably ingenious Carlyle's use of it may be is well illustrated by the following passage from a letter of 1823 to Jane Welsh in which two sequences of such epithets—the one suggesting littleness, the other suggesting brisk, meaningless activity—are combined with faint praise and abundant metaphor to damn one of his rivals for her hand, Dr. Fyffe, who was from her hometown, Haddington:

> The coach had just reached Workman's door in Moffat, and I was sitting calmly on my place, reposing after a hard ride on horseback of nearly 20 miles, when a voice below pronounced my name in a tone of gladness; and whose should the voice be but your little Doctorkin's! It was Fyffe himself travelling like a weaver's shuttle from Edinburgh and back to it: He took his place beside me on the roof, and we journeyed together. "Miss Welsh, Sir," said he, "arrived at her Grandfather's the night before last." This joyful intelligence was given with an air of knowingness and self-sufficiency which I relished very little. The topic of "Miss Welsh" I studied to avoid for the rest of the day. This Fyffe is a jewel of a creature; made of the kindliest clay, feels good will towards many persons, ill will towards none; and his little spirit mounts and swells and whirls about with all the briskness of the freshest can of penny-beer. I cannot but admire the man, a little more would make me envy him. The lion is ruler of the forest, but the

58. Letter to his wife, 10 April 1841, from the original letter at Trinity College, Cambridge.

squirrel leads a merrier life: one had sometimes rather be the squirrel. I shall always entertain a species of affection for your Doctor: he is of the *genus* cricket, and I like all crickets.[59]

It is difficult to see how the energetic little doctor could have had much of a chance with the fair lady after this. As a matter of fact, we know that he did not.

Another standard device for delineating character which Carlyle did not fail to use is that of comparing or contrasting one person with another. When he meets Fonblanque, famous editor of the *Examiner*, in 1831, "something metallic in the tone of his voice" reminded him of the voice of Professor John Austin.[60] The following passage from a letter to Emerson skillfully combines the use of character foils with metaphor in treating Frederic Henry Hedge and Carlyle's publisher, Chapman: "Hedge is one of the sturdiest little fellows I have come across for many a day. A face like a rock; a voice like a howitzer; only his honest kind gray eyes reassure you a little. . . . Hedge came to me with tall lank Chapman at his side,—an innocent flail of a creature, with considerable impetus in him: the two when they stood up together looked like a circle and tangent,—in more senses than one."[61] There is pathos in a letter of 1836 to his brother John in which he speaks of how two living friends, John Sterling and Henry Taylor, suggest to him complementary sides of a very dear dead one: "He [Sterling] and Taylor often seem to me very strangely like the two *halves* of Edward Irving, living apart; it is a singular feeling, of sight and remembrance, of sadness and kindliness. My poor Irving is snatched away from me: away, away!"[62]

The most striking characteristic of Carlyle's portraits, however, is his way of dominating his subjects completely, in every instance and in every detail. Here again he suggests Rembrandt. From the Queen of England down to the gruesome corpse of a lowly workman that Carlyle gazed upon in a Paris morgue, all that came before his eye was instantaneously seized upon as subservient to his emotions and artistic imagination, and subject to the interpretations and judgments

59. *Love Letters*, I, 220–21. In Jane Welsh's letter to Carlyle of 15 April 1824, she calls Fyffe "Dr. Thumb." Wilson, *Carlyle*, I, 323.
60. *Two Note Books*, pp. 213–14.
61. Of 31 Aug. 1847. *Correspondence of Carlyle and Emerson*, II, 170–71.
62. *New Letters*, I, 5.

dictated by his clearly defined sense of values. In this respect, the portraits are simply like everything else that Carlyle touched in his long life. The habit of dominance was not merely in every stroke of his pen but in his very appearance. Emerson observed it early; and shortly after Carlyle made his inaugural address as Lord Rector at the University of Edinburgh in 1866, the Secretary of the University, Alexander Smith, commented significantly: "Altogether, in his aspect there was something aboriginal, as of a piece of unhewn granite, which had never been polished to any approved pattern, whose natural and original vitality had never been tampered with. In a word, there seemed to be no passivity about Mr. Carlyle; he was the diamond, and the world was his pane of glass."[63] His portraits, therefore, are the product of his "veracity" with a difference—the difference made by the intensely active mind through which they passed. They are evaluative portraiture as truly and completely as the splendid pictures of his contemporaries that William Butler Yeats has left in this century.

The quality of such highly individualized work depends largely upon the quality of the mind and hand that produce it—upon the trustworthiness of the artist's power of observation, the degree with which he may act responsibly with a sense of fidelity to his subject, the extent to which he has achieved skill in the technique of presentation, and the acceptability of the system of values by which he judges his subjects. The artist's complete dominance of his subject may simply result in misrepresentation and distortion unless he can measure up to very exacting requirements. The question is whether Carlyle does so. There are those who emphatically think he does not. Professor René Wellek speaks competently for them:

On the whole, Carlyle's sense of individuality and human personality seems grossly exaggerated by his enthusiasts. . . . Carlyle rarely enters a man's mind sympathetically: he frequently is content with sketching his external physiognomy, with a "flame-picture" or, at worst, with the lurid light of the theater or the grimace of a caricature. His portraits of Coleridge or Lamb are the achievements of a superb caricaturist, his sneering condemnations of Shelley, Keats, Hazlitt, or August Wilhelm Schlegel mere ventings of prejudice and spite. Carlyle's narrow range of sympathy is in itself a contradiction of the true "historic spirit" and must account for the

63. Wilson, *Carlyle*, VI, 49.

most repulsive traits of his adoration of mere power, which comes out in his attitude to the Irish or Polish question, to the Negroes or the Czechs.[64]

Undoubtedly Carlyle's opinions *were* dogmatic, his feelings were often violent, and his art unusually bold. His reactions to people were definite and vigorous, and he made little effort to control and subdue his feelings. What the old Carlyle in 1875 told Allingham about his attitude toward Cardinal Manning is thoroughly characteristic of him: "I have often been invited to places with the temptation of meeting Manning; but he is perhaps of all human creatures the one I would most decidedly refuse to meet. If we did, it might possibly end in actual blows, old as I am."[65] Is this the unpredictable, intensified crankiness and spleen of a lifelong dyspeptic, or is it the firm and unyielding integrity of a great artist and man? Whatever else it is, it is consistent. Carlyle had his moods, but they had remarkably little effect on his convictions, judgments, and attitude toward people.

Yet Carlyle's intimate friend Sir Charles Gavan Duffy says that Carlyle could never have brought himself to the point of deliberately misrepresenting or falsifying a subject he was painting: "I knew that one of his most notable gifts was the power of making by a few touches a likeness of a man's moral or physical aspect, not easily forgotten. His portraits were not always free from a strain of exaggeration, but they were never malicious, never intentionally caricatured; they represented his actual estimate of the person in question."[66] Duffy was an Irishman who had known what it was to suffer from Carlyle's frank expression of his low opinion of most Irishmen. He had an independent mind and had many times maintained his opinions in the face of opposite ones held by his friend. If we accept his assertion, as I think we may, we can proceed to examine Carlyle's values and ask whether he knew a good man when he saw one.

When Emerson made that remarkable early visit to Carlyle at

64. "Carlyle and the Philosophy of History," *Philological Quarterly*, XXIII (Jan. 1944), 73–74.

65. *Diary*, p. 240. We are reminded of Dr. Johnson again, particularly of his manner of dealing with James Macpherson. This kind of rough-grained individualism seems to have gone out of fashion. My students are often shocked at the behavior of Johnson and Carlyle, and they would scarcely approve of that of Cavaignac described below. Yet many pride themselves upon their own nonconformity.

66. Duffy, *Conversations with Carlyle*, p. 50.

Craigenputtoch in 1833, he drew Carlyle out precisely in reference to this question. About one week later Emerson recorded what he had found out in a letter to Alexander Ireland: "But his respect for eminent men, or rather his scale of eminence, is about the reverse of the popular scale. Scott, Macintosh, Jeffrey, Gibbon,—even Bacon— are no heroes of his; stranger yet, he hardly admires Socrates, the glory of the Greek world; but Burns, and Samuel Johnson, and Mirabeau, he said interested him, and I suppose whoever else has given himself with all his heart to a leading instinct, and has not *calculated* too much."[67] Carlyle's lukewarm attitude toward Socrates we must attempt to explain later. But his judgment of Scott, Jeffrey, and Bacon, taken with Emerson's words about giving oneself entirely to a leading instinct and not calculating too much, suggests one of the chief criteria by which Carlyle judged people. He certainly could not admire people who surrendered to the values of what he called the "world," even if it became known as civilization, or who allowed their original force to be tamed by it. And to attempt to fight fire with fire, to pit one's own counterschemes against the complex and everramifying schemes of the world, or, as it were, to try to outwit the world was a kind of surrender to it, which always proved to be futile and foolish. Carlyle liked men who faced the world squarely and defied it. His own father, he believed, was such a man. Cromwell was another. Burns and Samuel Johnson also had been such men. Among his own contemporaries Carlyle was pleased to find this untamable quality in a highly bred Frenchman, Godefroy Cavaignac. He wrote to Mill, 2 May 1836: "Cavaignac . . . strikes me as the best Frenchman by many degrees whom I have met with. A courageous energetic man, with much free Nature and *bonhomie* in his composition; really a Son of Nature, tho' French and in this time."[68] Almost a year later he wrote to his brother: "By the bye, I continue to find Cavaignac a most true-hearted well gifted, natural genuine wild man and Frenchman; on the whole, one of the best Brother men I fall in with here. He comes about once in the ten days; a wild proud man; who takes considerably to me."[69] In the following vignette of a comically dramatic scene in a London drawing room Carlyle lets us see Cavaignac

67. *Correspondence of Carlyle and Emerson*, I, 5.
68. *Letters of Thomas Carlyle to John Stuart Mill, John Sterling, and Robert Browning*, ed. Alexander Carlyle (London, 1923), p. 124.
69. Of 23 April 1837, *New Letters*, I, 70.

in action. It is in a letter of 24 July 1836 to Carlyle's wife. The "world" to be avoided in this instance was Mrs. George Grote, wife of the historian, a formidably large woman known for her lion-hunting and boring talk.

But before quitting Cavaignac, I must tell you a thing I *saw* at Mrs. Buller's rout, but did not *discern* till a day or two after. Charles Buller led Cavaignac away to introduce him to a large lady, whom I afterwards perceived to be Mrs. Grote: Cavaignac went, without struggling, tho' verily like a sheep led to the slaughter; the presentation performed, he made I think *five* successive bows to Mrs. Grote (a very shower of rapid bows); then, without uttering a word, reeled back, like a sheep *from* the slaughter (or a *calf*, for you know how he *goes*), and landing in a very elegant attitude, stood, five paces off, with his hat behind his back, looking out into space, and the general movement of the rout,—this whole Introduction, Acquaintance, Friendship being begun, carried on, finished, and abolished with such incredible brevity as I describe. It was two days before this phenomenon presented itself rightly before me; and it has tickled me ever since.[70]

Mrs. Carlyle, whose judgment of men usually agreed with that of her husband, expresses admiration for the same quality when, after she had once been bored by a visit of several hours by Charles H. Terrot, Bishop of Edinburgh, she exclaimed: "Bah! I wish I could snort like Cavaignac."[71]

It was the lack of this kind of individual strength and power of resistance that Carlyle believed had greatly weakened Bacon, Jeffrey, and Scott, and had rendered the journalist and critic John Wilson ("Christopher North") almost completely impotent. Carlyle wrote of Wilson in 1833: "There is no man in the Island who has so wasted himself: a mass of Power standing on *no* basis; drifted about by every breath; lamed into the despicablest weakness."[72] Bryan Procter ("Barry Cornwall"), with his languid looks and the "dreamy mildness in his eye," was doomed to be a small poet, according to Carlyle, for his heart and intellect were not strong.[73] On the other hand, Carlyle found in Christ precisely the kind of personal force and strength

70. *New Letters*, I, 19.
71. *Letters and Memorials of Jane Welsh Carlyle*, I, 207.
72. Letter to J. S. Mill, 18 April 1833, *Letters of Carlyle to Mill, Sterling, and Browning*, p. 45.
73. *Love Letters*, I, 375. There is an important passage on Procter in an unpublished letter of Carlyle to John Forster, 26 Oct. 1874, in the Victoria and Albert Museum.

that he admired, so badly misrepresented, he thought, by the smooth, serene, peaceful pictures of the Italian Renaissance:

I do not find Christ that pound of fresh-butter character, which people have made of him. On the contrary, He is a man with a great deal of anger in Him; but the anger all on the right side. He always has a sharp word to return to the Pharisees. When one who has kept the Ten Commandments asks Him whether that is enough, He tells him no—"Leave all thy riches and follow after me." He goes to the Temple, and becomes indignant at the buyers and sellers there, and upsets their stalls with a kick of His foot, and takes a scourge and drives the money-dealers out of the holy place! I thought if anybody in our days should go in our Court of Chancery and do the like there, people would give him a different character from that of a pound of fresh-butter![74]

Yet to attempt to escape from the world, in Carlyle's eyes, was fully as weak as to surrender to it. Because he believed Keats did not show fortitude and courage in facing what was unpleasant, Carlyle could not join his friend Milnes in hearty admiration for the poet.[75] Even Socrates, if we may now return to him, seemed at times something of an escapist to Carlyle, taking his ease in the shady groves of the Academy and along the cool banks of the River Ilisus as he gave his mind to the delightful anodyne of his lovely dialectic.[76] Furthermore, Carlyle looked for what was solid and substantial in personality, for what yielded practical results in human activities, for what brought order out of chaos.

Did he also look for beauty? Writing to his brother Alexander in Canada on 3 July 1847, Carlyle said: "And train the children, each in its own little garden, to respect fruit-trees, honorable profit, *industry*, *beauty*, and *good-order*: it is the summary of all Gospels to man!"[77] Were these merely the values that strengthened and confirmed the

74. Letter to Joseph Neuberg, 12 Jan. 1850, in Sadler, "Carlyle and Neuberg," p. 283.
75. Allingham's *Diary*, p. 205.
76. Even Matthew Arnold, we know, was inclined to agree with the statement attributed to Carlyle that Socrates was "too much at ease in Zion" (*Culture and Anarchy*, chap. iv). John Burroughs reports that he once said to John Sterling, "Woe to them that are at ease in Zion"; but Burroughs also says of Carlyle: "His own genius came nearer the demon of Socrates than that of any modern man." Wilson, *Carlyle*, V, 581. Carlyle once in talking with Holman Hunt included Socrates in a list of those "brave-hearted creatures . . . who have helped to make us something better than wild beasts of rapine and havoc," who teach others to bear life "with patience and faith"; and who have "won or lost in the struggle to do what they deemed the justest and wisest thing." *Ibid.*, IV, 488. See also *ibid.*, I, 153, and Allingham, *Diary*, p. 213.
77. *New Letters*, II, 38.

Victorian middle class, Matthew Arnold's Philistines, in their ways? Carlyle includes beauty in his short list of highest values. The question whether he had an adequate sense of beauty is an important one, but it is much too difficult and complex to be dealt with here. However, two brief comments on the subject may be helpful. In the first place, Carlyle did not like to talk about beauty or hear others talk about it. He did not believe that those who talked about beauty most were sure to reach the level of the highest artists any more than that those who talk about Heaven most are sure to go there. In the second place, his sense of beauty was very much like Browning's. Reality was highly complex to both men, and they frequently discovered beauty amid surroundings that appeared strange, uncongenial, even grotesque. They sought for reality first and would not sift it in order to find and keep apart the pure grains of beauty. Nevertheless, many of Carlyle's portraits are lit up by intensely lovely flashes of beauty. As for order, the instinct for it was highly developed in Carlyle's nature. In the age of the Gothic revival, he cared nothing for Westminster Abbey but carried down to old age the feeling of wonder and admiration with which he first gazed upon St. Paul's. "It was and is," he told Allingham in 1874, "the grandest building I ever saw."[78] And he never grew tired of praising his wife for the skillful management that made it possible for him to live in an orderly household in Chelsea. Such values as these compose the essential fabric of ideas in *Past and Present*.

Undoubtedly these values count for much in the portraits. Samuel Wilberforce, he believed, had neither individual integrity nor substantiality in his nature; and so Carlyle dismisses him as one who "has got all he has by pure soapiness, suppleness, and sychophancy."[79] Witty spoof was no better substitute than frothy soapsuds for substantiality. Hence, Carlyle's rejection of Sydney Smith as an extremely boring person because of his everlasting desire and effort to be witty.[80] Hence also one of Carlyle's even more shocking heresies, his rejection of Charles Lamb. He was thrown with Lamb more than once on his visit to London in 1831 and each time was filled with disgust. Here is a passage from a letter of 29 August 1831: "We saw Charlie Lamb (Elia) at tea: a miserable, drunk-besotted, spindle-

78. *Diary*, p. 233.
79. Wilson, *Carlyle*, V, 65, 450.
80. Allingham, *Diary*, p. 236.

shanked skeleton of a body; whose 'humour,' as it is called, seemed to
me neither more nor less than a fibre of genius shining thro' positive
delirium and crack-brainedness (*verrückheit*), and would be to me
the most intolerable of all nuisances."[81] After seeing more of Lamb,
he made a detailed entry in his *Note Book* (2 November 1831):

> How few people speak for Truth's sake, even in its humblest modes! I
> return from Enfield, where I have seen Lamb, etc., etc. Not one of that class
> will tell you a straightforward story, or even a credible one, about any
> matter under the sun. All must be perked up into epigrammatic contrasts,
> startling exaggerations, claptraps that will get a plaudit from the galleries!
> I have heard a hundred anecdotes about W. Hazlitt (for example); yet
> cannot, by never so much cross-questioning even, form to myself the small-
> est notion of how it really stood with him. Wearisome, inexpressibly wea-
> risome to me is that sort of clatter: it is not walking (to the end of time you
> would never advance, for these persons indeed have no Whither); it is not
> bounding and frisking in graceful natural joy; it is dancing—a St. Vitus
> dance. Heighho!—
>
> Charles Lamb I sincerely believe to be in some considerable degree
> *insane*. A more pitiful, rickety, gasping, staggering, stammering Tom fool
> I do not know. He is witty by denying truisms, and abjuring good manners.
> His speech wriggles hither and thither with an incessant painful fluctua-
> tion; not an opinion in it or a fact or even a phrase that you can thank him
> for: more like a convulsion fit than natural systole and diastole.—Besides
> he is now a confirmed shameless drunkard; *asks* vehemently for gin-and-
> water in strangers' houses; tipples until he is utterly mad, and is only not
> thrown out of doors because he is too much despised for taking such
> trouble with him. Poor Lamb! Poor England where such a despicable
> abortion is named genius!— He said: There are just two things I regret in
> English History; first that Guy Faux's plot did not take effect (there would
> have been so glorious an *explosion*); second that the Royalists did not hang
> Milton (then we might have laughed at them); etc., etc.[82]

Carlyle never changed his mind about Lamb. Many years later he
spoke to Duffy about Lamb's "fantastic method of looking at things."
There was no practical sense in him, Carlyle said, and he had formed
the habit of turning into quips and jests whatever turned up; hence,
he was an ill example to younger men who had to live their lives in a
world that was altogether serious.[83] In the late 1870s Carlyle still

81. To his wife, Bliss, *Letters to His Wife*, p. 64.
82. *Two Note Books*, pp. 217–19.
83. *Conversations with Carlyle*, p. 86.

refused to yield to the slightest degree after W. H. Wylie warmly maintained that Lamb's humor was admirable. Lamb had no humor, Carlyle said; he had "only a thin streak of Cockney wit." He had known "scores of Scotch moorland farmers who for *humor* could have blown Lamb into the zenith!" The only thing really humorous about Lamb was his personal appearance: "His suit of rusty black, his spindle-shanks, his knee-breeches, the bit ribbons fleein' at the knees o' him: indeed he was humor personified!" And Carlyle ended, "Poor silly cratur!"[84]

Shelley, whom Carlyle never saw, he found even less substantial than Lamb. He was a poor shrieking creature who had said or sung nothing worth remembering. Carlyle was both blunt and frank in a letter to Browning of about 1850, when Browning still had almost unreserved enthusiasm for Shelley: "I am not sure but you would excommunicate me if I told you all I thought of Shelley. Poor soul, he has always seemed to me an extremely weak creature; a poor, thin, spasmodic, hectic, shrill and pallid being. . . . The very voice of him (his style, etc.), shrill, shrieky, to my ear has too much of the ghost!"[85] To Milnes he described Shelley in similar terms: "Shelley is always mistaking spasmodic violence for strength. I know no more *urned* books than his. It is like the writing of a ghost, uttering infinite wail into the night, unable to help itself or anyone else."[86]

To Carlyle, Swinburne was unsubstantial like Lamb and Shelley. His verses were froth, "a fuzz of words," and there was "not the least intellectual value in anything he writes."[87]

Far more formidable to Carlyle, however, than the thin insubstantiality of a Lamb, a Shelley, or a Swinburne, was an emptiness in some people, which, fortified behind the ostentation of vanity and the power of official position, could be willfully perverse and could even obstruct those who wished to do useful work. Shelley's insub-

---

84. *Thomas Carlyle*, pp. 331–33.
85. Wilson, *Carlyle*, IV, 110.
86. *Ibid.* See also Duffy, *Conversations with Carlyle*, pp. 63–64. Carlyle's opinion of Hazlitt, too, was low. "Have been reading Hazlitt's *Table Talk*: an incessant chew-chewing, the Nut never cracked, nothing but teeth broken and bleeding gums. The man has thought much; even intently and with vigor: but he has discovered nothing. One other sacrifice to the Time!" *Two Notebooks*, pp. 213, 217–19.
87. Wilson, *Carlyle*, VI, 137–38; Allingham, *Diary*, p. 258. Wylie (p. 315) reports that Swinburne replied to some of Carlyle's criticism by saying that the old man's words were the "sewerage of Sodom" and that "a foul mouth is ill matched with a white beard."

stantiality in its most inane and thin form was never in league with what Carlyle called "the world"; but there was a much more serious show of negative qualities that "the world" supported with fanfare and display of pride. Carlyle found it in Sir Anthony Panizzi, Keeper of Printed Books and later Chief Librarian of the British Museum. And his battle against Panizzi was a losing one. In our time Panizzi has been highly praised in the columns of London's *Times Literary Supplement* as one of the great builders of the British Museum Library.[88] The history of Carlyle's various conflicts with him is complex and cannot be fully discussed here, where we must concern ourselves with what Panizzi seemed to be to Carlyle, and with the values that Carlyle used in judging him. From the beginning to the end of his literary career, Carlyle was confronted, as many other writers and scholars have been, with the problem of gaining access to the books he needed and of finding a satisfactory place in which to work with them. He was thus greatly interested in library problems as such, as many important incidents in his life testify; for example, he took delight in using the Advocates' Library in Edinburgh in his early days, and he was a leader, about 1840, in founding the London Library. He was clearly convinced, moreover, that the chief duty of those who were officials in libraries was to do all they could to make it possible for readers to work with the books they needed in a satisfactory place of study. Panizzi, he believed, did just the opposite; was chiefly concerned with rules, red tape, and facts and figures concerning the growth of his library; and all in all was the most terrible ogre Carlyle ever encountered in dealing with such problems. Before he finally plunged into what he always considered the twelve-year-long nightmare of trying to write the life of Frederick the Great, he had hoped to write on an English subject instead, perhaps John Knox, but Panizzi and those in league with him seemed to block the way:

88. "Great British Libraries—V: The British Museum Library—I," 17 June 1955, p. 338. "Panizzi's temperament and methods brought him at times into conflict with both staff and trustees, yet the library owes more to him than to any other individual." Francis Espinasse, who for a time worked under Panizzi in the British Museum, presents him in an extremely unfavorable light in his *Literary Recollections*. He describes him as "a big, boisterous, rather blustering man, with likes and still more with dislikes, a dangerous foe, and if he was also a helpful patron his patronage was generally bestowed on those in whom he found subserviency and sycophancy united to mediocrity." See pp. 15, 72–73, and all of chap. 11, "The British Museum Library Fifty Years Ago, and After."

24 October 1851

Panizzi and the whole world (which Panizzi accurately enough represents) are a formidable barrier against any earnest work of the historical kind.[89]

14 November 1851

Being English,—I had much rather have an English hero, if it pleased Panizzi and Company,—which, alas, it does not do, nor can do! I find Panizzi the true representative of English dillettantism, Pedantry, Babblement, and hollow dining and drinking Nonsense of so-called "Literature" in this epoch; and therefore I have forgiven, or endeavored to forgive, the poor Man, fatal to me as he and the like of him have been and are.[90]

Working in the general reading room of the British Museum always gave him a headache, and he did not enjoy being bitten by the fleas that flourished there in great numbers. Once the decision to write on Frederick had been made, however, Carlyle swallowed his pride and applied to Panizzi in writing for the privilege of working in the quiet rooms where George III's library was stored. He was promptly refused, and in the long period in which he worked on Frederick had to depend mainly on his two friends Henry Larkin and Joseph Neuberg to do his research in the British Museum. (They did not seem to get the headaches or complain about the fleas.) Some of Carlyle's comments about Panizzi are as follows:

17 August 1853

Panizzi, whom I do not love, and who returns the feeling, *will* not, though solicited from various quarters—high quarters some of them—admit me to the silent rooms of the King's Library, to a place where I *could* read and inquire. Never mind! No matter at all! Perhaps it is even better so. I believe that I could explode the poor monster if I took to petitioning, writing in the "Times," etc. But I shall take good heed of that. Intrinsically he hinders me but little. Intrinsically the blame is not in him, but in the prurient darkness and confused pedantry and ostentatious inanity of the world which put him there, and which I must own he very fairly represents and symbolizes there. Lords Lansdowne and Brougham put Panizzi in; and the world with its Hansards and ballot-boxes and sublime apparatus put in Lords Lansdowne and Brougham.[91]

89. *New Letters*, II, 115–16.
90. To Lady Ashburton, in Wilson, *Carlyle*, V, 23.
91. Froude, *Carlyle*, II, 137. Carlyle shrewdly assumes that Panizzi would enjoy publicity if he gave it to him.

8 September 1853

George the Third's modest, solid and excellent Library is *worth* far more than Panizzi's huge expensive unsound and ostentatious one, and calls for a blessing yet on the faithful and really human soul of that simple King (instead of a *non-blessing* on certain other *in*human, pedantic, and merely showman souls).[92]

As time went by and he became more and more involved in his task, Carlyle's misery increased. On 23 September 1855 he wrote that he was working on "a history of Fritz which no Man *can* write, even if Vulture Panizzi were to offer pens from his own ugly person."[93]

Where Carlyle found substantiality and intelligent honesty and practicality, he bestowed his praise freely. In his early reading he found these qualities in John Hampden and George Washington:

26 March 1822

Hampden and Washington are the two people best *loved* of any in history. Yet they had few illustrious qualities about them; only a high degree of shrewd business-like activity, and above all that honest-hearted unaffected *probity*, which we patriotically name *English*, in a higher degree than almost any public men commemorated in history.[94]

In one of his most intimate and helpful friends, John Chorley, there was no pedantry or froth but rather solid learning, very extensive in its nature, combined with abundant common sense and practical ability; he was the kind of man that Swift would have admired. At the time of Chorley's death in 1867, Carlyle gave him highest praise in a letter to his brother: "I know no man, nor shall ever again know, nearly so well-read, so widely and accurately informed, and so completely at home not only in all fields of worthy literature and scholarship, but in matters practical over and above."[95] John Lockhart had his faults but also redeeming qualities of a very substantial sort: "A hard, proud, but thoroughly honest, singularly intelligent, and also affectionate man, whom in the distance I esteemed more than perhaps he ever knew. Seldom did I speak to him;

92. To Lord Ashburton, in Wilson, *Carlyle*, V, 45–46.
93. To Lady Ashburton, *ibid.*, p. 176. According to Wylie (p. 215), not only the Ashburtons but also George L. Craik and Payne Collier joined Carlyle in his complaint against Panizzi's management of the British Museum Library.
94. *Two Note Books*, 26 March 1822, p. 7.
95. Wilson, *Carlyle*, VI, 133–34.

but hardly ever without learning and gaining something."[96] He was a "tough, elastic man."[97] Bishop Connop Thirlwall was also someone that Carlyle could like as "a right solid honest-hearted man, full of knowledge and sense."[98] Rintoul, a Scotch printer who had become editor and proprietor of the *Spectator*, was never very profound, in Carlyle's opinion, but even so he had deeper insight than the other journalists of the day. He was a man "altogether free from romantic or visionary babblement or the ordinary echoes of parliamentary palaver." What he wrote was never mere wind; it always meant something. He was a diligent and upright man, and his *Spectator* was the best journal in England.[99] The Reverend Alexander Scott, likewise, Carlyle praised in a letter to Emerson as "one of the few distinguished thinkers of his time: a man of real intellect, earnestness, originality and depth," one who "by no means tells his secret at once" but most certainly "has his secret, many curious secrets."[100] David Laing, too, was a man whose "faithful solid accurate ways are worthy of all honor," a man whose head, moreover, was "full of Scotch good sense and prudence."[101] The scientist Sir Richard Owen was quite definitely substantial and useful. He was a man "of huge coarse head, with projecting brow and chin (like a cheese in the *last* quarter), with a pair of large protrusive glittering eyes," who nevertheless had real talent and worth: "Hardly twice in London have I met with any articulate-speaking biped who told me a thirtieth-part so many things I knew not and wanted to know. It was almost like to make me cry, to hear articulate human speech once more conveying real information to me,—not dancing on airy tiptoes, nowhence and nowhither, as the manner of the Cockney dialect is."[102]

Humor was another thing that Carlyle valued in people. Much has been written about his own vein of humor, his indebtedness to Swift

96. *Letters and Memorials of Jane Welsh Carlyle*, I, 107.
97. Letter to Varnhagen von Ense, 8 June 1845, *New Review*, VI (April 1892), 426. See also *Two Note Books*, p. 249.
98. Two letters to his wife, 18 and 19 July 1843, Bliss, *Letters to His Wife*, 169–71.
99. Duffy, *Conversations with Carlyle*, p. 85. See also Wylie, p. 165.
100. Letter to Emerson, 30 June 1858. Original in the Berg Collection of the New York Public Library. Quoted with permission.
101. Unpublished letter to Dr. John Carlyle, 11 May 1865, MS, NLS, 517.92; unpublished letter to C. E. Norton, 8 Dec. 1873, in the Houghton Library, Harvard.
102. Letter to his wife, 26 Aug. 1842, in Bliss, *Letters to His Wife*, pp. 155–56; letter to John Sterling, 29 Aug. 1842, in *Letters of Carlyle to Mill, Sterling, and Browning*, pp. 257–58.

and Sterne, and the power that his own loud, rich outbursts of laughter had to delight those who heard him talk.[103] When George Bancroft visited him in 1847, Carlyle was pleased to find in him "a certain small under-current of genial *humor,* or as it were *hidden laughter,* not noticed heretofore."[104] He enjoyed the humor in Sir David Wilkie's pictures. They contained, he said, "a great broad energy of humor and sympathy." Wilkie was a real painter, "alone among us since Hogarth's time."[105] Carlyle particularly enjoyed humor in Dickens, especially in Dickens' public readings. In Dickens as in Garrick the genius for humor manifested itself mainly through mimicry.[106] In Jane Welsh Carlyle, too, one of the qualities most endearing to her husband was her alert, sure sense of the ridiculous and her habit of exploding nonsense with laughter. A fine sense of humor was also in Carlyle's early friend and benefactor, Edward Strachey, grandfather of Lytton Strachey, to whom the grandfather may have bequeathed some of this quality. Carlyle describes him as one who above all things "loved Chaucer, and kept reading him." He was the colleague of Thomas Love Peacock and worked near him, so that the two were often found laughing together over the absurdities of the world. He had "a fine, tinkling, mellow-toned voice" and "a pretty vein of quiz." Humor was a part of the armor with which he faced the world:

[He was] a man sharply impatient of pretence, of sham and untruth in all forms; especially contemptuous of quality pretensions and affectations, which he scattered grinningly to the winds. Dressed in the simplest form, he walked daily to the India House and back [to Fitzroy Square], though there were fine carriages in store for the woman part; scorned cheerfully "the general humbug of the world," and honestly strove to do his own bit of duty, spiced by Chaucer and what else of inward harmony or condiment he had. . . . A man of many qualities comfortable to be near.[107]

To Carlyle, the greatest wit of the day was Charles Buller, nephew of Edward Strachey's wife and Carlyle's own pupil in the early Edin-

---

103. See esp. T. W. Higginson, "Carlyle's Laugh," *Atlantic Monthly,* XLVIII (Oct. 1881), 463–66; Wilson, *Carlyle,* VI, 386; and n. 3 above.

104. Letter to Emerson, 13 Nov. 1847, *Correspondence of Carlyle and Emerson,* II, 184.

105. Froude, *Carlyle,* III, 330–31.

106. Duffy, *Conversations with Carlyle,* pp. 74–76; Wilson, *Carlyle,* IV, 126, 418; Froude, *Carlyle,* IV, 270.

107. *Reminiscences,* ed. C. E. Norton (London and New York, 1887), II, 124–25.

burgh days. Buller's wit, according to Carlyle, was not based on pure
nonsense and insubstantiality like that of Charles Lamb. Buller was
a man of great practical abilities, of integrity, of "a constant veracity
of intellect and character." Neither was it like the contrived wit of
Sydney Smith, ostentatious and affected. It was a natural stream
of brilliance flowing from the mind, "an airy winged turn of thought,
flowing out in lambencies of beautiful spontaneous wit and fancy."
Buller expressed his inborn detestation of the base and false by
"showering witty scorn upon it, . . . in which, indeed, I never saw
his rival." Yet Buller's was "a kindly, genial nature; clear, productive,
with a rare union of decision and benignity." He died young, with
what appeared to be a brilliant career in the direction of colonial affairs ahead of him. At his death Carlyle wrote to Lady Ashburton, 29
November 1848: "Alas, alas, what sad tragedy is this,—the saddest,
I think, that ever befell among friends of mine! . . . And we shall never
see that blithe face more. . . . His presence was cheering and benef-
icent to all, and hurtful and afflictive to none that lived. But to you,
dear friend,—alas, it is a loss which I fear none of us can ever repair!
In his own form he was by far the brightest Soul in your circle, or
indeed in all the World, that I knew of." Buller's humor was not
merely intelligent and clever; it was the product of a remarkable humanity, fully vitalized, glowing, warm, and substantial.[108]

The indefinable humanity that Carlyle found in Buller counts for
much in various portraits as the artist evaluated his subjects. Carlyle
sought this quality out wherever it could be found, had a quick eye
to discover it or the lack of it, judged his subjects according to the
degree of it that they possessed, and had great skill in suggesting in
the portraits precisely how much humanity his subjects had. Here
again his portraits remind us of Rembrandt's. This quality of humanity he thought of in the manner that traditional humanism has
always thought of it—both as whatever in man's nature may raise
him above the level of the lower animals and as whatever liberated
his physical faculties, allowed the natural man to function, and displayed him, fully alive, as a creature of the earth. Jesus he praised as

---

108. *Letters and Memorials of Jane Welsh Carlyle*, I, 113–14; letter to J. S. Mill,
19 Nov. 1832, *Letters of Carlyle to Mill, Sterling, and Browning*, p. 23; Wilson, *Carlyle*,
V, 13–14; and Carlyle's "Death of Charles Buller," *Examiner*, 2 Dec. 1848. For a detailed discussion of Carlyle's relation to the Stracheys and Bullers and for other portraits of them, see my book *The Strachey Family* (Durham, N.C., 1953), pp. 108–46,
321–22.

"that grandest of all beings" who have helped to make us something better than "wild beasts of rapine and havoc."[109] Goethe he acclaimed as "a *man*, not a *dwarf* of *letters*."[110] "Be men," Carlyle said to the other authors of the day, "before attempting to be *writers*."[111] To friends in his old age he said that he had "tried to put some humanity" into Frederick II but that it was "hard work."[112] One of his early disappointments came from his discovery of what seemed to be a fundamental lack of humanity in the poet Thomas Campbell, whose poems he had read with admiration. The poet had a smirk on his face like that of an auctioneer; his eye had "the cold vivacity of a conceited worldling; his talk was small, contemptuous, and shallow; every detail of his dress proclaimed the literary dandy." Carlyle declared, "The aspect of that man jarred the music of my mind for a whole day." He concluded: "There is no living well of thought or feeling in him; his head is a shop, not a manufactory; and for his heart, it is as dry as a Greenoch *kipper*."[113] The same fundamental deficiency appeared in John Wilson Croker. Carlyle wrote in 1851, "No viler mortal calls himself man than old Croker at this time"; and he objected to an attack on Maurice, Kingsley, and other liberals that he had read in the *Quarterly Review* as "very beggarly Crokerism, all of copperas and gall and human *baseness*."[114] Lacking humanity, too, was the geologist Sir Charles Lyell, with his monotonous, uninspired voice and "the clear leaden twinkle of his small bead eyes."[115] When Carlyle visited Sir William and Lady Beecher in County Cork, Ireland, he was astonished to find in Lady Beecher, formerly the famous actress, Eliza O'Neill, no suggestion of human warmth or gracious hospitality, but instead cold rigidity and formality. Her eyes were cold and cruel. Her air was silent, reserved, disagreeable. She sternly and rigorously imposed her character upon her whole household. She lived in constant obedience to what she called her duty and was a thrall to the Thirty-nine Articles.[116] Very different to Carlyle was a true saint,

109. Wilson, *Carlyle*, IV, 488–89.
110. Letter to Jane Welsh, 28 Feb. 1825, *Love Letters*, II, 102.
111. Letter to Jane Welsh, 9 Jan. 1825, *ibid.*, II, 63. See also p. 92.
112. Wylie, p. 268.
113. Letter to Jane Welsh, 23 June 1824, *Love Letters*, I, 375; II, 58; Allingham, *Diary*, pp. 236–37.
114. Letter to Dr. John Carlyle, 7 Oct. 1851, *New Letters*, II, 113.
115. Wilson, *Carlyle*, III, 125; letter to his wife, 9 June 1865, Bliss, *Letters to His Wife*, p. 378.
116. Duffy, *Conversations with Carlyle*, pp. 98–100.

Martin Luther. When he saw in Germany a picture of Luther that he admired, he exclaimed: "Martin himself has a fine German face: eyes so frank and serious, a look as if he could take a cup of ale as well as wrestle down the devil in a handsome manner."[117] True humanity, to Carlyle, is never stiff or stuffy. One of the first of Lady Ashburton's tributes to Carlyle himself is significant here. After a visit to Oxford in 1853, she said, "Coming back to the society of Carlyle after the dons at Oxford is like returning home from some conventional world to the human race."[118] It is pleasant to know that Carlyle found plenty of unmistakable humanity in Ivan Turgenev, whom he got to know on the novelist's visits to England. He said, "A fine faculty is in that Russian big man; the heart of him somewhat too *sensual*, but full of noble melancholy, and fine qualities." Turgenev was good company and an excellent talker.[119] Carlyle's skill in suggesting what is indefinable in humanity is perhaps nowhere illustrated better than in his description of a corpse that he saw in Paris in 1824:

I turned aside into a small mansion with the name of *Morgue* upon it; there lay the naked body of an old grey-headed artisan whom misery had driven to drown himself in the river! His face wore the grim fixed scowl of despair; his lean horny hands with their long ragged nails were lying by his sides; his patched and soiled apparel with his apron and *sabots* were hanging at his head; and there fixed in his iron slumber, heedless of the vain din that rolled around him on every side, was this poor outcast stretched in silence and darkness forever. I gazed upon the wretch for a quarter of an hour; I think I never felt more shocked in my life.[120]

As Carlyle paints the picture, the death of the artisan is merely the last stroke in a long succession of blows by which the struggling man was beaten back and denied the possibility of fulfilling himself as a human being. It is well to note here, furthermore, that the many important questions which Carlyle raised concerning modern industrialized society have to do largely with its dehumanizing tendencies.

The touch that counts for most in Carlyle's portraits, however, is a magic one that defies analysis. With it he makes us suddenly aware that his subject belongs not merely to the earth but is a creature of infinitude, staring out at us from a strange, mysterious place where

117. Froude, *Carlyle*, IV, 132.   118. Wilson, *Carlyle*, V, 69.
119. Letter to his wife, 29 July 1858, Bliss, *Letters to His Wife*, pp. 331–32; letters to Dr. John Carlyle, 26 Nov. 1870 and 13 May 1871, *New Letters*, II, 272–73, 278–79.
120. Letter to Jane Welsh, 28 Oct. 1824, *Love Letters*, II, 28.

immensity and eternity meet. We are filled with awe and wonder, and exclaim with Hamlet: "What a piece of work is man!" This gift for suggesting the close conjunction of the natural with the supernatural seems to have been born in Carlyle. It operated in his treatment of places as well as persons. It sometimes frightened him. He wrote in 1843: "Sure enough I have a fatal talent of converting all Nature into Preternaturalism for myself: a truly horrible Phantasm-Reality it is to me; what of heavenly radiances it has, blended in close neighborhood, in intimate union, with the hideousness of Death and Chaos;—a very ghastly business indeed."[121] But this very gift accounts for the intensity of his vision and the splendidly luminous quality of his portraits of Coleridge in his *Sterling* and of Jeffrey and Jane Welsh Carlyle in the *Reminiscences*. It suggests, furthermore, a scale of values that refused to come to terms with the prevailing science, industrialism, and materialism. In the words of one of his contemporaries, "The marvels of industry did not awe him, the progress of humanity he did not place in the triumphs of matter; in his eyes a man was a man only on condition of being a tabernacle of the living God."[122] The shadows that are so important in Carlyle's portraits, as in Rembrandt's, suggest not merely depth but reveal to us earthly creatures partaking of eternity and infinitude.

The importance of Carlyle's work in handing down to posterity portraits of his contemporaries cannot be exaggerated. The scope and range of the gallery of Victorian portraits he has bequeathed to us are tremendous. He was consciously trying to do for those who came after him what he wished had always been done for him by those who came before him. His portraits vary greatly not only according to their subjects but also in the methods that he used in dealing with

121. Letter to Emerson, 31 Oct. 1843, *Correspondence of Carlyle and Emerson*, II, 40. In a review of Carlyle's *Cromwell*, J. B. Mozeley wrote: "Mr. Carlyle's Reality is a magnificent abstraction; it refuses to be caught and grasped, and will give no account of itself for the satisfaction of sublunary and practical curiosity. It wages an eternal war with shadows; it is a disperser of phantoms; lies flee before it; formulae shudder at its approach. This is all we know of its nature and its characteristics. It carries on a great aerial battle nobody knows where; and teaches with sublime infallibility nobody knows what." In the *Christian Remembrancer*, XI (1846), 243 ff. *Sartor Resartus* is in considerable part a probing into the nature of reality. So are *Hamlet* and *Don Quixote*, of course, and it is a significant fact that the Carlyles read and quoted Shakespeare constantly and were reading Cervantes in the Spanish during the period of incubation for *Sartor*. For this aspect of *Don Quixote*, see Richard L. Predmore, "El Problema de la Realidad en el *Quijote*," *Nueva Revista de Filologia Hispanica*, VII (1953), 489–98.
122. Wylie, p. 372.

them. Some are made up merely of a bold stroke or two, with charcoal on white paper. Many others are more full and complex, but in a brief, bright, compact manner that at times suggests Chaucer's *Prologue*. In this group we find portraits of Lady Holland, William Godwin, Samuel Rogers, Robert Southey, Sir James Stephen, Thiers, Daniel Webster, Hartley Coleridge, Bronson Alcott, Mazzini, Gladstone, Disraeli, and many others. A third group of portraits is that dealing with subjects who completely fascinated him or who had strongly gripped his mind, imagination, and emotions. These portraits, much fuller than any of the others, he returned to again and again through his various published writings and letters. They are thus composites of passages that he wrote through the years as his mind returned to them and his experience presented them in a fresh light. Such are his splendid portraits of his own father, James Carlyle, of Jane Welsh Carlyle, Edward Irving, Francis Jeffrey, S. T. Coleridge, John Sterling, Browning, Dickens, Emerson, Leigh Hunt, Macaulay, J. S. Mill, Ruskin, Thackeray, Tennyson, Wordsworth, and Queen Victoria. Those who jump to the conclusion that Carlyle's portraits always lack charity, are distorted by prejudice, or are hostile toward the Romantics should study the careful discrimination and remarkable balance in his portraits of Irving, Jeffrey, and Sterling, and the affectionate tolerance and warm friendliness that run through the many sketches of Leigh Hunt. We may be willing to forgive Carlyle for much when we remember that he could appreciate Jeffrey and could love Leigh Hunt.[123]

123. For a companion study, see "Carlyle's Pen Portraits of Queen Victoria and Prince Albert," in *Carlyle Past and Present*, ed. K. J. Fielding and Rodger L. Tarr (London and New York, 1976), pp. 216–38.

THE BACKGROUND OF CARLYLE'S
PORTRAIT OF COLERIDGE IN
THE LIFE OF JOHN STERLING

It is generally assumed that one of the most important and interesting relationships between British literary men in the nineteenth century was that between Coleridge and Carlyle and that one of the most brilliant and memorable verbal portraits of a contemporary produced by a Victorian writer is that of Coleridge in Carlyle's *Sterling*. The component elements in Carlyle's conception of Coleridge were complex, and the texture of his portrait of Coleridge is correspondingly rich, variegated, and consistent with the Boswellian formula which demands that in biography there should always be an interplay between the shadow and the light.

In the chapter on Carlyle in my book *Coleridge and the Broad Church Movement* (1942)[1] I studied the relation of the two men to one another and attempted to trace the origin of the component elements in Carlyle's portrait of Coleridge and to explain his attitudes and motivation in terms of his personal relation to Coleridge, his reading of Coleridge's works, and his relation to other persons who had known Coleridge. Since I wrote that book, however, so much new material bearing on the subject has been found that it now appears necessary to rewrite the part of the chapter dealing with the portrait of Coleridge in order to approximate the completeness that the complex subject demands and to include the new material, much of it from manuscript sources, now available.

In my earlier treatment of the subject I wrote:

Behind the luminious but not altogether complimentary picture of Coleridge in Carlyle's *Life of John Sterling* is a curiously mixed attitude. J. C. Hare's *Memoir* of John Sterling (1848) had accorded Coleridge almost unreserved praise. Coleridge was a major issue to Carlyle when in 1851 he set about writing a life of Sterling which he hoped would correct what he

---

1. (Durham, N.C.). Hereinafter *Coleridge and the Broad Church.*

considered some of the wrong impressions of Sterling created by Hare's biography. Although Carlyle was himself "an unconscious continuator of Wordsworth and Coleridge"[2] in more than one respect and although he owed something to Coleridge's influence, he was extremely reluctant to admit the indebtedness. His strong antipathy for Coleridge as a man, a poet, and a philosopher—an antipathy which made him unwilling to concede that Coleridge could contribute much of value to him, to Sterling, or to anyone else, and which made him scornful of the Coleridgeans of his generation—arose from some of his most deep-seated instincts, feelings, and convictions, which were frequently powerful enough to conquer him in spite of his own resolution to see justice done. The antipathy for Coleridge was, furthermore, an old one, born in him when he was still a young man and expressed in various forms throughout the years. The treatment of Coleridge in *Sterling* is really the culmination of a series of judgments on him stretching out over a period of about thirty years in which Carlyle struggled sometimes more and sometimes less to master his natural antipathy.

At least as early as 1816 Edward Irving, a Coleridge enthusiast, urged upon Carlyle the importance of reading Coleridge and of heeding Coleridge's advice to study the English writers of the seventeenth century as models of the best prose.[3] Although Carlyle responded to Irving's enthusiasm and read both Coleridge and the seventeenth-century writers, he tells us later that he had some misgivings: "We were all taught by Coleridge, etc., that the old English dramatists, divines, philosophers, judicious Hooker, Milton, Sir Thomas Browne, were the genuine exemplars; which I always tried to believe, but never rightly could *as a whole*."[4] Yet the rhythm of the prose style which he developed, as individual as it is, suggests that he may have learned something from reading these writers. "For all the jaggedness and incoherence of the new idiom he had evolved, echoes of the fullness of their cadence and reminiscences of their splendor of phrase remain."[5] It seems clear, however, that in these early years, as well as later, he read both the seventeenth-century writers and Coleridge with considerable discrimination. He praised Coleridge in a letter to Jane Welsh in May, 1822, in which he said, "Coleridge is not more celebrated for anything he has done than for his version of Wallenstein."[6] But an en-

2. Louis Cazamian, *Carlyle*, trans. E. K. Brown (New York, 1932), p. 54.
3. Emery Neff, *Carlyle* (New York, 1932), p. 34.
4. Thomas Carlyle, *Reminiscences*, ed. C. E. Norton (London and New York, 1887), III, 41.
5. Cazamian, p. 132.
6. *The Collected Letters of Thomas and Jane Welsh Carlyle*, ed. C. R. Sanders, K. J. Fielding, et al. (Durham, N.C., 1970), III, 109.

try in his notebook made in March, 1823, reads: "The distinction of Coleridge's, which he may have borrowed from Woltmann, about *talent* and *genius* is complete *blarney*—futile, very futile."[7]

Here ends the long quotation from my earlier treatment of the subject; with the introduction of fresh material that follows immediately I shall refrain from the practice of labeling what I use as old or new but instead attempt to blend the component elements and achieve chronological continuity and development.

On 22 October 1823 Carlyle wrote to Jane Welsh:

He [Irving] figured out purposes of unspeakable profit to me, which when strictly examined melted into empty air. He seemed to think that if set down on London streets some strange development of genius would take place in me, that by conversing with Coleridge and the Opium eater,[8] I should find out new channels for speculation, and soon learn to speak with tongues.[9] There is but a small degree of truth in all this. Of genius (bless the mark!) I never imagined in the most lofty humours that I possessed beyond the smallest perceptible fraction; and this fraction be it little or less can only be turned to account by rigid and stern perseverance thro' long years of labour, in London or any other spot in the universe.[10]

On 11 November of the same year he gave his brother John, then a student at the University of Edinburgh, a long list of authors to read that included Coleridge, described as "very great but rather mystical, sometimes absurd."[11] In his letter to Jane of 13 November the comment on Coleridge is more favorable and suggests some influence, however slight. "Your very diffidence is to me fresh evidence of the generous power that lies in the faculties of your heart and head. 'Genius,' says Schiller, 'is ever a secret to itself.' So it is, if my experience of men has taught me anything. Coleridge says he never knew a youth of real talents that did not labour under bashfulness and disbelief in his own ability. I could *prove* all this to you, if I had room; but it is not necessary."[12]

---

7. *Coleridge and the Broad Church*, pp. 147–49; Wilson, *Carlyle*, I, 278; *Two Note Books of Thomas Carlyle from 23 March 1822 to 16 May 1832*, ed. C. E. Norton (New York, 1898), pp. 46–47.

8. DeQuincey.

9. A rather remarkable anticipation of the way in which Irving's London disciples carried "speaking with tongues" to sensational and extravagant lengths.

10. *Collected Letters*, II, 459–60.

11. *Ibid.*, II, 468.

12. *Ibid.*, II, 472. The quotation from Coleridge has not been traced precisely, but

When Carlyle made his first visit to London in 1824–25, Irving and Mrs. Basil Montagu lost little time after his arrival in arranging for him to get his first glimpse of Coleridge and to hear him talk. Carlyle, no doubt, was very curious about him and was particularly eager to learn from him something about Kant. The resulting visit to Highgate, made in June 1824, was far from satisfying to him. Many years later, in his *Reminiscences,* he recorded his memory of it:

> On one of the first fine mornings, Mrs. Montagu, along with Irving, took me out to see Coleridge at Highgate. My impressions of the man and of the place are conveyed, faithfully enough, in the *Life of Sterling*; that first interview in particular, of which I had expected very little, was idle and unsatisfactory, and yielded me nothing,—Coleridge, a puffy, anxious, obstructed-looking, fattish old man, hobbled about with us, talking with a kind of solemn emphasis on matters which were of no interest (and even *reading* pieces in *proof* of his opinions thereon); I had him to myself once or twice, in *narrow* parts of the garden-walks; and tried hard to get something about *Kant* and Co. from him, about "reason" *versus* "Understanding," and the like; but in vain: nothing came from him that was of use to me, that day, or in fact any day. The sight and sound of a sage who was so venerated by those about me, and whom I too would willingly have venerated, but could not,—this was all. Several times afterward, Montagu, on Coleridge's "Thursday Evening," carried Irving and me out, and returned blessing Heaven (I not) for what we had received; Irving and I walked out more than once on mornings, too; and found the Dodona Oracle humanely ready to act,—but never (to me, nor to Irving either I suspect) explanatory of the question put. Good Irving strove always to think that he was getting priceless wisdom out of this great man; but must have had his misgivings. Except by the Montagu-Irving channel, I at no time communicated with Coleridge: I had never, on my own strength, had much esteem for him; and found slowly, in spite of myself, that I was getting to have less and less. Early in 1825 was my last sight of him. . . . On my second visit to London (autumn 1831), Irving and I had appointed a day for pilgrimage to Highgate; but the day was one rain-deluge, and we couldn't even try.[13]

This memory of the first impression made upon him by Coleridge was, in spite of the intervening years, remarkably similar to the record that he made at the time of the visit in a letter to his brother John,

---

Carlyle appears to be referring rather loosely to several passages in the *Biographia Literaria.*

13. *Ibid.,* II, 130–32.

dated 24 June 1824. Froude calls this record the "original sketch" of
the portrait of Coleridge in Carlyle's *Sterling*:

Besides Irving I have seen many other curiosities. Not the least of these
I reckon Coleridge, the Kantean metaphysician and quondam Lake poet.
I will tell you all about our interview *when we meet*. Figure a fat flabby
incurvated personage, at once short, rotund and relaxed, with a watery
mouth, a snuffy nose, a pair of strange brown timid yet earnest looking eyes,
a high tapering brow, and a great bush of grey hair—you will have some
faint idea of Coleridge. He is a kind, good soul, full of religion and affection,
and poetry and animal magnetism. His cardinal sin is that he wants *will*; he
has no resolution, he shrinks from pain or labour in any of its shapes. His
very attitude bespeaks this: he never straightens his knee joints, he stoops
with his fat ill shapen shoulders, and in walking he does not tread but
shovel and slide—my father would call it *skluiffing*.[14] He is also always
busied to keep by strong and frequent inhalations the water of his mouth
from overflowing; and his eyes have a look of anxious impotence; he *would*
do with all his heart, but he knows he dare not. The conversation of the
man is much as I anticipated. A forest of thoughts; some true, many false,
most part dubious, all of them ingenious in some degree, often in a high
degree. But there is no method in his talk; he wanders like a man sailing
among many currents, whithersoever his lazy mind directs him—; and what
is more unpleasant he preaches, or rather soliloquizes: he cannot speak;
he can only "*tal-k*" (so he names it). Hence I found him unprofitable, even
tedious: but we parted very good friends I promising to go back and see
him some other evening—a promise I fully intend to keep. I sent him a
copy of Meister about which we had some friendly talk. I reckon him a
man of great and useless genius—a strange not at all a great man.[15]

14. Scots *sklufe* or *skloof*: "to trail the feet along the ground in walking."
15. *Collected Letters*, III, 90–91. Coleridge's known references to Carlyle are scanty
but not without significance. In the opening letter of *Confessions of an Inquiring Spirit*,
intended to be included in *Aids to Reflection* (1825) although not published until 1840,
Coleridge wrote: "I employed the compelling and most unwelcome leisure of severe
indisposition in reading *The Confessions of a Fair Saint* in Mr. Carlyle's recent translation of the Wilhelm Meister [*Apprenticeship*, Book VI], which might, I think, have
been better rendered literally, *The Confessions of a Beautiful Soul*. This, acting in conjunction with the concluding sentences of your Letter, threw my thoughts inward on
my own religious experience, and gave the immediate occasion to the following Confessions." Earl Leslie Griggs believes that Coleridge is referring to Carlyle's "Schiller's
Life and Writings," *London Magazine* (Oct. 1823–Sept. 1824), rather than to a contribution to *Blackwood's*, when he speaks in a letter to Gioacchino de' Prati of 8 [9] May
1826 of his "vexation, namely, that you should have chosen a subject which had been
so recently and in different forms, Magazines, Reviews, and one separate work either
published or announced for publication, forestalled with the Public—and I had well
nigh said, hackneyed. And this was more unfortunate, that a Life of Schiller had already appeared in Blackwood's Magazine, the only Publisher, that could answer your

Writing to Jane Welsh the day before he wrote this letter, Carlyle had said near the end of his long letter, "Of Coleridge, and all the other originals I will not say a word at present: you are sated and more."[16]

It is well to note that Carlyle, in spite of his great curiosity about Coleridge, was skeptical about him before he met him, that he found in him, according to his own statement, about what he expected to find. There is no disillusionment in these visits to Coleridge. Making up Carlyle's impression of Coleridge here were component elements that would determine his attitude to the end: a thrifty, tidy-minded Scot's strong, instinctive feeling of repulsion at Coleridge's personal appearance and habits; a conviction that Coleridge could not be a great man and at the same time be so conspicuously lacking in self-discipline; the restlessness of one who liked to talk, and who himself had great genius for talking, at being subjected to a flood of seemingly unmethodical words that one had no opportunity to answer and that were spoken in accents that grated on Scottish ears; but at the same time a nervous, tantalizing feeling that the man Coleridge was not altogether bad or lacking in wisdom and that there was much in his teaching which one could not afford to ignore.

Other letters written during Carlyle's first visit to London reveal very much the same attitude. In a letter of 5 July 1824 to George Boyd of the Edinburgh publishing firm of Oliver and Boyd in which he proposed to produce a translation of Goethe's autobiography that would be greatly superior to that which Henry Colburn, the London publisher, had brought out, he said: "As to the *Life* [of Goethe] I confess my feeling that were it shorter it might please me (as well as the public) very much. I could also command *notes* to it from Coleridge if necessary; and from another gentleman personally known to Goethe [probably Henry Crabb Robinson], and familiar with all the late literary history of Germany as of England."[17] Although Carlyle clearly had established his relation to Coleridge on a satisfactory footing, it is certainly dubious whether he could have "commanded" notes on Goethe or on any other subject from him, since he did not respond very readily to commands from the high or the low. Never-

_____

purposes, over whom *I* possess the least influence" (*Collected Letters of Samuel Taylor Coleridge*, ed. E. L. Griggs (Oxford, 1956–71), V, 435; VI, 578).

16. *Collected Letters*, III, 85.

17. *Ibid.*, III, 103.

theless, such a translation by Carlyle with notes by Coleridge and Crabb Robinson would have been a thing to see, and we can only regret that it did not come into being.

The mixed attitude toward Coleridge continues to be apparent in other letters written during the first visit to London. On 24 August 1824 he wrote to Thomas Murray, one of his earliest friends and a fellow student at Edinburgh:

Coleridge is a steam-engine of a hundred horse power—with the boiler burst. His talk is resplendent with imagery and the shows of thought; you listen as to an oracle, and find yourself no jot the wiser. He is without beginning or middle or end. A round fat oily yet impatient little man, his mind seems totally beyond his own control; he speaks incessantly, not thinking or imagining or remembering, but combining all these processes into one; as a rich and lazy housewife might mingle her soup and fish and beef and custard into one unspeakable mass and present it trueheartedly to her astonished guests.[18]

In a letter to Jane of 15 November Carlyle wrote: "A man that is not standing on his own feet in regard to economical affairs, soon ceases to be a man at all. Poor Coleridge is like the hulk of a huge ship; his mast and sails and rudders have rotted quite away."[19] Again on 4 December Carlyle wrote Jane that there was "no truly intellectual person" on Irving's list and that "any thing resembling a 'great man,' a man exercised with sublime thoughts and emotions, able even to participate in such, and throw any light on them, is a treasure I have yet to meet with"; and in replying on 19 December Jane wrote somewhat mockingly: "There is no intellectual person you say on the Orator's list! Why, what has befallen his acquaintance? Where are all the eminent personages, the very salt of the earth[,] whom you and he told me of?" Then she named about half a dozen of the "eminent personages," including Coleridge, "the first of Talkers."[20] On 20 December Carlyle wrote Jane: "Coleridge is sunk inextricably in the depths of putrescent indolence."[21] On 22 January 1825, weary of London and pessimistic about what it could offer him, he wrote to his brother John:

That I shall return to Scotland pretty soon is I think the only point entirely decided. Here is nothing adequate to induce my continuance. The

18. *Ibid.*, III, 139.
19. *Ibid.*, III, 199.
20. *Ibid.*, III, 215–16, 228.
21. *Ibid.*, III, 233.

people are stupid, and noisy; and I live at the easy rate of five-and-forty shillings per week! I say the people are stupid, not altogether unadvisedly; in point of either intellectual or moral culture, they *are* some degrees below even the inhabitants of the "Modern Athens" [Edinburgh]. I have met no man of a true head and heart among them. Coleridge is a mass of richest spices, putrified into a dunghill: I never hear him *tawlk*, without feeling ready to worship him and toss him in a blanket.[22]

In a letter to Jane of 31 January he again expressed his low opinion of those poets in London who were seeking literary fame:

'Fame!'—The very sound of it is distressing to my ears. Oh that I could show you the worshippers of it whom I have met with here! To see how the shallow spirits of these scribes are eaten up by this mean selfish passion; how their whole blood seems to be changed by it into gall, and they stand hissing like as many rattle-snakes each over his small very small lot of that commodity! I swear to you I had rather be a substantial peasant that eat my bread in peace, and loved my fellow mortals, tho' I scarcely knew that my own parish was not all the universe, than one of these same miserable metre-ballad-mongers, whose heart is dead or worse, for whom creation is but a mirror to reflect the image of his own sorry self and still sorrier doings! An hour with Coleridge or Procter would do more for you, than a month of my talking. You would forswear *fame* forever and a day.[23]

In the same vein he wrote to his brother John on 10 February: "I saw Coleridge for the last time yesterday: he is an inspired ass,"[24] and again wrote to him on 7 March: "I heard Coleridge *tawlk* one night a fortnight since. He took an ounce of snuff, speculated in half intelligible Kantism, and vilipended universal nature, in all her productions, but himself. I will tell thee when me meet."[25]

After he had returned to Scotland, he wrote to Mrs. Basil Montagu on 18 July 1825: "Has Coleridge published his book,[26] or is he still merely *tawlking*, and taking snuff? Unhappy Coleridge! A seventy-four-gun ship, but water-logged, dismasted, cannot set a thread of sail!"[27]

Yet when Carlyle's *The Life of Friedrich Schiller* came out in book form in March of this same year, it carried words of hope and even praise concerning Coleridge. At one place in its text he declares: "The philosophy of Kant is probably combined with errors to its very core;

22. *Ibid.*, III, 260–61.
23. *Ibid.*, III, 271. For "metre-ballad-mongers," cf. *I Henry IV*, III, i, 130.
24. *Ibid.*, III, 280.   26. *Aids to Reflection.*
25. *Ibid.*, III, 300.   27. *Collected Letters*, III, 351–52.

but perhaps also, this ponderous unmanageable dross may bear in it the everlasting gold of truth! Mighty spirits have already laboured in refining it; is it wise in us to take up with the base pewter of Utility, and renounce such projects altogether? We trust, not." For this passage he provides a footnote: "Are our hopes from Mr. Coleridge always to be fruitless? Sneers at the common-sense philosophy of the Scotch are of little use: it is a poor philosophy, perhaps; but not so poor as none at all, which seems to be the state of matters here at present."[28] And in another passage in the book he again praises Coleridge's translation of *Wallenstein*:

Wallenstein has been translated into French by M. Benjamin Constant; and the last two parts of it have been faithfully rendered into English by Mr. Coleridge. As to the French version, we know nothing, save that it is an *improved* one; but that little is enough: Schiller, as a dramatist, improved by M. Constant, is a spectacle we feel no wish to witness. Mr. Coleridge's translation is also, as a whole, unknown to us: but judging from many large specimens, we should pronounce it, excepting Sotheby's *Oberon*, to be the best, indeed the only sufferable, translation from the German with which our literature has been enriched.[29]

There is further evidence that in spite of the strength of Carlyle's dislike of Coleridge at the end of his first visit to London he did not then or later entirely abandon him. In a postscript to a letter to Henry Crabb Robinson of 25 April 1826, he wrote: "What has become of Coleridge and his book of *Aids*? Where loiter the sweet singers of England, that no twang of a melodious string is heard throughout the Isle, nothing but the chink of yellow bullion? Alas! we are all Philistines together. But *veniet dies!*"[30] It appears also that in 1826 in deference to Coleridge he again began to read the old English writers.[31] Moreover, he did not totally ignore Coleridge's philosophy at this time but wrote in his journal on 3 December 1826: "Coleridge says, 'Many men live all their days without ever having an *idea*; and some of them with thousands of things they CALL *ideas*; but an Idea is not a Perception or Image, it cannot be *painted*, it is infinite.' Such was his meaning (not his words): I half or three-fourths seem to understand him."[32] In 1827 Carlyle began the novel *Wotton Reinfred* (of

28. *Works*, XXV, 114.
29. *Ibid.*, XXV, 151 n.
30. *Collected Letters*, IV, 82–83.

31. Wilson, *Carlyle*, II, 5.
32. *Two Note Books*, p. 78.

which he completed only seven chapters and which was not published until 1892). In this novel Dalbrook, identified with Coleridge, is a mystic philosopher and champion of transcendentalism, an "ardent seeker of truth and a worshipper of the invisible," who nevertheless is "incapable of action and without unity in himself."[33] In July of the same year, after an evening spent with John Wilson, an evening on which Wilson found great amusement in indulging in satire at Coleridge's expense, Carlyle recorded his delight in hearing Wilson's talk and his decided preference for it as compared with Coleridge's.[34]

Two articles published in 1827 and 1829 reveal the persistence of Carlyle's mixed attitude. In the first, the essay on "German Literature" published in the *Edinburgh Review*, Carlyle prefaced his somewhat detailed exposition of Kant's philosophy with statements that by implication denied Coleridge's right to be considered a metaphysical philosopher. The first step toward understanding Kant, Carlyle said, was to distinguish his teaching from all other teachings known to the British, particularly from metaphysical philosophy as taught in Britain, "or rather, what was taught; for, on looking around, we see not there is any such philosophy in existence at the present day"; philosophy in England had perished at the death of Dugald Stewart.[35] In the second article, "Novalis," published in the *Foreign Review*, he again said that Great Britain had had no philosophy since the passing of Dugald Stewart: "Now Philosophy is at a stand among us, or rather there is now no Philosophy visible in these Islands." In the same article, however, after declaring Coleridge to be neither so unintelligible nor so profound as Novalis, Carlyle said that the English reading public did not do justice to Coleridge's books such as *The Friend* and the *Biographia Literaria*. He even attempted to justify Coleridge's obscurity:

It is admitted, too, on all hands, that Mr. Coleridge is a man of "genius," that is, a man having more intellectual insight than other men; and strangely

---

33. W. S. Johnson, *Thomas Carlyle: A Study of His Literary Apprenticeship, 1814–1831* (New Haven and London, 1911), pp. 14–15, 30. For the text of *Wotton Reinfred*, see *Last Works of Thomas Carlyle*, ed. K. J. Fielding (Westmead, Hants, England, 1971), pp. 1–148. The quoted words above are Johnson's.
34. Wilson, *Carlyle*, II, 25–26.
35. *Works*, XXVI, 79. Cf. a passage in "Signs of the Times," *Works*, XXVII, 63, where Carlyle says very much the same thing.

enough, it is taken for granted, at the same time, that he has less intellectual insight than any other. For why else are his doctrines to be thrown out of doors, without examination, as false and worthless, simply because they are obscure? . . .

Never yet has it been our fortune to fall in with any man of genius, whose conclusions did not correspond better with his premises, and not worse, than those of other men; whose genius, when once it came to be understood, did not manifest itself in a deeper, fuller, truer view of all things human and divine, than the clearest of your so laudable "practical men" had claim to.[36]

Here again Carlyle was caught between a sincere desire to be fair to Coleridge and strong forces in his nature motivated by personal antipathy and considerable skepticism concerning Coleridge's mind.

Carlyle must have been considerably impressed by a statement made to him in a letter of 17 May 1830 by his brother John, educated to be a doctor, a brother whose mind and opinions were highly respected by Carlyle. Now in London, John wrote: "Coleridge has been unwell of late, but is now getting better. I saw him yesterday for the second time. I believe there is no man in the island puts more thought through himself."[37] Coleridge was certainly in the background of Carlyle's mind when he wrote "Characteristics," published in the *Edinburgh Review* for December 1831. In writing to Macvey Napier, editor of this review, on 8 October, just a few weeks before publication, Carlyle said of the article: "Coleridge has lately set forth a fragmentary Philosophy of Life; and I read a very strange one by Friedrich Schlegel, which he died while completing. It struck me that by grouping two or three of these together [he also mentions Thomas Hope's *Essay on Man* and William Godwin's *Thoughts on Man*], contrasting their several tendencies, and endeavouring, as is the Reviewer's task, to stand peaceably in the middle of them all, something fit and useful might be done."[38]

Coleridge died on 25 July 1834. Four days later Carlyle, now living in London, commented as follows in a letter to John Bradfute, an old friend in Edinburgh:

36. *Ibid.*, XXVII, 3–4, 38.
37. MS, NLS, 1775A.6o.
38. British Museum, Add. MS 34, 615, fol. 206. Carlyle probably refers to Coleridge's *Aids to Reflection* (1825, 1831) as well as to Friedrich Schlegel's *Philosophie des Lebens* (1828) and *Philosophische Vorlesungen* (1830), Thomas Hope's *An Essay on the Origins and Prospects of Man* (1831), and William Godwin's *Thoughts on Man* (1831).

Poor Coleridge, as you may have seen, died on Friday last: he had been sick and decaying for years; was well waited on, and one may hope prepared to die. Carriages in long files, as I hear, were rushing all round Highgate when the old man lay near to die. Foolish carriages! Not one of them would roll near him (except to splash him with their mud) while he lived; had it not been for the noble-mindedness of Gilman the Highgate Apothecary, he might have died twenty years ago in a hospital or in a ditch. To complete the Farce-Tragedy, they have only to bury him in Westminster-Abbey.[39]

A fairer and less cynical obituary is to be found in a letter to his mother of 5 August. In its simplicity, its rejection of rhetorical flourish and overemphasis, its balance, and its motivating spirit of sincerity and honesty, it is one of Carlyle's best pronouncements on Coleridge.

Coleridge, a very noted Literary man here, of whom you may have heard me speak, died about a week ago, at the age of 62. An Apothecary had supported him for many years: his wife and children shifted elsewhere as they could. He could earn no money, could set himself steadfastly to no painful task; took to opium and poetic and philosophical dreaming. A better faculty has not been often worse wasted. Yet withal he was a devout man, and did something, both by writing and speech. Among the London Literaries he has not left his like or second. Peace be with him![40]

To Emerson he wrote on 12 August: "Coleridge, as you doubtless hear, is gone. How great a Possibility, how small a realized Result. They are delivering Orations about him, and emitting other kinds of froth, *ut mos est*. What hurt can it do?"[41]

In spite of the desire to be fair reflected in his letter to his mother, the torrent of praise of Coleridge now being forced upon his attention intensified Carlyle's antipathy for the man. Not only in the letter to Emerson just quoted, but in more than one place elsewhere he reveals that he found what he considered the overpraise of Coleridge very distasteful. The attitude expressed in the following entry in his journal, 26 May 1835, is representative:

Coleridge's 'Table Talk' . . . insignificant for most part: a *helpless* Psyche, overspun with Church-of-England cobwebs; a weak, diffusive, weltering, ineffectual man. The *Nunc Domines* I hear chaunted about these two per-

39. D. G. Ritchie, *Early Letters of Jane Welsh Carlyle* (London, 1889), pp. 258–59.
40. MS, NLS, 520.31.
41. Joseph Slater, *The Correspondence of Emerson and Carlyle* (New York and London, 1964), p. 106.

sons [Wordsworth and Coleridge] had better provoke *no* reply from me: what is false in them passes; what is true deserves acceptance, speaks at least for a sense on their part.— . . .

Coleridge's Table Talk: insignificant; yet expressive of Coleridge. A great Possibility—that has not realised itself. Never did I see such apparatus got ready for thinking, and so little thought. He mounts scaffolding, pullies and tackle, gathers all the tools in the neighbourhood, with labour, with noise, demonstration, precept, abuse,—and sets three bricks. I do *not* honour the man; I pity him (with the *opposite* of contempt); see in him one glorious up-struggling ray (as it were), which perished, all but ineffectual, in a lax, languid, impotent *character* (*gemuth*): this is my theory of Coleridge,—very different from that of his admirers here. Nothing I find confuses me more than the admiration (the kind of man admired) I see current here. So measurable these infinite men do seem; so unedifying the doxologies chaunted to them. Yet in that also there is something; which I really do try to profit by. The man that lives has a real way of living, built on *thought* of one or the other sort: *he* is a *fact*; consider him; draw knowledge from him.[42]

Coleridge's championing of the Church of England, in which Carlyle had little faith, was a very real issue between the two men. Other issues, particularly those that Carlyle raised in connection with Coleridge's philosophical ideas and distinctions, were more assumed than real, since they involved much that Coleridge and Carlyle held in common.

The Church of England question and the value of Coleridge's teachings in general became very much an issue, however, soon after Carlyle met John Sterling at John Stuart Mill's office in the India House in February 1835. For years before, Sterling, like his old teacher of Plato at Cambridge, Julius Charles Hare, had been an enthusiastic admirer and champion of Coleridge. In his first letter to Carlyle, 29 May 1835, he praised Coleridge, who, he said, "by sending from his solitude the voice of earnest Spiritual Instruction came to be beloved studied & mourned for by no small or careless school of disciples."[43] Henceforth, until the death of Sterling in 1844, there was to be a kind of tug-of-war between the influence of Coleridge and that of Carlyle, with the mind and soul of John Sterling as the prize in the middle. Although critical of much that he found in Sterling, Carlyle

42. Froude, *Carlyle*, III, 45–46.
43. Harrold, *Sartor*, p. 308.

yet found much to admire in him and soon developed a deep affection
for him. In a letter of 27–30 November 1835 to his brother John,
Carlyle said: "Of all the people I see here John Sterling (the young
Clergyman) is the one I *love* most, different as our tempers and life-
theories are in all points. He is a frank brotherly all-hoping, most
childlike mortal, of very considerable genius; one feels as if he were
'too good to live'; which indeed his bodily constit*n* makes one anxious
about. He has fixed himself at Bayswater and comes often down to
me."[44] It is clear, however, that Sterling, even though Carlyle spoke
of him as childlike and even though he reciprocated Carlyle's admiration and affection, never became servile as a disciple of Carlyle
or allowed him to undermine completely his faith in Coleridge. "To
Coleridge," Sterling wrote Hare in 1836, "I owe *education*. He taught
me to believe that an empirical philosophy is none, that Faith is the
highest Reason, that all criticism, whether of literature, laws, or manners, is blind, without the power of discerning the organic unity of
the object."[45] It is clear, too, that Sterling had courage and would at
times challenge Carlyle in debate. The following entry in Carlyle's
journal for 15 May 1838 is significant:

> Dull dinner the day before yesterday—indeed, *hinc illae lacrymae*, for
> I had a cup of green tea too—at the Wilson's; Spedding, Maurice, John
> Sterling, and women. Ah me! Sterling particularly argumentative, babbla-
> tive, and on the whole unpleasant and unprofitable to me. Memorandum
> not to dine where he is soon, without cause. He is much spoiled since last
> year by really no great quantity of praise and flattery; restless as a whirling
> *tormentum*; superficial ingenious, of endless semifrothy utterance and
> argument. Keep out of his way till he mend a little. A finer heart was seldom
> seen than dwells in Sterling, but, alas! under what conditions? *Ego et Rex
> meus*. That is the tune we all sing. Down with ego![46]

The presence of Frederick Denison Maurice, who married the sister
of Sterling's wife and who for years had been a militant champion of
Coleridge, at this dinner must have been particularly irritating to
Carlyle. In *The Life of John Sterling* he wrote: "Of Coleridge there
was little said. Coleridge was now dead, not long since; nor was his
name henceforth much heard in Sterling's circle; though on occasion,

---

44. MS, NLS, 523.35.
45. John Sterling, *Essays and Tales*, ed. J. C. Hare (London, 1848), I, xv.
46. Froude, *Carlyle*, III, 138–39.

for a year or two to come, he would still assert his transcendent admiration, especially if Maurice were by to help."[47]

We may be sure, on the other side, that Sterling's "transcendent admiration" of Coleridge did not cause Carlyle to change his mind about the Highgate philosopher to the slightest degree. He was very much pleased when his brother John wrote him from the Continent that someone there had applied the phrase *krankhafte Dunkelheit* to Coleridge. "Krankhafte Dunkelheit [morbid gloom]," he wrote back on 2 July 1835, "was of all words the very word for Coleridge. I have amused several with it, to whom also it is *treffend* [a direct hit]. Mystic is *krankhafte* always."[48] Writing to the same brother again on 23 February 1836, he said: "On the whole, I often meditate on Christian things; but find as good as no profit in talking of them here. Most so-called Christians . . . treat me instead with jargon of metaphysic formulas, or perhaps shovelhatted Coleridgean moonshine. I admire greatly that of old Marquis Mirabeau (tho he meant it not for admiration): *Il a humé toutes les formules!* A man should 'swallow' innumerable 'formulas' in these days; and endeavour above all things to look with eyes."[49] When John Stuart Mill's well-known essay on Coleridge appeared in the *London and Westminster Review* in 1840, Carlyle felt that it reflected far too much credit on Coleridge. He wrote to his brother John on 17 March: "Mill has an Article on Coleridge in the last Review which some admire much. It is admirably *expressed*; but with that my admiration of it stops short."[50]

47. *Works*, XI, 129. For a somewhat detailed discussion of Maurice in his relation to Coleridge, Carlyle, and Sterling, see *Coleridge and the Broad Church*, pp. 157–59 n. On 30 June 1839 Sterling wrote to Carlyle: "I have also looked through Michelet's Luther with great delight & have read the *4th* vol of Coleridge's literary remains in which there are things that would interest you. He has a great hankering after Cromwell—& explicitly defends the execution of Charles" (MS in possession of Professor Frederick W. Hilles).

48. MS, NLS, 523.31.

49. MS, NLS, 523.37. Cf. *The French Revolution, Works*, II, 212. It is interesting to note that Jeffrey in a letter to Carlyle of 18 May 1837 praised *The French Revolution* with a phrase borrowed from Coleridge's comment in *Table Talk* on Kean's acting of Shakespeare: "It is no doubt a very strange piece of work, and is really, as Coleridge I think said of something else, like reading a story by flashes of lightning!" (Wilson, *Carlyle*, III, 9; Kathleen Coburn, *Inquiring Spirit: A Coleridge Reader* [New York, 1951, 1968], p. 294.)

50. MS, NLS, 523.78. John Sterling's article "On the Writings of Thomas Carlyle," in the *London and Westminster Review* (1839) and reprinted in Sterling's *Essays and Tales*, I, 252–381, though it contained much praise of Carlyle, did not altogether please him. Harriet Martineau wrote in her journal in Dec. 1839: "Striking review of Carlyle by Sterling in the London and Westminster. Carlyle writes to me that it is like the

Certain passages in Carlyle's lectures on *Heroes and Hero-Worship*, given in 1840 and first published in 1841, show, however, a definite and acknowledged influence of some of Coleridge's doctrines on Carlyle's thought. In "The Hero as Priest" he quotes with approval Coleridge on the subject of religious faith: "Souls are no longer *filled* with their Fetish; but only pretend to be filled, and would fain make themselves feel that they are filled. 'You do not believe,' said Coleridge, 'you only believe that you believe.' It is the final scene in all kinds of Worship and Symbolism; the sure symptom that death is now nigh."[51] In "The Hero as King" he approves Coleridge's doctrine of individual fulfilment: "The meaning of life here on earth might be defined as consisting in this: To unfold your *self*, to work what thing you have the faculty for. It is a necessity for the human being, the first law of our existence. Coleridge beautifully remarks that the infant learns to *speak* by this necessity it feels."[52] Even more important is a passage in his treatment of Dante in which he gives Coleridge due credit for the central thought in one of his own favorite doctrines concerning the relation of profound meaning to music and the precise way in which music is a component of great poetry, rather scarce in his time because of the failure of those who were trying to write it to grasp Coleridge's basic concept:

See deep enough, and you see musically; the heart of Nature *being* everywhere music, if you can only reach it. . . .

Coleridge remarks very pertinently somewhere, that wherever you find a sentence musically worded, of true ryhthm and melody in the words, there is some good in the meaning too. For body and soul, word and idea, go strangely together here as everywhere. Song: we said before, it was the Heroic of Speech! All old Poems, Homer's and the rest, are authentically Songs. I would say in strictness, that all right Poems are; that whatsoever is not *sung* is properly no Poem, but a piece of Prose cramped into jingling lines,—to the great injury of the grammar, to the great grief of the reader, for the most part! What we want to get at is the *thought* the man had, if he had any: why should he twist it into jingle, if he could speak it out plainly? It is only when the heart of him is rapt into true passion of melody, and the very tones of him, according to Coleridge's remark, become musical by the greatness, depth, and music of his thoughts, that we can give him

Brocken Spectre—a very *large* likeness and not very correct" (*Autobiography* [Boston and New York, 1877], II, 345).
    51. *Works*, V, 122.
    52. *Ibid.*, V, 225.

right to rhyme and sing; that we call him a Poet, and listen to him as the Heroic of Speakers,—whose speech *is* Song. Pretenders to this are many; and to an earnest reader, I doubt, it is for the most part a very melancholy, not to say an insupportable business, that of reading rhyme! Rhyme that had no inward necessity to be rhymed:—it ought to have told us plainly, without any jingle, what it was aiming at.[53]

In *Past and Present* (1843) Carlyle attacked again the shallow, artificial aestheticism and conception of poetic genius that he felt was prevalent in his age.[54] Moreover, in also attacking the idleness of the aristocracy, he used a metaphor drawn from his reading of *The Ancient Mariner*: "Idleness? The awakened soul of man, all but the asphyxied soul of man, turns from it as from worse than death. It is the life-in-death of Poet Coleridge."[55]

Yet the antipathy for Coleridge persisted in expressing itself, spasmodically but vigorously. It appeared as Carlyle was recording his impressions of a visit to Bruges in 1842: "Bruges in the thirteenth century had become the 'Venice of the North,' had its ships on every sea; the most important city in these latitudes was founded in a soil which, as Coleridge with a poor sneer declares, was not of God's making, but of man's. All the more credit to man, Mr. Samuel Taylor!"[56] Francis Espinasse reports that in the summer of 1843 he heard Carlyle repeat "with a certain glee" Hazlitt's verdict on Coleridge as a reasoner, "No premises, sir, and no conclusions." Espinasse also relates a story he had heard Carlyle tell at the expense of Coleridge and Coleridge's disciple John A. Heraud. Carlyle, it seems, was one of the audience to whom Heraud delivered a very eulogistic and rather high-flown funeral oration on Coleridge. He sat beside an obese, rubicund city man, who, when Heraud had ended turned to Carlyle, and giving "a great guff of port-wine" in his face, said, with due solemnity: "Sir, one drop of the blood of Christ is worth it all!"[57] Also in the 1840s he found all efforts of Coleridge's son Derwent and daughter Sara to be friendly with him decidedly distasteful and resisted them when he could. The following sentence from a letter to his brother John of 16 July 1844 is characteristic: "I am bound at present

53. *Ibid.*, V, 84, 90–91.
54. *Ibid.*, X, 292–93.
55. *Ibid.*, X, 285.
56. Wilson, *Carlyle*, III, 176.
57. *Literary Recollections and Sketches* (New York, 1893), pp. 67–68.

to a Tea with a certain stupid Derwent Coleridge here—ah me!"[58] In the summer of 1849, when Carlyle was touring Ireland with C. G. Duffy as his guide much of the time, he told Duffy that Coleridge had brought "the great ocean of German speculation" over into Great Britain and that Coleridge and Wordsworth had translated Teutonic thought into a "poor, disjointed, whitey-brown sort of English, and that was nearly all."[59] When the subject of Browning arose in Duffy's conversations with Carlyle, and Duffy maintained that Browning owed something to Coleridge, Carlyle argued with some heat that he did not:

Browning was the stronger man of the two, and had no need to go marauding in that quarter. . . . Whatever Coleridge had written was vague and purposeless, and . . . intrinsically cowardly, and for the most part was quite forgotten in these times. He had reconciled himself to believe in the Church of England long after it had become a dream to him. For his part he had gone to hear Coleridge when he first came to London with a certain sort of interest, and he talked an entire evening, or lectured, for it was not talk, on whatever came uppermost in his mind. There were a number of ingenious flashes and pleasant illustrations in his discourse, but it led nowhere, and was essentially barren. When all was said, Coleridge was a poor greedy, sensual creature, who could not keep from his laudanum bottle though he knew it would destroy him. . . .

There were bits of Coleridge fanciful and musical enough, but the theory and practice of his life as he lived it, and his doctrines as he practiced them, was a result not pleasant to contemplate.[60]

When Carlyle set about writing *The Life of John Sterling* in 1851, more than one force operated to compel him to exercise restraint in his representation of Coleridge and to evaluate his influence with unusual carefulness and discrimination. The maturity, effectiveness, and balance of the resulting portrait owe much to these forces. Although he actually wrote the biography very rapidly, after Bishop Connop Thirlwall and he had engaged in a theological wrangle that had provided the final impulse,[61] he may have entertained the notion

58. MS, NLS, 524.51. Similar expressions are in Carlyle's letters to his wife, 11 and 16 July, MSS, NLS, 611.175, 611.179.
59. *Conversations with Carlyle* (London, Paris, and Melbourne, 1896), p. 55.
60. *Ibid.*, pp. 58–62.
61. Sir Leslie Stephen, "Carlyle," *DNB*.

of writing the life as early as 1844, shortly after Sterling's death;[62] and then, after he and Hare, co-literary executors designated in Sterling's will, had agreed that Hare was to write the life, he had given up the idea for some years. Certainly the work that Carlyle finally wrote was one into which he poured experiences, impressions, and ideas that had been ripening in his mind over a period of years. Yet very few if any fundamental changes in Carlyle's attitude toward Coleridge and his influence took place through the years. The difference between the impression of Coleridge conveyed by Carlyle's *Sterling* and the earlier impressions that he recorded is a difference, almost altogether, of shaping, style, and scope, not a difference involving anything essential in Carlyle's judgment.

At his disposal when he wrote the life of *Sterling*, Carlyle had the letters and papers that Hare had used before him, together with his own considerable correspondence with Sterling, on which he draws largely.[63] He also had read and annotated two copies of Hare's two-volume edition of Sterling's *Essays and Tales*. The first copy he seems to have read and annotated very thoroughly, both Hare's memoir and Sterling's writings, soon after it was published in 1848.[64] In

62. F. D. Maurice wrote to Hare, in a letter dated 18 Nov. 1844, to inform him that Carlyle was interested in Sterling's papers. "When you pass through London, Carlyle wishes very much to see you, and to have some conversation with you about John's papers. Will you let me know beforehand how this may be arranged, either by his meeting you here or by your going to him at his house?" (Sir John Frederick Maurice, *The Life of F. D. Maurice, Chiefly Told in His Own Letters*, 3rd ed. [London, 1884], I, 387). Carlyle wrote to his mother on 12 Feb. 1848: "A Book consisting of my poor friend John Sterling's scattered writings has just come out; edited by one Julius Hare (an Archdeacon, soon to be a Bishop they say, a good man but rather a weak one);—with a *Life* of Sterling, which by no means contents me altogether. I think I shall send a copy of the Book up to you, by and by; probably one of my first tasks will be something in reference to this Work of poor Sterling's,—for he left it in charge to me too, and I surrendered my share of the task to the Archdeacon, being so busy with *Cromwell* at the time: but I am bound by very sacred considerations to keep a sharp eye over it, too; and will consider what can now be done" (MS, NLS, 521.66).

63. The Carlyle-Sterling correspondence is surprisingly extensive in the light of the fact that it covers a period of friendship of less than ten years. It contains fifty-five letters from Carlyle to Sterling, thirty letters from Sterling to Carlyle, fourteen letters from Jane Carlyle to Sterling, and two from Sterling to Jane. After John Sterling's death the Carlyles, particularly Jane, continued to correspond with his children. Many of the manuscript letters from Sterling to Carlyle, together with Carlyle's annotations, are now in the collection of Professor Frederick W. Hilles. In the biography Carlyle draws on a few of the letters in his correspondence with Sterling and a considerable number of Sterling's letters to members of his own family.

64. This copy is now in the Widener Memorial Collection of the Harvard Library. Miss Anne K. Tuell recorded and studied Carlyle's annotations in it in her article "Carlyle's Marginalia in Sterling's *Essays and Tales*" (*PMLA*, LIV [Sept. 1939], 815–

his marginalia here he comments on various things, including Sterling's portrait of Carlyle himself in his story "The Onyx Ring," beside which he writes an amusing "Moi!"[65] But his most significant comments are on Coleridge. When Sterling writes that the talk of Dr. Johnson was inferior to that of Coleridge, Carlyle declares, "Superior you mean." Many of his objections relate to quotations from Coleridge dealing with religious or theological matters. For instance, when Coleridge is quoted as saying that Christendom is obviously superior to the rest of the world in everything, Carlyle replies, "But there is much else here than 'Christendom.'" When Coleridge is quoted as saying that the Pelew Islanders possessed superstition rather than religion since they were ignorant of the personality of the Deity, Carlyle quotes Goethe in the margin, "*Wer darf Ihn nennen!*"[66] When Hare writes in the memoir, "At that time it was coming to be acknowledged by more than a few that Coleridge is the true sovereign of modern English thought," Carlyle exclaims in the margin, "Alas, alas." Hare's statement that Sterling owed more to F. D. Maurice than to any other man except Coleridge is scoffed at with a "Hoohoo" in the margin. Hare publishes, with some textual errors, Sterling's brilliant account of Coleridge's talk on his first visit to Highgate in 1827.[67] To this also Carlyle took exception, correcting Sterling: "Stoops much, shuffles in walking, does not seem to know exactly whence or whitherward in any respect. He always 'preaches' in a kind of melancholy, snuffling recitative."

Carlyle seems to have annotated the second copy of Sterling's *Es-*

---

24). See also Miss Tuell's book *John Sterling: A Representative Victorian* (New York, 1941).

65. Moncure D. Conway wrote of his conversations with Carlyle: "At every moment I was impressed by the truth of John Sterling's characterization of Carlyle in 'The Onyx Ring,' where as Collins he figures along with Goethe (Walsingham). I had read the story in my youth, and although in later years I do not accept the censorious estimates of Goethe, John Sterling's Carlyle has appeared to me as profound as Carlyle's Sterling" (*Autobiography* [London, Paris, and Melbourne, 1904], I, 355).

66. "Who dare NAME Him!" Cf. Harrold, I, *Sartor*, p. 317.

67. The manuscript of this is preserved, with a short notation in Carlyle's hand, in NLS, MS, 1765.62. Appended to it is a note, also in Sterling's hand: "I am very anxious that the following notes should not be lent or copied. They are in themselves of little importance,—& no one who rates Coleridge at his just value will ever think of making any unfair use of this very imperfect copy from his hasty sketches. But so much melancholy injustice has befallen the renown of great men from the circulation of similar slight records, that I should bitterly repent having ever written these minutes if I believed they could get beyond a few safe hands—or be exposed to the malignant stupidity of the mob. J. S. Sept. 17–1827."

says and Tales shortly before he wrote his own biography of Sterling. Most of the notes in it deal with Hare's memoir.[68] Here he scolds Hare for not giving the dates when Sterling wrote his account of Coleridge's talk—23 August–17 September, 1827—clearly given by Sterling himself on the manuscript, dates which might suggest that the description was written early by Sterling in his first burst of enthusiasm concerning Coleridge, not by the later Sterling in whom the influence of Coleridge had waned considerably. "Poor Coleridge," Carlyle writes in the margin, "I have heard his 'monologues' too, but found them very empty of nourishment to me; more elaborate futility tongue never spake in my hearing!"

When we consider the complexity of the materials and experiences that went into the making of the portrait of Coleridge in Carlyle's *Sterling*, we are certain to be greatly impressed by the degree to which imaginative synthesis or fusion based on heterogeneous, realistic materials has produced a work of art that richly deserves the high praise bestowed upon it through the years since 1851. Not merely restraint and balance, the Boswellian combination of light and shadow that Carlyle admired much in other biographers and in the great portrait painters, but moderation of tone and the introduction of atmosphere serve him well here. The beginning, which sets the key and the mood, is one of the finest passages of prose in Victorian literature:

Coleridge sat on the brow of Highgate Hill, in those years, looking down on London and its smoke-tumult, like a sage escaped from the inanity of life's battle; attracting towards him the thoughts of innumerable brave souls still engaged there. His express contributions to poetry, philosophy, or any specific province of human literature or enlightenment, had been small and sadly intermittent; but he had, especially among young inquiring men, a higher than literary, a kind of prophetic or magician character. He was thought to hold, he alone in England, the key of German and other Transcendentalisms; knew the sublime secret of believing by "the reason" what "the understanding" had been obliged to fling out as incredible; and could still, after Hume and Voltaire had done their best and worst with him, profess himself an orthodox Christian, and say and print to the Church of England, with its singular old rubrics and surplices at Allhallowtide, *Esto perpetua.* A sublime man; who, alone in those dark days had saved

68. This copy with Carlyle's annotations is preserved in the Duke University Library. Professor William Blackburn in "Carlyle and the Composition of *The Life of John Sterling*" (*Studies in Philology*, XLIV [Oct. 1947], 672–87) has recorded its marginalia and studied it in relation to Miss Tuell's work.

his crown of spiritual manhood; escaping from the black materialisms, and revolutionary deluges, with "God, Freedom, Immortality" still his: a king of men. The practical intellects of the world did not much heed him, or carelessly reckoned him a metaphysical dreamer: but to the rising spirits of the young generation he had this dusky sublime character; and sat there as a kind of *Magus*, girt in mystery and enigma; his Dodona oak-grove (Mr. Gil[l]man's house at Highgate) whispering strange things, uncertain whether oracles or jargon.

The critical spirit is fully alive in this passage but so is an understanding of the magnetism through which Coleridge drew young men like Sterling to him and exerted influence on them. The whole picture, furthermore, is wrapped in a softening haze of art, which gains much from the description of the Gillman's garden that soon follows it:

A really charming outlook, in fine weather. Close at hand, wide sweep of flowery leafy gardens, their few houses mostly hidden, the very chimney-pots veiled under blossomy umbrage, flowed gloriously down hill, gloriously issuing in wide-tufted undulating plain-country, rich in all charms of field and town. Waving blooming country of the brightest green; dotted all over with handsome villas, handsome groves; crossed by roads and human traffic, here inaudible or heard only as a musical hum: and behind all swam, under olive-tinted haze, the illimitable limitary ocean of London, with its domes and steeples definite in the sun, big Paul's and the many memories attached to it hanging high over all. Nowhere, of its kind, could you see a grander prospect on a bright summer day, with the set of the air going southward.

Thus, Carlyle provides a frame for his picture and through the use of physical perspective suggests psychological perspective and proper focus.

The whole treatment of Coleridge in this chapter is of very much the same quality and texture. None of his faults is spared: his attitude of bewilderment, his flabby and irresolute body, his shuffling walk, his lapses into floods of unintelligible talk, his addiction to monologue, his logical hocus-pocus, his queer nasal pronunciations, his inability to laugh heartily, his want of practicality and economic self-sufficiency, and, to Carlyle, his unreasonable defense of the Church of England. The strong effort to be fair to Coleridge is here, too, and Carlyle writes of his talk: "Glorious islets, too, I have seen rise out of the haze; but they were few, and soon swallowed in the general element again. Balmy sunny islets, islets of the blest and the intelligible:—on which

occasions those secondary humming groups would all cease humming, and hang breathless upon the eloquent words." In a similar
vein Carlyle writes, "Let me not be unjust to this memorable man.
Surely there was here, in his pious, ever-labouring, subtle mind, a
precious truth, or prefigurement of truth; and yet a fatal delusion
withal. . . . What the light of your mind, which is the direct in-
spiration of the Almighty, pronounces incredible,—that, in God's
name, leave uncredited; at your peril do not try believing that." Likewise, Carlyle speaks thus of Coleridge's natural gifts: "To the man
himself Nature had given, in high measure, the seeds of a noble endowment; and to unfold it had been forbidden him. A subtle lynx-
eyed intellect, tremulous pious sensibility to all good and all beautiful;
truly a ray of empyrean light;—but imbedded in such weak laxity
of character, in such indolences and esuriences as had made strange
work with it. Once more, the tragic story of a high endowment with
an insufficient will." [69]

It would certainly be an error to conclude that Carlyle, however
hard he may have tried, succeeded in being fair to Coleridge in his
biography of Sterling. The roots of his preconceptions and prejudices
ran too deep for him to be able to remove them by mere act of will.
He did succeed in producing impressive art, but it was also highly
subjective art.[70] Not merely John Sterling, F. D. Maurice, J. C. Hare,
and others, but he himself had been considerably influenced, sometimes unconsciously, by Coleridge. Moreover, the personality and
mind of Coleridge held a strange fascination for him, reflected to
some degree in Coleridge's portrait in *Sterling*, but also manifesting
itself many times throughout the years after he had written *Sterling*
as well as before. He could never surrender completely to the spell
of Coleridge; but neither could he leave him alone. In writing his
Reminiscences soon after the death of his wife in 1866, he recorded
recollections of Coleridge that, as we have seen, indicated hardly
any change in his impressions of Coleridge throughout the years; here
also he expressed satisfaction with his treatment of Coleridge in
his *Sterling*.[71] When Carlyle called upon Tieck in Germany on 7

69. *Works*, XI, 52–54, 56–57, 60–61.
70. Cazamian (*Carlyle*, pp. 257–58), in writing on Carlyle's attitude toward Coleridge, speaks of an "egocentric feeling" that he says is "an element of the greatest importance in Carlyle's personality: it decides for his thought and teaching at what point
the bold sincerity of his mind gives place to the subtle spell of his instincts."
71. See esp. pp. 282–83, where Carlyle quotes DeQuincey as saying in his articles

October 1852 and Tieck began talking about Coleridge, Carlyle "broke into uncontrollable laughter." Tieck asked Carlyle to tell him why he laughed, and Carlyle stopped laughing and said, "I know quite well that about Coleridge much is to be said seriously." "Then why did you laugh?" demanded Tieck; but Carlyle gave him no further answer.[72] On 8 October 1867 Carlyle wrote to James Hutchinson Stirling that he had read his article "De Quincey and Coleridge upon Kant" in the current issue of the *Fortnightly Review* and agreed entirely with its conclusion that "neither De Quincey nor Coleridge had read anything considerable of Kant, or really *knew* anything about him at all."[73] Carlyle also wrote to his brother John on 20 November 1875: "I have also two altogether paltry French letters, one of them from a young man just coming out of the school & all aflame to write a book on Coleridge, as the Lamp of England & Trismegistus of Men, —but wishing greatly withal, that I would set him on his way. Which you may judge how altogether likely I am to do. . . . *O Curas hominum!*"[74] But, as we have said, the fascination that Coleridge had for Carlyle lingered on too. D. A. Wilson records a rather charming story of a visit Carlyle made to Highgate in his old age. One day in the 1870s, when he and the historian Lecky were taking one of their delightful walks together, and after what seemed to Lecky much aimless strolling, Carlyle suddenly said: "What brought me here today was a desire to see Coleridge's house once more. In old times I went there to see him on several occasions, but I can't remember the house." Although Lecky was pessimistic about finding the house, Carlyle was confident that he was in the right neighborhood and persisted in looking for it. On discovering an old lady approaching, he spoke to her, "took off his hat, and with great politeness" asked: "Can you be so good as to inform me, madam, which house hereabout was once inhabited by the poet Coleridge?" A look of pleasure spread over the old lady's face, and she answered readily, "Certainly I can, sir. I can point out the very house to you. There it is." She turned and indicated it with the stick upon which she had been leaning. "It belonged to

---

in *Tait's Magazine* both that "Coleridge had the greatest intellect perhaps ever given to man" and that he lacked common honesty in applying it, which to Carlyle appeared to be "a miserable contradiction in terms."

72. Wilson, *Carlyle*, IV, 442–43.
73. *Ibid.*, VI, 142.
74. MS, NLS, 528.44.

my brother, and Coleridge was his tenant. I am a sister of Dr. Gillman."[75]

Actually, we know that the ideas of Coleridge and Carlyle, both great readers of German literature and philosophy, have much in common.[76] But because personality meant much to Carlyle, even more than ideas, he could rarely apprehend Coleridge's ideas except as they filtered to him through his intervening impression of Coleridge's personality and through the very powerful emotions associated in him with that impression. Accordingly, he more than once failed to recognize in Coleridge some reflections of himself. And he proved once more, as had often been proved before, that out of strange mixtures of the elements of human life and human relations great art can be born. Although it deals with a minor literary figure of the nineteenth century, certainly not a Carlylean hero, Carlyle's *Sterling* is perhaps the best one-volume biography written in England in its century; and it clearly demonstrates that the dynamics of conflict, both external and internal, in biography as well as in drama, can serve the writer well.

75. *Carlyle*, VI, 314.
76. For comparative studies of Coleridge's and Carlyle's ideas, see Osbert Burdet, *The Two Carlyles* (Boston and New York, 1931), pp. 136–37 and *passim*; Cazamian, *passim*; C. F. Harrold, *Carlyle and German Thought: 1819–1834* (New Haven, 1934), pp. 50–54; and *Coleridge and the Broad Church*, pp. 163–76.

THE CARLYLES AND BYRON

Carlyle's characteristic and habitual use of emphasis often leads the reader to make hasty and oversimple conclusions about his attitudes. Nothing could be more emphatic or apparently plain than the often-quoted passage on Byron and Goethe in *Sartor Resartus*: "What Act of Legislature was there that *thou* shouldst be Happy? A little while ago thou hadst no right to *be* at all. What if thou wert born and pre-destined not to be Happy, but to be Unhappy! Art thou nothing other than a Vulture, then, that fliest through the Universe seeking after somewhat to *eat*; and shrieking dolefully because carrion enough is not given thee? Close thy *Byron*; open thy *Goethe*." And in opening Goethe, Carlyle emphasizes his Christian doctrine of self-denial, re-nunciation, or *Entsagen*.[1]

The explosive finality with which Carlyle closes our Byron for us suggests an absoluteness of judgment which may lead us to conclude that in *Sartor Resartus*, written and published in the years 1830–34 at the very end of the Romantic Period, we have symbollically a clear transition from Romantic individualism and self-centeredness to Vic-torian social-mindedness, that all of Byron and what he stands for has been considered only to be rejected, and that all of Goethe is to be welcomed as salutary for the new age.

Furthermore, those who thus interpret the passage in *Sartor* can find some confirmation for their view in other passages in that work as well as in Carlyle's correspondence and notebook entries at the time when he was writing *Sartor*. In *Sartor* Carlyle says that the ways of a Byron or a Napoleon, great as they may seem for a while, are not lasting: "the very Napoleon, the very Byron, in some seven years, has become obsolete, and were now a foreigner to his Europe."[2] Then, too, in *Sartor* Byron is not merely a hungry vulture but like Beau Brummel, Count D'Orsay, and Bulwer-Lytton, a member of the Dandy class, a class always to be derided. Byron had also caught

---

1. Harrold, *Sartor*, pp. 191–92. Harrold comments: "This is Carlyle's announce-ment that the age of *Kraftmänner* (Power-men) like Byron, which had followed on the age of Voltaire, has given place to a new era of practical idealism, the age of Goethe in his *Wilhelm Meister*" (p. 192 n.).

2. P. 47.

the disease of view-hunting and, like Wordsworth and De Quincey, enjoyed luxuriating in his feelings as he discovered beautiful and picturesque natural landscapes. Carlyle's Professor writes: "Some time before Small-pox was extirpated, there came a new malady of the spiritual sort on Europe: I mean the epidemic, now endemical, of View-hunting. Poets of old date, being privileged with Senses, had also enjoyed external Nature; but chiefly as we enjoy the crystal cup which holds good or bad liquor for us; that is to say, in silence, or with slight incidental commentary." They never exclaimed, like the poets of the present, "Come let us make a Description! Having drunk the liquor, come let us eat the glass!"[3] Charles Frederick Harrold writes that Carlyle's objection in *Sartor* to the maxim "Know thyself" is based on his belief that it leads to morbid self-analysis, the disease of metaphysics, and Byronic despair.[4] Long after the publication of *Sartor*, Carlyle is reported to have told Francis Espinasse that Byron would be "forgotten in fifty years."[5]

While Carlyle was composing *Sartor*, he was giving considerable thought to Byron and seriously considering writing an essay on him. Thomas Moore's life of Byron appeared in 1830. Francis Jeffrey read it with great pleasure and in April 1830 wrote Carlyle a letter in which, despite the fact that he had at times been the target of Byron's satire, he spoke in the most glowing manner about Byron. "I have been reading Moore's *Byron*, or rather Byron's own *Byron*, for the charm is almost entirely in his own letters and fragments, with intense interest, pity and delight. I feel sure we should have been such friends, if we had met! and can scarcely help gnashing my teeth with spite that we never did, and alas never can. There are some traits of mysticism about him, for which you should like him all the better, and I believe I do not like him less. It is miserable that he should have perished in the golden prime of his days!"[6] Jeffrey's words, coming to Carlyle at a time when he was planning a trip to meet Goethe at Weimar, possibly suggested to him that it might be worth his while to develop

3. Pp. 58, 151–52. Carlyle also asserted that the younger Goethe with his *Sorrows of Werter* had had much to do with creating this taste (*ibid.*). Furthermore, most of Byron's work reflected the same stage of development as Goethe's earlier work: "Your Byron publishes his *Sorrows of Lord George*, in verse and in prose, and copiously otherwise" (*Sartor*, pp. 156–57). The Goethe opened in *Sartor* is not the whole Goethe but the older, mature Goethe.

4. *Sartor*, p. 163 n.

5. *Literary Recollections and Sketches* (London, 1893), p. 228.

6. Wilson, *Carlyle*, II, 152.

and put in order his thoughts concerning Byron. On 23 November 1830 Carlyle wrote from Craigenputtoch to Macvey Napier, editor of the *Edinburgh Review*:

Occasionally of late I have been meditating an Essay on *Byron*; which, on appearance of Mr Moore's Second Volume, now soon expected, I should have no objection to attempt for you. Of Mr Moore himself I should say little; or rather perhaps, as he may be a favorite of yours, nothing: neither would my opinion of Byron prove very heterodox; my chief aim would be to *see* him and show him, not, as is too often the way, (if I could help it) to write merely 'about him and about him.' For the rest, tho' no Whig in the strict sense, I have no disposition to run *amuck* against any set of men or of opinions; but only to put forth certain Truths that I feel in me, with all sincerity; for some of which this *Byron*, if you liked it, were a fit enough channel. . . .

I have been thinking sometimes likewise of a Paper on Napoleon, a man whom tho' handled to the extreme of triteness, it will be long years before we understand. . . . This however were a task of far more difficulty than *Byron*, and perhaps not so promising at present.

For *Byron* no Books were wanted except Mr Moore's two vo[lumes] to which Galt's might be added: except the *Plays* and Don Juan, which also would be needed, all his Poems are already here.[7]

Napier was not ready for Carlyle's essay on Byron at this time. When almost two years later he asked Carlyle to write an article on Byron for the seventh edition of the *Encyclopedia Britannica*, of which he was general editor, the mood had passed in which Carlyle felt that he could deal with the poet in a judicious, balanced fashion. Furthermore, the concise narrative of facts characteristic of an encyclopedia article was not what he had intended writing on Byron. On 28 April 1832 he wrote to Napier:

If it can gratify any wish of yours, I shall very readily undertake that little piece on *Byron*: but it will be *tacente Minervâ*, without inward call; nor indeed am I sure that you have fixed on the right man for your object.

In my mind, Byron has been sinking at an accelerated rate, for the last ten years, and has now reached a very low level: I should say *too* low, were there not a *Hibernicism* involved in the expression. His fame has been very great, but I see not how it is to endure; neither does that make *him* great. No genuine productive Thought was ever revealed by him to man-

7. From the manuscript letter in the British Museum, 34,614, fol. 436, published in R. H. Shepherd, *Memoirs of the Life and Writings of Thomas Carlyle* (London, 1881), I, 74–77.

kind; indeed no clear undistorted vision into anything, or picture of anything; but all had a certain falsehood, a brawling theatrical insincere
character. The man's moral nature too was bad, his demeanor, as a man,
was bad. What was he, in short, but a huge *sulky Dandy*; of giant dimensions, to be sure, yet still a Dandy; who sulked, as poor Mrs Hunt expressed
it "like a schoolboy that had got a plain bunn [*sic*] given him instead of a
plum one." His Bunn was nevertheless God's Universe with what Tasks
are there; and it had served better men than he. I love him not; I *owe* him
nothing; only pity, and forgiveness: he taught me nothing that I had not
again to forget.

Of course, one could not wilfully propose to astonish or shock the general feeling of the world, least of all, in a quiet Dictionary of Arts and
Sciences. Indeed, I suppose nothing is wanted but a clear legible Narrative, with some little summing-up, and outline of a Character, such as a
deliberate man may without disgrace in after times be found to have
written down in the year 1832. Whether you dare venture to have this
spirit traceable in it, I must now leave you to judge; adding only (if that
be necessary) that you *are* freely left; that I can in no wise esteem it a
slight or a disadvantage, should you see good, as perhaps I might do in
your case, to employ some other hand.

If, on the contrary, you still persist, then be so good as transmit me your
copy of *Moore's Life of Byron* (the second volume of which I have never
seen), and word along with it, How many Edinburgh Review pages three
or four of the Encyclopedia make. . . .[8]

It is not to be wondered at that Napier did not give Carlyle an immediate signal to write the article. In early May, just after finishing
his essay on "Corn-Law Rhymes," Carlyle wrote in his notebook:
"Purposed next to draw up an Encyclopedia memoir of Lord Byron
(for N[apier] and *purely* in compliance with his request); had accordingly jotted down some pages of it: but now an uncertainty arises
whether my service (as I explained the possibility of rendering it)
is wanted; which uncertainty will soon become a certainty that said
service cannot be had. I had no manner of call to speak *there* about
Lord Byron; and had much rather eschew it."[9] Thus, neither the essay
nor the article on Byron was written. It is a pity, for, in the essay
especially, Carlyle seemed ready to attempt a just and balanced estimate of the poet such as he was to give of Coleridge many years

8. From the manuscript letter in the British Museum, 34,615, fol. 328, published
in Shepherd's *Carlyle*, I, 104–107.
9. *Two Note Books of Thomas Carlyle from 23 March 1822 to 16 May 1832*, ed.
C. E. Norton (New York, 1898), pp. 267–68.

later, even though he had found just as many faults in Coleridge as in Byron. As it is, the general reading public has felt itself justified in interpreting "Close thy Byron; open thy Goethe" in the simplest terms possible.

But just as it is now possible to go back through Carlyle's letters and other writings before 1851 and discover in their primal freshness the materials that Carlyle with remarkable consistency and very high art wove into the portrait of Coleridge in his *Life of Sterling*, it is possible to find many threads of various colors in Carlyle's early writings that very probably would have been woven into his essay on Byron if he had written it. Both the lights and the shadows would have been in this essay, as Carlyle's letter to Napier of 1830 hints, for he had not only learned well his lesson from Boswell but his own experience in reading Byron through the years before 1830 had been a complex one, and the busy shuttle of his mind had been at work through all this time. Strong-minded reader and critic as he was, he more than once had had to reckon with the opinions of others concerning Byron, not the least important being those of Jane Welsh Carlyle.

The essay on Byron would not have been merely a Victorian estimate of a Romantic poet. Even dates are significant here. Carlyle had been born in 1795, the year in which Keats was born and the year in which Matthew Arnold's *father* was born. If he had died in 1835, he would have been classified as a Romantic essayist, critic, and philosopher much given to German transcendentalism who had written a highly fantastic and imaginative Romantic novel in a philosophical vein. Carlyle read and criticized Byron as a contemporary and, in many important respects, as one Romantic speaking of a fellow Romantic.

Moreover, Carlyle shared with Byron a feeling of indebtedness to the eighteenth century that many of their contemporaries did not share. Just as Byron adhered in theory to the principles of neoclassicism and admired Pope, Carlyle read early the works of Swift, Smollett, Sterne, Johnson, and Boswell and admired them throughout his long life. As enemies of the "world," both Byron and Carlyle found in satire an effective weapon, and behind their satire was the great satire of Butler's *Hudibras*, of Swift and the eighteenth century, and of Cervantes. Furthermore, Calvinism was rooted deeply in the minds of both men. Hence, Carlyle did not always shout down the spirit of Byron across a great chasm of time, taste, temperament, and conviction, but often found him standing near at hand, even on common ground.

Often tempestuous in mood and style, both of them were writers such as Keats objected to in "Sleep and Poetry" because they used "ugly clubs" and were "Polyphemes/ Disturbing the grand sea," not "might half slumb'ring on its own right arm." In both writers, furthermore, as in Swift, the tone of indignation and defiance appears again and again. Carlyle challenges and rejects the Everlasting No with his whole soul, and Byron's Manfred defies all the powers of Earth, Hell, and Heaven that would attempt to bring his invincible soul into subjection. No Romantic tendency is more pronounced in them than that manifested by independent and self-sufficient individualism. Yet neither their lives nor their writings were governed entirely by the spirit of vigorous action and romantic excitement: both fully appreciated the importance of coming to rest and of enjoying peace in tranquil moods; both wrote well when they expressed the intensity of stillness.

Both were writers whose imaginations found effective stimulus in history. Relics of old time and past events and brave men struggling, conquering, or dying moved them deeply. The sense of drama in history was what affected them most; history to them was always something acted out on a stage where only the most important characters and the most stirring and significant incidents were allowed to appear. Yet to some extent both Byron and Carlyle were saved from the purely theatrical in their interpretation of history by a down-to-earth sense and a humanizing touch, Carlyle more so than Byron. They loved to associate the faraway, the grand, and the relatively unknown with the local, the commonplace, and the familiar. For instance, there was Scottish blood in Byron as well as in Carlyle; and no Scotchman ever failed to be noticed by Byron and Carlyle, whether in Wellington's army at Waterloo, in Greece, or at Weimar or Berlin.

It is well to linger briefly on what Byron and Carlyle had in common because it is not only important but easy to overlook. In the main, however, they are strongly contrasting men and writers who throw one another into bold relief. It is sufficient to observe that there was a warp as well as a woof in the thoughts and experiences relating to Byron that Carlyle had up to 1834.

In 1814, at the age of nineteen, D. A. Wilson tells us, Carlyle was reading much poetry. *Hudibras* was one of the works he liked most, and among living writers he preferred Scott and Byron.[10] In the spring of the following year he discusses "The Corsair" briefly in a letter to his friend Robert Mitchell.[11] Two years later he met a certain Thomas Cuvallo, born at Istanbul, a Greek sailor who had had many Byronic adventures in the Near East.[12] In May 1818, after reading Canto 4 of *Childe Harold*, he praised Byron's "deep-toned" and "emphatic" style.[13] But two months later he objected to Byron's tendency to complain about his lot in life and contrasted him with Epictetus greatly to the advantage of the Stoic philosopher:

Complaint is generally despicable, always worse than unavailing. It is an instructive thing, I think, to observe Lord Byron surrounded with the voluptuousness of an Italian Seraglio, chaunting a mournful strain over the wretchedness of human life; and then to contemplate the poor but lofty-minded Epictetus—the slave—of a cruel master, too—and to hear him lifting up his voice to far distant generations, in these unforgotten words: [Carlyle quotes a passage from the *Encheiridion*, which C. E. Norton translates as follows: "It is the way of an uninstructed man to blame others for what falls out ill with him; of one beginning to be instructed to blame himself, but of one well-instructed to blame neither another nor himself."] [14]

In a more slapdashing mood he wrote to his friend John Fergusson on 5 August 1820: "Mark only—if Fortune do not mend, it is not certain but I may become a *roaring* philosopher. Byron is at the head of this school: but I doubt it does not answer—tho' the blaspheming

10. *Carlyle*, I, 91.

11. MS, Arched House, Ecclefechan; published in *Early Letters of Thomas Carlyle, 1814–1826*, ed. C. E. Norton (London and New York, 1886), pp. 19–22.

12. Wilson, *Carlyle*, I, 142–43.

13. MS, 25 May to Robert Mitchell, Arched House, Ecclefechan; published in *Early Letters of Thomas Carlyle*, pp. 71–75, incomplete, and in Moncure D. Conway, *Thomas Carlyle* (New York, 1881), pp. 167–68, also incomplete.

14. To Thomas Murray, 28 July 1818, in *Early Letters of Thomas Carlyle*, p. 79. Epictetus, however, did not become one of the "props" for Carlyle's mind as he did later for Matthew Arnold's. Carlyle found in his philosophy an aloofness and an unsocial quality that made too much of solitude. "Connected with mankind by sympathies and wants which experience never ceases to reveal, I now begin to perceive that it is impossible to attain the solitary happiness of the Stoic—and hurtful if it were possible. How far the creed of Epictetus may require to be modified, it is not easy to determine; that it is defective seems pretty evident. I quit the stubborn dogma, with a regret heightened almost to remorse; and feel it to be a desire rather than a duty to mingle in the busy current which is flowing past me, and to act my part before the not distant day arrive, when they who seek me shall not find me. *What* part I shall act is still a mystery." To James Johnston, 8 Jan. 1819, *ibid.*, p. 99.

line is worse. This is the age of philosophers—and in good truth I am of opinion that when all that tumultuous and fiery stuff, which so many of our poets are busy with, has once been moulded and fashioned rightly, many splendid results will follow."[15] His more detailed comments on Byron in a letter to William Graham of 28 January 1821 are not more favorable:

I suspected what the French call *mystification*, when you talked to me of poetry and Byron. Alas! my dear Sir, if discontented thoughts and reckless familiarity with whatever is at first sight more appalling in our inexplicable destiny, were all that went to form Giaours and Childe Harolds, there would indeed be a plentiful supply of that commodity. The corroding strife of will against Necessity, the vain tho' desperate efforts we make to reconcile the world within and the world without, are not confined to Byron: thousands feel this deeply; but the magic voice that gives it utterance, and clothes it all with splendor and beauty are the lot of one or two. I might write "last speeches" and "dying words": poetry—alas!—I do not regret this deficiency. Poets such as Byron and Rousseau are like opium eaters; they raise their minds by brooding over and embellishing their sufferings, from one degree of fervid exaltation and dreamy greatness to another, till at length they run *amuck* entirely, and whoever meets them would do well to run them thro' the body. Peace to the unfortunates! They find repose at last.[16]

This is the first of many passages in which Carlyle finds something psychologically and spiritually unhealthy in Byron's poetry.

In late May of 1821 Carlyle met Jane Welsh, whose enthusiastic admiration for Byron was for a time almost unbounded. In 1816, at the age of fifteen (she was now twenty), she had written laudatory verses to Byron that have been preserved. The last lines of the poem read:

> Byron, thy noble, lofty mind,
> Has been the sport of passions blind;
> Phrenzy has havocked in thy brain,
> With all her desolating train.

15. MS, NLS, 568.5.
16. *Letters of Thomas Carlyle to William Graham*, ed. John Graham (Princeton, 1950), pp. 19–21. It has been impossible to proofread the quotation from this letter and that from the letter to James Johnston, 21 Sept. 1823 (n. 40 below) against the MS letters, which have not been found. All other quotations from printed letters in this study have been proofread against the MS letters, whether the notes give the whereabouts of the MS letters or not, and some discrepancies appear between the printed texts and the passages as quoted here.

But that is past—and now you roam
Far from your wife, your child, your home,
Joys which might still have been your own.
But shall I love my Byron less,
Because he knows not happiness?
Ah, no! tho' worlds condemn him now,
Though sharp-tongued fame has sunk him low,
The hapless wand'rer still must be
Pitied, revered, adored by me.[17]

Jane's interest in Byron intensified Carlyle's own for a while, and he did not dare to cross swords with her immediately upon a point of taste in which her feelings were very much involved. Furthermore, there was much he himself could say sincerely in favor of Byron. Edward Irving, a highly valued friend of both Carlyle and Jane, had disapproved of Jane's reading Rousseau and Byron, authors whom he felt could not be counted on to build up a young lady's moral strength; but she continued to read them anyway and declared to her friend Bess Stodart that she felt all the better morally for having done so. "I never felt my mind more prepared to brave temptation of every sort than when I closed the second volume of this strange book [La Nouvelle Héloise]. I believe if the Devil himself had waited upon me [in] the shape of Lord Byron[,] I would have desired Betty [the maid] to show him out."[18] In January 1822, after Carlyle had sent her the manuscript of his "Faustus" and some of Byron's latest plays to read, she wrote to him: "I have read the Tragedies—I thank you for them—They are Byron's[;] need I praise them[?] I have also read your eloquent history of Faust."[19] This is the first bracketing together of the names of Byron and Goethe in the correspondence between them; a little later a tug-of-war developed between the two poets in the minds of Carlyle and Jane Welsh. For the moment, however, Carlyle was willing to go along with Jane. On 23 June 1822 in giving his younger brother John a list of what to read, he included the works of Byron: "You ought to read all Scott's Novels at odd

17. Early Letters of Jane Welsh Carlyle, ed. D. G. Ritchie (London, 1889), p. 102 n.
18. Ibid., pp. 30–31. The maid was Betty Braid, with whom Jane maintained an affectionate correspondence until her death in 1866 and with whom Carlyle corresponded for some years afterward.
19. The Love Letters of Thomas Carlyle and Jane Welsh, ed. Alexander Carlyle (London and New York, 1909), I, 20. Carlyle seems to have sent Jane the volume of Byron's plays that had been published on 19 Dec. 1821, containing Sardanapalus (dedicated to Goethe), The Two Foscari, and Cain.

hours—and Byron's poetry—and Shakespear—and Pope—and the like. These things are of the very highest value."[20] Meanwhile, Jane's feelings about Byron were expressed without restraint. She brooded imaginatively over the plight of Byron's little daughter Ada and in July 1822 even suggested that Carlyle write a poem about the child:

Dear Byron—sinner as he is there is no body like him—I have got his likeness; better done than the one I had. I can scarcely help crying when I look at it and think I may chance to go out of the world without seeing its original—What nonsense! . . . I have been thinking of a subject for you. Will you try it? an address to Lord Byron from his daughter. If she is *a genius* she might be writing verses by this time—those people are always in my head—I began to think yesterday, in church, of his child's feelings towards him. and when the people rose to pray I continued sitting—I did not wake out of my dream till the Dr prayed God to 'carry us in safety to our respective places of abode['] and then I saw all the people staring at me—[21]

A few days later, before Carlyle had replied, she wrote again about Ada: "I hope you have made something of Ada—I have made a precious nursery song of it."[22] Carlyle did make an effort to do something with Ada, but the results, though somewhat characteristically heavy-handed, were not gratifying to him or to anyone else. He wrote to Jane on 13 July 1822: "I did my best endeavor to conceive the feelings of poor little Ada, and throw some ornament over them; I had even proceeded so far as to *intend* saying something of the Stork with her bosom torn up to feed her young, of the Greenland bear whose cubs the English sailors interfered with—greatly to their cost; and I *intended* to draw a very notable moral from the whole: but alas! just as I was beginning, the 'Devil' came for *copy*, the Bullers came . . . , and lastly Irving came."[23] We cannot feel quite the same regret for these interruptions as we do for that of Coleridge's "gentleman from Porlock."

It was not like Carlyle, however, to be swept along by the tide of Jane's enthusiasm for Byron without some resistance. Recently he had become the tutor of Charles and Arthur Buller, and the boys' mother, a lady of high social standing and considerable culture, did

20. *Early Letters of Thomas Carlyle*, p. 222. On 8 Sept. 1824 John Carlyle wrote to his brother Thomas that he had read all of Byron except *Don Juan*. MS, NLS, 2883.36.
21. *Love Letters*, I, 61–62.
22. MS, ca. 11 July 1822, NLS, 2883.255.
23. *Love Letters*, I, 63–64.

not admire Byron. Carlyle felt compelled to convey Mrs. Buller's opinion to Jane in a letter of late July 1822: "I am sorry . . . that I cannot bring her to a right sense of Byron's merit; she affirms that none admire that noblemen [*sic*], so much as boarding-school girls and young men under twenty—which she reckons a sure sign of his being partly a charlatan."[24] Mrs. Buller's opinion, however, did not change Jane's or at this time affect Carlyle's to any considerable extent. As Byron's writings continued to be published, the two followed and read them with great interest. In October 1822 Carlyle wrote to Jane: "There is a new Periodical work coming out; in which it is said Byron is to take a large share. It will be the cleverest performance extant in that case. I will send it to you whenever it arrives."[25] The new periodical, which Leigh Hunt edited and which contained some of Byron's writings, was the *Liberal*. After the first issue appeared a few days later, Carlyle wrote to Jane: "Byron's Magazine or rather Hunt's 'the Liberal' is arrived in town; but they will not sell it—it is so full of Atheism and Radicalism and other noxious *isms*. I had a glance of it one evening; I read it thro' and found two papers apparently by Byron, and full of talent as well as mischief. Hunt is the only serious man in it, since Shell[e]y died: he has a wish to preach about politics and bishops and pleasure and paintings and nature, honest man; Byron wants only to write squibs against Southey and the like. The work will hardly do. If possible you shall see this number."[26] Carlyle wrote in a similar vein to A. Galloway on 6 November: "At present the honest people 'of letters' are much shocked at the appearance of Byron's and Hunt's Magazine 'The Liberal,' which hardly one of the Bibliopolists will venture to sell a copy of. The first two articles, seemingly Byron's, are exceedingly potent—very clever and very wicked: the rest is in Hunt's vein, and no better or worse than a common Examiner."[27] It was sometime later before Jane saw this issue of the *Liberal*, but she wrote to Carlyle on 11 November: "Ah poor poor Byron, I, even I must give him up."[28] Even so, she was not really ready to give him up. Neither

24. *Ibid.*, I, 69.
25. *Ibid.*, I, 79.
26. *Ibid.*, I, 95–96.
27. MS, NLS, 3278.117. To this first number of the *Liberal* Byron contributed "The Vision of Judgment," "A Letter to the Editor of 'My Grandmother's Review,'" and "Epigrams on Lord Castlereagh." See Leslie A. Marchand, *Byron: A Biography* (New York, 1957), III, 1026.
28. *Love Letters*, I, 101.

was Carlyle, who wrote to her protesting against such a hasty decision. At the same time he sent her Byron's *Werner* to read. "I hope this Tragedy of Byron's will amuse you for an hour or two: I meant to send it on Saturday, but was too late by some minutes in finishing it myself. You must not entirely 'give up' his Lordship yet; he is a person of many high and splendid qualities, tho' as yet they have done little for him: I still hope he will improve. If I had his genius and health and liberty, I would make the next three centuries recollect me. Tell me what you think of this *Werner*."[29] Jane's response was what might be expected: "Many thanks for 'Werner,' of which I might never have heard in this barbarian borough [Haddington]. is it not a masterly performance? he is my own matchless Byron after all!—"[30] Carlyle's own admiration for Byron as a dramatist was not great, but in another letter to Jane he objected to comparisons that the newspapers were making between *Werner* and another new play much inferior in quality, Lord John Russell's *Don Carlos*:

The Newspapers say Lord Byron is greatly obliged to his brother Lord, the latter having even surpassed "Werner" in tameness and insipidity; so that Byron is no longer author of the dullest tragedy ever printed by a Lord. This is very foul to Byron; for tho' I fear he will never write a good play, it is impossible he can ever write anything so truly innocent as this "Don Carlos." I would have sent it to you; but it seemed superfluous. There is great regularity in the speeches, the lines have all ten syllables exactly— and precisely the same smooth ding-dong rhythm from the first page to the last; there are also little bits of metaphors scattered up and down at convenient intervals, and very fine whig sentiments here and there: but the whole is cold, flat, stale and unprofitable, to a degree that "neither gods nor men nor columns can endure." You & I could write a better thing in two weeks, and then burn it.[31]

In a letter of 23 December 1822 to Robert Mitchell, one of his earliest and best friends, Carlyle returned to the subject of the *Liberal*: "Have you seen the 'Liberal'? It is a most happy performance, Byron has a 'vision of Judgement' there, and a letter to the Editor of 'My Grandmother's Review', of the wickedest and cleverest turn you could imagine. The Vice Society, or Constitutional Assoc^n are

29. *Ibid.*, I, 111.
30. Letter of 6 Dec. 1822, *ibid.*, I, 113.
31. *Ibid.*, I, 131–32. *Don Carlos: or, Persecution, a Tragedy in Five Acts* was first published in 1822.

going to prosecute. This is a wild fighting, loving, praying, blaspheming, weeping, laughing sort of a world! The literati and literatuli
with us are wrangling and scribbling; but effecting nothing, except
to 'make the day and way alike long.' "[32] A few days later there were
rumors that the second number of the *Liberal* was off the press.
Carlyle found it hard to get. On 12 January 1823 he wrote to Jane:
"I have not seen . . . Moore's *loves of the Angels,* or the second number of the Liberal, with Byron's Heaven and Earth (another 'loves of
the Angels') in it. I thought to get the Liberals for you yesterday, but
could not. The vice-society is prosecuting for Byron's articles, and
men are shy of selling them. Mr Bradfute I think is the publisher here
—you will see them when you come to Town."[33] About a week later
he suggested Madame de Staël and Byron as possible subjects for an
essay by Jane.[34]

As time went on, Goethe loomed larger and larger in Carlyle's
thinking and in his correspondence with Jane, more often than not
in some sort of association with Byron. The essay "Faustus," which
had been published in the *New Edinburgh Review* for April 1822
and which we know Jane read in manuscript and commended, had
raised what has now become the new time-worn question of how
much Byron owed to Goethe. Before its publication Carlyle had
written to a Mr. Hodgkin: "I do not say that Byron took the idea [of
the wicked and clever remarks in *Don Juan*] from Mephistopheles;
it is unhappily easy for many a one to find such ideas nearer home
if he is blackguard enough to indulge in them. I only meant to say
that Byron might have found his fundamental conception realised in
Goethe's play."[35] In the essay itself, frequently overlooked today because it is not in the various sets of Carlyle's collected works, there
is an important passage in which Carlyle discusses in some detail
what *Manfred* as well as *Don Juan* owes to Goethe. Full of admiration for Goethe, Carlyle writes with a full and intimate knowledge
of both poets and with a discrimination that does full justice to Byron:

32. *Early Letters of Thomas Carlyle,* pp. 252–53.
33. *Love Letters,* I, 148. John Bradfute, of Bradfute & Bell, Edinburgh booksellers,
was the uncle of Jane's intimate friend, Eliza Stodart. Jane frequently stayed in his
home on visits to Edinburgh before her marriage.
34. *Ibid.,* I, 159.
35. March 1822. Quoted from Wilson, *Carlyle,* I, 237. This essay is to be found
in *Collectanea Thomas Carlyle 1821–1855,* ed. S. A. Jones (Canton, Pa., 1893), pp.
59–92.

We cannot take leave of Faust, without adverting to the controversy
which has arisen respecting its connection with Manfred. The charge of
plagiarism, which Goethe brought forward against Byron, some time ago,
in a German Journal—and still more his mode of bringing it forward—gave
us pain; we thought it unworthy of Goethe; it shews too much of the author,
too little of the man. Goethe may be at ease about his laurels. It has been
his fortune to live through a change of dynasty in European poetry, and
to be himself, more than any other, instrumental in causing that change.
He has created a new literary era in his own country; and none will dispute
him the glory not only of having furnished many scattered ideas—but what
is far more honorable—much important intellectual training, to every one
of the great minds, with whose fame all Europe, and particularly England
"rings from side to side." The man whose writings served to nourish and
direct the genius of Sir Walter Scott,—whose *Götz von Berlichingen* paved
the way for the poetizing of Border Chivalry, and this prepared, afar off,
the elements of the Scot's novels, has no need to higgle with Byron about
even the property of Manfred. It is not our business at present to enter
upon the discussion of the point in dispute. A cursory perusal of Faust and
Manfred, we think, will satisfy any one, that both works stand related to
each other,—that if Faust had never seen the light, neither in all probability
would Manfred. Yet it does not appear to be apparent, but as forerunner,
that Faust is related to Manfred. The idea of man's connection with the
invisible world is the same in both; but in Byron it is treated solemnly; in
Goethe it often furnishes matter of laughter. Manfred, too, is not the same
character with Faust; he is more potent, and tragical, less impetuous and
passionate, and the feeling of remorse is added to that of the uncertainty
of human knowledge. In the management of the plot, the two pieces have
no similarity, and the impressions they leave on the reader are as different
as possible. Byron is not a copyist, but a generous imitator, who rivals
what he imitates. We have not heard that Goethe has given in any claim to
a right of property in Don Juan. Perhaps he might, with some prospect of
success; but the advantage of succeeding would be small. Mephistophiles
[*sic*] is unfortunately, not a character very difficult to conceive; nor has our
countryman presented it under a form likely ever to become very pleasing,
or permanently useful. The German devil is a much shrewder fellow than
the biographer of Don Juan; he sneers as keenly and as comprehensively;
he despises with fully more sprightliness and tact; and the taste for physical
impurity in all its most disgusting shapes, which his English rival manifests
so strongly, is one of the few qualities which the great "Denyer" seems to
have acted wisely in denying.[36]

36. *Collectanea Thomas Carlyle*, pp. 90–92.

Unquestionably to Carlyle even in these early years Goethe was a much greater poet than not only Byron but Wordsworth. After Carlyle had recommended that Jane read Goethe and she had found him difficult to read at first, he insisted that she persevere and more and more sought to convince her that he was superior to all other living poets:

This Goethe has as much in him as any ten of them [other poets of that time]: he is not a mere bacchanalian rhymester, cursing and foaming and laying about him as if he had breathed a gallon of nitrous oxide, or pouring forth his most inane philosophy and most maudlin sorrow in strains that "split the ears of the groundlings"; but a man of true culture and universal genius, not less distinguished for the extent of his knowledge and the profoundness of his ideas and the variety of his feelings, than for the vivid and graceful energy, the inventive and deeply meditative sagacity, the skill to temper enthusiasm with judgement, which he shews in exhibiting them. Wordsworth and Byron! They are as the Christian Ensign and Captain Bobadil before the Duke of Marlboro! [37]

In the spring of 1824, while Carlyle was translating *Wilhelm Meister*, Jane scolded him for wasting his genius in such work and confessed that she found little in the novel to admire. She spoke lightly of the characters in it: "The unaccountable propensity to kissing which runs through all your dramatis personae perplexes me sadly." [38] Carlyle replied: "So you laugh at my venerated Goethe and my *Herzenskind* poor little wood-eating Mignon! O! The hardness of man's and still more of woman's heart! . . . You will like Goethe better ten years hence than you do at present." Then turning his thought toward the money that he hoped to make through his translation, he added: "Me it would make happy, at least for half a year, if I saw the certain prospect before me of making £500 per annum: a pampered Lord (e.g. Byron) would turn with loathing from a pyramid of ingots. I *may* be blessed in this way: he never. Let us be content!" [39] While translating Goethe's book, however, Carlyle himself sometimes lost patience with the author. He wrote to one of his old friends: "In the meantime I am busily engaged every night in translating Goethe's *Wilheim Meister*: a task which I have undertaken formally and must proceed with, though it suits me little. There is poetry in the book,

---

37. Letter of 4 March 1823, in *Love Letters*, I, 178.
38. Letter of 4 April 1824 in *ibid.*, I, 352.
39. Letter of 15 April 1824, *ibid.*, I, 357.

and prose, prose for ever. . . . Goethe is the greatest genius that has lived for a century, and the greatest ass that has lived for three. I could sometimes fall down and worship him; at other times I could kick him out of the room."[40] And while he continued to insist that Jane read Goethe, he kept her informed about Byron and his latest publications. On 6 April 1823 he wrote to her: "Byron has sent us a new poem the *Age of Bronze*: it is short, and pithy—but not at all poetical. Byron may still easily fail to be a great man. You shall see his *Bronze* (a political squib) when you arrive; and another *Liberal* which is on the way."[41]

When Byron died on 19 April 1824, the blow to Jane was sudden and great. Carlyle joined with her in her feeling of grief and loss. On 19 May he wrote:

Poor Byron! Alas poor Byron! The news of his death came down upon my heart like a mass of lead; and yet, the thought of it sends a painful twinge thro' all my being, as if I had lost a Brother! O God! That so many sons of mud and clay should fill up their base existence to its utmost bound; and this, the noblest spirit in Europe, should sink before half his course was run! Late so full of fire, and generous passion, and proud purposes, and now forever dumb and cold! Poor Byron! And but a young man; still strug-gling amid the perplexities, and sorrows, and aberrations, of a mind not arrived at maturity or settled in its proper place in life. Had he been spared to the age of three score and ten, what might he not have done, what might he not have been! But we shall hear his voice no more; I dreamed of seeing him and knowing him but the curtain of everlasting night has hid him from our eyes. We shall go to him, he shall not return to us. Adieu my dear Jane! There is a blank in your heart, and a blank in mine, since this man passed away— Let us stand the closer by each other![42]

Though we may suspect that Carlyle, without being insincere, was in part attempting to express Jane's feelings for her and may even as a lover have been enjoying the companionship of grief, the central statement in this obituary is important. It runs through many of Carlyle's later pronouncements about Byron. Byron, "the noblest spirit in Europe," was one of the "inheritors of unfulfilled renown." He was immature but full of promise; if he had lived, he probably would have done mighty things. This was more than Carlyle was

40. To James Johnston, 21 Sept. 1823, in *Early Letters of Thomas Carlyle*, p. 286.
41. *Love Letters*, I, 195.
42. *Ibid.*, I, 366.

willing to grant to the other younger Romantic poets, Shelley and Keats, who to him showed no such promise.

Jane's grief was absolute and complete. She wrote to Carlyle on 20 May: "And Byron is dead! I was told it all at once in a room full of people. My God if they had said that the Sun or the Moon was gone out of the heavens it could not have struck me with the idea of a more awful and dreary blank in the creation than the words Byron is dead. I have felt quite cold and dejected ever since. All my thoughts have been fearful and dismal."[43] Five days later she wrote to him: "Every hour is bringing you nearer!—thank God! I have you again— Byron's death made me tremble for all that I admire and love."[44] The sincerity of Carlyle's own feelings is attested in his letter to Jane of 27 May: "I had such a fight to-day with Brewster and a gothic German for the memory of our poor Byron!"[45]

During Carlyle's first visit to London the poet Bryan W. Procter ("Barry Cornwall") gave him a fragment of a letter from Byron. On 22 July 1824 he wrote excitedly to Jane: "I have got a whole sheaf of poetic autographs—and among them a piece of Lord Byron's writing. I will send them the first frank I can get."[46] It was December, however, before Jane received the autographs. Just before they were sent, Goethe's first letter to Carlyle came; and Carlyle sent that to Jane too. On 3 January 1825 she wrote to him to express her delight. The letter from Byron was even more valuable to her than the one from Goethe. "The Autographs you have sent me, have all of them a value in my curiosity-loving eyes; but Byron's handwriting—my own Byron's—I esteem, not as a *curiosity* merely, but rather as a relic of an honoured and beloved Friend. Will you believe it? it is more precious to me than even Goethe's letter; flattering tho' it is for you to have received, and for me to be made the Depository of such a letter from so illustrious a Personage."[47] To Eliza Stodart on 18 January Jane wrote even more ecstatically of Byron's letter: "You cannot think how it affected me! This, then, was *his* handwriting! *his* whose image had haunted my imagination for years and years; whose wild,

43. *Ibid.*, I, 369.
44. *Ibid.*, I, 370.
45. *Ibid.*, I, 372. Dr. David Brewster had invited Carlyle to write biographical articles for the *Edinburgh Encyclopedia*, which have been collected in *Montaigne and Other Essays Chiefly Biographical*, collected by S. R. Crockett (London, 1897).
46. *Love Letters*, I, 388.
47. "Eight New Love Letters of Jane Welsh Carlyle," ed. Alexander Carlyle, *Nineteenth Century and After*, LXXV (Jan. 1914), 104–105.

glorious spirit had tinctured all the poetry of my Being! *he*, then, had seen and touched this very paper,—I could almost fancy that his look and touch were visible on it[!] And *he*—where was he now? All the sentiment in me was screwed up to the highest pitch; I could hardly help crying like a child or Dugald Gilchrist, and I kissed the seal with a fervour which would have graced the most passionate Lover."[48] In the meantime, however, on 9 January Carlyle wrote to warn her against narrowing the basis of her life by making "Literature" written large her all-in-all. Life and human nature were broader than literature. He himself had had to learn this lesson at a high cost. In arguing his point, Carlyle found it convenient to refer to Byron's way of life and to quote Goethe.

I have lost them [health, equanimity, and regular, profitable, and natural habits of activity], by departing from Nature; I must find them by returning to her. A stern experience has taught me this; and I am a fool if I do not profit by the lesson. Depend on it, Jane, this literature, which both of us are so bent on pursuing, will *not* constitute the sole nourishment of any true human spirit. No truth has been forced upon me, after more resistance, or with more invincible impressiveness than this. I feel it in myself, I see it daily in others. Literature is the *wine of life*; it will not, cannot, be its *food*. What is it that makes Blue-stockings of women, Magazine-hacks of men? They neglect household and social duties, they have no household and social enjoyments. Life is no longer with them a verdant field, but a *hortus siccus* [parched garden]; they exist pent up in noisome streets, amid feverish excitements; they despise or overlook the common blessedness which Providence has laid out for *all* his creatures, and try to substitute for it a distilled quintessence prepared in the alembic of painters and rhymers and sweet singers. What is the result? This *ardent spirit* parches up their nature; they become discontented and despicable, or wretched and dangerous. Byron and all strong souls go the latter way; Campbell and all weak souls the former. "*Hinaus!*" as the Devil says to Faust, "*Hinaus ins frey Feld!*" ["Out into the wide open field!"] There is no soul in these vapid "Articles" of yours: away! Be *men* before attempting to be *writers!*"[49]

48. *Early Letters of Jane Welsh Carlyle*, pp. 101–102. Dugald Gilchrist had wept wildly shortly before when Jane rejected his proposal of marriage.

49. *Love Letters*, II, 63. Campbell is Thomas Campbell, of whom Carlyle had written in Aug. 1824: "Hardship, I suspect, has withered out the sensibilities of his nature, and turned him, finally, into a whisking, antithetical little editor. There is no significance in his aspect. His blue frock, and switch, and fashionable wig, and clear, cold eyes, and clipt accents, and slender *persiflage* might befit a dandy." Conway, *Carlyle*, p. 194.

Behind Goethe in this important passage is the precedent of Milton, often quoted by Carlyle; and looming out of the passage is a prophetic sign, somewhat *larger* than a man's hand, betokening the broad basis upon which Victorian literature sought to establish itself. It is worth noticing that the passage does not attack Byron; it attacks a conception of literature that would too much restrict the free, vigorous, magnanimous spirit of a Byron.

Until the Carlyles married in October 1826 most of their thoughts concerning Byron had taken the form of a dialogue between them conducted through letters. After the marriage Jane rarely mentioned the subject in writing, and Carlyle expressed his opinions chiefly through *Sartor* and articles written for magazines, with occasional references to Byron in his notebook and letters to relatives and friends. Books like Leigh Hunt's *Lord Byron and Some of His Contemporaries* and Thomas Moore's *Life of Byron* he found particularly interesting and provocative. By 1826 his opinions concerning Byron were fairly well formed. A highly articulate man, in the next few years he made them very clear indeed.

To his notebook he communicated on 3 December 1826: "Byron, good, generous, hapless Byron! And yet when he died he was only a *Kraftmann, Power-man* as the Germans call them. Had he lived he would have been a Poet."[50] He expanded this thought in his "State of German Literature," which appeared in the *Edinburgh Review* in October 1827: "Our Byron was in his youth but what Schiller and Goethe had been in theirs: yet the author of *Werter* wrote *Iphigenie* and *Torquato Tasso*; and he who began with the *Robbers* ended with *Wilhelm Tell*. With longer life, all things were to have been hoped for from Byron: for he loved truth in his inmost heart, and would have discovered at last that his Corsairs and Harolds were not true. It was otherwise appointed."[51] The state of public taste for poetry in these years, Carlyle believed, was very bad. The genuine poets had either died or were too discouraged to write. "Our Poets are silent; and nothing is heard for the time but the chirping of a thousand thousand sparrows in the light printwork of the day."[52] He wrote to Eckermann on 9 December 1828 that in England poets like Thomas Moore and

50. *Two Note Books*, p. 71.
51. See *Works*, XXVI, 69.
52. To Dr. N. H. Julius, 15 April 1827, MS in the Speck Collection, Yale University Library.

other *Kraftmänner* had silenced the real poets and had the stage all to themselves:

The aspects of our Literature at present, had one a weak Faith, are in fact discouraging enough: our real Poets, Wordsworth, Coleridge driven into silence by the state of public taste; and the air filled with nothing, as it were, but the chirping of ten thousand grasshoppers, each firmly believing that it is a mighty Singer. . . . Thomas Moore is nothing better than one of your *Heinses*, or other *Kraftmänner*; he has published an *Epicurean*, re-splendent with gold-leaf and Bristol diamonds, and inwardly made of mere Potter's-clay. Walter Scott manufactures Novels. Peace be with them! But the spirit of England is not dead, only asleep; neither, as I firmly believe, is the day distant when these men will be for most part swept into the lumber-room, and quite another scene enacted.[53]

Goethe, who was granted the gift of years as well as other very high gifts, set a splendid example to other poets of his day and to all later poets by outgrowing and rising above the *Kraftmann* side of his nature. He won the victory that Byron could only dimly sense:

Werter is but the cry of that dim, rooted pain, under which all thoughtful men of a certain age were languishing: it paints the misery, it passionately utters the complaint; and heart and voice, all over Europe, loudly and at once respond to it. True, it prescribes no remedy; for that was a far dif-ferent, far harder enterprise, to which other years and a higher culture were required; but even this utterance of the pain, even this little, for the present, is ardently grasped at, and with eager sympathy appropriated in every bosom. If Byron's life-weariness, his moody melancholy, and mad stormful indignation, borne on the tones of a wild and quite artless melody, could pierce so deep into many a British heart, now that the whole matter is no longer new,—is indeed old and trite,—we may judge with what vehe-ment acceptance this *Werter* must have been welcomed, coming as it did like a voice from unknown regions; the first thrilling peal of that im-passioned dirge, which, in country after country, men's ears have listened to, till they were deaf to all else. For *Werter*, infusing itself into the core and whole spirit of Literature, gave birth to a race of Sentimentalists, who have raged and wailed in every part of the world; till better light dawned on them, or at worst, exhausted Nature laid herself to sleep, and it was discovered that lamenting was an unproductive labour. These funereal choristers, in Germany a loud, haggard, tumultuous, as well as tearful class,

53. W. A. Speck, "New Letters of Carlyle to Eckermann," *Yale Review*, XV (July 1926), 739. The original letter is in the Speck Collection at Yale.

were named the *Kraftmänner*, or Power-men; but have all long since, like sick children, cried themselves to rest.

Byron was our English Sentimentalist and Power-man; the strongest of his kind in Europe; the wildest, the gloomiest, and it may be hoped the last. For what good is it to "whine, put finger i' the eye, and sob," in such a case? Still more, to snarl and snap in malignant wise, "like dog distract, or monkey sick"? Why should we quarrel with our existence, here as it lies before us, our field and inheritance, to make or to mar, for better or for worse; in which, too, so many noblest men have, ever from the beginning, warring with the very evils we war with, both made and been what will be venerated to all time?[54]

Goethe, however, triumphed gloriously over his difficulties, fully as formidable and multifold as those about which Byron complained loudly. "Did he not bear the curse of the time? He was filled full with its scepticism, bitterness, hollowness and thousandfold contradictions, till his heart was like to break; but he subdued all this, rose victorious over this, and manifoldly by word and act showed others that come after, how to do the like. Honour to him who first 'through the impassible paves a road'! Such, indeed, is the task of every great man."[55] Earlier, Cervantes had demonstrated his genuine strength by rising to just such a great victory. In contrast with him, a Power-man like Byron seemed very weak indeed:

A certain strong man, of former time, fought stoutly at Lepanto; worked stoutly as Algerine slave; stoutly delivered himself from such working; with stout cheerfulness endured famine and nakedness and the world's in-gratitude; and, sitting in jail, with the one arm left him, wrote our joyfulest, and all but our deepest, modern book, and named it *Don Quixote*: this was a genuine strong man. A strong man, of recent time, fights little for any good cause anywhere; works weakly as an English lord; weakly delivers himself from such working; with weak despondency endures the cackling of plucked geese at St. James's; and, sitting in sunny Italy, in his coach-and-four, at a distance of two thousand miles from them, writes, over many reams of paper, the following sentence, with variations: *Saw ever the world one greater or unhappier?* This was a sham strong man. Choose ye.[56]

This passage, eloquent in its treatment of Cervantes, a major in-fluence on Carlyle when he was writing *Sartor* and later, is unfair to

---

54. "Goethe," *Foreign Review*, July 1828. See *Works*, XXVI, 217–18. The two quotations are from *The Comedy of Errors* and *Hudibras*, respectively.
55. "Death of Goethe," *New Monthly Magazine*, June 1832, *Works*, XXVII, 379.
56. "Goethe's Works," *Foreign Quarterly Review*, Aug. 1832, *Works*, XXVII, 436.

Byron, who did fight in some very good causes and whose *Don Juan*, as Carlyle himself appears once or twice to have discerned, was like *Don Quixote* a great triumph of the human mind and spirit.

But the indictment of Byron Carlyle repeated over and over, not merely emphatically, as in the passage just quoted, but at times in words almost savage in tone. To his notebook he confided on 23 December 1831: "Byron we call 'a Dandy of Sorrows, and acquainted with grief.' That is a brief definition of him."[57] Byron's morbid outlook on life was in striking contrast to the fundamental courage and cheerfulness of writers like Ebenezer Elliott, author of the *Corn-Law Rhymes*, William Cobbett, and Sir Walter Scott. "In good truth, if many a sickly and sulky Byron, or Byronlet, glooming over the woes of existence, and how unworthy God's Universe is to have so distinguished a resident, could transport himself into the patched coat and sooty apron of a Sheffield Blacksmith [Elliott], made with as strange faculties and feelings as he, made by God Almighty all one as he was,—it would throw a light on much for him."[58] Carlyle deplored what he considered the general unhealthiness of English literature in the 1830s, which, he said, despite the example of good health set by Cobbett and Scott, "lay all puking and sprawling in Werterism, Byronism, and other Sentimentalism tearful or spasmodic."[59] The spectacle of himself that Byron had permitted the general public to watch was indeed a pitiful thing:

Is there, for example, a sadder book than that *Life of Byron* by Moore? To omit mere prurient susceptivities that rest on vacuum, look at poor Byron, who really had much substance in him. Sitting there in his self-exile, with a proud heart striving to persuade itself that it despises the entire created Universe; and far off, in foggy Babylon, let any pitifulest whipster draw pen on him, your proud Byron writhes in torture,—as if the pitiful whipster were a magician, or his pen a galvanic wire struck into the Byron's spinal marrow! Lamentable, despicable,—one had rather be a kitten and cry mew! O son of Adam, great or little, according as thou art lovable, those thou livest with will love thee.[60]

57. *Two Note Books*, p. 230.
58. *Corn-Law Rhymes*, *Edinburgh Review*, July 1832, *Works*, XXVIII, 158.
59. "Sir Walter Scott," *London and Westminster Review*, Jan. 1838, *Works*, XXIX, 39.
60. *Ibid.*, pp. 52–53. "Rather be a kitten and cry mew": Carlyle quotes Hotspur, *Henry IV, Part One*, III, i.

It was inevitable that Carlyle, with his Scottish Puritan respect for thrift and industry and with the Gospel of Work that he preached with great emphasis, should find in idleness one of the roots of the malady from which Byron suffered. Only work, he repeated many times, could enable a man to find and profit from his highest nature. Hence, on 13 November 1831 he wrote to his brother John, then the private physician of the Countess of Clare: "I fully agree with you that Employment would be the best of all medicines for your Patient. Neither is Employment, or can it be in a world existing by Labour, impossible to find; whether for Peasantess or Princess. Unfortunately, however, it is often very difficult to find: thus Swing burns ricks, thus Byron writes Satanic Poetry. What man wants is always that the highest in his nature be *set* at the top, and actively reign there."[61] And in developing this idea more fully in *Past and Present*, he finds an opportunity to attack the "Greatest-Happiness" theory of the Benthamites:

We construct our theory of Human Duties, not on any Greatest-Nobleness Principle, never so mistaken; no, but on a Greatest-Happiness Principle. . . . You are men, not animals of prey, well-used or ill-used! Your Greatest-Happiness Principle seems to me fast becoming a rather unhappy one.—What if we should cease babbling about "happiness," and leave *it* resting on its own basis, as it used to do!

A gifted Byron rises in his wrath; and feeling too surely that he for his part is not "happy," declares the same in very violent language, as a piece of news that may be interesting. It evidently has surprised him much. One dislikes to see a man and poet reduced to proclaim on the streets such tidings: but on the whole, as matters go, that is not the most dislikable. Byron speaks the *truth* in this matter. Byron's large audience indicates how true it is felt to be. . . .

The only happiness a brave man ever troubled himself with asking much about was, happiness enough to get his work done. . . . The night once

61. MS, NLS, 522.105. The *O.E.D.* indicates that a fictitious "Captain Francis Swing" wrote letters threatening to burn ricks and barns, some of which were actually burned in 1830–31. The name "Swing" thus became accepted as generic for "rick-burner," like Kilroy for the ubiquitous GI of World War II. Earlier Carlyle had quoted a well-known line from *Childe Harold* (Canto III, stanza 42) to spur another brother, Alexander, on to work: "There is not on the earth so horrible a malady as idleness, voluntary or constrained. Well said Byron: 'Quiet to quick bosoms is a hell.' So long as you are conscious of adding to your stock of knowledge or other useful qualities, and feel that your faculties are fitly occupied, the mind is active and contented." *Early Letters of Thomas Carlyle*, p. 291, letter of 2 Nov. 1823.

come, our happiness, our unhappiness,—it is all abolished; vanished, clean gone; a thing that has been: "not of the slightest consequence" whether we were happy as eupeptic Curtis, as the fattest pig of Epicurus, or unhappy as Job with potsherds, as musical Byron with Giaours and sensibilities of the heart.[62]

Kraftmann or not, Lord Byron had had his merits. Carlyle did not like to see him dealt with unjustly by his old friend and benefactor Leigh Hunt. When Hunt's controversial book on Byron appeared in 1828, Carlyle found it difficult to get a copy to read but feared that there was only too much truth in what the reviews were saying about Hunt's unjust and ungrateful treatment of Byron. On 17 January he wrote to Bryan W. Procter: "What is this periodical of Leigh Hunt's, and have you seen that wondrous Life of Byron? Was it not a thousand pities Hunt had borrowed money of the man he was to disinhume and behead in the course of *duty* afterwards? But for love or money I cannot see Hunt's Book, or anything but extracts of it, and so must hold my tongue. Poor Hunt! He has a strain of music in him too, but poverty and vanity have smote too rudely over the strings."[63] To his brother John he wrote on 10 June: "Farther, except continued abuse of Leigh Hunt for his *Lord Byron & some of his Contemporaries*, there seemed no news in 'The Literary world,' or rather universe, for was there ever such a *world* as it has grown?"[64] After Carlyle and Hunt met in 1831, they became close friends. Carlyle found much to admire in Hunt despite marked differences in their characters and opinions. But he also had experiences similar to those that Byron had had with Hunt as a perennial borrower of money and as one who had little sense about money.

Perhaps Carlyle achieved a clearer and truer perspective in his consideration of Byron when he compared him, not with such great

62. Ed. A. M. D. Hughes (Oxford, 1934), pp. 139–41. Hughes writes of "eupeptic Curtis": "A family of this name has been doctors and botanists for over a century. I can only guess that Carlyle is referring to some system of diet, or possibly some pill or medicine, associated with one of them" (p. 322).

63. Conway, *Carlyle*, pp. 244–45. The original letter is in the Speck Collection, Yale University Library. Hunt's periodical the *Companion* published its first number on 9 Jan. 1828 and its last on 23 July of the same year. On 1 Feb. Carlyle wrote to his brother John that he had intended to get a copy of *Lord Byron and Some of His Contemporaries*, "a book which fills the magazines at present," but upon learning that the price would be, not seven shillings, but three guineas, decided to "decline the Article." From the MS, NLS, 522.65.

64. *Letters of Thomas Carlyle, 1826–1836*, ed. C. E. Norton (London and New York, 1889), p. 116.

writers as Cervantes and Goethe, but with the Scottish poet Burns, who like Byron was born with very rare gifts but who died, Carlyle believed, without realizing them completely or bringing them to maturity. Every schoolchild who has read Carlyle's essay on Burns contributed to the *Edinburgh Review* for December 1828 knows with what tremendous admiration Carlyle treats his subject. This admiration he kept throughout his long life. Yet Carlyle acknowledges in more than one passage that Burns failed in precisely the same struggle in which Byron failed—the struggle toward intellectual and spiritual maturity, and that the differences between them so far as progress was concerned were differences merely of degree.

Furthermore, Carlyle asserts that it is great error to assume that in this struggle all the advantages lay with Byron—with one who had inherited a great fortune and a high position in society. "The worst-educated man is usually your man of Fortune. *He* has not put forth his hand upon anything, except upon his Bell-rope. Your scholar proper, generally too your so-called man of Letters, is a thing with clearer vision—thro' the hundredth part of an eye. A Burns is infinitely better educated than a Byron."[65] The taste of the British public had been perverted by the Gigmen and Philistines of the day who evaluated literature in terms of the extent to which it reflected the wealth, social standing, and accepted respectability of the author. The mind of Byron himself had been tainted with this belief:

On the whole, what a wondrous spirit of gentility does animate our British Literature at this era! We have no Men of Letters now, but only Literary Gentlemen. Samuel Johnson was the last that ventured to appear in that former character, and support himself on his own legs, without any crutches, purchased or stolen: rough old Samuel, the last of all the Romans! . . .

Has the Poet and Thinker adopted the philosophy of the Grocer and Valet in Livery? Nay, let us hear Lord Byron himself on the subject. Some years ago, there appeared in the Magazines, and to the admiration of most editorial gentlemen, certain extracts from Letters of Lord Byron's, which carried this philosophy to rather a high pitch. His Lordship, we recollect, mentioned, that "all rules for Poetry were not worth a d–n" (saving and excepting, doubtless, the ancient Rule-of-Thumb, which must still have place here); after which aphorism, his Lordship proceeded to state that the great ruin of all British Poets sprang from a simple source; their ex-

65. *Two Note Books,* 2 Nov. 1831, p. 223.

clusion from High Life in London, excepting only some shape of that High
Life below Stairs, which, however, was nowise adequate: he himself and
Thomas Moore were perfectly familiar in such upper life; he by birth,
Moore by happy accident, and so they could both write Poetry; the others
were not familiar, and so could not write it.— Surely it is fast growing time
that all this should be drummed out of our Planet, and forbidden to return.[66]

Actually Byron was the supreme example of the truth that he denied
—that wealth, birth, and social position were not great advantages
to a poet. Yet Burns too had to struggle against formidable obstacles.
The glory of both Burns and Byron was that they did make the struggle, even though they did not win a complete victory. Neither was
willing to join the ranks of the Philistines and become a worshipper
of idols. A fundamental integrity in the soul of each made him prefer
to perish in the battle rather than to do that.

We hope we have now heard enough about the efficacy of wealth for poetry, and to make poets happy. Nay, have we not seen another instance of
it in these very days? Byron, a man of an endowment considerably less
ethereal than that of Burns, is born in the rank not of a Scottish ploughman,
but of an English peer: the highest worldly honours, the fairest worldly
career, are his by inheritance; the richest harvest of fame he soon reaps,
in another province, by his own hand. And what does all this avail him?
Is he happy, is he good, is he true? Alas, he has a poet's soul, and strives
towards the Infinite and the Eternal; and soon feels that all this is but
mounting to the house-top to reach the stars! Like Burns, he is only a proud
man; might, like him, have "purchased a pocket-copy of Milton to study
the character of Satan"; for Satan also is Byron's grand exemplar, the hero
of his poetry, and the model apparently of his conduct. As in Burns's case
too, the celestial element will not mingle with the clay of earth; both poet
and man of the world he must not be; vulgar Ambition will not live kindly
with poetic Adoration; he *cannot* serve God and Mammon. Byron, like
Burns, is not happy; nay, he is the most wretched of all men. His life is
falsely arranged: the fire that is in him is not a strong, still central fire,
warming into beauty the products of a world; but it is the mad fire of a
volcano; and now—we look sadly into the ashes of a crater, which ere long
will fill itself with snow!

Byron and Burns were sent forth as missionaries to their generation, to

66. "Jean Paul Friedrich Richter," *Foreign Review*, Jan. 1830, *Works*, XXVII, 130,
133. Wilson (*Carlyle*, II, 112) says that the expression of this opinion about Byron
may have caused Macvey Napier not to accept Carlyle's proposal to write an essay
on Byron in 1830.

teach it a higher Doctrine, a purer Truth; they had a message to deliver, which left them no rest till it was accomplished; in dim throes of pain, this divine behest lay smouldering within them; for they knew not what it meant, and felt it only in mysterious anticipation, and they had to die without articulately uttering it. They are in the camp of the Unconverted; yet not as high messengers of rigorous though benignant truth, but as soft flattering singers, and in pleasant fellowship will they live there: they are first adulated, then persecuted; they accomplish little for others; they find no peace for themselves, but only death and the peace of the grave. We confess, it is not without a certain mournful awe that we view the fate of these noble souls, so richly gifted, yet ruined to so little purpose with all their gifts. It seems to us there is a stern moral taught in this piece of history,—*twice* told us in our own time! Surely to men of like genius, if there be any such, it carries with it a lesson of deep impressive significance. Surely it would become such a man, furnished for the highest of all enterprises, that of being the Poet of his Age, to consider well what it is that he attempts, and in what spirit he attempts it. For the words of Milton are true in all times, and were never truer than in this: "He who would write heroic poems must make his whole life a heroic poem." If he cannot first so make his life, then let him hasten from this arena; for neither its lofty glories, nor its fearful perils, are fit for him. Let him dwindle into a modish balladmonger; let him worship and be-sing the idols of the time, and the time will not fail to reward him. If, indeed, he can endure to live in that capacity! Byron and Burns could not live as idol-priests, but the fire of their own hearts consumed them; and better it was for them that they could not. For it is not in the favour of the great or of the small, but in a life of truth, and in the inexpugnable citadel of his own soul, that a Byron's or a Burns's strength must lie.[67]

Although neither poet achieved victory, Carlyle believed that Burns approached it more nearly. "Nay, in our own times, have we not seen two men of genius, a Byron and a Burns; they both, by mandate of Nature, struggle and must struggle towards clear Manhood, stormfully enough, for the space of six-and-thirty years; yet only the gifted Ploughman can partially prevail therein: the gifted Peer must toil and strive, and shoot-out in wild efforts, yet die at last in Boyhood, with the promise of his Manhood still but announcing itself in the distance."[68] The struggle was indeed a difficult one. Very few

67. "Burns," *Edinburgh Review*, Dec. 1828, *Works*, XXVI, 315–16.
68. *Corn-Law Rhymes*, *Works*, XXVIII, 140. In "Burns" (XXVI, 293) Carlyle writes: "Byron was, at his death, but a year younger than Burns; and through life, as it might have appeared, far more simply situated: yet in him too we can trace no such

men in any generation had both the courage to undertake it and the strength to see it through as Goethe had done. Byron was almost alone in making the struggle in his generation: "Among our own poets, Byron was almost the only man we saw faithfully and manfully struggling, to the end, in this cause; and he died while the victory was still doubtful, or at best, only beginning to be gained. We have already stated our opinion, that Goethe's success in this matter has been more complete than that of any other man in his age; nay, that, in the strictest sense, he may almost be called the only one that has so succeeded." [69] Burns and Byron had at least shown of what sort of metal they were made, and this in itself was a significant accomplishment.

The clearest analysis that Carlyle gives us of the precise nature of the progress Byron did make and the extent of that progress is to be found in another passage from "Burns." It reminds us of the important fact that Carlyle had read all of *Don Juan* when the various cantos first appeared and indicates that he was not entirely blind to qualities in it that suggested maturity.

Byron, for instance, was no common man: yet if we examine his poetry with this view, we shall find it far enough from faultless. Generally speaking, we should say that it is not true. He refreshes us, not with the divine fountain, but too often with vulgar strong waters, stimulating indeed to the taste, but soon ending in dislike, or even nausea. Are his Harolds and Giaours, we would ask, real men; we mean, poetically consistent and conceivable men? Do not these characters, does not the character of their author, which more or less shines through them all, rather appear a thing put on for the occasion; no natural or possible mode of being, but some-

---

adjustment, no such moral manhood; but at best, and only a little before his end, the beginning of what seemed such." And he emphasizes the difficulty of the struggle that each had to make: "But even for the Byron, for the Burns, whose ear is quick for celestial messages, in whom 'speaks the prophesying spirit,' in awful prophetic voice, how hard is it to 'take no counsel with flesh and blood,' and instead of living and writing for the Day that passes over them, live and write for the Eternity that rests and abides over them; instead of living commodiously in the Half, the Reputable, the Plausible, 'to live resolutely in the Whole, the Good, the True!' Such Halfness, such halting between two opinions, such painful, altogether fruitless negotiating between Truth and Falsehood, has been the besetting sin, and chief misery, of mankind in all ages." ("Schiller," *Fraser's Magazine*, March 1831, *Works*, XXVII, 173.) He also writes to Mrs. Basil Montagu on 27 Oct. 1830: "In Hazlitt, as in Byron and Burns and so many others in their degree, there lay some tone of the 'eternal melodies,' which he could not fashion into terrestrial music, but which uttered itself only in harsh jarrings and inarticulate cries of pain." Conway, *Carlyle*, pp. 251–52.

69. "Goethe," *Works*, XXVI, 243.

thing intended to look much grander than nature? Surely, all these stormful agonies, this volcanic heroism, superhuman contempt and moody des-
peration, with so much scowling, and teeth-gnashing, and other sulphurous
humour, is more like the brawling of a player in some paltry tragedy, which
is to last three hours, than the bearing of a man in the business of life,
which is to last threescore and ten years. To our minds there is a taint of
this sort, something which we should call theatrical, false, affected, in
everyone of these otherwise so powerful pieces. Perhaps *Don Juan*, especially the latter parts of it, is the only thing approaching to a *sincere*
work, he ever wrote; the only work where he showed himself, in any
measure, as he was; and seemed so intent on his subject as, for moments,
to forget himself. Yet Byron hated this vice; we believe, heartily detested
it: nay, he had declared formal war against it in words. So difficult is it
even for the strongest to make this primary attainment, which might seem
the simplest of all: to *read its own consciousness without mistakes*, without errors involuntary or wilful![70]

Perhaps if Carlyle had reread *Don Juan* and other later poems by
Byron closely associated with it in order to write the essay for Macvey
Napier, he would have found other elements of maturity in these
poems that we find today and that he had missed on his first reading.
No one in the nineteenth century, not even Meredith, was more interested in laughter and the nature of its function in literary art; and
what Carlyle would have had to say about the relation of the comic
spirit, as it dances brilliantly through Byron's great poem, and intellectual and spiritual maturity would be a very good thing to have.
But he did not write the essay or tap this rich vein. As it is, he leaves
Byron in a state where he has conquered the Everlasting No, is passing through the Center of Indifference where his sense of humor has
been fully emancipated and has achieved dominance over lesser
senses, and appears to be in sight of the country of the Everlasting
Yea with its positive beliefs, its constructive action, its higher individualism, and its Entsagen.

Closing Byron in *Sartor Resartus*, then, was not a thing of thunder-
ous finality like Nora's slamming the door at the end of *A Doll's
House*. Not all of Byron was shut out; not all of Goethe was invited
in. Burns, Byron, and Goethe were all among those rare souls who
fight the good fight, although differing in the degree to which they
realized victory. The passage in *Sartor*, moreover, did not by any

70. P. 269.

means indicate the end of Carlyle's interest in Byron. Many not unpleasant signs of this interest appeared in the long years that followed the composition of *Sartor*. Carlyle was quick to read a new unsigned article on Byron which appeared in *Fraser's Magazine* for March 1833, and entered into a lively discussion concerning its authorship with John Stuart Mill.[71] Jane's picture of Byron, we have reason to believe, kept its place on the walls at Craigenputtoch as long as the Carlyles lived there, where it was appropriately near a small bronze statue of Napoleon and medals that Goethe had sent. On 27 August 1833, Carlyle wrote to his brother John: "Napoleon, as too large for his station, has been moved into this Library of mine, under his Kinsman Byron, and your little Italian vase, with Goethe's medals in it and other *etceteras*, now stands in his place."[72] In May 1840 Carlyle, now famous, was pleased to discover at his lecture on "Heroes and Hero-worship" Lady Byron, widow of the poet, in his audience busily taking notes.[73] In *Past and Present* (1843) Carlyle again classified Byron with the great champions of mankind who refuse to bow down to the idols of the world but who, like Samson, endure torture rather than submit: "These are they, the elect of the world; the born champions, strong men, and liberatory Samsons of this poor world: whom the poor Delilah-world will not always shear of their strength and eyesight, and set to grind in darkness at *its* poor gin-wheel! Such souls are, in these days, getting somewhat out of humour with the world. Your very Byron, in these days, is at least driven mad; flatly

71. Pp. 303–17. The article, "Critical Illustrations of Lord Byron's Poetry," emphasizes the same point that Carlyle emphasizes, namely, the belief that Byron did not achieve maturity. In a letter of 9 March 1833 (MS, NLS, 618.16) Mill asks Carlyle whether he knows who wrote the article and adds: "It looks like the production of some half-fledged pupil of yours." On 18 April 1833 Carlyle replies to Mill: "The writer of that Byron (according to my guess) is no disciple of mine, but of Coleridge's: one Heraud, who lives at Tottenham, and looks better on Paper than otherwise; a meritorious creature nevertheless, who from the depths of some Law-Stationer's shop could contrive to appropriate an Idea or two (even in Coleridge's sense), and now re-echoes them, in long continuance,—I fear, as from *unfurnished chambers*." *Letters of Thomas Carlyle to John Stuart Mill, John Sterling, and Robert Browning*, ed. Alexander Carlyle (London, 1923), p. 49. John Abraham Heraud (1799–1887) edited the *Sunbeam*, 1838–39, and the *Monthly Magazine*, 1839–42. Carlyle habitually refers to him as unclean-looking in his personal appearance and Coleridgean in his intellectual tendencies.

72. *Letters of Thomas Carlyle, 1826–1836*, p. 371. In an unpublished and undated letter to Leigh Hunt, probably written in the summer of 1837, Carlyle wrote: "I pass these days in a very low condition of soul; reading Byron's letters; extremely sorry for him, for myself, and all mankind." From the MS letter owned by Gordon N. Ray.

73. Wilson, *Carlyle*, III, 84.

refuses fealty to the world."[74] In 1846 he was pleased when told by William Dougal Christie, who had been helpful in founding the new London Library, that "a natural son of Lord Byron's" was writing a biography of his father and commented: "I hope it may turn to something!"[75] In 1850, after Carlyle had come to admire Sir Robert Peel very much, he enjoyed a conversation with Peel about Byron at Harrow, where Peel and Byron had been schoolfellows, and he was delighted to tell Peel that Byron in a note to one of his poems, probably "The Age of Bronze" twenty-five years before, had heaped abuse on Castlereagh and spoken of the great promise of Peel. Peel had not known of the note, which was dropped in later editions.[76] In 1860 Carlyle spent five weeks with Sir George Sinclair, who had also been in school with Byron at Harrow and who, even then widely read in several languages, had been called by Byron "the prodigy of our schooldays." Sir George, a great admirer of Carlyle, told him many delightful anecdotes about Byron and about Napoleon, whom he also had known.[77] In 1867, while sitting for G. F. Watts to paint his portrait, Carlyle got into an argument with Watts over the extent to which physiognomy was significant of character and ability. Carlyle had just seen the Elgin Marbles and was disappointed because many of the figures had what he considered inadequate jaws. He exclaimed: "Depend upon it, neither God nor man can get on without a jaw." When they debated the importance of other features and Carlyle insisted that a long upper lip was a sign of intellect, Watts cited Napoleon, Goethe, and Byron as examples to the contrary.[78] On Saturday, 5 April 1874, Carlyle went with William Allingham to visit the studio of J. E. Millais and saw Byron's old friend, rival in arms and athletic prowess, and fellow adventurer Edward J. Trelawney sitting for the figure of the old mariner in "The Northwest Passage."[79] Carlyle must have thought of his meeting with Cuvallo in 1816. The great wave of Byronic romanticism had reached so far and was not yet dead! But in the long sequel to *Sartor Resartus* with its "Close

74. P. 260.
75. MS letter, NLS, 524.64. J. L. Armstrong published a *Life of Lord Byron* (London, 1846), but I am not certain that this is the author and work referred to.
76. Wilson, *Carlyle*, IV, 253. Carlyle asked Francis Espinasse, who worked at the British Museum, to look for Byron's note in early editions of his poems. I do not know whether he found it.
77. Wilson, *Carlyle*, V, 395.
78. *Ibid.*, VI, 131.
79. *Ibid.*, VI, 333.

thy Byron," the most interesting incident has to do with Harriet
Beecher Stowe and her attack on Byron in the *Atlantic Monthly* for
September 1869. On 26 October G. W. Novice, an artist and author
of *Lights in Art*, wrote a letter to Carlyle from Edinburgh protesting
against what he considered Mrs. Stowe's unfair and slanderous treatment of Byron and urging him to write an answer to her. "You have
already," Novice said, "and most thoroughly, vindicated the character
of Oliver Cromwell, the great Protector and *expander* of our empire,
yet, before your own time, one of the most abused of men. [Para-
graph] Allow me to mention that were you *now* to write something,
however brief, concerning the character of Lord Byron, whose memory is ruthlessly assailed by a popular lady more in love with gold
than with truth, I am sure you would confer a noble benefit upon
society, at home and abroad."[80] Carlyle's answer to this letter, if
there was one, has not come to light. But he must have decided, as
he did when Napier wanted him to write the encyclopedia article on
Byron, that he was not the man for the job. He did not like Mrs.
Stowe and her "Uncle Tommism," as he called it; and he probably
disapproved of her attack on Byron. But Byron was not Cromwell,
and there were limits beyond which Carlyle could not reach, as he
well knew, in defending a character such as Byron's. The pertinent
evidence, too, not all of which scholars have even today, would have
been extremely hard for him to get. Furthermore, he was well versed
in the psychology of literary controversy, and he did not wish to
honor the lady by attacking her. Byron's honor would suffer little
from his neglect at this time, just as it had suffered little from his
attention and efforts to make a just and honest appraisal in earlier
years. Most important, he probably did not see fit to discuss Byron's
case in terms of the issues raised by Mrs. Stowe and still made much
of by modern scholarship. He himself had already established what
he considered the really important issues for Byron. How much, he
may well have asked himself, did the battle between the sexes, even
when sexual aberrations were involved, matter in the struggle within
himself that a strong man and poet had made to find his soul and his
full strength? Not very much, Carlyle had once answered in the relation of King David to Bathsheba. Despite Bathsheba, King David's
life had in the main been "the faithful struggle of an earnest human

80. From the MS letter in the collection of Professor Frederick W. Hilles.

soul towards what is good and best." His comment on Mohammed, likewise, is pertinent here: "I believe we misestimate Mahomet's faults even as faults: but the secret of him will never be got by dwelling there."[81] Perhaps students of Burns and Byron may find something to ponder in Carlyle here.

81. *Heroes, Hero-Worship, and the Heroic in History, Works*, V, 46–47.

THE CORRESPONDENCE
AND FRIENDSHIP OF
THOMAS CARLYLE AND LEIGH HUNT

THE EARLY YEARS

Almost alone among the English Romantics, Leigh Hunt enjoyed the affection and esteem of Thomas Carlyle. Even more remarkable is the fact that Hunt, who had been an intimate friend of Byron, Shelley, and Keats, and who never once wavered in preaching a philosophy based on unrestrained optimism and love of beauty, found great delight in the companionship of the Calvinistic Carlyle and his acid-tongued wife, in spite of their Scottish Presbyterian background and the deep shadows in which they often lived and thought. The friendship was a complex one that had to overcome great difficulties on both sides. It flourished upon a basis of clearly understood differences of opinion, character, and ways of life. It persisted despite each friend's sharp awareness of the other's faults. Lasting through many years and vicissitudes and tested in many various situations, it proved itself to be a friendship of a very rare and high quality that reflected great credit on the humanity of both men.

Carlyle did not meet Hunt before his visit to London of 1831–32. But he had read some of Hunt's writings much earlier and by no means had been always favorably impressed. "Is Happiness our being's end and aim?" Carlyle wrote on 7 June 1820; ". . . L. Hunt I do not like."[1] About two years later he wrote to Jane Welsh: "Hunt is the only serious man in it [*The Liberal*], since Shelley died: he has a wish to preach about politics and bishops and pleasure and paintings and nature, honest man."[2] And while in London in 1824 he wrote to her: "Leigh Hunt writes 'wishing caps' for the Examiner, and lives

1. To Matthew Allen. From the MS letter in the John Rylands University Library of Manchester. For help with the text and annotations of these letters I am indebted to my colleagues Arthur Tillo Alt and Thomas M. Simkins, Jr., and to Mrs. Janet Ray Edwards.

2. *The Love Letters of Thomas Carlyle and Jane Welsh*, ed. Alexander Carlyle (London and New York, 1909), I, 95–96.

on the lightest of diets at Pisa."[3] Up to this time Carlyle had discovered that Hunt was serious, honest, and critically disposed toward politics and bishops; but he had found little else congenial with his own way of life and philosophy.

The correspondence and friendship began through a gesture of Hunt's when the Carlyles were in London in early 1832. He sent a copy of his *Christianism*, just published, addressed to the author of the essay "Characteristics." Carlyle promptly wrote to thank him and to suggest a meeting.

Letter 1. Carlyle to Leigh Hunt.[4]

4 Ampton Street, Gray's Inn Road
8 February 1832

The writer of the essay named "Characteristics" has just received, apparently from Mr. Leigh Hunt, a volume entitled "Christianism," for which he hereby begs to express his thanks. The volume shall be read: to meet the author of it personally would doubtless be a new gratification.

T. Carlyle

Hunt's reply, although delayed for almost two weeks, was written in the same spirit.

Letter 2. Hunt to Carlyle.[5]

18. Elm Tree Road
St. John's Wood—
Feb. 20 [1832].

Dear Sir,

(For so I hope the spirit of your writings, and the kindness of your note, will allow me to call you) it was not I that sent you the book, but it was sent *at my request*; & I notice this difference, merely to account in part for the delay in answering your communication, which did not come to me first. The rest has been occasioned by a conspiracy of petty obstacles which I sometimes curiously suffer to hinder me from doing what I wish, precisely because I wish it to be done in the best & most attractive manner,

3. 20 Dec. MS letter in the NLS, 530.29. The essays that Hunt was writing for the *Examiner* were called "The Wishing Cap."
4. "Eight Unpublished Letters of Thomas Carlyle," ed. Richard Garnett, *Archiv für das Studium der Neueren Sprachen und Litteraturen*, N.S. II (1899), 327. Also in Moncure D. Conway, *Thomas Carlyle* (New York, 1881), p. 64. The MS letter is at the State University of Iowa. See Luther A. Brewer, "Leigh Hunt Association Books," *Books at Iowa*, No. 1 (Oct. 1964), pp. 4–10. For fuller information about the first meeting and the role played by John Forster, see *Collected Letters*, 6:117–18.
5. MS letter in the Luther A. Brewer Collection at the State University of Iowa. See

—and after all it shall have nothing to shew for itself!—Your note gratified me very much, especially as I had long been desirous of personally knowing you, and thanking you, among other things, for enabling me to become acquainted with Wilhelm Meister. I shall take my chance of finding you at home some day this week, about noon; and venture to hope, that I may by & by see you at a new abode into which I move tomorrow morning,— No. 5. York Buildings, New Road.

Your obliged servant,
Leigh Hunt

P.S. Be kind enough, among the causes that induce me to give way to the obstacles I speak of, to bear in mind a good deal of ill health, & much troubled business.— I do not allow the excuse myself; so I must get my friends to do it for me. Perhaps you will write me a line to say when it would be most convenient to yourself to be at home.

Carlyle was again prompt in reply.

Letter 3. Carlyle to Hunt.[6]

4 Ampton Street, Gray's Inn Road,
20th February, 1832.

Dear Sir—

I stay at home (daily scribbling) till after two o'clock, and shall be truly glad, *any* morning, to meet in person a man whom I have long, in spirit, seen and esteemed.

Both my Wife and I, however, would reckon it a still greater favor, could you come at once in the evening, and take tea with us, that our interview might be the longer and freer. Might we expect you, for instance, on Wednesday night? Our hour is six o'clock; but we will alter it in any way to suit you.

We venture to make this proposal, because our stay in Town is now

---

Luther A. Brewer, *My Leigh Hunt Library: The First Editions* (Cedar Rapids, Iowa, 1932); the same, *My Leigh Hunt Library: The Holograph Letters* (Iowa City, 1938); and Frank S. Hanlin, "The Brewer–Leigh Hunt Collection at the State University of Iowa," *Keats-Shelley Journal*, VIII (Autumn 1959), 91–94. Thornton Hunt could not find his father's letters to Carlyle when he was editing the correspondence soon after his father's death in 1859. See *The Correspondence of Leigh Hunt,* ed. Thornton Hunt (London, 1862), I, 321. Alexander Ireland made copies of many of Hunt's letters to Carlyle. The copies have been preserved in the Ireland Collection of the Manchester Public Library. They were studied by Professor George D. Stout of Washington University in his Harvard dissertation for the Ph.D., "Studies Toward a Biography of Leigh Hunt," 1928.

6. Published by Garnett in "Eight Unpublished Letters," pp. 327–28, and by Conway in *Carlyle*, p. 66.

likely to be short, and we should be sorry to miss having free speech with you.

Believe me, dear sir, very sincerely yours,

Thomas Carlyle

This time Hunt, too, replied promptly.

Letter 4. Hunt to Carlyle.[7]

Elm Tree Road—Feb. 21 [, 1832]. Tuesday.

My dear Sir,

The invitation which Mrs. Carlyle and yourself have been good enough to send me, is just the one that suits & pleases me best, and I shall be with you, at the hour you mention, tomorrow evening. In fact, you cannot conceive how much it has gratified me; for since the death of some dear friends, I have lived almost entirely out of the pale of intellectual acquaintance,— a toiling solitary; and with the spring, many unlooked-for comforts seem to await me, of which this is one.

Very truly yours,
Leigh Hunt.

Since there is no evidence to the contrary, then, we may assume that the first meeting of Hunt with the Carlyles took place at 4 Ampton Street on the evening of Wednesday, 22 February, just a few weeks before the Carlyles returned to Craigenputtoch. The meeting seems to have pleased everyone who was there, and soon the Carlyles met Marianne, Mrs. Hunt, and there was visiting back and forth. Mrs. Hunt was much older than Jane Carlyle, and there was very little else to make the two congenial; but in this early period they at least made an effort to become good friends.

Letter 5. Hunt to Carlyle.[8]

Dear Sir,

Will M^rs. Carlyle & yourself favour us with your company to tea at six, either tomorrow or Saturday evening, whichever suits you best,—supposing one of them to be not inconvenient?— The servant, who saw you at the gate

7. MS, NLS, 665.35. Among Hunt's "dear friends" who had died were Keats, Byron, and Shelley. Shelley he seemed to miss particularly; and the radiant optimism of "Prometheus Unbound" seems to have lighted his way for the rest of his life.

8. MS, NLS, 665.68. The "new paper" that had to stop at the end of three weeks was the *Plain Dealer*, also called the *Critical Plain Dealer*, in which Hunt briefly had a hand. See Louis Landré, *Leigh Hunt* (Paris, 1935–36), II, 495–96; George D. Stout, "Leigh Hunt and the Plain Dealer," *Modern Language Notes*, XVII (June 1927), 383–85.

yesterday, is new to us, otherwise she would not have talked of my going
to dinner.— I have had a great blow since I saw you, which knocks up my
prospect of half-week leisures; & the worst of it was, that it was knocked up
in the most childish manner, the Proprietors of a new paper, which they
had got me to conduct, putting a stop to it at the end of three weeks, because it did not *flourish* in that time! I never had so tremendous a compliment paid me before, or one that ended in so frightful a rebuke.— But the
prospect, like the extemporaneous orchard they looked for, was too romantic to last. I am therefore setting about new tasks, as "lovingly &
cheerfully," as a man all over fatigue & jaundice well can; & as a help to
them, hope my friends will come & see me.

Very truly yours,
Leigh Hunt.
5. York Buildings – New Road.
March 1 [,1832].—

Letter 6. Hunt to Carlyle.[9]

Dear Sir,

Mrs. Hunt hopes that Mrs. Carlyle will be well enough, with the help
of an omnibus, to favor her with her company this evening; though she
begs it to be understood, that she by no means takes any such thing for
granted, being a terrible stayer at home herself, & knowing enough of illness
to be aware that night-airs & visits are not always to be trusted, even at a
short distance. For the rest, I can only say that my wife is a proper house-
wifely woman, very maternally given, who will take as much care of yours
as if she were her eldest daughter.

Very truly yours,
Leigh Hunt.

March 3 [,1832].—York Buildings.

An entry in Carlyle's notebook for this month sums up the beginning of the friendship and provides the first of several inimitable
pen portraits of Hunt that he drew:

9. MS, Brewer Collection, State University of Iowa. An undated one-page letter
from Jane Carlyle to Marianne Hunt listed in Maggs catalogue 306 and dated about
March 1832 is written in thanks for the gift of a copy of Hunt's novel *Sir Ralph Esher*
(1830, 1832). It is quoted as follows:
    "I like it for the great purity and tenderness of the serious parts; for the sweet grace
that is over the whole; I like it because it is the same as Mr. Hunt talking to us, and
because it falls in with my own sentiments about many things, and gives me a surer
and more affectionate hold of them.
    "You will not include this among those 'compliments on your Husband's talents' for
which you express such mortal aversion (justly, for nothing can be more nauseous).

Leigh Hunt and I have come into contact by occasion of the *Character-istics*: he sought me out, and has been twice here; I once with him. A pleasant, innocent, ingenious man; filled with *Epicurean Philosophy*, and steeped in it to the very heart. He has suffered more than most men; is even now bankrupt (in purse and repute), sick, and enslaved to daily toil: yet will nothing persuade him that man is born for another object here than to be *happy*. Honor to tenacity of conviction! *Credo quia impossible.*— A man copious and cheerfully sparkling in conversation; of grave aspect, never laughs, hardly smiles; black hair shaded to each side; hazel eyes, with a certain lifting up of the eyebrows that has no archness in it, rather sentient, well-satisfied self-consciousness. He is a real lover of Nature, and even singer thereof; and, for the rest, *belongs to London in the opening of the 19th century.*[10]

After Mrs. Carlyle's death in 1866 Carlyle spoke again of this early period in their friendship with Hunt in a note to one of her letters: "Among the scrambling miscellany of notables and quasi-notables that hovered about us, Leigh Hunt (volunteer, and towards the end) was probably the best; poor Charles Lamb (more than once, at Enfield, towards the middle of our stay) the worst. . . . Leigh Hunt came in sequel (prettily courteous on his part) to the Article *Character-istics*; his serious, dignified and even noble physiognomy and bearing took us with surprise, and much pleased us. Poor Hunt! Nowhere or never an ignoble man!"[11]

After the Carlyles' return to Craigenputtoch in late March 1832, there seems to have been a temporary lull in the correspondence with Hunt. But there was no chance that Carlyle would forget or lose interest in him. About August he sent Hunt a short letter that seems to have been lost. In the autumn he sent John Stuart Mill a note of introduction to Hunt accompanied by some sentences giving a balanced appraisal of the man:

I enclose you here a small Note for Leigh Hunt. If you like to make use of it as a Note of introduction, send your card up with it. . . . Hunt, worthy

---

But if I like the book and the writer of it, and I do, with my whole heart; and if I feel pleasure in saying I like them (and that I do also) I may say it, may I not, with impunity? . . ."

10. *Two Note Books of Thomas Carlyle*, ed. C. E. Norton (New York, 1898), pp. 256–57.

11. *New Letters and Memorials of Jane Welsh Carlyle*, ed. Alexander Carlyle (London and New York, 1903), I, 34–35. The original note and most of Carlyle's notes on his wife's letters are in the Henry W. and Albert A. Berg Collection of the New York Public Library.

man, is of those unfortunate people whose *address* is often *changing*. . . .
You will find Hunt a most kindly, lively, clear-hearted creature, greatly to
be sympathized with, to be honored in many things and loved; with whom
you will find no difficulty to get on the right footing, and act as the case will
direct. Hunt is a special kind of man; a representative of London Art, and
what it can do and bring forth at this Epoch; what was too contemptuously
called the "Cockney School," for it is a sort of half-way-house to something
better; and will one day be worth noting in British Literary History.[12]

The following letter to Hunt was enclosed in Mill's letter.

Letter 7. Carlyle to Hunt.[13]

Craigenputtoch, Dumfries
20th Nov[r] 1832—

My Dear Sir,

I sent you a little Note, by some conveyance I had, several months ago;
whether it ever came to hand is unknown here. We learned soon afterwards, from a notice in the New Monthly Magazine, that you were again
suffering in health.

If that Note reached you, let this be the second, if it did not then let this
be the first little Messenger arriving from the Mountains to inquire for
you, to bring assurance that you are lovingly remembered here, that nothing befalling you can be indifferent to us.

Being somewhat uncertain about the Number of your House, I send
this under cover to a Friend who will punctually see that it reaches its
address. If he deliver it in person, as is not impossible, you will find him
worth welcoming: he is John Mill, eldest son of India Mill; and, I may
say, one of the best, clearest-headed and clearest-hearted young men now
living in London.

We sometimes fancy we observe you in *Tait's* and other Periodicals.
Have the charity some time soon to send us a token of your being and well-
being. We often speak of you here, and are very obstinate in remembering.

I still wish much that you would write Hazlitt's *Life*. Somewhat of History lay in that too luckless man; and you, of all I can think of, have the
organ for discerning it and delineating it.

As for myself I am doing little. The Literary element is one of the most
confused to live in, at all times; the Bibliopolic condition of this time renders
it a perfect chaos. One must write "Articles"; write and curse (as Ancient
Pistol ate his leek); what can one do?

12. MS, dated 19 Nov. 1832, NLS, 618.11. Published in *Letters of Thomas Carlyle
to John Stuart Mill, John Sterling, and Robert Browning*, ed. Alexander Carlyle (London, 1923), p. 23.
13. MS, British Museum, 33, 515, fol. 37. Published in Conway's *Carlyle*, pp. 203–4.

My Wife is not with me today; otherwise she would surely beg to be remembered. You will offer my best wishes to Mrs Hunt, to Miss, and the little grey-eyed Philosopher who listened to us.

I asked you to come hither and see us, when you wanted to rusticate a month. Is that forever impossible?

I remain always,

My Dear Sir,
Yours truly & kindly
T. Carlyle.

Letter 8. Hunt to Carlyle.[14]

5. York Buildings—New Road—London
December 1st 1832.

My Dear Sir,

I know not what you and Mrs. Carlyle will think of me, when I tell you that I received your first letter; but I trust that your knowledge & your kindness will induce you to think me not unpardonable, when you know all. Twice, nay thrice, I encountered the most singular & painful obstacles, when about to send off a packet; till at last, because I had delayed so much, & must have seemed in spirit to have delayed so much more, shame conspired with accident to make me still more dilatory. There is a story of an old gentleman, who being about to get on horseback before some ladies, begged them to count "eighty." I would beg you & Mrs. Carlyle on this occasion to count great illness, great trouble of all sorts, and in the first instance a singular conspiracy of obstacles. I have now this minute, while writing to you, a great weight in my head, another in my side (from an attack of liver) and the doctor is coming to me, and I have domestic anxieties beside, of various & *extreme* kinds, with which I will not shadow too much the face of your forgiveness. Suffice to whisper into ears that will husband the secret for me from vulgar ones, and as a specimen of what I have been accustomed to go through for the last year, that not long after you wrote to me, I had an execution on my house for six weeks. It was owing to my not receiving my payments from the True Sun, the difficulties of which paper have distressed me exceedingly, & forced me, much against my will, to suspend my contributions to it.— I have let out more than I meant to tell; but my heart flows towards you for the kind things you say to me, & you must be content to take some of the bitter water with the sweeter. These have been by no means the worst of my troubles; but I support myself by an indestructible love of my calm, same-faced old friends, Nature & books; and by such kind words as other friends give me. Pray do not think me ungrateful, &

14. MS, Brewer Collection, State University of Iowa. "My book was out yesterday" —*The Poetical Works of Leigh Hunt*, published this year by Edward Moxon.

above all, write me as speedily as possible another letter, that I may be sure you have got this. My book was out yesterday to subscribers, and I expect in the course of a week to be taken out of the worst possible situation in certain matters, & put in such a one as I have not known—God knows for how long. You will therefore understand me when I say, that I shall take it as a very kind & delicate thing of you, if you will not wait for conveniences of conveyance, but send me a letter by the general post at once, both to ease my mind & flatter my new riches. I want to know particularly how *large* a packet I may venture to send you, because I have some *enormous* books in which I flatter myself you will both find occasional entertainment on a rainy day,—at all events such as I can send with less immodesty to a solitary place afar off (expense apart) than I could to one where reading is more immediately to be had. Colburn is re-printing the Indicator; which I shall send you also. Meanwhile here is Mr. Shelley's Masque of Anarchy,—& another book which I have persuaded myself you will accept as some proof of the atonement I wish to make for my delay. I am aware that a certain name is in my subscribers' list, & I am proud of my patron; but this copy comes to my friend.

And now—at this point of my letter—not before—I have taken courage to open your second— Not that I thought it would be unkind— My self-love was even greater than that—but because I could not read it, till I had discharged some of my duty. Mrs. Hunt, who is very much yours, read it for me to herself, & said it was "all nice."

Alas! I wish so *very* much that I could come & see you, that I will try to hope I may do so in the spring; but cares like mine, & a family of eight children all at home, & half of them are so large they ought to be away, are terrible obstacles. Tell me again about it however, that I may indulge my fancy, & strive.— I wrote one article in Tait (as you guessed)— The World of Books, & one in the New Monthly, or Indicator; both of which articles, at least the latter, I will send you with divers others, of older or coming date in my huge & proper parcel,—for the present (with the exception of my friends great heart in it you are to take only in earnest. Upon your writing I pounce whenever I meet with it, in pieces or magazine, & recognize the head & heart flowing together with a depth & copiousness beyond any other living writer I know. "Miss" returns her best compliments, & the "little grey-eyed philosopher" is delighted. He hugs [begs?] his "Flora"[?]. Dear Sir, & dear Mrs. Carlyle, I am truly & thankfully yours,

Leigh Hunt.

P.S. Mr. Mill did not bring his letter himself. I wish you would rebuke him for it, for I should like to know him much.

P.P.S. Mind—my verses claim praise only for animal spirits, & for truth & consistency of *some* kind, though far from what I could wish it: so I do not expect my friends to put their consciences to any trouble for me. My greatest praise has been, that kind eyes have shed tears over some of them. This I know, & therefore cannot give up the "glory" of it, as the French say.

Letter 9. Carlyle to Hunt.[15]

18. Carlton Street, Stockbridge, Edinburgh,
28th Feb^y, 1833—

My Dear Sir,

Last night, after tea, a Bookseller's Porter came in, with two Parcels; in one of which we found your two Books and your Letter; both of which kind presents awakened the gratefullest feelings here. As for your Letter, written with such trustfulness, such patient, affectionate Hope, Faith and Charity, I must report truly that it filled the heart,—in one of our cases, even to *overflowingly the eyes.* We will not dwell on this side of it. Let me rejoice rather that I do see, on such terms, such a Volume as yours. The free outpouring of one of the most purely *musical* natures now extant in our Earth; that *can* still be musical, melodious even in these harsh-jawing days; and out of all Discords and Distresses, extract Harmony and a mild Hope and Joy; this is what I call *Poetical,* if the word have any meaning. Most of these Pieces are known to me of old; you may be sure, in their collected shape, I shall carefully prize them, and reperuse them for their own sake and yours.

It was not till I had read your Letter a second or even third time, that I found the date of it to be the 2nd of December! Where, whether at Moxon's, or at Longman's the Parcel may have lain hid these three months can only be conjectured: I had determined in any case to write by return of Post; and now, on that vexatious discovery, had almost snatched my pen, to write before I went to sleep; as if that could have got you word a little sooner. It is very provoking, and to me at the moment doubly so, for a cheerful illusion was dispelled by it.

Alas, then, it is too likely that sorrowful Paragraph we read in the Newspapers was *true*; and the modest hopes your Letter was to import to me were all misgone before its arrival! Would I could help you. Tell me at least without delay, how it stands; that we may know if not what to do, at least what to wish. Meanwhile I again preach to you: Hope! "Man," says

15. MS, Brewer Collection, State University of Iowa. Published in "Concerning Leigh Hunt," *Cornhill Magazine,* LXV (May 1892), 488–90. The "German Friend" quoted in the third paragraph is Goethe. The "Lord Advocate" is Francis Jeffrey. The Carlyles left Craigenputtoch for Edinburgh in early January and remained there through April.

a German Friend of mine whom I often quote, "is properly speaking founded upon Hope; this world where he lives is called the *Place of Hope.*" Time and Chance, it is written, happen unto *all* men. Your good children, now like frail young plants, your chief care and difficulty, will one day stand a strong hedge around you, when the Father's hand is grown weary, and can no longer toil. Neither will the sympathy of kind hearts, so far as that can profit, ever fail you. Esperaunce!

I too am poor, am sick; and, in these wondrous chaotic times, dispirited, for moments, nigh bewildered. Let us study to hold fast and true even unto the death; and ever among the Sahara sands of this "wilderness journey," to look up towards loadstars in the blue still Heavens! We were not made to be the sport of a Devil or Devils' servants; my Belief is that a GOD made us, and mysteriously dwells in us.

However, let us now turn over to a more terrestrial leaf, and talk of this journey to Craigenputtoch, which we here cannot consent to abandon. It is not a piece of empty civility, it is a firm scientific conviction on my Wife's part and mine that you would both get and give true pleasure in our Nithsdale Hermitage. She says emphatically, I must *press* you to come. You shall have her Pony to ride; she will nourish you with milk new from the Galloway Cow; will etc. etc. In sober prose, I am persuaded it would do us all good. You shall have the quietest of rooms, the *firmest* of writing-desks: no soul looks near us more than if we were in Patmos: our day's work done, you and I will climb hills together, or saunter on everlasting moors, now cheerful with speech; at night the Dame will give us music; one day will be as peaceable and diligent as another. Why cannot you come? The way thither, and back again, is the simplest. You embark at your Tower Wharf in a Leith Ship (Smack it is called); where under really handsome naval accommodation, sailing along shores which grow ever the finer, and from Flamborough Head onwards can be called beautiful, you land at Leith; say, after a voyage of four days, the whole charge Two pounds Sterling. An omnibus takes you to the inn door: whence that very night, if you like, a Coach starts for Dumfries; and seventy miles of quick driving bring you safe into my old Gig, which in two hours more lands you at Craigenputtoch house-door; and you enter safe and *toto divisus orbe* into the oasis of the whinstone wilderness. Or there is another shorter day-light way of getting at us from Edinburgh; which a Letter of mine could be lying here to describe and appoint for you. Will nothing be temptation enough! Nay, we are still to be here till the first week of April; could lodge you in this hired Floor of ours, show you Edin^r, and take you home with us ourselves. You must really think of this; Mrs Hunt, for your sake, will consent to make no objection; your writing work, one might hope, would proceed not the slower but the faster. You see two Friends; innumerable stranger Fellow-men; and lay in a large stock of impressions that will be new, whatever else they be.

As for the projected Book-parcel, fear not to overburthen me with Books: at home, I am quite ravenous for these. Fraser (Magazine Fraser) the Bookseller of Regent Street will take charge of anything for me, and have it forwarded; at the utmost, for five-pence per pound. Or perhaps your better way (if the Colburns are punctual people) were to direct any Parcel simply "to the care of Messrs Bell & Bradfute, Edinburgh" (with whom they *infallibly* communicate every Magazine-day), by whom, also at the lowest rate, such as themselves pay, it will be carefully forwarded.

My Paper is nigh done; yet I have told you little or nothing of our news. The truth is happily there is almost none to tell. Mrs Carlyle is still sickly, yet better than when you saw her; and rather seems to enjoy herself here, —almost within sight of her birthplace. For me I read Books, and scribble for better for worse. We left home some two months ago, once more to look at men a little. The style of thought and practice here yields me but little edification; as indeed any extant style thereof does not yield one much. I too have some of your "old same-faced Friends"; and rummage much in the Libraries here, searching after more. A thing on *Diderot* of my writing will be out by and by in the *F.Q. Review*.

This sheet comes to you under cover to the Lord Advocate. If he call on you some day with a card of mine, you will give him welcome. He is a most kindly sparkling, even poetic man; with a natural drawing towards all that is good and generous. Fortune has made strange work with him; "not a Scottish Goldoni, but a Whig Politician, Edin' Reviewer and Lord Advocate": the change, I doubt has not been a happy one. And now my dear Sir, good night from both of us, and peace and patient endeavour be with you and yours! We shall often think of you. Write soon, as I have charged you.

Ever faithfully,
T. Carlyle

Carlyle was no more an unmitigated pessimist than Hunt was an unadulterated optimist. In this letter, as we have seen, he preached hope and courage to Hunt, just as he was to do a little later to another even more robust optimist, Robert Browning.[16] Hunt's optimism was fine-woven in its texture and of great radiance and beauty; Carlyle's was thrown in bold relief by massive shadow and given strength by a quality of granite-like intellectualism; Browning's was militant, aggressive, and irresistible.

16. See my "Carlyle, Browning, and the Nature of a Poet," *Emory University Quarterly*, XVI (Winter 1960), 197–209.

Letter 10. Hunt to Carlyle.[17]

5. York Building—New Road
March 7 [1833].

My Dear Sir,

Great was the comfort your letter gave me yesterday; especially as I had begun to think—not that you were offended with me (for I knew you were too wise & kind for that)—but that out of some subtle intention or other of doing me good, you had resolved not to write to me except at long intervals. I had endeavoured to persuade myself that my packet might have been delayed, but I had no notion of its being delayed so long. I saw Mr. Moxon in the afternoon, & he explained it by a mistake he had made relative to the road it was necessary for it to take:—at least so I understood him during a brief & interrupted interview; but he said he was going to write to you on the subject. Luckily I shall now know what to do in future, & your books shall come accordingly at the beginning of the month. Would to heaven that I could come myself! You have no conception how much I desire it, for you do not know from under what a daily & deadly load of cares I should slip away for the time, freshening my wings in your pure northern air, amidst the breath of wildflowers, & the converse of the wise-hearted. Your walks, & your talks, and your music would all be most de-lightful to me; & the very offer & notion of it is so:—nay, if I can at all manage to be master of my time & movement any time within these two years, most certainly will I come to you, and meanwhile I shall look upon it as a good thing which I have in a *sort* of *posse*,—as a pleasure which I can fly to, if I can fly any where,—a friend's *locale* at my service,—an own other-man's possession & country-house, which is mine when I can go to it. This is much, believe me; & reminds me of one of the greatest pleasures I had in the world, which was, that wherever Shelley had a roof over his head, there I had a bit of it to put over mine, in case I chose to seek it,—whether he was abroad or at home, in England or Italy, or had gone to China. He once thought of taking a voyage to India; & I immediately felt as if I had a house in Calicut, or the Himalaya mountains.

Saturday March 9.

I was obliged to leave off here in order to go to Town upon business; & during my absence *Jeffrey* called. Imagine my disappointment. I called upon him however myself yesterday, & found him at home, & most pleasant. He is full of life & evident good-heartedness, & is a boy still, in spite of the bar, & his wig, & the Whig (with the aspirate in it) and criticism, & Lord Advocacy. He finds it hard to Germanize; but loves those that can, & is

17. MS, Brewer Collection, State University of Iowa.

full of respect for you & yours. I am to see him again, & speedily; so I shall write you further about him, for now that we have a Parliament again, there are members in town, & I can get franks. I will make him give me some. He shall be, in all senses of the word, *Frank* Jeffrey with me. (I hope, in your universalities, you do not exclude the humanity of a pun. I want you to see that I have some animal spirits left,—especially for my friends when they write me such kind & consolatory letters.)

And now, by way of shewing you the excess to which they will carry me, I have a very impudent thing to say. Yet impudence is not at the heart of it, or I could not propose it. You are kind enough to ask me to come & see you: I cannot do so at present: there are a hundred reasons, connected with a family of eight children, great & small, & all at home, which prevent me; besides matters of business which I *must* attend to on the spot, on pain of losing both money & good name. I shall hope to come, & shall keep the visit in prospect; & with that I must content myself. But my eldest boy (man rather, for he is past twenty-one) has lately made us anxious about the state of his health: the doctor recommends that he should go from home a little, into fresh air; & I am unable to send him; & this gives me remorse, & makes me think it criminal in me to be no richer. Will you allow me, dear Sir, to send him to you for a week or two, as my substitute? I will make no apology for the proposal, because you will understand my feelings as much as I do myself, & I cannot pretend & suppose that you will think ill of them. All I request is, that if you are going from home any where, by any new chance of necessity in the interval since you wrote, you will be ingenuous with me,—or on any other score of hindrance, if such there be. *Au reste*, I shall take it for granted that you will not be sorry to see him. He is an intelligent youth, indeed of no common order of intelligence (as Lamb prophesied for him when a child, & Hazlitt could have borne witness to you in his riper years); & he is capable of deriving knowledge from you, & I think, of contributing his share of reasonable entertainment as a guest. In the course of a few months, he begins his career as an artist, having had a regular education for it these three years, & the greatest encouragement from the critics; and should it not be inconvenient to you to receive him, I have another favour to beg; which is, that you will let him make an essay at taking a portrait of you for his father. He would bring canvas & all appurtenances with him, for that purpose. Of music he is passionately fond; so that he would be enabled to enter into all your pastimes. Finally, he is a *good fellow*;—and has ever treated his father's scantiness of means with a considerate & unaffected delicacy, and a cheerfulness of self-denial, which sometimes brings a bitter tear out of my very delight. But I hope all will turn to good account with him in the end. Better have his difficulties first,

& his pleasures afterward, than the reverse. I endeavour to console myself with thoughts like these; but it is sometimes hard. Heaven send I may live to see him healthy & strong, & in the dawn of worldly prosper[ity.]

And now, my dear Sir, never say a word to me again in kind allusion to your own scantiness of means, with reference to myself. I think, & indeed know, I made some good guesses about you, as soon as I had the pleasure of your acquaintance; for Jeffrey did not enlighten me as to the spirit, though he did as to the letter of your position; and I venture to tell you (without grudging what generosity you might have shewn me had you been as rich in pocket as in nature) that, as far as myself am concerned, I feel an especial delight in a certain moneyless & scholarly sympathy from a man like yourself, & in the refuge I can take in the thought of you from all thoughts of money & whatsoever belongs to it. I only regret that the want of it will not enable us to do just what we please, to go any where & have what books we like, & shew what an indifference we have for it. Has not your own good faith given me a corner in your heart for belief in mine; and do you not tell me of tears of sympathy that have come into womanly eyes? I am rich enough, believe me, Scotland-wards.

Tuesday March 12.

I have been again hindered from closing my letter & fear I shall not be able to get it franked till tomorrow. The Lord Advocate has not been here again; but I expect him. I forgot to say, that in the midst of his praises of you, your benevolence included, he said you were "austere." "Austere!" cried I. "Oh, yes," cried he: "he is indeed: he is quite austere." I said it was one of the last epithets I should have given you, & that if you were austere, it was like the austere rind of a fruit round a heart of sweetness. So you see, though not a Lord Advocate, I am an advocate fit to talk of you among lords. I suppose he fancied you not dulcet enough towards those men of the world, with whom he pretends to identify himself.

Do you see a newspaper? Would you like to see an evening one, the True Sun, the most radical of radicals? I have long ceased to write in it, not having been able to go on struggling with it, in addition to my own struggles; but it is making its way; it is still sent us; & I could frequently transmit it to Craigenputtoch. Cobbett's speeches in Parliament make the debate quite a new thing. He talks Registers; & keeps up a note, very provoking, about "rich & poor," in which, for my part, I cannot help rejoicing. I like to see people going to the elements of things, & telling the whole truth, instead of agreeing to keep the worse part of it a convenient secret. But then how much of the passions & will there is in the thing, & how little philosophy! for the same man talks against the "blasphemous Jews!" and asks what is to become of Christianity if we treat them well. "However, a sledge-hammer is not a sun-beam." I must not omit to tell you that I am better than when I saw you last. The subscription has not been what it was hoped it would; but it has still served me much, & saved me from some more distressing things which I fear could have gone nigh to bear me down. About six weeks ago I had some new & alarming pains in the fore part & side of my head, accompanied with a terrible cloudiness of feeling; but they suddenly disappeared, & instead of being worse, I have ever since been better.

Dear Sir, I am

Most sincerely yours,
Leigh Hunt

This letter reflects two qualities of mind that Hunt shared with Carlyle: a genuine radicalism that cut through the conventions of thought and insisted on "going to the elements of things, & telling the whole truth," and a sharp awareness of the formidable obstacles that poverty could place before literary men.

On 16 March Carlyle wrote to his mother that Hunt was proposing to send his oldest son to Craigenputtoch and added, "We shall *see* what will come of it."[18] Generously, even magnanimously, they invited Hunt's son Thornton to spend some time at their home on the Scottish moors.

Meanwhile, Carlyle gave Mill a not uncritical appraisal of Hunt in a letter dated 21 March. "Leigh Hunt says, I must 'rebuke you' for not bringing that Note yourself: he has long had a desire to know you. So whenever you feel called that way, the road is open. The return also will be open; that is to say, Hunt is a most *harmless* man. I call him one of the ancient Mendicant Minstrels strangely washed ashore into a century he should not have belonged to. For the rest, unless you feel *called*, it is not worth while to go: he has nothing to teach you, nothing to show you—except himself, should you think that worthy."[19]

Letter 11. Carlyle to Hunt.[20]

Edinburgh, 1st May, 1833—

My Dear Sir,

From amid what is well named the "agonies of Packing," I write you a hasty line, for memento and farewell. It is not farewell either, for in

18. MS, NLS, 520.16.
19. MS, NLS, 618.17. Published in *Letters of Carlyle to Mill, Sterling, and Browning*, pp. 42–45.
20. Addr: 5. York Buildings/New Road. PM: 2.A. NOON. 2/4. MY/1833. MS: British Museum, Ad. 38523, f. 124.

fact we are coming seventy miles nearer you: but somehow at every change of abode one so feels it.

We leave Edinburgh on Tuesday morning,[21] and in two days more shall be at Craigenputtoch, in the old Hermitage Establishment, as it was, and as we were. I carry down some Books with me; contradictions enough to meditate on, and make into *coalitions*; little else that is worth carrying. The winter has been sickly, dispiriting, stagnant; pleasant neither for the outward nor the inward man. Such a dreary morass of Dulness, Halfness, Unbelief; embarrassment, poverty spiritual and economical, it seems to me I never dwelt in: the truth is, Ruin, here as elsewhere is advancing with quite notable rapidity, and still darker days are in store for us. The overloaded Ass will lie down, and roll itself on its rider and squelch him; for any higher enterprise it has neither light nor heart: that is my prediction. I declare the aspect of the whole matter quite pains and saddens me; your whole mind is filled with pity, indignation, shame and sorrowful forebodings; and gladly escapes (if it can) into other contemplations.

So leaving things in general to fare as they may, let us have a word on things in particular. That "Thornton comes to Scotland" is a settled point with us; we wish now that you would, while time favours, get him what the sailors call "under way". Our moors will have on their best cloak before May is done: there are long dawns and *gloamings* (dusks); and sunsets (perhaps sunrises) that he and I must look at from mountain-tops together. Tell him to set his Packages in order, and take the road; there are friends waiting him at the end of it. We promise to send him back a healthier and a wiser man.[22] When I once know his time, I will write to himself a note of directions; if he come by Edinburgh, we shall try to have some friend waiting for him here to do the honours: you yourself little as you may be aware of it, have kind even ardent friends in this cold city. Let us be warned therefore in due time; it will all be easily arranged.

The True Sun,[23] which amuses us not a little, will not after Saturday night (your London Saturday) find us here; but be doubly welcome in the wilderness, "Craigenputtoch Dumfries." The unfortunate Book-parcel will also certainly get thither one day or other: I used to buy single *Tatlers*[24] in London; I shall find use enough for it among the moors, either in rainy days or dry, where all are alike lonely, unvisited of any excitement, except the beginning of work and the ending of it.

21. On 7 May.
22. Cf. the next to the last line of *The Ancient Mariner*: "A sadder and a wiser man."
23. *The True Sun* was a newspaper published from 5 March 1832 to 23 Dec. 1837. In 1832 Hunt reviewed new books for it.
24. The *Tatler* was a daily journal of literature and the stage, published in London from Sept. 1830 to 1832.

Jeffrey has not written to me for many months: indeed till two weeks ago I was in his debt in that point. Whatever you may have written to him, I do not think he will in the long run misunderstand it, still less take it ill. He affects indeed the philosophy of a man of the world, and has no settled *creed* of any higher sort: but there is a perpetual noble contradiction to it in that poetical heart of his. He loves all men, and especially loves the love of all men.

My good Dame sends her affectionate re[gards] to all of you; especially to Thornton that is "coming to Scotland." Our ad[dres]s then (after Saturday) is "Craigenputtoch Dumfries." Write to us so[on;] good news if the Fates will! I am ever, / My Dear Sir, / Yours most truly,

T. Carlyle

Letter 12. Hunt to Carlyle.[25]

5. York Buildings—New Road
May 28. 1833.

My Dear Sir,

I snatch a hurried moment to write to you, because it is the first in which I am able to break my silence, Thornton not having had it in his power to state confidently at what time he could be prepared to set off, though expecting to have been enabled to do so every day. He now begs me to give his best respects & kind wishes, & say that he can set off whenever you give him signal. He comes by sea, because he thinks it will do good to his health, which has been very poor, especially of late; & I must add here, while I think of it, that his diet is of the most moderate description, & that we have no wine at our table. He is very glad, nay very anxious to come, & is making himself as much acquainted with you as possible by reading all such of your writings as he can get at. He has been long acquainted with Wilhelm Meister, has just read the article on Diderot, and is now in the midst of the Life of Schiller. That is an admirable article on Diderot, full of niceties & depths of all sorts, the extremes of refinement, & of knowledge. I read you always, every bit, with an earnestness not to let slip any thought or implication, & I master you thoroughly, & love & admire you as I go. But why do you put Hazlitt with such names as Derrick & Dermody etc., men from whom he was surely as different as great from small, or a brain from an old hat—? And do you not beg the question (very

---

25. MS, Brewer Collection, State University of Iowa. Carlyle's essay on Diderot appeared in the *Foreign Quarterly Review*, XVI (April 1833), 261–315. Diderot's given name was Denis. Carlyle clearly sympathized with Diderot's wife Sophie when he betook himself to mistresses; she was, he said, "too good a wife for such a husband." Carlyle's reference to Hazlitt that Hunt objects to reads: "Nay, could many a poor Dermody, Hazlitt, Heron, Derrick and suchlike, have been trained to be a good Jesuit, were it greatly worse than to have lived painfully as a bad Nothing-at-all?"

subtilly as well as with dignity, I allow, and with just rebuke to some of the vagaries of "Denis") in favour of that very odd & most on-all-hands— proposed "sacrament" of marriage? an experiment which I should hardly think can be said to have succeeded in the world, even in this chaste & hyprocritical & Mamma-sacrificing country of England, where, if I like, as I do everywhere, the fine capable human being, I hate as hard as I can the *nation boutiquière* [nation of shopkeepers], with their love of pence & lords, & their sacrifice, in the metropolis, of a sixth part of the poor female sex for the convenience of prudential young gentlemen & the preser- vation of chastity in the five remaining classes of shrews & scolds, & women good & bad, & wives happy, unhappy, & crimcon-ical [?]. The love of two loving people I love & revere, & wish & believe they remain together to all eternity, whether they think as I do on the subject of marriage or not; but my notions, I own, are more Golden-Aged on this point than those of the Kirk & the cutty-stool,—the bishops & Miss Hannah Moore, whom I am Christian enough to wish had *not* been an old maid, for then she would have been more virtuous & tolerant. Truth is my point of honour,—truth, fair dealing & no deception, grave or gay, with man, woman, or child,—& this I would have to be the point of honour with all the world,—& let every thing else take its chance. [I] do not trust much harm could come of it, if there were no secrets, & no [belief] that we had a right to sacrifice any body's happiness to our own, whether belonging to us or not, which is assuredly the case, in a thousand shapes, with our present legitimatized institutions. In short I would have as many kindly feelings left open, & as many hard & selfish ones discountenanced as possible, & make virtue be- loved upon Plato's principle, because she was seen as she really is. Con- cealment is a great ingredient, I grant, in the present composition & ap- parent providence of the world, & so is lying & tyranny & monopoly & a hundred miseries which providence provides that we shall fight against. If this mixture is the right thing, & must continue, it will do so; but I hope not, & that the fight will be victorious. As to "Dennis," I hate his treatment of his wife, if she was the woman she appears to have been, & I cannot comprehend how he could write about his bodily ailments in that manner to his "Veneres Cupidinesque"; except that the French have an art of neutralizing the grossest things by putting on a face of impudent innocence about them. But I delight in your quarrelling with him as you do, & then finding out something good to make you charitable. I have been afraid, since I wrote to you about Jeffrey, that I have been in need of your char- itable constructions myself, after seeing me button up my patriotic & fatherly sides in that manner; & trying to behave like a man of this world; but you will smile when you see an article I was writing at the time for Tait, & which would damn me with any prudential Whig, however good-natured. Jeffrey, I must tell you, has been very kind & got me upwards of 20 subscribers, but he says I have been "indiscreet." I have indeed: the pioneers & preservers of the sacred fire of Liberty, when others give it up, are apt to be so, & so I shall continue, whatever fancy I may have got into my head that there was some obscure corner of preferment, Scotch or English, in which they might have thrust an old soldier of Reform, who has done his part in its cause, & who has the comfort of knowing he must go on, whether he fight any better or not.

You must have been surprised at not receiving any more True Suns. I am very sorry, as you say they amused you; but the dictatorship of the paper has fallen into new hands,—trustees I believe, & they have cut off my privileges in common with others. It was not very handsome, because the paper was indebted to me; but trustees are not bashful & it is a great thing to be a creditor. So I am dignified & forgiving.

Best compliments on all hands to Mrs. Carlyle,

Ever truly yours,
Leigh Hunt

P.S. I have at length discovered, to my irrepressible & daily delight, in spite of innumerable cares & the other tasks that took me away from it, a subject that suits all the poetical feelings that I ever had in me, & which, I feel certain will put them in the best & most refined[?] light they ever appeared in, or are capable of manifesting. It is the first time I ever felt *my nature versified,*—without some confusion of art & misgiving; & the poem will either be fifty-fold the best thing I ever did, or a huge mistake. For my part, I am impudent enough to be full of confidence.

I forgot to notice something you said in a letter or two back. Pray do not say that some day or other you shall succeed in "tempting" me to come to Scotland. It looks as if I did not wish it; which is very provoking, if you knew all. Thornton will tell you how delighted I should be to get a holiday with a friend,—an expectation[?] absolutely unknown to me; & he will *explain* to you how *impossible* it is for me to do it.

Letter 13. Carlyle to Hunt.[26]

Craigenputtoch, 13th June, 1833—

My Dear Sir,

Will you read this to your young Artist; and let him consider it as addressed equally to himself. The unfortunate Frank is bursting, or I should give you both better measure.

Your Letter, tho' dated 28th May, was only franked for the 4th of June, and only arrived here yesternight. It has taken the longest possible time;

26. MS, Carlyle House, Chelsea.

so I lose none in saying that my Friend Thornton will be welcome whenever he can set out. The following is for hi[s c]*arte de route.*

The cheapest sea-passage, and perhaps in good weather the pleasantest, is by a Leith Smack: these vessels lie about the Tower Wharf; ask for the London & Leith Shipping Company, in case there be any counterfeits. The voyager receives his berth beforehand; it is not likely to be crowded. Say four days brings him to Leith. If it is night, or towards night, he can stay on board till morning, and then equip himself there at leisure. If it is day, let him step ashore (trunk and all), and get into one of the Edinburgh "Stages"; or failing that give some idle youth his luggage, and walk; it is only a mile.

Henry Inglis (pronounced Ingl*es* and the "W.S." means *Writer to the Signet*), to whom I have already spoken, and will in the interim write, is a young friend of mine with a fair young wife and household; a most pleasant, gifted, goodhearted fellow; in whom Thornton will see a Scotch Galantuomo, and friendly Host, whose house is to be his lodging and resting place while he pleases so to honour it. This was Henry's own proposal, and I think ought to be accepted.— Suppose now Edinburgh seen, the Traveler finds a Coach every alternate day (Tuesday is one) starting (from 2. Princes Street) for Dumfries and Thornhill: he takes out his place for Thornhill, is landed there about 3 in the afternoon; sees me (if I be duly warned); or in the other case, asks for Templand (a little furlong off), finds my Mother-in-law there apprised of his coming; and has landed *at home.* Remark that our *only* p[ost]day is Wednesday, the Monday night of London, the Tuesday night of Edinburgh. But Templand *always* stands in the place.— This as the Quakers say, seems "the needful"; and surely nothing more. I am in boundless haste. And so Good Night to all!

Ever faithfully yours,

T. Carlyle.

P.S. A still more brief independent and direct method, whereby Edinburgh is omitted altogether (and can be seen in returning) is this: A Dumfries Mail Coach leaves Edin^r every night at half past nine (the starting-place, quite in the road from Leith, and known to all); take a place in this *forthwith*; you are in Dumfries next morning; write there to me, which a Boy will carry for a shilling; then go to bed (if you have not slept in the leathern convenience, or go and see Burns's Mausoleum etc. if you have); before you are well awake I am there with a gig.— In any case "do the impossible" to give us warning of the *day* you are to arrive on; that will make it all smoother.—

But Thornton Hunt did not get to Craigenputtoch. In late June he did arrive in Edinburgh, where he stayed with Henry Inglis, as Carlyle had suggested. After just two nights there, however, he was overwhelmed and his illness greatly intensified by homesickness. On July 1 he wrote Carlyle to say that he was returning to London as soon as possible and to attempt such explanations as he could make.[27] The Carlyles seem to have been disappointed but accepted Thornton's letter in a kindly spirit.

Letter 14. Carlyle to Hunt.[28]

Craigenputtoch, 18th July, 1833—

My Dear Sir,

There seems no hope now of our good Thornton; so these two Letters, memorials of what might have been and was so near being, must now go the road they came. We had still an expectation; for I wrote off, to the care of Inglis, the instant I had Thornton's Letter, who however I conclude was already gone. We are really vexed all of us; we think how happy your son could have been and we with him in these fine July days; my Brother here too to have doctored him, and nothing but the shine of wholesome skies, and the sound of green woods all round us. Thornton's Letter, so ingenuous so true and gentle looking, had not a little increased our interest. But what can we do? Pray only that the good youth may have got home to his own again, and feel his great misery (to me well known) assuaged a little. After such a misventure it looks foolish to say more about visits: I will only repeat however that I took you at your word in that kind imagination of your also having a house in Nithsdale; be it well understood then that *so* stands it. For the rest give our love and sympathy to Thornton, our prophecy that he will rise to be a Man and Painter, in spite of all hindrances; there looks thro' him that fair openness of soul which, besides its intrinsic price and pricelessness, I have ever found the surest presage of all other gifts.

And now, my dear Sir, let us beg a Letter from *you*, to knit up these

27. MS, Brewer Collection, State University of Iowa.
28. MS, Brewer Collection, State University of Iowa. "Craigcrook" is Jeffrey's home in Edinburgh. It was later the home of Carlyle's friend John Hunter, mentioned below as an admirer of Leigh Hunt. On 28 July Jane Carlyle wrote to her friend Eliza Stodart: "Young Hunt is not come or coming. He got the length of Edinburgh, where he was kindly entertained by Henry Inglis, as we had arranged for him. But the fatigue of the journey and the separation—his first separation—from his own people increased his nervous ailments to such a degree, that he could resolve on nothing but to go back with all despatch the way he came." *Early Letters of Jane Welsh Carlyle*, ed. David G. Ritchie (London, 1889), pp. 243–44.

ravelments; so much lies uncertain to us. That you labour, and continue thro' all weather to labour, with such undying cheerfulness and hope, we rejoice to believe: but pray give assurance of it; let us sympathize with you if it is not so. I say *we* and *us* in all this matter; for my Wife and I are at one in it.

What you mention about the new Poetical subject might awaken one's curiosity; but perhaps you are of Goethe's mind (which I think a very good one) that if you *blab* in seeking hidden treasure, the spirits will rise, and whisk it (and oneself too) to the Devil. I can heartily give you joy of the mood you hint at; it is one I have fancied often enough, but never was at any time near to. Go on and prosper, were the times never so prosaic! There is an ear and a heart in man; if not in this man or in that man, yet in some man: let us forever have faith in man. We are this morning reading your *Rimini*; with praise enough on all hands; with a *clear* feeling on my part if not of the Art yet of the Artist: sunny Italy with her children of the Sun, all is so freely mirrored there.

As for myself I am idle, all but a little reading; chiefly of French Revolution *Mémoires*, and such other *Realities* as I can come at. My Brother has all manner of things to say about Rome and Naples, even the poor old purple or rather scarlet old woman of a Holy Father is worth looking at. To me Italy face to face were perhaps almost wearisome at present. Spiritually I feel myself in a kind of crisis; the best I can do is to stand still a little; my road will disclose itself again (let me hope, to still higher countries, pleasanter or not) by and by. I have found it generally so with me; from time to time I have a kind of sick moulting-season; but after that new feathers[;] without great previous pain I never made any advancement.

Many thanks for your attentive perusal of my poor *Diderot*. A few such readers, and careful writing were worth while; that one such thinks me worth reading is encouragement. Pity that I were not with you to hear your whole *Miserere* over the Marriage-state; which I wholly agree with you is at present miserable enough. Nevertheless I would stand by my argument that the Covenant of Marriage m[ay] be perennial; nay that in a better state of society there will be other pere[nnial] Covenants between man and man, and the home-feeling of man in this world [of] his be all the kindlier for it. For instance, could two Friends, good men both, declare themselves Brothers, and by Law make themselves so! Alas, Friendship were again possible in this Earth; and not as at present only Dining-together. But as for the unfortunate-females and so forth, I declare I can see *no* remedy except in improvement of the individual: till people learn again what *god*like meaning is in Duty and practice self-denial which is the beginning of all, what can you do for them by Laws? All machinery of Laws will entangle itself in new confusion before it is well set up; because the *hinges* are naught; I mean the four Cardinal virtues are not there. Finally I will most heartily agree with you, nay I often vehemently assert the same myself that at whatever rate we value chastity, it is brutish and delirious to punish only the weaker for want of it. The fault I continue to declare is (in spite of all genealogy barbarisms) alike for both; and so indeed our worthy old Cutty Stool (which I reverence much even in its worm-eaten state) has always most honestly regarded it. Praise to the Cutty Stool, for its day, then! I pray only to Heaven that we had a new one—of better structure if you will;—but *a new one*, the *principle* that made the old one, this is to me the grand want of wants. Thus you see we could discourse most eloquent musical discords for a week, or year.

What of the Advocate now? It is months since we heard a syllable of him, except by the Newspapers. I fear he is vexed and worried; the people and their Editors are grunting at him not a little here and there. I wish he were well out of that scandalous Cockpit, and back again to Craigcrook. — Do not wait for Franks when none are convenient. Nothing is better worth its price (even taxed price) than a Letter of yours. And so all Good with you and yours! My Wife joins with me in that prayer.—

Ever affectionately
T. Carlyle

I expect some Tait's Magazines soon, and will ferret you out.

Letter 15. Hunt to Carlyle. A short letter from Thornton Hunt to Carlyle is written across a page and a half of this letter.[29]

4. Upper Cheyne Row, Chelsea, near London.
Monday—July 29 [,1833].

My dear Sir,

I should have written to you before, but I have been more than usually unwell, with a great pain in my right side, & another, not so physical, in my left; but I have resorted to my good angel, Patience; & have been helped by him[?] as well; & which I have not seldom found after more than ordinary trouble, I have the pleasure of telling you, that I have just experienced a more than ordinary improvement in my position, having, as you will see by my new address, got at last into another far cheaper yet better house,—at least to my taste; for it is of the good old solid wain-scotted fashion, such as reminds me of the times of my father & mother; & instead of paying a hundred & sixty guineas a year for paltry heavy

---

29. MS, Brewer Collection, State University of Iowa. "A Day with the Reader," intended to be a very long, comprehensive poem, was never finished, and only fragments of it were published.

furniture of the people, it costs me thirty guineas with honest furniture of my own; & instead of being swept all day by a tempest of carts and omnibuses, [it] is as quiet as if it were a hundred miles from town,—a remnant of the rustic part of the old village, up in a corner where there is no thorough-fare, no houses to overlook us, with gardens & trees back & front, & I have got a tree to look at as I write, with a cottage window peeping under it, amid a nest of green & you have no conception,—as the phrase is (for you *have*) of the comfort this is to me, & how my head seems to bathe itself in the quiet. We are all of us the better for it, Thornton included.

But to speak more of him, I was astonished one day, on returning home, to find him sitting, not at Craigenputtoch, but in one of the drawing-room chairs, impudently smiling in my face, as if nothing had happened. I was alarmed at first, but not long; & though he has been very ill since, he has not been as ill as at Edinburgh, & upon the whole is better than when he left us. We all regret, & he not the least of us, that his journey was unfinished; especially as in you he had found another friend who could have understood him in his strength as well as weakness, & encourage & sustain him, & do all, & perhaps more, than any other friend. Yet I must tell you, that these trials are not unknown to his father; sometimes I fear to inherit a tendency to them from me, as I did from one of my own parents—another of whom gave me perhaps more animal spirits to vary them than belong to him. Yes, my experiences have been very bitter, & at any rate have the benefit of what I can tell him to comfort him & how to manage himself; & he sees me come home, in spite of all my troubles, able to "take the good the gods provide me," & realizing consolations & an amount of years, which I never expected to see. At the same age with himself, I fell into a hypochrondriacal illness, which stirred up sources of thought in me frightful as if I had seen the gulfs of time & place opened. I had another, sometime after, which lasted me four years & a half, in midst of which I had to go into prison; and I had a third but shorter, more severe, about three years ago, since which I feel as I should have been better in my general health than before, if I had not had so many other anxieties. In the intervals of all these attacks, I have enjoyed a natural tendency to a flow of spirits singular for one who has suffered so much; and I have never ceased to extract a certain delight from Nature (so called), even when she pressed too strongly upon my consciousness, & seemed to cut me with too much distinctness, except upon one point which also turns to a great pleasure when I can entertain the thought of it. But enough of myself. Thornton writes to you across this letter, & both of us are thankful for what you say about franks, which in truth have at times nearly driven me out of my wits, as the saying is,—owing to the cross-

purposes they have occasioned & the uncertain movements of the bestow-
ers of them. I did not like to write without them, because being the man
you are, I felt as if I could not be certain that it might not inconvenience
you at the moment, well off or not as you might be in general; or if this
is too moneyless a fancy, I must own that it may have originated in circumstances experienced [by] myself;—not *now* experienced however; &
it will be a grace in you if you will take me at my word in this as in the
other instance, & act as if you did; for I assure you, my letters must be
welcome to you indeed if they are half as much so as yours to me. I was
going to say *as* much instead of half; but my animal spirits, in my time,
have got me into such bad reputation with some people for vanity—I mean
the critics—that they have made me jealous sometimes of their getting
me into a scrape with my best friends; & I feel that the perplexity somewhat sophisticates me. I now believe I ought to have lived in the south,
or in my father's West Indian island, that allowance be made for extra-
vivacity, and that way so called mental as well as personal gesticulation,
or (to lump metaphors together accordingly) for that foliage of manners,
which however relevant and superfluous, may yet contain some fruit with
a sound core to it underneath. Scotchmen, I think, have understood me
worse than any other people; but I have at length met with one, who is
inclined to construe me so handsomely, that I am anxious to obtain that
revenge over his countrymen, even at the hazard of being thought a little
too well of. I endeavour to persuade myself, that if he thinks too well of
me in some things, I could almost piece out his good opinion in some
other points,—if he knew all. But here is more of myself, & yet I must needs
give you more still, to answer what you say about my verses. Next time, I
will talk to you of marriage, & all sorts of other matters, abstract & concrete, & endeavour to interchange minds & fancies with you. I can see
what you very goodnaturedly find to like in the Story of Rimini; and that
you cannot help finding deficients in it; and I am equally sure, that I agree
with you in your objections. There is at once too much art in it, & too
little: too much in the conventional sense, & too little in the high, artistical.
Neither, in spite of this better knowledge, do I believe that I shall ever
be where I could wish to be in poetry, but I do certainly believe that I
can get a footing in the enchanted ground beyond what I have yet shewn
any abundant marks of; & I have got a strong persuasion upon me, that
I am now getting it. My subject, at all events (which I will disclose to *you*,
& of course to your other you, in spite of what Goethe says & says truly)
is one, for the first time, that suits my whole nature, its gravity, & its levity;
its experiences, & its wishes; & if I have any poetry in me at all, there it
will be found. The poem is entitled A Day with the Reader, & its object
is to shew how *the common-places of life may be enriched* by feeling &

fancy, not omitting his breakfast, with his China teacups, his dinner, his bed, his room with the most trivial things around him, his walks on the streets, & his restings in the country. It is to[o] long, & I think of publishing a portion at a time, beginning with morning, for I propose to enrich his eyesight[?] the moment he wakes, let the day be never so rainy & so to accompany him around through the four & twenty hours till he wakes again. I do not know whether you ever saw a little periodical publication of mine called the Indicator, which is thought by my friends the best thing I ever did. I shall send you a copy of it shortly, for Colburne is re-publishing it. Well, the papers in that collection have a similar object to the poem; I used often to feel, while writing it, a propensity to put my thoughts in verse, which with great impatience I was forced not to do, because I wrote for the day that[?] went over my head. The poem will be [a] sort of "Indicator" in verse, but more connected; & I am so full of it, that I shall let my pen run as it pleases, thinking no more of what the Edinburgh critics will say, than a bee. It is in blank verse, in order that I may be as headlong or otherwise as I please.

I have got much to say to you about *"marriage,"*—which I love, be it known, in the particular, but think naught & horrible in the general. So my kindest regards to the "gode wife," & to her "guide, philosopher, & friend," & may all blessings be with the good hearts of Craigenputtoch, quoth their obliged & affectionate friend,

Leigh Hunt

Since "The World of Books," I have written nothing in Tait but "Wishing-Caps." I have seen nothing more of Jeffrey, but mean shortly to call upon him. I shall get franks again, & be able, I trust, to do all things with proper planetary order & swiftness, once I have got out of a chaos indescribable.

Letter 16. Carlyle to Hunt.[30]

Craigenputtoch: 29th October, 1833

My Dear Sir,—

It is above two long months since the sight of your handwriting last gratified me at Dumfries. I was there in person, I remember; and read the

30. Published in "Concerning Leigh Hunt," pp. 491–95. The "cynical Extravaganza of mine" is *Sartor Resartus,* which appeared in *Fraser's Magazine* for Nov. and Dec. 1833, and for Feb., March, April, June, July, and Aug. 1834. "Amid the Cannon vollies, shrieks and legislative debates, the laughter and tears": Carlyle had already begun the reading that prepared him to write *The French Revolution.* Sir Samuel Egerton Brydges (1762–1837) wrote bibliographical and genealogical works. His *Censura Literaria,* in ten volumes, was published at London by Longman, Hurst, Rees, and Orme from 1805 to 1809. He is said to have written two thousand sonnets in one year. Richard Porson (1759–1808), English classical scholar, edited Aeschylus and made

kind lively sheet, with a pipe and tumbler (of water), taking with double relish "mine ease at my inn." Why I have not answered sooner, looks foolish to tell. I waited for "opportunities"; had but *one* and missed it by pressure of haste. A Reformed Parliament having now, by Heaven's grace, taken itself into retirement, there are henceforth no "opportunities" possible. What can I do but what I should have done six weeks ago—*make* an opportunity? You shall pay thirteen pence and odds into His Majesty's impoverished Exchequer; and on this long sheet get talk from me enough: —soon, I hope, through the same channel, repaying with interest, to the Patriot King's benefit and mine.

Your new situation looked so cheerful and peaceful, I almost fear to inquire what it has become. Chances and changes hardly leave us a week at rest in this fearful Treadmill of a World. The prophet said "Make it like unto a wheel": that is the kind of wheel I think we are made like unto. Meanwhile, ever as I figure you, that cheerful Tree, seen from your window, rises leafy and kind on me; I can hardly yet consent to have it leafless, and its kind whisper changed into a loud October howl. Be patient, and nestle near the chimney corner: there is a Spring coming. Nay, as I hope, one day, an Eternal Spring, when all that is dead and deserved not to die, shall bloom forth again, and live for ever!

You must tell me more specially what you are doing. How prospers your Poem? Has the winter checked it; or is it already branching out to defy all storms both of outward and of inward weather?

I see nothing here; scarcely more of you than a small "wishing-cap" incidentally in *Tait*, and even that not lately. The Newspapers told us you had been engaged for the Theatrical department of some new *Weekly True Sun*: I can hardly imagine it, or you would have sent us an old paper, some day, by way of sign. The whole Literary world seems to me at this time to be little other than Chaos come again; how should I see your course in it, when I cannot see my own? This only is clear for both of us, and for all true men: mix not, meddle not with the accursed thing there; swim stoutly, unweariedly, "if not towards landmarks on the Earth, then towards loadstars in the Heaven!" For the rest, as our good Scotch adage has it: Fear nothing earthly; there is ever Life for the Living.

Since I wrote last, I have read all your Poems; the whole volume, I believe, without missing a line. If you knew with what heart-sickness I in general take up a volume of modern rhymes, and again with a silent curse

---

important contributions to knowledge of iambic and trochaic verse. "Peter Pindar" was the pseudonym of John Wolcot (1738–1819), a physician who wrote witty but coarse satires. Carlyle was greatly influenced by Dr. Johnson's biography of the comparatively obscure Richard Savage, which he certainly had in mind when he wrote his *Life of John Sterling*, a much better biography than either his *Cromwell* or his *Frederick the Great*.

of Ernulphus, (for where were the good of making a spoken one?) lay it down, this fact would have more meaning for you. I find a genuine tone of *music* pervade all your way of thought: and utter itself, often in the gracefullest way, through your images and words: this is what I call your vocation to Poetry: so long as this solicits you, let it in *all* forms have free course. Well for him that *hath* music in his soul! Indeed, when I try Defining (which grows less and less my habit), there is nothing comes nearer my meaning as to poetry in general than this of *musical thought*: the unpardonable poetry is that where the word only has rhythm, and the Thought staggers along dislocated, hamstrung, or too probably rushes down altogether in shameful inanition. One asks, *why* did the unhappy mortal write in *rhyme*? That miserablest decrepit Thought of his cannot even walk (with crutches); how in the name of wonder shall it *dance*? But so wags, or has wagged the world literary: till now, as I said, the very sight of *dancing*, drives an old stager like me quick into another street. More tolerable were the Belfast Town and Country Almanack, more tolerable is the London Directory, or McCulloch's Political Economy itself in the Day of Judgment than these! To come a little to particulars: we all thought your *Rimini* very beautiful; sunny brilliancy and fateful gloom most softly blended, under an *atmosphere* of tenderness, clear and bright like that of Italian Pictures. Beautifully *painted*; what it wanted to be a *whole* (and a picture) I believe you know better than I. *Leander* also dwells with me; I think, that of his "bursting into tears," when he feels the waves about to beat him, is eminently natural. Thank you also for the two children's pieces: I remember, some seventeen years ago, seeing *Dick's* one quoted by a Quarterly Reviewer, as an instance of "bad taste" (may the Devil, in his own good time, take "taste," and make much of it!): but the effect on me quite baulked the Reviewer. In the same Article, I first saw that picture of the mother ("a poor, a pensive, but a happy one"), singing as she mended her children's clothes, when they were all asleep; and never lost it, or am like to lose it.

You shall now get quit of criticism; and hear a little about Craigenputtoch. For a long while, for eight or nine months almost, I have been not idle, yet fallow; *writing* not a word. A cynical Extravanganza of mine is indeed beginning to appear in *Fraser's Magazine,* and will continue there till you are all tired of it but it was written wholly three years and a half ago: it was some purpose of publishing it as a Book that brought me up to London. The last thing I wrote was a *Count Cagliostro* in that extraordinary Periodical. When I shall put pen to paper next is quite a problem. It ought to be when I have *mended my ways*; for nothing is so clear to me at present as that, outwardly and inwardly, I am *all in the wrong*. I believe, one is hardly ever all in the right. Let us not mourn over that. But the strange thing at present with me is the outward economic state of Literature. Bookselling I apprehend to be as good as dead; without hope of revival, other than perhaps some galvanic one: the question therefore arises, what next is to be done? A monstrous question, which I think it may take two centuries to answer well. We, in the mean time, must do—the best we can. I have various projects, some of which may become purposes; I reckon, I may see you again in London by and by, for one thing.

This winter, at all events, and who knows how much more, we mean to spend here in the depths of the wilderness; divided from all men. Probably it may be a healthier winter; probably a happier and usefuller one. London I liked much, but the fogs and smoke were pestiferous; Edinburgh I find has left but a sad impression of hollowness and dulness on me: however, both might yield profit; and now a solitary winter, filled to overflowing with Books (for I have discovered a Library here), may be the profitablest of all. You, as a determined Book-moth, will appreciate my felicity, when you hear that I read some ten hours often at a sitting, divided by *one*, for a walk, which I take like physic. My head grows a perfect "Revolt of Paris;" nothing occurring to divert me; only the little Table-clock (poor little fellow) suggesting now and then that I am still in the world of time. I fall asleep at last towards midnight, amid the Cannon vollies, shrieks and legislative debates, the laughter and tears, of whole generations;—for it is mainly History and Memoirs that I am reading. Now and then I shall perhaps write something, were it only for Prince Posterity. Thus you see us with winter at our door; but with huge stacks of fuel for the body's warmth, and for the mind's.

A benevolent artist arrived lately, moreover, and rehabilitated the Piano: a little music is invaluable to me; better than sermons; winnows all the bitter dust out of me, and for moments makes me a good man.

Pray think of us often; send now and then a Paper Messenger through the snow to us; to which I will not fail to reply.

I had innumerable questions to ask you about matters literary in London. Who manages the New Monthly Magazine now? For I see Bulwer has given it up long ago. What else is stirring? Pray tell me all you can think of, about such things: remember that here simply *nothing* reaches me of its own accord. Do you know an English Book, of date 1709, reprinted some twenty years ago, named *Apuleius' Golden Ass?* I fancied it a translation of the old story; found it only an Imitation; full of questionable and of *un*questionable matter. It surprised me a little; especially as a Queen Anne performance. Farther, can you in [a] few words inform me who or what Sir Egerton Brydges is? Was his *Censura* published in London? Much of it is perfectly useless for me; but the man has a small vein of real worth in him, and knows several things: the whining in his Prefaces struck me as the strangest.— I still continue to wish much you would undertake the Life of *Hazlitt*: though in my ignorance of the position matters stand in, to *advise* it were beyond my commission. Of all imaginable Books *True* Biographies are the best, the most essential. Hazlitt *should not* be forgotten. How I have lamented too that Porson studied, and drank, and rhymed, and went to the Devil, in vain! Peter Pindar too! We should have *Lives* of all such men: not of the "respectable" sort (far from it!); but of the *true* sort; painted *to the life*, as the men actually looked and were. There are hardly any readable Lives in our language except those of Players. One may see the reason too.

But now, alas, has my time come. Accept in good part this flowing gossip. If I had you here, you should have ten times as much. Answer me soon, though I have no right to ask it. Our kindest regards to Mrs. Hunt to Thornton and all the rest; not forgetting that smallest *listening Philosopher*, who has forgot me though I have not him. Adieu!

Ever faithfully,
T. Carlyle.

There was another lull in the correspondence after Carlyle sent this letter. On 30 January 1834 he wrote to Henry Inglis: "We have heard no whisper of Hunt these many months. Your notice of Hunt junior was news; for it seemed too possible something had got wrong. Poor Leigh has the toughest battle to fight; it is never up till he is down again. The Battle must last too till—*Night*! God help him; and us."[31]

Letter 17. Hunt to Carlyle.[32]

4. Upper Cheyne Row, Chelsea
Monday, April 8. 1834.

My dear Sir,

I write to you in pure despair of being able to write as I could wish. I am always hoping to send you long letters, with full, true, & particular accounts of all that I am doing, thinking, writing suffering, & enjoying; & the consequence, it seems, is, that I write none at all; which is a meeting of extremes that must not be. But I get so knocked up with writing every day, that I literally dread to put pen to paper again for the remainder of it. I forget that I might write something less for my task, & devote the

---

31. MS, NLS, 1796.35. Published in the *Glasgow Herald*, 16 Feb. 1882.
32. MS, Brewer Collection, State University of Iowa.

time I save from it to my friends; or rather, I get so bitter with my task while about it, & think it necessary to say such heaps of all sorts of superfluous things, that my time is swallowed up before I am aware of it, & my cheek & head begin to burn before I have done what I undertake. No more of this. I will be wiser.— I beg your acceptance of the two vols. of Essays herewith sent you, which were first published sometime back (the Indicator & Companion), and also of the numbers that have hitherto appeared of a new three-halfpenny periodical, which is to be an English Chalmers, and much honester than its richer brethren, ergo, more effective in what it has of good in it. You will like the good-will in it at all events.— You must know I was mystified enough when your Sartor Resartus first appeared, to take it for a satire on "Germanick[?ism]" itself from the pen of the editor of the magazine, also nevertheless appeared to me to intimate a number of serious & deep things in it, for which I gave him a great lift in my imagination. I soon found out my mistake; but by some unaccountable chance I had overlooked—forgotten rather, that part of your letter in which you had advised me of it. I shall send you, when I think this letter has arrived (otherwise I will not mystify *you* by the abrupt entrance of an old newspaper or two) the number of the True Sun, in which I spoke of it; & they shall be followed by a few essays in the *Weekly* True Sun, which may amuse you for want of something better. I have had a flitting engagement in both the papers, but have ceased with the one, & am about to do so with the other.

But they tell me you are coming to live in London, & that you wish to live in a house like mine? *Is it true?* & may I look out for such a house? & shall it, or can it be, any where in this neighborhood? Tell me so, & it will be the best news I have heard from you, since the day on which a gentleman came to us & said he had a proposal to make to assure competence to my family (this new project, to wit); for my first want is to see my labours turn to some lasting account for the little people about me; & my need is the want of a companion. If you lived here, I should have somebody to walk with & talk with, and you should be some gainer too, as you are of the sociable order of philosophers, especially as huge literary London could be close to you, & companions endless; for though you have Mrs. Carlyle with you, & music, etc. yet the best & most loving human beings cannot live wholly upon spices—at least, so they say—without some ordinary food for the staple commodity of their dish; & so I hope you will come & make your dumpling out of us, & be still happier than before with the plums with which God has blessed you.

Ever indeed yours
Leigh Hunt

P.S. Thornton has been uneasy at never hearing from Mr. Inglis. He was constrained on his abrupt departure from Scotland to borrow five pounds of him, which he returned after the lapse of a good many weeks; and he sometimes fears he may have most involuntarily given offence; sometimes hopes that Mr. I. thought it unnecessary to write.

Letter 18. Carlyle to Hunt.[33]

Craigenputtoch, 18th April, 1834—

My Dear Sir,

Your Letters are rare, too rare, in their outward quality of sequence thro' the Post; but happily still rarer in their inward quality: the hope and kind trustful sympathy of new Eighteen dwelling unworn under hair, which you tell me is getting tinged with grey! It is actually true that we are coming to London; so far have Destiny and a little Resolution brought it. The kind Mrs Austin, after search enough, has now (we imagine) found us a House; which I hope and believe is not very far from yours: it shall be farther than my widest calculation, if I fail to meet your challenge, and walk and talk with you to all lengths. I know not well how Chelsea lies from the Parish Church of Kensington; but it is within sight of the latter that we are to be; and some "trysting-tree" (do you know so much Scotch?) is already getting into leaf, as yet unconscious of its future honour, between these two suburbs of Babylon. Some days too we will walk the whole day long, in wide excursion; you lecturing me on the phenomena of the region, which to you are native: my best amusement is walking; I like, as well as Hadrian himself, to mete out my world with steps of my own, and so take possession of it. But if to this you add Speech! Is not Speech defined to be cheerfuller than Light, and the Eldest Daughter of Heaven? I mean articulate discourse of reason, that comes from the internal heavenly part of us; not the confused gabble, which (in so many millions) comes from no deeper than the palate of the mouth; which it is the saddest of all things to listen to, a thing that fills one alternately with sorrow and indignation, and at last almost with a kind of horror and terror. As if the world were a huge Bedlam; and the sacred Speech of men had become an inarticulate jargon of hungry cawing rooks!

We laid down your description of your House, as the Model our kind Friend was to aim at: how far we have prospered will be seen. In rent it appears we are nearly on a par; we also anticipate quiet and some visitations of the heavenly air: but for the rest, ours will be no "high-wainscotted dwelling," like Homer's and yours; no, some newfangled brick-booth, which will tremble at every step, in which no four-footed thing can stand

33. MS in the British Museum, 33,515, fol. 39. Published in Conway's *Carlyle*, pp. 204–207. The Carlyle's friend Mrs. John Austin (Sarah Austin) (1793–1867) trans-

but only three-footed; such as "Holland Street, Kensington", in this year of grace, can be expected to yield. However, there is a patch of garden, or indeed two patches; I will have some little crib for my Books and Writing-table; and do the best that may be. Inn[umerable], immeasurable vague forebodings hang over me as I [write]; meanwhile there is one grand assurance: the feeling [that] it was a duty, almost a necessity. My Dame too [is] of resolution for the enterprise, and whatsoever may follow it; so, Forward in God's name!

I have seen nothing of you for a long time, except what of the "Delicacies of Pigdriving" my Examiner once gave me. A most tickling thing; not a word of which can I remember, only the whole *fact* of it pictured in such subquizzical sweet-acid geniality of mockery, stands here, and, among smaller and greater things, will stand. If the two volumes are of that quality, they will be worth a welcome. I cannot expect them now till the beginning of May; or perhaps I may even still find them with Fraser at Whitsuntide. Here among the Moors they were best of all.

The starting of your *Journal* was a glad event for me; it seemed one of the hopefullest projects in these days; and surely it must be a strange Public, one would think, in which Robert Chambers (a very silly kind of man) prospers and Leigh Hunt fails. You must bear up steadily *at first*; it is there, in this as in all things, that the grand difficulties lie.

Thornton need be under no uneasiness about Henry Inglis, from whom we heard not long ago, with some remark too of a very friendly character about the Traveller in question, and not the faintest hint about pounds or shillings.

I am writing *nothing*; reading, above all things, my old *Homer* and Prolegomena enough; the old song itself with a most singular delight. Fancy me as reading till you see me; then must *another* scene open.— Your Newspapers will interest me; as for the unhappy *Sartor* none can detest him more than my present self; there are some ten pages rightly *fused* and harmonious; the rest is only *welded* or even agglomerated, and may be thrown to the swine.

All salutations from us both! valete et nos amate!

T. Carlyle

---

lated and edited German and French historical works. Shakespeare, Bacon, and Coleridge, like Carlyle, have an exalted conception of "discourse of reason" and distinguish between it and such communication as the lower animals may be capable of. "Delicacies of Pigdriving": Carlyle had read a review of Hunt's *The Indicator and Companion*, 2 vols. (London: published for H. Colburn by R. Bentley, 1834), in the *Examiner* for 12 January 1834, in which Hunt's essay "On the Graces and Anxieties of Pig-Driving" had been quoted at some length. *Leigh Hunt's London Journal* appeared weekly from 2 April 1834 to 25 Dec. 1835.

Letter 19. Carlyle to Hunt.[34]

Craigenputtoch, 1st May, 1834—

My dear Sir,

In your last Letter you asked to be permitted to look us out a House in your neighbourhood. By a strange turn of the cards, it chances this day that we find ourselves in the very state to profit by your bounty. Our expected Kensington House has evaporated, and we are here, alone, with all the world before us where to choose.

In a fortnight, accordingly, I expect to see you, on that quest. Mrs Austin is still angling in Kensington for us. If you will fish Chelsea, I shall almost at once know what I am about. The more necessary as the time is rapidly expiring!

As you have not only two eyes of your own, but who knows how many other pairs of *younger* ones (and as bright as any in England), perhaps you may discover something. At all events, this commission may amuse your walks a little; you have here the announcement of a visit which I know will agreeably occupy your thoughts; and so with hopes of a speedy meeting and prayers that it may be a glad one, I remain,

My Dear Sir, / Yours most faithfully
Th: Carlyle

(in great haste)

By 13 May Carlyle was himself in London. He looked at houses in Kensington, Brompton, Camden Town, Primrose Hill, and Hampstead before finally deciding to take one at 5 Great Cheyne Row, just a short distance from Leigh Hunt's house on Upper Cheyne Row. Mrs. Carlyle soon joined him after they had decided through correspondence to take the house in Chelsea, and on 10 June they moved into it. It would be their home for the rest of their lives.

Letter 20. Carlyle to Hunt.[35]

[Early May 1834]

Thanks, my dear Sir, for your kind M[essage] and most hospitable offer. I must, on no account, think of leaving my own bed; for otherwise, I *leave sleep* along with it; the meaning of which latter circumstance is, I fear, too well known to yourself.

Meanwhile, I will be with you very shortly after Henry; and investigate the capabilities of Chelsea, with all intentness, under your guidance. If Mrs Hunt some time in the afternoon will give me some six ounces

34. MS, NLS, 1796.39.
35. Carlyle to Hunt, early May. MS in Yale University Library.

avoirdupois of Beefsteak and two Potatoes, the Patriot King[36] could not offer me a better dinner.

I am my own till towards six o'clock, when I must be in Edwardes Square Kensington, for a second examination of a place I saw there. Alas, it is Noah's Raven[37] that I am like for the present! But we must and will be thro' it.

Ever faithfully,
T. Carlyle—

As here indicated, Hunt had been helpful in this quest and was delighted when the choice of the house near him was made. During the search Carlyle had seen the inside of Hunt's house and had written his wife a vivid description of the bizarre household:

At length came Chelsea, and Cheyne Row; a set of young bronze coloured gypsey faces were idly looking thro' a window; I asked them with a half-presentiment where Hunt lived; they answered, Here, and that he was from home. I enter: O ask me not for a description till we meet! The Frau Hunt lay drowsing on cushions "sick, sick" with [a] thousand temporary ailments; the young imps all agog to see me jumped hither and thither, one strange goblin-looking fellow, about 16, ran ministering about tea-kettles for us: it was all a mingled lazaretto and tinkers camp, yet with a certain joy and nobleness at heart of it: faintly resembling some of the maddest scenes in *Wilhelm Meister*, only madder. They had looked at no houses, knew not what I meant by them; gave me to fancy that perhaps at that hour you might be reading a new Letter of Hunt's asking further instructions of me. They gave me tea, would fain have given me the Husband's shoes (à la Shelley, for I was to be the new Shelley): finally the goblin, "Percy Hunt," a very good sort of fellow, I think, inquired me out an omnibus to Temple Bar: and I came *hirpling* [limping with the uneven gait of a hare] home, with a determination at least to have my old shoes next day.[38]

A week later Carlyle wrote a similar description of the Hunt household and the "Huntlets" for his notebook: "Nondescript! unutterable! Mrs. Hunt asleep on cushions, four or five beautiful, strange, gipsy-looking children running about in undress, whom the lady ordered to get us tea. . . . a sallow, black-haired youth of sixteen, with a kind of dark cotton nightgown [dressing-gown] on, went whirling about

36. The current monarch, William IV.
37. Cf. Gen. 8:7: he "went forth to and fro."
38. MS, NLS, 610.23. Published incomplete in *Thomas Carlyle: Letters to His Wife*, ed. Trudy Bliss (Cambridge, Mass., 1953), pp. 90–97.

like a familiar, providing everything: an indescribable dreamlike household."[39]

Once the Carlyles were actually neighbors of the Hunts, they found much in the relationship that proved highly gratifying, but also much that indicated that these were neighbors who had to be treated with some degree of caution. Leigh Hunt himself they both developed real affection for; and they found the personal charm of the man irresistible despite marked differences in his philosophy of life and that of Carlyle. Hunt is mentioned favorably in Carlyle's letter to his mother of 12 June 1834, the first letter that he wrote from his Chelsea home: "Hunt, who is close by, is not only the kindest but the politest of men; has never been near us (which we reckon very civil), but will always be delighted when I go and rouse *him* for a walk; and indeed a sprightly, sensible talker he is, and very pleasant company for a stroll. Jane greatly preferred his 'poetical Tinkerdom' to any of the unpoetical Gigmandoms (even Mrs. Austin's) which I showed her. The Hunts, I think, will not trouble us, and indeed be a pleasure so far as they go."[40] About two weeks later he described Hunt and his family in greater detail in a letter to his brother Alexander:

Hunt is always ready to go and walk with me, or sit and talk with me to all lengths if I want him. He comes in once a week (when invited, for he is very modest), takes a cup of tea, and sits discoursing in his brisk, fanciful way till supper time, and then cheerfully eats a cup of porridge (to sugar only), which he praises to the skies, and vows he will make his supper of at home. He is a man of thoroughly London make, such as you could not find elsewhere, and I think about the *best* possible to be made of his sort: an airy, crotchety, most copious clever talker, with an honest undercurrent of reason too, but unfortunately not the deepest, not the most practical—or rather it is the most *un*practical ever man dealt in. His hair is grizzled, eyes black-hazel, complexion of the clearest dusky brown; a thin glimmer of a smile plays over a face of cast-iron gravity. He never laughs—can only titter, which I think indicates his worst deficiency. His house excels all you have ever read of—a *poetical Tinkerdom*, without parallel even in literature. In his family room, where are a sickly large wife and a whole shoal of well-conditioned wild children, you will find half a dozen old rickety chairs gathered from half a dozen hucksters, and all seemingly engaged, and just pausing, in a violent *hornpipe*. On these

---

39. Entry of 24 May 1834. From Lawrence and Elisabeth Hanson, *Necessary Evil: The Life of Jane Welsh Carlyle* (London, 1952), p. 183.
      40. MS, NLS, 520.29.

and around them and over the dusty table and ragged carpet lie all sorts of litter—books, paper, egg-shells, scissors, and last night when I was there, the torn heart of a half-quartern loaf. His own room above stairs, into which alone I strive to enter, he keeps cleaner. It has only two chairs, a bookcase, and a writing-table; yet the noble Hunt receives you in his Tinkerdom in the spirit of a king, apologizes for nothing, places you in the best seat, takes a window sill himself if there is no other, and there folding closer his loose-flowing 'muslin-cloud' of a printed nightgown in which he always writes, commences the liveliest dialogue on philosophy and the prospects of man (who is to be beyond all measure 'happy' yet); which again he will courteously terminate the moment you are bound to go; a most interesting, pitiable, loveable man, to be used kindly but with discretion. After all, it is perhaps rather a comfort to be near honest friendly people—at least an honest, friendly man of that sort. We stand sharp but mannerly for his sake and for ours, and endeavor to get and do what good we can, and avoid the evil.[41]

The growing intimacy and free discussion soon intensified the philosophical differences between the two men. On 22 July Carlyle wrote to his brother John:

Hunt is always at hand, but as the modestest of men *never* comes unless sent for: his theory of life and mine have already declared themselves to be from top to bottom at *variance*, which shocks him considerably: to me his talk is occasionally pleasant, is always clever and lively; but all too *foisonless* baseless and shallow. He has a theory that the world is or should and shall be a gingerbread Lubberland, where Evil (that is *Pain*) shall never come, a theory in very considerable favor here; which to me is pleasant as streams of *un*ambrosial dishwater, a thing I simply *shut my mouth* against, as the shortest way. With Hunt*dom* we find it quite possible and simple to manage altogether with[out] and keep nearly wholly *clear* of it, except when we can[not] help it, which is seldom. I pity Hunt and love him.[42]

About two weeks later he wrote to his mother:

Hunt, nor the Hunts, does not trouble us more than we wish: he comes in when we send for him; talks, listens to a little music, even sings and plays a little, *eats* (without *Kitchen* of any kind, or only with a little sugar) his allotted plate of Porridge, and then goes his ways. His way of

41. Froude, *Carlyle*, II, 439–40. Warlocks and witches presided over by Auld Nick dance wild hornpipes in Burns's "Tam O'Shanter."
42. MS, NLS, 523.23. Published in Froude, *Carlyle*, II, 440–43. "*Foisonless*": thin, unfruitful, lacking substance.

thought and mine are utterly at variance; a thing which grieves him much, not me. He accounts for it by my "Presbyterian upbringing," which I tell him always I am everlastingly grateful for. He talks forever about "happiness," and seems to me the very miserablest man I ever sat and talked with. Poor fellow! And one can do nothing for him, except *letting* him eat his plate of porridge, and sit and talk there. He has a whole "scrow" of children, all coming up without the slightest nurture, like wild asses' colts; some of them one can see little outlook for except the Hulks or Treadmill; and yet *he* talks about "the world getting wiser, and one day all-wise!"[43]

On 8 September Carlyle wrote in his journal: "Hunt himself seems almost scared off by my Puritanic Stoicism; talks in a quite tremulous way when he does come. A mind *shattered* by long misery into a kind of unnatural quivering eagerness, which before and instead of all things covets *agreement* with it? A *good* man."[44]

The first year as a neighbor of the Hunts in Chelsea was undoubtedly somewhat trying at times for Jane Carlyle. From the beginning she had liked Leigh Hunt himself, and soon after moving to London she had written to Elizabeth Stodart: "For the rest, our society, with a few additions, [is] much the same that we had when here formerly, only I find it much pleasanter now, being in better case for enjoying it. John Mill, Leigh Hunt, and Mrs. Austin remain my favorites."[45] Mrs. Hunt had slack ways of keeping house and of borrowing without being sure to return promptly all that had been borrowed. She seemed slovenly and irresponsible to Mrs. Carlyle's thrifty and punctiliously correct Scotch mind. With her eminently practical nature, Jane also found Mrs. Hunt's Bohemian aestheticism ridiculous. On 1 September 1834 she wrote to Carlyle's mother:

I told Mrs. Hunt on one day I had been very busy *painting*. "What?" she asked, "is it a portrait?" "O no," I told her, "something of more importance; a large wardrobe." She could not imagine she said "how I could have patience for such things." And so having no patience for them herself what is the result? She is every other day reduced to borrow my tumblers, my teacups, even a cupful of porridge. A few spoonfuls of tea are begged of me because "Missus has got company and happens to be out of the

43. MS, 5 Aug. 1834, NLS, 520.31. "*Scrow*": "crowd, swarm" (Dumfriesshire Scottish).
44. *Reminiscences*, ed. C. E. Norton (London and New York, 1887), I, 174 n.
45. *Jane Welsh Carlyle: A Selection of Her Letters*, ed. Trudy Bliss (London, 1959), p. 49.

article"—in plain and unadorned English because "Missus is the most wretched of managers and is often at the point of having not a copper in her purse." To see how they live and waste here, it is a wonder the whole city does not bankrape and go out o' sight—flinging platefuls of what they are pleased to denominate "CRUSTS" (that is, what I consider all the best of the bread) into the ash-pits. I often say with honest self-congratulation in Scotland we have no such thing as "crusts." On the whole, tho' the English ladies seem to have their wits more at their finger ends, and have a great advantage over me in that respect, I never cease to be glad that I was born on the other side of the Tweed and that those who are nearest and dearest to me are Scotch.[46]

Some weeks later her feeling toward Mrs. Hunt was approaching dangerously near the point of complete exasperation: "Mrs. Hunt I shall soon be quite terminated with, I foresee. She torments my life out with borrowing. She actually borrowed one of the brass fenders the other day, and I had difficulty getting it out of her hands; irons, glasses, teacups, silver spoons are in constant requisition, and when one sends for them the whole number can never be found. Is it not a shame to manage so, with *eight guineas* a week to keep house on! It makes me very indignant to see all the waste that goes on around me when I am needing so much care and calculation to make ends meet."[47]

Whatever differences there may have been in the way of life of the two families and however sharply defined the differences of opinion between the two men may have been, Leigh Hunt proved himself to be a true friend of Carlyle during his first difficult years in London before the publication of the *French Revolution* in 1837 made him famous and removed many financial difficulties. There are numerous quotations from Carlyle and favorable references to him in *Leigh Hunt's London Journal* for 1834–35 when he badly needed recognition.[48] Hunt published two poems by him: "Drumwhirn Bridge," 22 October 1834; and "The Wish," 26 November 1834. Hunt also undertook to provide Carlyle with a copy of the *Examiner* each week, which Carlyle usually sent to his relatives in Scotland, often with one or

46. *Letters and Memorials of Jane Welsh Carlyle*, ed. J. A. Froude (London, 1883), I, 1–4. Charles Lamb, whom the Carlyles met and detested, expressed the other point of view, that of the London Englishman as he considers the Scotchman, in his "Imperfect Sympathies."
47. *Letters and Memorials of J. W. Carlyle*, I, 11–12.
48. See William H. Wylie, *Thomas Carlyle* (London, 1881), pp. 221 ff.

two strokes of the pen upon it that conveyed brief messages concerning health and such matters. Carlyle was duly appreciative and spoke of "our good neighbour Leigh Hunt,—who also is one of the most elastic, unconquerable, innocent-minded mortals I ever met with."[49]

Absolute regularity was beyond the power of Hunt, however, and sometimes the *Examiner* was not forthcoming from him at the times when it was expected. In late October 1834 Carlyle felt compelled to write to his mother: "There was no *Examiner* this week; Hunt bids me tell you that whenever one is missed there will be *two* next week: he is a much-harassed confused poor man; sits in the middle of a distracted uproar that would make many a one mad. I borrowed an *old* Paper from him, that you might not be altogether disappointed: he sent me one of *Jan. 7 last*; ten months old; which I should think is among the oldest ever went by post."[50]

Letter 21. Carlyle to Hunt.[51]

[?1834]

My Dear Sir,

Arthur Coningsby's Father and Mother are expected to Tea with us tomorrow evening; also the mathematical Mrs Sommerville[*sic*], and perhaps John Mill; all of them well affected towards you, and *good* people as people go. Will you come too, and do us all a real kindness? Say "Yessir"; or what were better (for I am quite idle and solitary) come over straightway, and say it with the lips.

Here is *Kean* again, with many thanks.

Your's always
T. Carlyle

Wednesday ev[g]

The mixed nature of Carlyle's feelings concerning Hunt, however, are revealed by his comments made in late 1834. "We see comparatively little of the Hunts for some weeks; they have sickness in the house, and many sad cares: poor Hunt himself I think one of the

49. MS letter to his sister Mrs. James Austin, 24 Oct. 1834, NLS, 511.29.
50. MS, NLS, 520.33.
51. MS, Brewer Collection, State University of Iowa. "Arthur Coningsby's Father and Mother" are Mr. and Mrs. John Sterling. Sterling's novel *Arthur Coningsby* (1833) is not to be confused with Disraeli's *Coningsby* (1844). Mary Somerville (1780–1872), wife of Dr. William Somerville, wrote on mathematics and physical science. She brought out in 1831 a popularized English version of Laplace's *Mécanique Céleste*. Somerville College, Oxford, is named after her. Carlyle seems to have been reading Bryan W. Procter's *The Life of Edmund Kean*, 2 vols. (London, 1835).

most innocent men I ever saw in man's size; a very boy for clear innocence, tho' his hair is grey, and his face ploughed with many sorrows."[52] "[Alexander Aitken, Carlyle's maternal uncle] had a hard battle to fight, but fought it, too, like a man; and so left the *best* inheritance for those he loved. I am often reminded of him here: there is a queer kind of *sub*-likeness to him in our neighbor Leigh Hunt,— who also is one of the most elastic unconquerable innocent minded mortals I ever met with."[53] "Hunt is also a 'friend of the species,' but we make an exception of him; tho' nowise of the Doctrine as held by him: indeed I find my Cameronian rigour, and denouncement of all paltering, poltroonery a[nd 'cry]ing for the want of *taffy*' has quite scared him into seclusion; and he comes now only some once in the fortnig[ht, and] gives us really a most musical evening (for he is far the most ingenious creature I speak with here), concent[rating] many visits into one: I never in my whole life met with a more innocent childlike man; transparent, many-glancing, really beautiful, were this Lubberland or Elysium, and not Earth and England. His family also are innocent, tho' wholly fools and donothings. We get no harm from them, and some little good: God help him and them! is our hearty prayer for them."[54]

Early in 1835 the friendship was subjected to a new test. Leigh Hunt's son John, for many years a problem to his father and other members of the family, appealed to Carlyle for help and forced him into a difficult situation where he had to do what he could wisely to help the son and yet if possible in so doing to avoid offending the father. Carlyle gave a detailed statement of the case in a letter to his mother:

Yesterday afternoon a son of Leigh Hunt's sent me a Letter to say that he was out of his Father's house, could not get back again, and wanted "a few shillings," being in a "starving" state! We sent for him to come and get some meat; shillings we could not give him. I find on talking with the poor youth (about 22, strong and healthy) that he is very much what I supposed: a creature grown up to manhood without the slightest nurture or admonition, with wild hungry wishes in[him], with very considerable natural faculty, but without *any* the faintest principles of conduct; whom accordingly (for what else could happen?) they have had to keep for the last 20 months or more up in a garret, none of them speaking to him,

52. Carlyle to his mother, 23 Oct., Norton, *Letters, 1826–36*, p. 452.
53. Carlyle to Jean Carlyle Aitken, 24 Oct., MS, NLS, 511.29.
54. Carlyle to John Aitken Carlyle, 28 Oct., MS, NLS, 523.26.

from which state he is at last broken out—into the street, and a "starving state." I gave him numerous "good advices"; without much hope that he could (with all his wish to do so) profit much by them. "Do you think I should go into the *Army*, Sir?" I had been telling Jane a few minutes before that I saw nothing under the Sun he could or should do but that. However I counselled him to try *all* other honest shifts first; in the meanwhile *not* to go back to his garret (from whence he would certainly have to break forth again) if there remained a resource for him on Earth: but above all to know and lay deeply to heart that without quite a total change in his *inner* man, and way of thinking and managing himself, *no* thing whatsoever could or would go well with him. He stared on me with his keen black eyes, astonished, not unthankful looking; and went his way, with our "best wishes," but not "best hopes"; nor no pressing invitation to come back, for, as I calculate, one is better *out* of all that folly, and could do no good *in* it. Hunt is a fool surely (tho' very clever too): but this is quite a common method of correction here. The people have no wisdom, no religion, no principle of any kind; this is the result it leads to.[55]

Carlyle did more than lecture to John Hunt. He spoke to Mill about his desperate situation, and Mill provided some work for the youth to do. On 2 February Carlyle wrote to Mill as follows:

Here is poor Ishmael Hunt, of whom I spoke: the news that you had work for him was like a reprieve from death.

As I find he is *totally* without cash at this moment, I have promised that you will pay him five shillings in advance; I said too that the longer he could make this serve him, both you and I would think the more of him. The *rate* he seems to say is "a penny for 72 words"; but he will be thankful for any rate. It will perhaps be kindest to him that you do not pay him *more* than what is strictly earned. As he has all the *virtues to acquire*, the one most within his reach, and most important for him were probably *thrift*. How singular if this copying of your manuscript should be the beginning of salvation for a living man! Alas, it is too dubious: *ich stehe für Nichts.*[56]

Ten days later he wrote to Mill again:

Hunt will be at you tomorrow, or at farthest on Saturday; hungry as a hyaena. To cut off from him the very temptation to play false, I beforehand

55. MS, 28 Jan. 1835, NLS, 520.39. In a letter to his brother Alexander of 28 Jan. 1835 Carlyle wrote: "We have not seen Leigh Hunt for almost three months! There was no quarrel either: but I believe the poor man is very miserable, and feels shocked at my rigorous Presbyterian principles; in short is afraid of me! I pity him much; but think too, he is perhaps as well where he *is*, and I where I am." Norton, *Letters, 1826–36*, p. 484.

56. MS, NLS, 618.60. *Ich stehe* etc.: "I can't guarantee anything."

furnish you with the enclosed receipt; testifying visibly that he has already (with your five) eaten twenty shillings of his wages. His work, what part of it I have seen, seems very tolerably done; nor have I, of my own insight, anything (except that crime of hunger) to urge against him. He has not even intruded himself on me, unless when driven by necessity stronger than an armed man. Poor devil! And yet one can do nothing for him, so good as leave him almost if not altogether alone. *Wer nicht anspannt, dem kann man nicht vorspannen,* is one of the truest proverbs in the world.[57]

Carlyle found himself, however, in an awkward position in relation to Leigh Hunt, and his position became even more awkward after Hunt discovered that John had applied to Carlyle for help. Carlyle was compelled to write the father a note of explanation.

Letter 22. Carlyle to Hunt.[58]

[ca. February 1835]

My Dear Sir,

I regret you should have heard at all of poor John's having ever applied to me: nothing else but the hope you might not hear could have excused me for not apprising you instantly. Nevertheless be of comfort; all I do trust may still be well. Let this line meanwhile assure you that the poor boy has spoken no word, given no faintest hint to prejudice me against you, which indeed no hint or word of his (or I think of anybody's) could have done; he seems to me to love you as a son should, to be in short a wild untamed creature with considerable stuff in him,—whom the world will tame. So much suffice at present. Tonight I fear I shall be engaged; but if not, I will certainly step over to you: at all events, tomorrow. Pray explain nothing to me that you feel it painful to speak of. I have trust enough in you; and, I may say, no *dis*trust at all.

Yours always
T. Carlyle

The sequel to this episode in the life of Hunt's second son, however, was a sad one. He married, drifted from one job to another and from one degree of poverty to a lower one until his early death, about ten years after his interview with Carlyle. Carlyle was one of many who from the time when John was a young boy had tried to save him. Thornton Hunt speaks of a natural deficiency in John's nature that may have rendered all efforts hopeless, but he adds that nothing

57. Thursday [12 Feb. 1835]. *Letters of Carlyle to Mill, Sterling, and Browning,* p. 105. Carlyle translated the proverb: "Him that will not yoke, you cannot help with tracing."
58. MS, Brewer Collection, State University of Iowa.

could ever make John lose his affection for his father.[59] We can only speculate whether Carlyle's moral instruction, if it had been given earlier, would have done any good.

Although Carlyle's judgment of men was usually penetrating and sound, he sometimes let his prejudices sweep him off his feet in dealing with a man as different from himself as Leigh Hunt was. The best that can be said for the appraisals in the following passage from a letter written by Carlyle to his brother John, 16 February 1835, is that Carlyle knew his own mind: "Mill is very friendly; he is the nearest approach to a real man that I find here; nay as far as negativeness goes he *is* that man, but unhappily not very satisfactorily much farther. It is next to an impossibility that a London-born man should not be a stunted one. Most of them (as Hunt) are dwarfed and dislocated into the merest Imbecilities. Mill is a Presbyterian's grandson, or he were that too."[60]

But allowance must be made in such descriptions for Carlyle's fondness for exaggeration. His esteem for Hunt was real, and he was always ready to encourage him. When this year Hunt sent him a copy of his newly published poem, "Captain Sword and Captain Pen," he was generous with his praise.

Letter 23. Carlyle to Hunt.[61]

[ca. 1 April 1835]

My Dear Sir,

I had thought of sending over to you for a loan of these two belligerent *Captains*; the more welcome to me is your gift; for which, many kind thanks. I read the book over last night without rising (*sedens sede in una*). What Aristotle and The Schlegels or even the British Able Editors might say of it I know not; but to me it seemed to be a real *Song*, and to go dancing with real heartiness and rhythm in a very handsome way, thro' a most complex matter.— To me you are infinitely too kind; but it is a fault I will not quarrel with.

Here are two wall-flowers, pledge of the Spring and of Hope. Why do you not come to see me? Depend upon it, whatever hinders is most probably a mistake or an absurdity.

59. *Correspondence of Leigh Hunt*, I, 273–75; also Edmund Blunden, *Leigh Hunt and His Circle* (New York and London, 1930), and *passim*, pp. 70, 86.
    60. Froude, *Carlyle*, III, 25.
    61. MS, Brewer Collection, State University of Iowa. Published in "Concerning Leigh Hunt," p. 495. "Sedens sede in una": "I read it at one sitting." Jeffrey was elevated to the judicial bench as Lord Jeffrey in May 1834.

Jeffrey is in Town; he that was Francis and is my Lord,—somewhat of the Francis having oozed out (I fear) in the interim. He "will with the greatest pleasure" come hither to meet you some night. Will you come? That is to say, will you *actually* come?— Pray do not promise if it is to embarrass you.

Depend on the goodwill and perfect trust and esteem of both me and mine. I know you do care for it.

Always most truly,
T. Carlyle.

Letter 24. Carlyle to Hunt.[62]

[ca. June 1835]

My Dear Sir,

Accept kind thanks from both of us for the volume you have sent my Wife. We are glad to see the *London Journal* in a new shape promising more of permanency. One may hope that at a future epoch some fit eye searching for what was good and graceful in an age when so very much was the reverse, may find something here to dwell upon and treasure.

I am afraid you take too much trouble about that *Examiner.* As hinted today, I have now generally another Newspaper which I can address to Scotland; and that was mainly the thing I wanted. For my own share, Fonblanque has lost nine tenths of his worth now when he is to be read not at Craigenputtoch but at Chelsea.

You would far misconstrue us both if you supposed that our natural regret at your temporary cessation of visits, had ended or was like to end, in irritation, suspicion or other unworthy humour. I can fancy causes enough of the phenomenon without implying disregard, or even diminution of regard on your part. Much must and should in all such cases be left to individual determination, grounded on such insight as is to be had. To me two things only are clear: that there is no man in London I like better to commune with from time to time; and that seen or unseen, I can feel nothing towards you but esteem and goodwill, and am and remain,

My dear Sir, Very faithfully Your's
T. Carlyle

And Carlyle's power of sympathy was unfailing. When *Leigh Hunt's London Journal* collapsed in late 1835, Carlyle was one of the first to try to help. On 18 January 1836 he wrote to his mother:

---

62. MS, Brewer Collection, State University of Iowa. *Leigh Hunt's London Journal* was merged with the *Printing Machine* with the issue of 27 May 1835. See Landré, II, 497. Albany Fonblanque (1793–1872) edited the *Examiner* from 1830 to 1847.

No *Examiner* came last week, for I got none; Hunt is very unpunctual. His *Journal*, poor fellow, by which he lived, has broken down suddenly, and he is now without work, without support, and eight or nine of a most thriftless ravenous family hanging on him: a man whom all men may justly pity! What he will do one cannot see rightly; he cannot dig, to beg he is ashamed. I have seen him twice lately; not for a long time previously: he speaks of trying the *Journal* (it was a Three-halfpenny weekly Paper) under a new form. I pray heartily he may succeed in it.— Did I mention last night that his son was drawing my Picture in oil colours? The poor young man requested it, as a thing that might do him good; and I could not refuse, tho' the task proved wearisome. Whether he will make a Likeness after all is very dubious: the figure at present is one of the toughest, grimmest[?] with "a look that would split a pitcher," as the Irish say![63]

A few days later he wrote to his brother John: "As to the Specklets in the eye, let me not forget to say that I know you Doctors call such things *muscae voliantes*, and make light enough of them; neither do I mind it. John Mill has had one jigging about daily these four years; Leigh Hunt has whole trains of them. . . . Poor Hunt's Journal is broken down with him; and he is once more, suddenly, in straits; yet not so great as he has known. He is a man of much infirm worth, and purest humanity; whom I *gelten lass*, when we meet; which is very rarely, for long." To this letter Jane Carlyle added the following postscript: "He ought to have told you that he is setting for his portrait to Thornton Hunt and is getting himself depicted one of the sulkiest commonplace men in the Island. I also am in progress and am if possible still *more* odious, with a frightful mechanical smile covering over the most vulgar Devilishness. Fortunately we give only our time."[64] At the same time Carlyle was trying to help his friend in ways more tangible than extending his sympathy and encouraging an artist son.

Letter 25. Carlyle to Hunt.[65]

[ca. 15 January 1836]

My Dear Sir,

Yesterday a Gentleman, sympathizing with the late mischance of the London Journal, asked me, whether I thought I could, without offence

63. MS, NLS, 523.36.
64. MS, dated 26 Jan. 1836, NLS, 520.50. *Muscae voliantes*: "flies on the wing." *Gelten lass*: "approve."
65. MS, Yale University Library.

to your feelings, hand you the inclosed little Paper on the part of a Name-less Friend? I answered, after consideration: Yes. The little gift is one of honourable goodwill; which why may not honourable goodwill accept? It falls nameless; like a little drop of manna in the wilderness, coming (truly) from *Above*: a devout heart, I think, may lift it, and say piously, "It is *twice* blest."

If I have gone wrong, I pray you forgive me for the intention's sake. It was part of my bargain that you were never so much as to *ask* me for the Name; that we were never to speak of the matter at all after this hour.

Believe me always,

My Dear Sir, Faithfully Your's
T. Carlyle.

Leigh Hunt was proud, however, and for the moment at least refused the gift, kindly tendered as it was.

Letter 26. Hunt to Carlyle.[66]

Sunday. January 24. 1836.

My dear Sir,

With the deepest sense of your kind feelings & those of your friend, & a delight to find another jewel to hang in my memory with the thought of his offer, I trust that neither you nor he will think ill of me in seeing it come back. Your delightful & truly delicate letter does me but justice in making no doubt of my sentiments on such an occasion, supposing the necessity to exist, & the friend to be of a nature worthy to comfort it (as I have no doubt he is, thus coming hand in hand with yourself); but all the difficulties of the moment have been *more* than done away by other generous friends; & I have no prospective right to let other purses unclose for me, seeing that myself & my family have now got *time*, & that we may have health & strength enough to neutralize the real struggle before it comes. Not to mention, that the most generous people are not always the richest, & that I might be drawing upon the resources of one whose purse might ill spare them, whatever his heart might do. Should a very frightful hour however still come some day, to which other friends would not be all-sufficient, I will call to mind,—indeed, I shall never forget,—that I have an unknown friend in your circle, to whom, if you will then tell me his name, & assure me that the application would not be more incon-venient than it would now have been, I will send & say (or you shall for me) "My necessity is arrived." And to tell you the truth, I should like to know his name now, & shall endeavour to convince you that I ought to know it, purely that I may have the pleasure of repeating it to my thoughts,

66. MS, Brewer Collection, State University of Iowa.

& because (though I should not like to make such a confession in Change Alley) gratitude, even for pecuniary favours, is so far from being to me a burden, that it gives me wings (always supposing the object to be worthy of it), and I am now this minute pruning them, & mustering up my forces during this burst of sunshine amidst my storm, and making myself as light-hearted & strong as possible, nay, absolutely *dandifying* the objects about me; for I have been giving some old perishing books on my shelves fine new cloth covers, which the very sunbeams seem to love to come & kiss; and if I had silks & satins in my wardrobe, & it were the fashion to wear them (for the rich), I think I should put them on, like my old friend Sir John Suckling when he lost at the gaming-table, & so absolutely shame Fortune into treating so fit a companion better. One thing helps particularly to keep me in spirits; which is,—that my head was very bad, & my health seemed fairly breaking down with it; but this involuntary rest has taken out of it its worst feelings, & you cannot conceive what new comfort & life this has given me, little as my appearance at present may have to show for it. The colds, & rheumatism, & head-aches, that beset me, are like the Lilliputians about Gulliver, compared with that giant of an ailment.— But to come to matters both serious & secret, the communication of which is due to your Kindness,—see now how well off I am, to meet this conjunctive; for one dear friend has secured us at all times from starvation (a dread which I *have* had, at one time—so at least to speak; for no fairly [un]certain condition of life is allowed perhaps absolutely to perish for want of sustenance); and another, as soon as my peril was heard of, sent me a hundred pounds to meet it with (fortunately not so great a sum for the giver's resources, as your friend's smaller sum is perhaps for *him*, nor half of it); and for eight weeks from the beginning of the year, I continue to receive eight pounds a week from Knight, partly for work done, partly for some I am to do, or to be otherwise accounted for by things which he may republish out of the journal (my handwriting is getting bad with my head). Thus I have one hundred pounds a year certain (as far as the funds will let them be) and one hundred & sixty-four, to give us time to look about us; and though I cannot but be anxious with so large a family all at home (but one), yet we are all inclined to hope & do the best; & so I have many blessings still for which I have reason to be grateful, & among them, dear Sir, is that of your friendship, & the offer of my kind unknown.

Affectionately yours,
Leigh Hunt

P.S. Pray send your friend this letter,—I need not add, to a nature like his,—in confidence. For my part, I confess I would fain have no secrets from any body; but then the world, not being yet come to generous man's estate, is apt to make mistakes. It is still more needless to add that no secret of course is to be made with M^rs. Carlyle, if she has any curiosity to read what I write, as she may have,—reckoning, as I know I may do, upon her kind wishes. It is one of my dreadful theories, you know, that husband & wife are the last people who ought to keep any secrets from one another.

P.P.S. I have just received a prodigious hamper from some anonymous friends in the country, containing an absolute poulterer's & pastry-cook's shop. Among the contents is a Twelfth Cake, which I shall keep for your Mozart evening, & a pig, a quarter of which (already dressed) will beg admittance at your small table today, sure of not being refused.

Hunt's worries about money, nevertheless, were not at an end. Possibly the following undated note from Carlyle indicates that Hunt was forced by circumstances to change his mind and take the money after all.

Letter 27. Carlyle to Hunt.[67]

[ca. 1 March 1836]
Thursday Morning

My Dear Sir,

Here is the old piece of Paper from the unknown Friend; with many satisfactions that it can do you a service. Courage!

I understand that there is decidedly hope of the Pension; that persons [of] all colours are striving in it, voting for it. A little while! *Post nubila Phoebus!*

Ever affectionately
T.C.

Hunt did not get his pension at this time, despite the efforts of Mill, Jeffrey, and others who were spurred on by Carlyle. Shortly before Carlyle had written to his brother John: "I was out with poor Hunt till near ten last night, and good for little when I came home. His *London Journal* (did I tell you?) has fallen to the ground; so with bad health, incipient old age, and thoughtless imbecility all round him, he has the sorriest outlook; yet keeps up his heart amazingly: 'a man of genius (real genius) in the shape of a Cockney'." Jane Carlyle's postscript to this letter speaks of Carlyle "having several calls tonight, one to go and speak comfort to Leigh Hunt, on things

67. MS, Brewer Collection, State University of Iowa. *Post nubila Phoebus*: "After cloudy weather comes the sun" (Latin Proverb).

in general."[68] An effort also was made to continue the encouragement to Thornton Hunt; but the portrait of Carlyle that he was making seemed so bad that Carlyle finally stopped sitting for it. "The picture Hunt's son was drawing has yet come to nothing. It grew so dreadfully ugly, and promised to be so little like one's own ugliness, and was withal such a wearisome thing, that I shirked off, by some good opportunity, and never came back again."[69] Yet in the early spring of 1836 there still seemed a chance that Hunt would soon be given a pension. Carlyle wrote to John Sterling: "By the bye, Jeffrey has taken Hunt's Pension in hand: may he prosper in it! Mill I find has as yet made small way."[70]

When a little later Hunt's financial situation became desperate, Carlyle was indefatigable in helping to find a scheme that would at least give him temporary relief.

Letter 28. Carlyle to Hunt.[71]

[?June 1836]
Sunday Night 11 o'clock

My Dear Sir,

I had a long conversation with Mr Talfourd; whom I found to be a most polite humane man, exceedingly well disposed towards you.

After much frank communication, both of us agreed that of the two Schemes the one suggested by Jeffrey did seem the hopefuller; that as both could not be followed, this latter must for the present be exclusively aimed at,—in the track and by the methods which Mr Talfourd and other Friends had already decided on.

The grand point for the moment being that you should have the means of meeting this existing perplexity, I took pains to ascertain how you were to act so that the result (of getting money to pay the debt, tomorrow morning) might be "*infallible.*" This was the manner of procedure,

That you were to call at Mr Foster's [*sic*] tomorrow morning at 10 o'clock; when Mr F., furnished with Lord Melbourne's Letter and instruc-

68. MS, 23 Feb. 1836, NLS, 523.37.

69. MS, Carlyle to his mother, 22 March 1836, NLS, 520.52.

70. MS, 12 April 1836, NLS, 531.12.

71. MS, Bodleian Library, Oxford. Sir Thomas Noon Talfourd (1795–1854), judge and poet, edited Charles Lamb's letters and memorials and defended Edward Moxon when he was prosecuted for publishing Shelley's *Queen Mab.* John Forster (1812–76), whose name Carlyle misspells in this letter, became a close and lasting friend of Carlyle about 1840, when they worked together in founding the London Library. Journalist, historian, biographer, he is best known for his life of Dickens.

tions how to act, would go with you, and get what money (£35 or £40) might be needful; the remainder to be put into some Bank, to lie there as a nucleus for the Subscription, which ought thereupon to be directly proceeded with.

Knowing the pressure of the case, and to secure "infallibility," I obtained farther that if you missed Mr Foster, or if by any accident Mr Foster and you could not obtain the money, then Mr Talfourd (who, or some substitute for him, was to be at the Court of Common Pleas) would himself advance the money on the security of that Letter.

I am in great haste. I write this down that the servant may carry it to you, at 6 tomorrow morning. There was nothing more to be said, even if I *had* seen you tonight. Good night my dear Sir.

Yours always
T.C.

As the year wore away, Mrs. Hunt, who was a much better artist than housekeeper, found an opportunity to redeem herself in the eyes of Mrs. Carlyle. In September Jane Carlyle found, upon returning home from a summer jaunt, a gift from Leigh Hunt consisting in what she considered a fine bust of Shelley made by Mrs. Hunt. She wrote to one of her aunts: "I found all at home right and tight; my maid seems to have conducted herself quite handsomely in my absence; my best room looked really inviting. A bust of Shelley (a present from Leigh Hunt) and a fine print of Albert Dürer, handsomely framed (also a present) had *still further ornamented* it during my absence."[72] And a few days later she wrote to a friend in Scotland:

The Hunts go on in the old way. Leigh Hunt himself looks well and is in good spirits tho' without any regular employment yet. . . .

Since I am come so unexpectedly on the subject of furniture, I must tell you some acquisitions I have made since you were here in which you will feel a friendly interest. *The piano* which refused any longer to do the service of one, is exchanged for a horizontal grand one of age *very advanced* indeed, but retaining much of its original sweetness. Then, on one of the tables stands that really admirable bust of Shelly [*sic*] which you may have read in the newspapers has lately been executed by Mrs. Hunt.[73]

---

72. MS, 5 Sept. 1836, NLS, 601.40. The bust of Shelley, by Marianne Hunt, owned in 1940 by A. S. W. Rosenbach, is shown in Newman Ivey White, *Shelley* (New York, 1940), II, opp. 400.
73. MS, to Susan Hunter, 11 Sept. 1836, NLS, 20.5.25.

The Carlyles themselves did not admire Shelley the poet and man, but they were aware of the Hunts' great admiration for him and could fully appreciate the significance of this gift to them.

Late in the year Carlyle seems to have approached Mill, as editor of the *London and Westminster Review*, in search of employment for Hunt and with the suggestion that he might write a review of Lord Wharncliffe's new *Letters and Works of Lady Mary Wortley Montagu*. He further praised Hunt in language reminding one in its fine generosity of Dr. Johnson's words for Goldsmith: "There was nothing he touched that he did not adorn." "In fact I know not what," Carlyle wrote Mill, "Hunt would deliberately undertake that he would not render worth reading."[74] Mill gave Hunt the assignment; but again Hunt's path seemed to be dogged by difficulties. The review was scheduled to appear in the number for April 1837, but there were awkward delays in getting a copy of the book into Hunt's hands.

Letter 29. Carlyle to Hunt.[75]

[January 1837]

My dear Sir,

Here is Mill's answer about the *Wortley*: I suppose the Book will come one of these days.

T.C.

Letter 30. Carlyle to Hunt.[76]

[February 1837]

My Dear Sir,

Mill, the other day, when I told him that you had never yet got your *Wortley*, almost flew into a fury, quiet man as he is and philosopher,—at some Editor or Sub-Editor or Manager he has who had shamefully neglected that duty. He means to pay off the said negligent Manager. He went forthwith and ordered the Book himself; and here it is: he did not know your address. Pray welcome it, and take to it as you would have done, had no fret (I know how fretting these things are) occurred in the business.

74. Undated, Nov. or Dec. 1836, NLS, 618.73.
75. MS, Brewer Collection, State University of Iowa. Carlyle's note is written on the one from Mill, which reads: "My dear Carlyle[,] Let it be Wortley by all means, & I will immediately get the book."
76. MS, Brewer Collection, State University of Iowa. On the back of the envelope Carlyle asks: "Have you the New Monthly?"

There is something in one or the other of those *Biog. Univ.* volumes you have which I want to see. Can you send them?

> Ever faithfully Yours
> T. Carlyle.

We are at home and alone every night.

Letter 31. Carlyle to Hunt.[77]

> [24 February 1837]
> Friday Morning

My dear Sir,

I have just received a Letter from Mill; of which this is the first paragraph:

"Mr Hunt's Article will be in time if it be not later than the 12th of March: and whether it be printed or not in this N° (tho' I am anxious that it should) I undertake that he shall be paid for it."

Hand to the work, therefore! And best speed to you! So says,

> Your's always
> T. Carlyle

With all his love for Burns, for rural Scotland, and for the simple ways of people dwelling in Annandale and Nithsdale, Carlyle was no primitivist. Bronson Alcott, an "acorn Quixote," with his efforts to convert the whole world to vegetarianism, smacked too much of the backwoods for him. He preferred Piccadilly and St. Paul's, symbols to him of the ways of civilized men. Hence, Leigh Hunt's fine urbanity did not go unappreciated. In May 1837 Carlyle saw it dramatized and thrown into clear relief through the visit to London of his highly esteemed old Annandale friend, Ben Nelson. In earlier years Carlyle had called Ben "the cleverest, most intelligent man I have ever met; with head enough to furnish half a dozen Outerhouse Authors, and Gaze[teers], and yet employed only in importing timber and exchanging Wool with Tar!"[78] Nelson visited Carlyle briefly in late April while on his way to Germany to take care of his son, who was seriously ill. His son died, however, before he could reach his bedside; when Nelson returned to London with the sad news, Carlyle sought for ways to comfort him. To bring about a meeting of his old Scotch friend with Leigh Hunt, with his "purest humanity," suggested itself to him as one resource.

77. MS, Cornell University Library. Hunt's review duly appeared in the April issue, pp. 130–64.
78. MS, to William Tait, 27 Jan. [1830], NLS, 3823.17.

Letter 32. Carlyle to Hunt.[79]

[ca. 16 May 1837]

My dear Sir,

There is a worthy old-friend of mine here at present, an intelligent good man, Burgher of the little Scotch Town of Annan, whom I have known since my school days. He is to be with us this evening. I would not have him leave London without an image of at least one man worth carrying so far. Our tea is at six. There will be none here but Friend Ben Nelson and we. Can you give us an hour? I am sure you will like Ben, and he you. Refuse frankly if you cannot.

There is a kind of possibility that I may catch John Mill too; but no certainty, perhaps hardly likelihood.

Yours ever
T. Carlyle.

Hunt obligingly came, but the meeting with Ben Nelson was far from successful. Carlyle gave this account of it to his brother John: "Ben seemed to bear the matter [the death of his son] with hard Dutch Stoicism; not without natural emotion, yet not with very much of it. I never before had discovered what a dogged sort of man he is; obstinate, obdurate, and carries the mark of that too in his physiognomy. I studied to be as kind to him as I could, went to West^r Abbey etc with him, and saw him often: but he did not prove very presentable here; one night when I brought out Hunt to see him, he made an almost absurd figure; contradictory, pedantic, à la 'Ewart's shop'; at which poor Hunt could only arch his brows."[80] The perfect eloquence of Leigh Hunt's arched brows was clearly not lost on Carlyle. But Ben Nelson was not merely a foil to set off some of the quality of Leigh Hunt; in the eyes of Hunt he was also a foil to set off some of Carlyle's.

Letter 33. Carlyle to Hunt.[81]

[ca. 17 May 1837]

My dear Sir,

When you quitted us last night with my astonishing "worthy old friend," I knew not whether to begin crying or begin swearing, or what to do: but I finished, at least this morning I do finish with heartily laughing.

79. MS, University of Virginia Library.
80. MS, 30 May 1837, NLS, 523.49. See also Carlyle's letter to his mother of 19 May 1837, NLS, 3823.230. "Ewart's shop": probably a reference to an earlier experience in Scotland when Nelson behaved in a similar fashion.
81. MS, British Museum, Add. 38523, fol. 203.

Who could have thought I was inviting you yesterday to meet a new Scioppius[82] or Julius Caesar Nelson Scaliger in the person of my astonishing friend with his three circulating Library Books, and his three thoughts which he thought he was thinking! My amazement was great. The instantaneously polemical side our Annan Scioppius turned up was the thing I was least of all prepared for. In fact I have seen little of him, and nothing at all of that, these three and twenty years; and had rashly supposed the thing was altogether extinct: that it could awaken in this instance was not more to be expected than one of those miracles of which Attile Schmelzle says "there are examples in the history of the middle ages."[83] But in truth the business brings back to me a very ugly side of Scotch existence, which in my solitude among the mountains I had lost sight of. God grant us all some more suitable "*Moral Coolture*," and "re-stra*ient*" fit for guiding us in this life! And O heaven how the soft sheet lightning began playing about this rhinoceros, and the thick hide tho' a non-conductor felt strangely tickled by it! I think there are few scenes in Ben Johnson [*sic*] equal to such a combination. Absurder figure made by a man of some sense I do not remember to have observed. Nothing remains for my astonishing friend (a man of worth at bottom too) but to walk out with a pound of butter on his head, and bless heaven.

But you, I pray you in pity come over to me again without delay, this night if you can, and let us laugh together; and reduce the absurdity into the region of the absurd.

Since I began writing your messenger has come. I am for the *Guide* and a contemplative pipe of tobacco down-stairs. Good be with you my dear friend; and many thanks.

T. Carlyle

Certainly Ben Nelson's argumentativeness did not prevent the friendship between Carlyle and Hunt from continuing as usual.

Letter 34. Carlyle to Hunt.[84]

[Early July 1837]

My dear Sir,

Here is the *Atlas* with many thanks and apologies. As I still see the *Examiner*, and do not make much of Newspapers, I think it will perhaps be better that you do not trouble yourself farther about this *Atlas* (which seems stupid enough); or at least only send it to me (with perhaps a pen-

---

82. Latinized form of the name of Kaspar Schoppe (1576–1649), German classical scholar and controversialist; became a Roman Catholic in 1598; attacked Scaliger, James I of England, and others.

83. See Carlyle's translation "Army-Chaplain Schmelzle's Journey to Flætz," by Jean Paul Richter, *Works*, XXII, 140.

84. MS, Gordon N. Ray.

cil-mark or snip of paper at the place) when you find anything interesting in it.

[I will] send over the fragment of Müll[n]er,[85] not that I think it will
ever be of any use to you; but that it may shew I was willing to be of use
had the disastrous eclipse or magnetic sleep I have been living in of late
permitted me. Everybody says, the *Repository* is quite a new thing, so
attractive, humane &c; as I myself say, and much more. May it "attract"
purchasers enough, and be a blessing to all parties.

You must come and see me surely? If not I will come and see you.

I pass these days in a very low condition of soul; reading Byron's Letters;[86] extremely sorry for him, for myself, and all mankind.

Ever faithfully Your's,
[T. Carlyle]

THE LATER YEARS

The year 1838 was a somewhat turbulent and mixed one for the
friendship. It involved, among other things, the usual asking and
doing of favors. Count Carlo Pepoli in the following letter was an
Italian nobleman who was one of several foreign protegés whom Jane
Welsh Carlyle had gathered around her. In 1839 he married Elizabeth Fergus, sister of Carlyle's old Edinburgh friend, John Fergus.

Letter 35. Carlyle to Hunt.[87]

[ca. 1 January 1838]

My dear Sir,—

Count Pepoli, who is at present Candidate for a Professorship in the
London University, wishes much for a sight of your Book *Le Imprise di
G. Ruscellai*; meaning, I think, to testify that he is properly of *British*

85. Almost certainly a reference to an unpublished manuscript on Amadeus Gott-
fried Adolph Müllner (1774–1829), German playwright, not to be confused with the
treatment of the same writer incorporated in "German Playwrights," *Foreign Review*,
3 (Jan. 1829), 94–125. The manuscript, now in the Beinecke Collection at Yale, 19
double-spaced typewritten pages long when transcribed, is prefaced by Carlyle as follows: "*Müllner* (a *Dud*)— What thou knowest about M. thou *canst* write down: write
it then, and be done with it.— Saturday Noon, 9*th* October, 1831." He ends the manuscript with the date "21*st* October 1831—" and "*Müllner*— The threads of a *Dud!*"
Hunt, who had recently succeeded R. H. Horne as proprietor of the *Monthly Repository*,
must have thought the "Müllner" a dud also, since he did not publish it. See Mineka,
The Dissidence of Dissent: The Monthly Repository, 1806–1838 (Chapel Hill, 1944),
pp. 382–93.

86. Probably Thomas Moore's *Letters and Journals of Lord Byron, with Notices of
His Life*, 2 vols. (London, 1830).

87. MS, Cornell University Library.

descent, connected with King John Lackland, and therefore entitled etc! Can you let him have it for a while?— Also for me, is the *Repository* out?

T.C.

Letter 36. Carlyle to Hunt.[88]

[ca. January 1838]

My dear Sir,

You will do us a real favour if you can consent to come over and take tea with us tonight. Two *violets* are coming (in a voluntary manner); great friends of yours: Miss Martineau; and Mrs Marcet[?]: whose works I do not know, but whose face pleases me much. There are only these two; perhaps even these may not come.

Now your plan would be, if you had the proper audacity, to let us see your face about six, to tea with *ourselves*: we should then have our own talk, independently of all people. When the *Violets* come, you could take a look of them; and, if you did not like them (which is infinitely improbable, for Harriet too is really an excellent creature), leave them to their fate!

Finally, my dear Sir, if you cannot come, scruple not for a moment to refuse. Alas, I know too well the moods one gets into; the engagements one may have, unseen save to oneself; and how impertinent a thing Speech may be, tho' otherwise said to be cheerfuller than light itself.

I am held very busy with Printers Devils. I remain always,

Most heartily your's,
T. Carlyle

Harriet Martineau wrote in her journal early this year: "Leigh Hunt tells Carlyle that his troubles will cease at five-and-forty; that men reconcile themselves, and grow quiet at that age."[89] Carlyle himself wrote to his brother John on February 1: "Hunt is in the sere and yellow leaf; has not been seen here above once since my return."[90]

Beginning April 30, Carlyle gave two lectures a week over a period of six weeks on the history of European literature. Leigh Hunt attended most of the lectures and reviewed them in the *Examiner*. It soon became clear to his readers that despite considerable praise he

88. MS, NLS, 3823.269. *Violets* are "Blue-Stockings," ladies who make a considerable show of being intellectual. Carlyle refers to Hunt's "Blue-Stocking Revels; or, the Feast of Violets," *Monthly Repository,* July 1837, pp. 33–57. "Miss Martineau" is Harriet Martineau (1802–76), who at this time had published books on economics. Mrs. Jane Marcet (1769–1858) was a writer on science and political economy who influenced Miss Martineau.
89. *Autobiography* (Boston and New York, 1877), II, 335. Entry dated 21 Jan. 1838.
90. MS, letter, NLS, 523.55.

accorded the lecturer he was far from being uncritical. In the May 6 number he said:

He again *extemporizes*: he does not read. We doubted, on hearing the Monday's lecture, whether he would ever attain, in this way, the fluency as well as depth for which he ranks among celebrated talkers in private; but Friday's discourse relieved us. He "strode away," like Ulysses himself; and had only to regret, in common with his audience, the limits to which the one hour confined him. He touched, however, in his usual masterly way, what may be called the mountain-tops of his subject—the principal men and themes. . . . and last, not least startling, Socrates, whom, though Mr Carlyle did him credit as to good life and intention, he beat about the head and ears as Mr Hazlitt once did a plaster-cast of the Emperor Alexander, and as though he was the representative of all the logical and moral *twaddle* that takes a masculine success out of nations. We confess we cannot take this view of the admired of Plato, and of Milton, and all ages; nor think any such "foremost men of all the world" (to use a favorite term of Mr Carlyle's) have such little "*significancy*" in them, or were so little intended to affect the improvement of coming time. Mr Carlyle was heartily greeted with applause at the close of his first week's eloquence; and we doubt not has now found the secret (whatever it is) of speaking with like triumphant volubility to their conclusion.

In the *Examiner* next week Hunt seized upon Carlyle's word *thrift*, used in praise of the Romans in the fourth lecture, and subjected it to a close examination and evaluation. It was not, he said, altogether a virtue in the conquest-loving Romans.

Mr. Carlyle described the earliest character of Rome as consisting in a spirit of steady agricultural *thrift*, a quality which he considered "the germ of all other virtues"; meaning, we presume (for he sometimes gives his auditors too great credit for making the most of his sententious brevity), the inclination to turn every little power we possess to its utmost, in a right direction; but his allusions to the *Dutch* and Scotch hardly tended to do justice to the higher part of his inferences on this point. This thrifty faculty in the Romans became turned into the "steady spirit of conquest," for which they soon grew famous,—all "by method" and the spirit of "the practical"; and the lecturer made some striking remarks on the vulgar objection to the early Romans, as thieves and robbers. He said they were only a tribe of a superior character, gradually, and of necessity, forcing the consequences of their better knowledge upon the people around them. The Carthaginians, he considered, in comparison with the Romans, as a mere set of money-hunters, with "a Jewish pertinacity" affecting their whole character.

Hunt also took exception to other ideas in this lecture and suggested that Carlyle had scarcely done justice to such writers as Ovid, Tacitus, Lucretius, Plautus, Catullus, and Cicero.[91]

Carlyle quickly sensed the questioning spirit of Hunt's reviews and on May 15 wrote in his journal: "Hunt's criticism no longer friendly; not so in spirit, though still in letter; a shade of spleen in it; very natural, flattering even. He finds me grown to be a something now. His whole way of life is at death-variance with mine. In the 'Examiner' he expresses himself afflicted with my eulogy of *thrift*, and two days ago he had *multa gemens* to borrow two sovereigns of me. It is an unreasonable existence *ganz und gar*."[92] A week later he discussed Hunt in the same vein in a letter to his mother.[93]

Hunt's reviews of Carlyle's other lectures in 1838 continued in the tone of his earlier reviews. In the *Examiner* for May 20 he approved of Carlyle's praise of Shakespeare but said that he overrated the kindliness of Dante, in whom spleen was the ruling habit. He liked very much Carlyle's comments on Cervantes, who "ended with being in good heart and hope with everything," and on Mohammed, who was no imposter but a sincere religious teacher attempting to substitute a higher religious faith for a lower one. On May 27 he treated favorably Carlyle's praise of Luther and Alfred the Great but questioned his enthusiasm for John Knox and suggested that Carlyle's comments on Erasmus and Milton were inadequate. On June 3 Hunt said that Carlyle was inclined to underrate both the French people and "their great *littérateur* Voltaire." Carlyle also was inadequate in dealing with Montaigne and neglected Molière, Marot, and Claude Lorrain. He underrated Steele and Hume and overrated Dr. Johnson. But his remarks on Johnson, Hume, and Boswell were nevertheless delightful. Hunt's review of June 10 was short, rather general, and more purely critical. He spoke ironically of Carlyle as a denouncer of disbelief in society who was himself, "at any rate, in high eloquent condition of belief of some sort; though what that is, most of his hearers will perhaps wait with some anxiety to be told; since at one minute he seems to think that morality, or doing that which we think right, is sufficient for all social purposes; and the next (in the confidence of

---

91. For an excellent discussion of Hunt's reviews of Carlyle's lectures, see Wylie, *Carlyle*, pp. 165 ff.

92. Froude, *Carlyle*, I, 136. "*Multa gemens*": "with many a groan." "*Ganz und gar*": "in every respect."

93. MS, 22 May 1838, NLS, 511.51.

his virtue, which we most heartily believe in) he startles unmetaphys-
ical listeners with ridiculing the notion that virtue is sufficient to
make men happy. What then, it will be asked him, is the object of
society itself, or the existence of anything?" On June 17 Hunt sum-
marized the teaching that Carlyle had got from Goethe and Christ
that "happiness was not the right thing to seek; that man has nothing
to do with happiness, but with the discharge of the work given him
to do" and then, without explicitly objecting to it, said: "The two
highest qualities we admire in a man are lovingness and sincerity;
and if the former of these appears to be occasionally obscured a little
in Mr Carlyle by impatience with those whom he thinks not hearty
enough in any good cause, or opposed to it, it is his bile that speaks
in him, and not his heart, which in all his final judgments is sure to
find him in a state of the largest-minded kindness towards all men."
In all his disagreements with Carlyle through the years, this was a
belief to which Hunt returned again and again.

The two notes that follow from Carlyle to Hunt are difficult to
date, but a passage in Mrs. Carlyle's letter to her husband of 10 September 1838 may at least suggest the general period to which they
belong. She wrote: "Baron von Alsdorf [*sic*] came here the other
night, seeking your address, to write to you for a testimonial. I was
obliged to give him Sandy's, having then no other, which will probably cost you a postage. 'Such is the lot of celebrity i' the world.' "94
Since the notes appear to have been written earlier, when Carlyle and
Hunt were first becoming acquainted with Alzdorf, possibly they
were written in the early summer of this year.

Letter 37. Carlyle to Hunt.95

[?July 1838]

My dear Sir—

I saw Baron Alzdorf last night, and made a kind of conditional promise
to him that I "would go if I *could*." The meaning of the *subjunctive* mood
is that I am to be out (what is very unusual with me) tonight too and on

94. *Letters and Memorials of Jane Welsh Carlyle*, I, 108. Carlyle's notes on this
letter state that the quotation is parodied from Schiller. On 12 Oct. 1838 Carlyle wrote
to Mrs. Anna Jameson: "Baron Alzdorf got a Testimonial from me, as he, so backed,
was doubly and trebly entitled to do: but whether it and all the rest did him any
service I have not yet learned. I saw him in Regent Street the day before yesterday,
but he would not see me or my signals, and the vehicle had to drive on." MS, Gerald
E. Hart Collection, Isabella Stewart Gardner Museum, Boston.
95. MS, British Museum, 37,210, fol. 180.

Saturday, and am like to have my poor nerves shattered all to shreds. I cannot yet be *indicative*. The prospect of your company up and down is my greatest or almost only chance. But be not guided by me. Be indicative for yourself; and think that I shall regret much if I cannot go with you. He seems a very good fellow the Baron.—Adieu!

Ever yours
T.C.

Letter 38. Carlyle to Hunt.[96]

[?Early July 1838]

My dear Sir—

Do you go to Baron Alzdorf's? If you go, I go; if not, not. My only condition is that we set off *soon*; for I must start homewards again before 10 o'clock.— He said "any time after six." There is Tea here five minutes hence if you will come over.

T.C.

It has been assumed that Hunt wrote his delightful rondeau "Jenny Kissed Me" in 1838 after, having been ill for a long time, he had one day suddenly appeared at Jane Carlyle's front door to announce in person that he was now much better, and had been rewarded with a kiss from the surprised Jane, who had sprung up with delight at seeing him.[97] She was not given to kissing men other than her husband and close relations, but she enjoyed a flirtation and unquestionably found Leigh Hunt, like Tennyson, an extremely attractive man. Three years before she had been greatly amused when her friend Susan Hunter, daughter of a professor at St. Andrews and later Mrs. James Stirling, on a visit to her in Chelsea had been completely swept off her feet by Hunt's masculine charm. Hunt had not failed to respond to what Carlyle called "Susan's mild love . . . sparkling through her old-maidish, cold, still exterior."[98] Jane had described in detail the behavior of the two in a letter to her husband:

Our visiting has been confined to one dinner and *two teas* at the Sterlings and a tea at Hunts!! You must know Susan Hunter came the day after you went and stayed two days. As she desired above all things to see Hunt I wrote him a note asking if I might bring her up to call. He replied he was just setting off to town but would look in at eight oclock. I supposed

96. MS, Brewer Collection, State University of Iowa.
97. Wilson, *Carlyle*, III, 30. The poem first appeared in the *Monthly Chronicle* for Nov. 1838 with the title "Nellie Kissed Me."
98. *Letters and Memorials of Jane Welsh Carlyle*, I, 16.

this as usual a mere off put but he actually came—found Pepoli as well as Miss Hunter was amazingly lively, and very lasting; for he stayed till near twelve— Between ourselves it gave me a poorish opinion of him to see how uplifted to the third Heaven he seemed by Susan's compliments and sympathizing talk. He asked us all with enthusiasm to tea the following Monday. Susan came from town on purpose and slept here— Mrs Hunt behaved smoothly and looked devilish and was drunkish. He sang, talked like a pen gun [Scottish for a gun with a quill barrell for shooting peas], ever to Susan, who drank it all in like nectar; while my Mother looked cross enough and I had to listen to the whispered confidences of Mrs Hunt— But for me, who was declared to be grown *"quite prim and elderly"* I believe they would have communicated their mutual experiences in a retired window seat till morning— *"God bless you Miss Hunter"* was repeated by Hunt three several times in tones of everincreasing pathos and tenderness as he handed her down stairs behind me. Susan for once in her life seemed of apt speech. At the bottom of the stairs a demur took place: I saw nothing but I heard with my wonted glegness—what think you?—a couple of handsome *smacks*! and then an almost inaudibly soft God bless you Miss Hunter! Now just remember what sort of looking woman is Susan Hunter and figure this transaction! If he had kissed me it would have been intelligible but Susan Hunter of all people![99]

Mrs. Carlyle and Hunt both had quick-witted, playful minds that took great pleasure in light combat. Their relation was in general highly congenial. The spirit of banter governing it is reflected in the two following undated letters that could belong to the year 1838.

Letter 39. Mrs. Carlyle to Hunt.[100]

[?1838]

My dear Sir

My Husband is just gone out leaving orders with me to write you a note inviting you to come to tea— I said it was of no use, you were predetermined *not* to come, especially if *I* asked you— He answered I could try at least, and write you he had finished his days work and was really very desirous you would come. So behold I try! and what can I do more? I cannot annihilate your laziness, or dislike, or pet, or caprice or whatever it is that makes you so obstinately stay away— I cannot make you as happy to come

99. MS, NLS, 601.34. Mrs. Welsh, Jane's mother, also seems to have been very much impressed by Hunt's masculine charm.

100. MS, British Museum, Add. 38,523, fol. 207. The Carlyles' old friend Edward Irving had had like Hunt an expansive, glowing mode of utterance. Jane Carlyle enjoyed chuckling over the phrase "good joy," which one of Hunt's children had used at the sight of flowers. *Letters and Memorials of Jane Welsh Carlyle,* I, 104.

to us, as we are to have you come. I can but (as Edward Irving commands in all such emergencies) *"pray to the Lord"*! and assure you, that in your solitary instance at least, I break thro my established principles of liking, in throwing away a very large quantity of affection on you which you seem totally insensible of and of course ungrateful for— Mrs Hunt also takes but a [moth]erless charge of me— Bless you all nevertheless

Yours sincerely
Jane W Carlyle

Letter 40. Hunt to Mrs. Carlyle.[101]

[?1838]

Dear clever & querulous,

(For I will not call you "Madam" lest I should appear solemn, nor Mrs. Carlyle lest you should think me ceremonious, nor Jane or Jenny, lest I should take a liberty which may be deemed presumptuous,—so I take refuge, between familiarity & fatherliness, in two epithets of manifest truth,—the second, I own, somewhat daring, but my zeal must protect me)—you misconstrue me very much throughout the whole of that list of causes, to which you are pleased to attribute my remaining so much at home of an evening. The simple truth is, generally speaking, that the badness of my health, which is worse than my natural spirits make it appear, conspires with my work & my household cares to render me too often unfit for any thing of an afternoon but to sit, as patient as I well can be, in the arm-chair in which I find myself after my morning's walk; & just now, I am suffering under a cold & fever, of nearly a fortnight's duration. I have not been from home after dinner, since I saw you. As to any want of consideration for kind friends who honour me with their good opinion, I hope I am not very capable of it in any instance, & I am sure the charge would not be just against me in this. I often think of both of you, when you do not see me; & never without wishing that I could cram you both full of health & contentment. Believe me indeed truly your grateful friend

L.H.

P.S. I am so unwell just now, that the writing this letter has brought all the blood up in my cheeks & head.

Hunt undoubtedly had great admiration for Mrs. Carlyle and did much to spread her reputation as an extremely clever woman and talker. That there was some dissent to his high opinion of her is indicated by the following undated manuscript note that seems to have been written by Carlyle's brother, Dr. John A. Carlyle:

101. MS, Brewer Collection, State University of Iowa.

A few years ago Tom's wife was getting into reputation as a rapid & great talker. I never had much patience with her Galloway Doric, &, not then knowing her, could very well contrive to keep out of ear shot. Leigh Hunt took to saying that she was really an eloquent woman, & Hunt's disciples [( )of whom he had always a considerable number) repeated the dictum, &, as usual, going further than their master, began to speak of her as quite a woman of genius. One night, at Creik's [Craik's], L——— said that Mrs Carlyle was a Scotch Madame de Staël. "Yes" rejoined W——— [?Wordsworth], "& a *very* Scotch one."[102]

Mrs. Carlyle, for her part, never permitted her sense of Hunt's personal charm to paralyze her critical faculty. Hunt, like Dickens, greatly respected her as a literary critic, but she did not always tell him what he wanted to hear about his own writings. In September 1838 she wrote to her husband:

Leigh Hunt wrote me a gracious little note inviting me to come and hear his play read and "*stand by him with some new friends,*" the said new friends turning out to be of the Taylor set,—Margaret Gillies and her sister, etc., etc. . . . As for the play, it is plain as a pikestaff why Macready would not play it—it is something far worse than "immoral," "anti-conventional," —it is mortal dull—a beautiful insipidity reigns throughout—and for the regenerating truths it is calculated to teach the conventional heart, they would need to be *shot at it* (as we do our truths) from the mouth of a cannon, not timorously, *pleadingly tendered* to it, before it were fair to expect that they should take the least effect.[103]

"As we do our truths—" Mrs. Carlyle usually agreed with her husband. She knew that a strong bond uniting her husband and herself with Leigh Hunt was the fact that all three of them refused to accept the platitudes of conventional thinking. But her preference for Carlyle's thundering vigor and her own intensified sprightliness over Hunt's graceful gestures with a lady's fan in the effort to get unconventional truths accepted is definite and clear, and the contrast of methods is a significant one. It is the difference between a powerful

102. What is apparently a copy of Dr. Carlyle's note is preserved in the British Museum, Add. 39,776, fol. 65v.

103. Bliss, *Jane Welsh Carlyle*, p. 82. "The Taylor set": probably the friends of Mr. and Mrs. John Taylor, namely W. J. Fox and the Flower sisters. After a long Platonic love affair and Mr. Taylor's death, Mrs. Taylor married John Stuart Mill. Margaret Gillies (1803–87), miniature and water color painter. W. C. Macready (1793–1873) was manager of Covent Garden Theater in 1838. A friend of Carlyle and John Forster, he produced Browning's *Strafford* (1837).

unblinded Polyphemus and Shelley's gentle, long-suffering, but persevering and confident Prometheus.

The year 1838 had been a full and interesting one in the history of their friendship. Toward the end of the year Carlyle appropriately wrote to Emerson: "Leigh Hunt, 'a man of genius in the shape of a Cockney,' is my near neighbor, full of quips and cranks, with good humor and no common sense."[104]

In May 1839 Hunt reviewed Carlyle's new series of lectures "On the Revolutions of Modern Europe" in the *Examiner*.[105] There was no change in the critical tone he had established in his reviews the year before. He asserted that Carlyle was too ready to condone Dante's almost diseased bitterness and gloom and to forget the fact that to unhealthy eyes "the blue of the firmament itself would turn yellow." He added, "We are recommended to become as 'little children,' not as jaundiced great men." In commenting on one of Carlyle's usual attacks on logic, Hunt said that there was much truth in Carlyle's position but that logic, "if of little use in establishing the best of things," was "a helper towards saving them from the worst,—from corruption and superstition." He praised the convincing manner in which Carlyle spoke his hearty convictions from the lecture platform and testified as to its effectiveness with the fashionable London audience. But he believed that Carlyle, in dealing with English Protestantism, was much too kind to Cromwell and much too hard on "poor decapitated Charles." Concerning Cromwell, Hunt asked, "In what did *he* succeed, except in making himself for a short time an unhappy prince?" And why did Carlyle neglect such master spirits as Vane and Milton? Carlyle's treatment of the eighteenth century did not do justice to Voltaire, Hunt said; he was considerably more than a "mere scoffer" deficient in sympathy, as Carlyle had declared; and to call him a "Frenchman all over" was assuredly not to condemn him since Frenchmen have "infinite social virtues" and are "no small constituent part of the great human family." But in dealing with some of the evils resulting from the revolution begun by Arkwright and the spinning jenny, Carlyle spoke eloquently and unforgettably of "the melancholy spectacle of a human being willing to labor but forced to starve." On the other hand, Carlyle's moral judgments concerning

104. *The Correspondence of Thomas Carlyle and Ralph Waldo Emerson, 1834–1872*, ed. C. E. Norton (Boston and New York, 1894), I, 199.
105. See numbers for 5, 12, and 26 May.

many important figures in the French Revolution were "more like the talking of his Scottish ancestors than his own candid philosophy." Moreover, Carlyle admired Cromwell too much and was too hard on Napoleon. Hunt definitely preferred Napoleon to Cromwell, with his "dreary, bad blood."

Probably there was further frank discussion of Dante among the two friends. Carlyle was to give considerable attention to Dante in his lecture "The Hero as Poet" the following May. An undated letter from Carlyle that belongs to this period reflects the common interest which the two had in that poet.

Letter 41. Carlyle to Hunt.[106]

[1838 or 1839]

My dear Sir,

The Italians have a saying "round as the O of"—some Painter, who dashed one off very round indeed at one stroke of his brush. Can you tell me the Painter's name? I need it in some scribble I am doing.

Likewise, and for a like reason, can you send me the passage of Dante you mentioned to me one day, where he speaks about the toil of his *Divine Comedy* having made him grey?— I have a notion to borrow that Copy of Dante again, and go fairly thro' it; having made unexpected way when I had it last.

Do not trouble yourself much or at all about either of these questions; I can manage *without* the answers very well, if they do not lie ready.

Finally will you lend me the last *Repository*? There is no use in giving me one; for really the loan of it till I read what you write is altogether equivalent,—especially as I know every copy, and setting of a letter, costs *you* somewhat.

I have a great deal of cold, have grown half deaf, altogether stupid, and am in a poor cowering way. The rule is, as the Scotch say, to "*jook* (duck), and let the *jaw* (rushing wave) go by." An excellent rule. I will see you soon; and hear you, were it with an ear-trumpet.

Ever most heartily Yours,
T. Carlyle.

In another undated letter Carlyle makes similar requests.

106. MS, Columbia University Library. Giotto demonstrated his skill in the presence of Pope Boniface VIII by drawing a perfect circle with one stroke. See Browning's "Old Pictures in Florence," 11. 133–35. In "The Hero as Poet" Carlyle emphasizes Dante's saying that writing his poem made him "*lean* [not *grey*] for many years." 12 May 1840.

Letter 42. Carlyle to Hunt.[107]

[Late 1839?]

My dear Sir

Thanks for your almanacs and books, for your kind remembrance of me. I am sorry to hear how the cold affects you. I too have got sore throat, and am entirely uncomfortable in such temperature. By the course of Nature and the Almanac, things must mend ere long.

If you have the other volumes of *Vasari*,[108] I will take a look at them by and by. A small slip of paper containing a request to that effect went over to you some weeks ago; but I believe it escaped your notice. I am in no haste about *Vasari*; nor indeed have I time for it at present, being busied with the Purgatorio of Dante. I have used your English edition so far; but now it leaves me, and now my own is as good as any of the others.

When your friend has done with Jean Paul Richter,[109] a lady wants to see it, having fallen in love with the large man.

Pray make my kind compliments to Mr Orger,[110] and thank him without delay for his gift which "T Carlyle, Armiger," (Penniger were better) is justly proud of. As it happens, I have no other complete Anacreon's, and I rather think no Sappho at all.[111] I design to read both; with the not unwelcome help of that English at the foot of the page. Mr Orger's esteem of me is as good as a Lord Chancellor's; perhaps better; that of a wise and good man—seated not on a woolsack, but a chair.—

Surely I shall see you soon? If you have not the last N° of the L and Westminster Review I can lend it you for a day.— Courage! Let us hope for spring, sunshine, and better luck every way.—

Yours faithfully always
T. Carlyle.

After many vain attempts, Hunt finally wrote a play, *A Legend of Florence*, which was successfully produced and well received by the

---

107. MS, British Museum, 38523, fol. 205. The letter must predate removal from 4 Upper Cheyne Row in the spring of 1840 and seems to have been written when Carlyle was working on the lectures for 1840, in which Dante is treated in "The Hero as Poet."

108. Giorgio Vasari (1511–74), Italian painter, architect, and art historian, wrote a series of biographies of Italian artists entitled *Vite de' Più Eccelenti Pittori, Scultori, ed Architetti Italiani* (1550), highly important for the information it gives about Italian Renaissance artists.

109. Probably Carlyle's translations in *German Romance, Works*, XXII, 117–332, though possibly Carlyle's essays on Richter, *Works*, XXVI, 1–25, XXVII, 96–159.

110. Mr. Orger is unidentified.

111. Mr. Orger appears to have given Jane Carlyle copies of Anacreon and Sappho; Carlyle prefers "Penniger" ("pen-bearer") to "Armiger" ("armor-bearer") as an epithet for her.

audience. It opened at Covent Garden on 7 February 1840. Queen Victoria went to see it more than once. Hunt was elated and thought that he had now found his calling. But he could not get his later plays produced. Carlyle saw the play and praised it in a letter to his brother John of 11 February 1840: "Hunt's Play was what they call successful; it really seemed to me as if here and there the audience did feel it in their heart;—as if the Play might run for some time, which is the grand result. The account in the *Examiner* is not favorable enough, written in a negatory spirit. Heraud sat behind us in the Box; as dirty and joyful as ever. I have not seen Hunt since."[112] Actually, whatever merits or deficiencies Heraud may have had as a critic of drama, he did not have a chance with two such formidable opponents as Carlyle and Hunt, who together impaled him like an insect with their phrases. A few months later Carlyle wrote to Emerson: "Heraud is a loquacious scribacious little man, of middle age, of parboiled greasy aspect, whom Leigh Hunt describes as 'wavering in the most astonishing manner between being Something and Nothing.' "[113]

In 1836 another of Carlyle's friendships had had its beginning, that with Robert Browning. Both Carlyle and Browning testify that they first met at Leigh Hunt's. Through the years to come Carlyle found much to admire in Browning and he steadfastly encouraged him when the public was slow to receive him. But he believed that Browning was too susceptible to Hunt's influence as well as to other influences from which he did not gain strength. Some years later he wrote of him: "He has decidedly a good talent; but is unluckily, and now bids fair to continue, in the valley of the shadow of Man George-Sandism, Mazzini-ism, Leigh Huntism: one cannot help it; tho' it is a pity!"[114]

Probably the most significantly revealing and dramatic account of

112. MS, NLS, 523.73. John Abraham Heraud (1799–1887), journalist and critic who edited the *Sunbeam*, 1838–39, and the *Monthly Magazine*, 1839–42, was something of an authority on German literature. On 6 Feb. Carlyle had written to his brother John: "Tonight, as we learn suddenly, Hunt's play is to come *out*; and we have (alas for it!) to go and *assist*. I augur little certain except a headache: you shall hear how it turns." *New Letters of Thomas Carlyle*, ed. Alexander Carlyle (London and New York, 1904), I, 185. Carlyle may have heard Hunt read this play or another one from his pen at a private gathering in 1838. Hunt wrote to Robert Bell in October of that year that he was inviting Knowles, Procter, Dickens, and him to the reading and added: "I expect Carlyle, who is looked for every day from Scotland." *Correspondence of Leigh Hunt*, II, 322.

113. *Correspondence of Carlyle and Emerson*, I, 302.

114. MS, 26 Sept. 1855 to his brother John, NLS, 525.10. See also *William Allingham: A Diary*, ed. H. Allingham and D. Radford (London, 1907), pp. 240, 310.

a debate between Carlyle and Hunt is that which an Edinburgh
lawyer, John Hunter, entered in his diary during 1840. Hunter, the
brother of the Carlyles' friend Susan Hunter, whose affection for
Hunt Mrs. Carlyle has described, had known Carlyle many years. He
was a discriminating disciple of Hunt's, had read him for a long time,
and in the words of Carlyle was "often actually *subventive*"[115] to him.
It was not Hunt's "rose-water philosophy," however, that he admired
but his poems and "the sunny, loving spirit of the man." On professional visits to London he saw Carlyle and Hunt together more than
once. Although he found in Carlyle "what Coleridge wanted, great
power of concentration and vigor of talent," he also observed what
seemed to him "one singular defect in Carlyle's mind . . . the entire
want of all perception of grace and beauty in outward form or expression." This explained, Hunter said, his depreciation of such poets
as Petrarch, Milton, Wordsworth, and Coleridge. Carlyle, despite
"bursts of laughter which made his 'lungs crow like Chanticleer,'"
was not a happy man, and his "powers were not in harmony with each
other." On the other hand, Hunter delighted in the way the conversation became livelier and happier and turned to the sunny side of
things the moment that Leigh Hunt entered the room. He and Carlyle both enjoyed Hunt's singing, particularly the marching song from
The Beggars' Opera. But the most dramatic debate between Carlyle
and Hunt described by Hunter is that which took place at George L.
Craik's home on Wednesday, 8 April.

Carlyle and Hunt were in great force, and came out in the course of
the evening in their full strength. They form decided contrasts to each
other in almost every respect, and the occasional collisions that took place
between them drew out the salient points and characteristic powers of
each in the most striking manner possible. I never saw Carlyle in such
vigor, and was delighted, even when I most differed from him, with the
surging floods of his sonorous eloquence which he poured forth from time
to time, illuminated, as they always were, by the coruscations of a splendid fancy, sometimes lurid enough, to be sure, and heated to boiling
fervor by the inextinguishable fire of deep emotion that is forever gnawing
his heart and brain. Hunt again was all light and air, glancing gracefully
over all topics, and casting the hues of his own temperament on every subject that arose. I do not mean to make any attempt at giving an account of
the conversation. That is out of the question in the present instance. It

115. Froude, *Letters and Memorials,* I, 16.

lasted without interruption from five till near twelve o'clock, and embraced the most multifarious subjects. We had the Scottish Kirk, Wordsworth, Petrarch, Burns, Knox and Hume, the Church of England, Dante, heaven and hell, all through our "glowing hands"; and strange work was made with most of them. I gave some offense to Carlyle, but he recovered from it so swiftly, and redeemed himself so generously, that it heightened my admiration of him. He had been declaiming against Wordsworth, whom he represented as an inferior person to Cowper, adding that from the *débris* of Robert Burns a thousand Wordsworths might have been made. We laughed at all this, especially when we found that he had never read, or, at least, had no recollection of "Laodamia" and various other things in which Wordsworth's finest powers are exhibited. We next came to Petrarch, whom he crushed to sapless nothing in his grasp. I stood out a good while on this subject, as did Hunt and Craik. At last Carlyle said —"All I have to say is, that there is one son of Adam who has no sympathy with his weak, washy twaddle about another man's wife. I cast it from me as so much trash, unredeemed by any quality that speaks to my heart and soul. And now you may say whatever you like of him or of me." I answered hastily—"Then I would say of you that you are to be pitied for wanting a perception which I have, and which I think, and the world in general will think, I am the richer for possessing; and I would just speak of what you have now uttered in these words:—

> Say, canst thou paint a sunbeam to the blind,
> Or make him feel a shadow with his mind?"

A slight shade passed over his face at this, and he said—"Well, I admit you are right to think so, whatever I may think of the politeness of your saying it as you have now done." Hunt interposed to the rescue with, "Well, that's very good. Carlyle knocks down all our idols with two or three sweeps of his arm, and having so far cleared his way to us, he winds up by knocking down ourselves; and when we cry out against this rough work, he begins to talk of—politeness!" This was followed by a peal of laughter, in which Carlyle joined with all his heart; and then addressed me cordially and kindly—"I believe, after all, you are quite right. I ought to envy you. I have no doubt you have pleasures and feelings manifold from which I am shut out, and have shut out myself, in consequence of the habit I have so long indulged of groping through the sepulchral caverns of our being. I honor and love you for [the] lesson you have taught me." This was felt to be very noble. "There is Carlyle all over," said Hunt; "that's what makes us all love him. His darkest speculations always come out to the light by reason of the human heart which he carries along with him. He will at last end in glory and gladness."

Towards the conclusion of the evening we had a regular discussion be-

tween Carlyle and Hunt, involving the whole merits of their several sys-
tems, if I may so call Hunt's fantastic framework of *agreeabilities*, which
Carlyle certainly shattered to pieces with great ease (though without disconcerting Hunt in the slightest degree) in order to substitute his eternal
principles of right and wrong, responsibility, awe of the Unseen—the
spiritual worship of the soul yearning out of the clay tenement after the
infinitely holy and the infinitely beautiful. Hunt's system, I told him,
would suit nobody but himself.[116]

R. H. Horne in his *New Spirit of the Age* tells a somewhat different
story of a debate over optimism and pessimism that also took place at
G. L. Craik's about this time or a little later.

The conversation rested with these two—both first-rate talkers, and the
others sat well pleased to listen. Leigh Hunt had said something about
the Islands of the Blest, or El Dorado, or the Millennium, and was flowing
on in his bright and hopeful way, when Carlyle dropped some heavy tree-
trunk across Hunt's pleasant stream, and banked it up with philosophical
doubts and objections at every interval of the speaker's joyous progress.
But the unmitigated Hunt never ceased his overflowing anticipations, nor
the saturnine Carlyle his infinite demurs to these finite flourishings. The
listeners laughed and applauded by turns; and had now fairly pitted them
against each other. . . .
    The contest continued with all that ready wit and philosophy, that mix-
ture of pleasantry and profundity, that extensive knowledge of books and
character, with their ready application in argument or illustration, and
that perfect ease and good-nature which distinguished each of these men.
The opponents were so well matched that it was quite clear the contest
would never come to an end. But the night was far advanced, and the
party broke up. They all sallied forth and leaving the close room, the
candles and the arguments behind them, suddenly found themselves in
[the] presence of a most brilliant star-light night. They all looked up.
"Now," thought Hunt, "Carlyle's done for! He can have no answer to
that!" "There!" shouted Hunt, "look up there, look at that glorious harmony, that sings with infinite voices an eternal song of hope in the soul
of man.["]
    Carlyle looked up. They all remained silent to hear what he would say.
They began to think he was silenced at last—he was a mortal man. But
out of that silence came a few low-toned words, in a broad Scotch accent.
And who on earth could have anticipated what the voice said? "Eh! It's a

116. Walter C. Smith, "Reminiscences of Carlyle and Leigh Hunt," *Good Words*,
XXIII (Feb. 1882), 96–103.

sad sight!" Hunt sat down on a stone step. They all laughed—then looked very thoughtful.[117]

In the spring of 1840 Hunt moved from Chelsea, where he had been Carlyle's neighbor for about six years, to 32 Edwardes Square, Kensington. Carlyle's feelings about losing such a neighbor were mixed, and he wrote as follows to his brother:

Leigh Hunt has left this quarter, for Edwardes Square, Kensington; we are decidedly rather sad of it. Our intercourse lately had reduced itself altogether to the *lending of sovereigns*. Poor Hunt had great difficulty to get away at last; had to prowl about, borrowing etc. etc. He has dissatisfied all his friends by his late behavior during what he reckoned his theatrical *success*, which proves to be no success either, for they do not now act his play. He is a born fool. His son has got out of the Glasgow *Argus*, and is here too. They are a generation of fools. They are better in Edwardes Square.[118]

Letter 43. Hunt to Carlyle.[119]

32, Edwardes Square
Kensington—Feb. 4 [1841]

Is dear Thomas Carlyle master of a strange sum of three pounds in his treasury, for a fortnight to come?— I sigh, rather than blush, to ask it,— knowing the man to whom I speak; & at all events *he* knows that I am punctual in my re-payments.

Plays are delicious things to write & lovely in their proceeds!—but alas for some of the struggles in the intervals to those who have not a half-penny worth of certainty to retreat upon.

117. Wilson, *Carlyle*, III, 211–12. See also Wylie, *Carlyle*, pp. 236–37.

118. MS, 22 June 1840, to Dr. John A. Carlyle, NLS, 523.88.

119. MS, Brewer Collection, State University of Iowa. William Farren (1786–1861) was an English actor and manager. Madame Vestris (1797–1856), actress and opera singer, married Armand Vestris in 1813 and Charles James Mathews, actor and playwright, in 1838. The following story told by Augustus Hare in *The Story of My Life* is probably spurious but in spirit it is close to the truth: "One day when Mr. [James] Hannay went to the house [Carlyle's], he saw two gold sovereigns lying exposed in a little vase on the chimney-piece. He asked Carlyle what they were for. Carlyle looked—for him—embarrassed, but gave no definite answer. 'Well, now, my dear fellow,' said Mr. Hannay, 'neither you nor I are quite in a position to play ducks and drakes with sovereigns: what *are* these for?'— 'Well,' said Carlyle, 'the fact is, Leigh Hunt likes better to find them there than that I should give them to him.'" Quoted in Blunden, *Carlyle and His Circle*, p. 257. A letter of 14 May 1841 from Carlyle to an unknown correspondent, possibly G. H. Lewes, shows that he continued to keep a friendly eye on Hunt's children when he could: "You provided for young Hunt, I think—tho' the lad himself never came to tell me of it. You did a charitable helpful act." From the MS letter in the collection of Professor Frederick W. Hilles.

On Sunday next I read to the managers—I hope, finally—some alterations which have given me a great deal of trouble & anxiety; but they bring Farren & Madame Vestris into the play, in the place [?] of actors of less pretension, and I trust will be of great service.

Dear Sir, if you are unable to do what I ask, you know you are thoroughly understood by the heart of yours ever truly,

Leigh Hunt.

For a few years after Hunt moved away from Chelsea the friendship and correspondence between the two men seems to have been comparatively inactive. There is no evidence that they continued the long walks and talks that they had enjoyed earlier. Perhaps they felt that they had already said all that could be said in their debates and that further discussion would simply have meant tiresome repetition. Probably Hunt was weary of Carlyle's moral earnestness and gloom, always associated with an unrelenting habit of dominance. Certainly Carlyle was weary of Hunt's borrowing habits, always associated with radiance and blue skies. This was by no means, however, the end of the friendship. It simply came to rest and was the better later for having done so. The one sure way to do permanent damage to a friendship is to force it.

In June 1847 Hunt finally got his pension, a gratifying one of £200 a year granted by Sir Robert Peel's government. Carlyle had been one of those most active in his behalf, just as he had been active in behalf of Tennyson a few years before. He drew up the petition to the government that summed up the reasons why he and other friends believed Hunt should be given the pension. Though fitted to Hunt's special case, it is in some sense a forceful statement of the claims upon society's respect and wealth that any competent and courageous man of letters has the right to make.

Memoranda concerning Mr. Leigh Hunt.[120]

1. That Mr. Hunt is a man of the most indisputedly superior worth; a *Man of Genius* in a very strict sense of that word, and in all the senses which it bears or implies; of brilliant varied gifts, of graceful fertility, of clearness, lovingness, truthfulness; of childlike open character; also of most pure and even exemplary private deportment; a man who can be

120. Published in "Leigh Hunt's Poetry," *Macmillan's Magazine*, VI (July 1862), 239; Richard Herne Shepherd, *Thomas Carlyle* (London, 1881), II, 2–4; and in many other places.

other than *loved* only by those who have not seen him, or seen him from a distance through a false medium.

2. That, well seen into, he *has* done much for the world;—as every man possessed of such qualities, and freely speaking them forth in the abundance of his heart for thirty years long, must needs do: *how* much, they that could judge best would perhaps estimate highest.

3. That, for one thing, his services in the cause of Reform, as founder and long as editor of the *Examiner* newspaper; as poet, essayist, public teacher in all ways open to him, are great and evident: few now living in this kingdom, perhaps, could boast of greater.

4. That his sufferings in that same cause have also been great; legal prosecution and penalty (not dishonourable to him; nay, honourable, were the whole truth known, as it will one day be): unlegal obloquy and calumny through the Tory press;—perhaps a greater quantity of baseless, persevering, implacable calumny, than any other living writer has undergone. Which long course of hostility (nearly the cruellest conceivable, had it not been carried on in half, or almost total misconception) may be regarded as the beginning of his other worst distresses, and a main cause of them, down to this day.

5. That he is heavily laden with domestic burdens, more heavily than most men, and his economical resources are gone from him. For the last twelve years he has toiled continually, with passionate diligence, with the cheerfullest spirit; refusing no task; yet hardly able with all this to provide for the day that was passing over him; and now, after some two years of incessant effort in a new enterprise that seemed of good promise, it also has suddenly broken down, and he remains in ill health, age creeping on him, without employment, means, or outlook, in a situation of the painfullest sort. Neither do his distresses, nor did they at any time, arise from wastefulness, or the like, on his own part (he is a man of humble wishes, and can live with dignity on little); but from crosses of what is called Fortune, from injustice of other men, from inexperience of his own, and a guileless trustfulness of nature:—the thing and things that have made him unsuccessful make him in reality *more* loveable, and plead for him in the minds of the candid.

6. That such a man is rare in a nation, and of high value there; not to be *procured* for a whole nation's revenue, or recovered when taken from us, and some £200 a year is the price which this one, whom we now have, is valued at; with that sum he were lifted above his perplexities, perhaps saved from nameless wretchedness! It is believed that in hardly any other way could £200 abolish as much suffering, create as much benefit, to one man, and through him to many and all.

Were these things set fitly before an English minister, in whom great part of England recognises (with surprise at such a novelty) a man of insight, fidelity and decision, is it not probable or possible that he, though from a quite opposite point of view, might see them in somewhat of a similar light; and, so seeing, determine to do in consequence? *Ut fiat!*

T.C.

No doubt the Hunts enjoyed their new prosperity. "The Hunts give splendid *soirées*," wrote Mrs. Carlyle to her husband on 9 October 1847.[121]

It will be recalled that early in their friendship Carlyle and Hunt had shown great interest in the question of sexual morality. An entry made by Emerson in his journal, 25 April 1848, while he was on a visit to England, records a discussion of the question with particular reference to incontinence in males at one of John Forster's dinners where Carlyle, Dickens, and others were present and took part in the talk. Leigh Hunt was not there, but Dickens conveyed his interesting opinion.

There were only gentlemen present and the conversation turned on the shameful lewdness of the London Streets at night. "I hear it," he [?Forster] said, "I hear whoredom in the House of Commons. Disraeli betrays whoredom, and the whole House of Commons universal incontinence, in every word they say." I said that when I came to Liverpool, I inquired whether the prostitution was always as gross in that city as it then appeared, for to me it seemed to betoken a fatal rottenness in the state, and I saw not how any boy could grow up safe. But I had been told it was not worse nor better for years. Carlyle and Dickens replied that chastity in the male sex was as good as gone in our times; and in England was so rare that they could name all the exceptions. Carlyle evidently believed that the same things were true in America. He had heard this and that of New York, etc. I assured him that it was not so with us; that, for the most part, young men of good standing and good education, with us, go virgins to their nuptial bed, as truly as their brides. Dickens replied that incontinence is so much the rule in England that if his own son were particularly chaste, he should be alarmed on his account, as if he could not be in good health. "Leigh Hunt," he said, "thought it indifferent."[122]

When Carlyle toured Ireland in the late summer of 1849, Charles Gavan Duffy was his guide much of the time. The notes made by Duffy on his conversations with Carlyle include the following ac-

121. Froude, *Letters and Memorials*, II, 16.
122. *Journals* (Cambridge, Mass., 1914), VII, 440–43.

count of a discussion concerning the comparative merits of Wordsworth and Leigh Hunt as talkers:

> I inquired if I might assume that Wordsworth came up to this descrip-
> tion of him as the best talker in England.
>
> Well, he replied, it was true you could get more meaning out of what
> Wordsworth had said to you than from anybody else. Leigh Hunt would
> emit more pretty, pleasant, ingenious flashes in an hour than Wordsworth
> in a day. But in the end you would find, if well considered, that you had
> been drinking perfumed water in one case, and in the other you got the
> sense of a deep, earnest man, who had thought silently and painfully on
> many things.[123]

In 1850 Hunt's excellent *Autobiography* appeared. It contained a
long passage on Carlyle in which Hunt attempted to provide somewhat the same kind of balanced critique of his friend as Coleridge
had provided for Wordsworth in the *Biographia Literaria*. He gave,
among other things, his final statement of the arguments dealing with
the main issues that he and Carlyle had been debating through the
years.

> Here [at Chelsea], also, I became acquainted with Thomas Carlyle, one
> of the kindest and best, as well as most eloquent of men; though in his zeal
> for what is best he sometimes thinks it incumbent on him to take not the
> kindest tone, and in his eloquent demands of some hearty uncompromising
> creed on our parts, he does not quite set the example of telling us the
> amount of his own. Mr. Carlyle sees that there is a good deal of rough
> work in the operations of nature: he seems to think himself bound to con-
> sider a good deal of it devilish, after the old Covenanter fashion, in order
> that he may find something angelical in giving it the proper quantity of
> vituperation and blows; and he calls upon us to prove our energies and
> our benevolence by acting the part of the wind rather than the sun, of
> warring rather than peace-making, of frightening and forcing rather than
> conciliating and persuading. Others regard this view of the one thing
> needful, however strikingly set forth, as an old and obsolete story, fit only
> to be finally done with, and not worth the repetition of the old series of
> reactions, even for the sake of those analogies with the physical economy
> of the world, which, in the impulse which nature herself gives us towards
> progression, we are not bound to suppose everlastingly applicable to its
> moral and spiritual development. If mankind are destined never to arrive
> at years of discretion, the admonition is equally well-founded and unneces-

---

123. *Conversations and Correspondence with Carlyle* (New York, 1892), p. 54.
Most of this correspondence is preserved in the National Library of Ireland, Dublin.

sary; for the old strifes will be continued at all events, the admonition (at best) being a part of them. And even then, I should say that the world is still a fine, rich, strenuous, beautiful, and desirable thing, always excepting the poverty that starves, and one or two other evils which on no account must we consent to suppose irremediable. But if the case be otherwise, if the hopes which nature herself has put into our hearts be something better than incitements to hopeless action, merely for the action's sake, and this beautiful planet be destined to work itself into such a condition as we feel to be the only fit condition for that beauty, then, I say, with every possible respect for my admirable friend, who can never speak but he is worth hearing, that the tale which he condescends to tell is no better than our old nursery figment of the *Black Man and the Coal-hole*, and that the growing desire of mankind for the cessation of bitterness, and for the prevalence of the sweets of gentleness and persuasion, is an evidence that the time has arrived for dropping the thorns and husks of the old sourness and austerity, and showing ourselves worthy of "the goods the gods provide us."

Mr. Carlyle's antipathy to "shame," is highly estimable and salutary. I wish Heaven may prosper his denouncements of them, wherever they exist. But the danger of the habit of denouncing—of looking at things from the anti-pathetic instead of the sympathetic side—is, that a man gets such a love for the pleasure and exaltation of fault-finding, as tempts him, in spite of himself, to make what he finds; till at length he is himself charged with being a "sham"; that is to say, a pretender to perceptions and virtues which he does not prove, or at best a willing confounder of what differs from modes and appearances of his own, with violations of intrinsical wisdom and goodness. Upon this principle of judgment, nature herself and the universe might be found fault with; and the sun and the stars denounced for appearing no bigger than they do, or for not confining the measure of their operation to that of the taper we read by. Mr. Carlyle adopted a peculiar semi-German style, from the desire of putting thoughts on his paper instead of words, and perhaps of saving himself some trouble in the process. I feel certain that he does it from no other motive; and I am sure he has a right to help himself to every diminution of trouble, seeing how many thoughts and feelings he undergoes. He also strikes an additional blow with the peculiarity, rouses men's attention by it, and helps his rare and powerful understanding to produce double its effect. It would be hard not to dispense with a few verbs and nominative cases, in consideration of so great a result. Yet, if we were to judge him by one of his own summary processes, and deny him the benefit of his notions of what is expedient and advisable, how could he exculpate this style, in which he denounces so many "shams," of being itself a sham? of being affected, unnecessary, and ostentatious? a jargon got up to confound pretension with performance, and reproduce endless German talk under the guise of novelty?

Thus much in behalf of us dulcet signors of philanthropy, and conceders of good intention, whom Mr. Carlyle is always girding at, and who beg leave to say that they have not confined their lives to words, any more than the utterers of words more potential, but have had their "actions" too, and their sufferings, and even their thoughts, and have seen the faces of the gods of wonder and melancholy; albeit they end with believing them to be phantoms (however useful) of bad health, and think nothing finally potential but gentleness and persuasion.

It has been well said, that love money as people may, there is generally something which they love better: some whim, or hobby-horse; some enjoyment or recreation; some personal, or political, or poetical predilection; some good opinion of this or that class of men; some club of one's fellows, or dictum of one's own; with a thousand other *somes* and probabilities. I believe that what Mr. Carlyle loves better than his fault-finding, with all its eloquence, is the face of any human creature that looks suffering, and loving, and sincere; and I believe further, that if the fellow-creature were suffering only, and neither loving nor sincere, but had come to a pass of agony in this life, which put him at the mercies of some good man for some last help and consolation towards his grave, even at the risk of loss to repute, and a sure amount of pain and vexation, that man, if the groan reached him in its forlorness, would be Thomas Carlyle.[124]

In this carefully drafted statement of his arguments, the strength and weakness of his own as well as Carlyle's position were clearly indicated and were, as it were, placed on record. The sincerity of his praise of Carlyle is not to be doubted. It is consistent with what he had said before; and elsewhere in the *Autobiography* he also praised him. "I admire and love all hearty, and earnest, and sympathizing men, whatever may be their creed— . . . the Carlyles and Emersons, the Hares, Maurices, Kingsleys,"[125] he wrote toward the end of the book; and he joined those who spoke of the wonder of Carlyle's eyes: "The finest eyes, in every sense of the word, which I have ever seen in a man's head (and I have seen many fine ones) are those of Thomas Carlyle."[126] This is high praise from one who had seen the eyes of Wordsworth, Coleridge, Byron, Shelley, Keats, Tennyson, Browning, Dickens, Emerson, and many other eminent men.

124. Ed. J. E. Morpurgo (New York, 1948), 425–28.
125. *Ibid.*, p. 448.
126. *Ibid.*, p. 256.

Carlyle liked the book, and the letter to Hunt in which he expressed his admiration is one of his finest.

Letter 44. Carlyle to Hunt.[127]

Chelsea, 17 June, 1850—

Dear Hunt,

I have just finished your *Autobiography*, which has been most pleasantly occupying all my leisure these three days; and you must permit me to write you a word upon it, out of the fulness of the heart, while the impulse is still fresh to thank you. This good Book, in every sense one of the *best* I have read this long while, has awakened many old thoughts, which never were extinct, or even properly *asleep*, but which (like so much else) have had to fall silent amid the tempests of an evil time,—Heaven mend it! A word from me, once more, I know, will not be unwelcome, while the world is talking of you.

Well, I call this an excellently good Book; by far the best of the auto-biographic kind I remember to have read in the English Language; and indeed, except it be Boswell's of Johnson, I do not know where we have such a Picture drawn of a human Life as in these Three Volumes. A pious, ingenious, altogether *human* and worthy Book; imaging, with graceful honesty and free felicity, many interesting objects and persons on your life-path,—and imaging throughout, what is best of all, a gifted, gentle, patient and valiant human soul, as it buffets its way thro' the billows of the time, and will not drown, tho' often in danger; *cannot* be drowned, but conquers, and leaves a track of radiance behind it: that, I think, comes out more clearly to me than in any other of your Books;—and that I can venture to assure you is the best of all results to realise in a Book or written record. In fact this Book has been like an exercise of *devotion* to me: I have not assisted at any sermon, liturgy or litany, this long while, that has had so *religious* an effect on me. Thanks in the name of all men. And believe along with me that this Book will be welcome to other generations as well as to ours. And long may you live to write more Books for us; and may the evening sun be softer on you (and on me) than the noon sometimes was!

127. This letter appeared in print as early as July 1862 in "Leigh Hunt's Poetry," cited in n. 120 above, pp. 239–40. Wylie, Conway, and Shepherd all published it in their biographies of Carlyle that came out in 1881. It is almost the only letter by Carlyle for which I have found evidence of forgery. At least five libraries in Europe and America have facsimiles that have been mistaken for the original letter. The paper in the facsimiles has yellowed much more than that which Carlyle used in other letters written near this date, and all the facsimiles are on paper that shows the watermark "Superior Bath Vellum," which appears on none of the paper that Carlyle used. The whereabouts of the original letter is still uncertain.

Adieu dear Hunt (you must let me use this familiarity, for I am an old fellow too now as well as you). I have often tho^t of coming up to see you once more; and perhaps I shall one of these days (tho' horribly sick and lonely, and beset with spectral lions, go whitherward I may): but whether I do or not, believe forever in my regard. And so God bless you,—prays heartily

T. Carlyle

Hunt knew that Carlyle could have taken exception to much that he had written concerning him in the *Autobiography* but had not done so. He was extremely grateful.

Letter 45. Hunt to Carlyle.[128]

Kensington—June 21, 1850.

My dear Carlyle,

After having been so often flustered & rendered inoperative by pains & troubles, I have been treated in the same manner, this week past, by an incursion of pleasures; letters, to wit, from valued friends, making much of me beyond anything I had looked for, and indeed taking away, as it were, the very breath of my responsiveness, yours most of all, so that I did not know what to say or where to begin; and you may imagine how extreme the pleasure was in your instance, when it surmounted, nay, wholly drowned the very pain I felt at your giving me no pain at all, not a single word of spleen or reproof, but a very torrent of nothing but honey,—pure love, & self-forgetfulness, or only such self-remembrance as made the sweet the sweeter, and superiority to every thing but the desire of all good hearts to find some ground for humanity to rest upon between this world & the next. It did not astonish me; for I knew what honey there was in the jaws of Samson's lion, & I have always said that of such stuff your secret inner nature was altogether made; though I confess I did not think sufficiently well of myself to suppose that I should ever be the man to awaken thus its whole manifest fountain. Nor, believe me, do I think that it is myself that has done it even now, in spite of all the kind things which you say of me, and which assuredly you therefore feel. I know not what objections you withhold, nor how far accord with my mere self has anything to do with the matter; nor reverence for you, my dear friend, apart, do I care; for I merge, as you do, the smaller thing in the greater, and only

128. MS, Brewer Collection, State University of Iowa. Printed in *New Letters of Thomas Carlyle*, II, 95–97. R. H. Shepherd records a visit made to Carlyle in 1868 during which Carlyle seemed to have forgotten the memorandum he had written to help Hunt get a pension but remembered the letter he had written to Hunt about his *Autobiography* and the effusive gratitude of Hunt and his wife at their next meeting with the Carlyles after reading it. *Carlyle*, II, 275–76.

rejoice to see your great & strong spirit sitting, even if it be but to refresh yourself for new combats, in that region of peace which others have found for us, and to attain which, in some finality or other, can be the only last object of all greatness & all strength, unless combat itself under a sense of dissatisfaction & heart-discord (a very different thing, I conceive, from combat physical, or the concordias discors of the elements) be our sole human destiny & mode of being; which is what the whispers of the great Spirit of the Universe to our hearts do not seem to allow.

At all events I thank you from the bottom of my heart for your letter, and cannot but feel very proud of it, whether my pride be right or wrong. As to visits, I know all about them, & have *reciprocated* with you a thousand *in velle*: for is a being in *velle* as well as in *esse* & *posse*. I know how great the distance is sometimes between *ailer* & *ailer*, however short the parish measurement. I was more than half a year the other day, without crossing the threshhold even to see a neighbour; & I am only now seeing my neighbour & my very son at Hammersmith. But on Tuesday next, if you are not engaged that evening, I propose to come after tea & take my good old North-British supper with you. Pray tell Vincent if I may come, & believe me, dear kind Carlyle, your ever

respectful & affectionate friend,
Leigh Hunt.

P.S. Those unctuous blots you see in my letter are not quite as vile as they seem. They are honest effluences of good palm candle, used in sealing a letter.— Pray accept the book I send, however superfluous.

Carlyle received this letter and replied to it on the day when it was written.

Letter 46. Carlyle to Hunt.[129]

Chelsea, 21 June (Friday Ev^g) [1850]

Dear Hunt,— Many kind thanks! I saw the Book, and sent thanks for it by Vincent; but I did not know, till this minute, what other pleasant thing lay in the Letter itself, which the dusk and the hurry would not suffer me to read at the moment.— By all means, Yes, Yes! My Wife is overjoyed at the prospect of seeing you again in the old good style: Courage, and do not disappoint us. We are here, quite disengaged, and shall be right glad to see you.

I hope Vincent explained what a miscellaneous uproar had incidentedly

129. MS, British Museum, 33,515, fol. 41. William Wetmore Story (1819–95), son of Joseph Story (1779–1845), associate justice of the U.S. Supreme Court, was a painter, sculptor, and musician who became the friend of the Carlyles, the Brownings, Landor, and other Europeans.

[*sic*] got about me tonight; and how for want of *light* as well as of time, I missed the kernel of the Letter altogether.—— Tuesday, remember! We dine about 5; and tea comes naturally about 7,—sooner if you will come sooner.

One of my people tonight, an accomplished kind of American, has begged a card of introduction to you: he is a son of a certain noted Judge Story; is himself, I believe, a kind of *Sculptor* and Artist as well as Lawyer: pray receive him if he call; you will find him a friendly and entertainable and entertaining man.

And so— till Tuesday Ev⁹—

Yours with all regard
T. Carlyle

Despite his pension and the merits of his *Autobiography*, Leigh Hunt was not by nature one who could tread the path of smooth success for long. Toward the end of 1850 he was ready for a new journalistic venture. An enterprising young business man of Manchester, John Stores ("Turpentine") Smith agreed to put up the capital for reviving *Leigh Hunt's Journal*. Prospects seemed rosy to Hunt. He wrote to Carlyle to invite contributions from him but suggested, no doubt with the angry tone of Carlyle's *Latter-Day Pamphlets* (which had been appearing throughout the year) in mind, that they come from the benign side of Carlyle's nature.

Letter 47. Hunt to Carlyle.[130]

Kensington—Nov. 7ᵗʰ [1850].
32, Edwardes Square.

My dear Carlyle,

You may have seen the announcement of a certain "Leigh Hunt's Journal"—for the 7th December. Is it possible that we could have the honour & glory of your name in it, and the more sequestered side of your nature? that is to say, the un-antagonistic part of it,—the more obviously loving or sympathetic portion—or anything *not actually opposed to us & our pacifics*, —essay, memoir, criticism, pleasantry, pathos, or what not? Our size is "Chambers" (in his late lesser shape) with the type of "Household Words," and your articles would be leaded,—the pay (that is to say, *your* pay) two guineas a page, and two pages at a time? I wish it were two and twenty. Pray delight & oblige, if you can, your affectionate friend,

Leigh Hunt.

---

130. MS, Brewer Collection, State University of Iowa. Carlyle did provide a not too happy heading for his articles: "From a Waste-paper Bag of Thomas Carlyle."

P.S. I need not say that I should hope to put you in good company, or at all events none altogether unworthy. Of my own you would have plenty. — I should like much to see your articles under one head, of your own choosing, like the Spectator or Rambler. Think of the volume they would make, when collected. The copyright, of course, would be your own.

When Carlyle responded promptly and favorably, Hunt wrote with enthusiasm to William Allingham on 22 November: "Carlyle is hearty for us, and will glorify our first number with a contribution."[131] Carlyle actually had misgivings, which turned out to be well founded. He wrote to his brother John on November 23: "Leigh Hunt, Ballantyne, little Turpentine Smith are about setting up 'Leigh Hunt's Journal' again; poor little Smith (who has just married and came hither to live by Literature) investing his little fortune in the speculation,—not a good one at all, I should say! I walked up one night, and found poor old Hunt, supping on gruel and sherry, in clean linen and immense cloud of cotton nightgown, full of the old kindly follies, good soul!"[132] But Carlyle did make his promised contribution: "Two Hundred and Fifty Years Ago: Duelling"[133] began to appear in the first number, 7 December, and continued in the numbers for 21 December and 11 January. Smith had been disappointed with the way in which the public had received the journal, had withdrawn his capital, and had returned to Manchester, where he became rich. It was a cruel blow to Hunt in his old age.

Letter 48. Hunt to Carlyle.[134]

2 Phillimore Terrace
Kensington—June 30 [1851].

My dear Carlyle,

A gentleman wishes to know who wrote the communication respecting Strauss in the late luckless Journal.— May I tell him? I did not know but it might be wished to be kept secret.

131. *Correspondence of Leigh Hunt*, II, 120.

132. MS, NLS, 513.60. The journal appeared seventeen times between 7 Dec. 1850 and 29 March 1851. See Hunt's *Autobiography*, p. 495. For "Turpentine" Smith, see Blunden, *Leigh Hunt and His Circle*, pp. 307–308; Wilson, *Carlyle*, IV, 328.

133. Reprinted in *Works*, XXIX, 384–96.

134. MS, Brewer Collection, State University of Iowa. "Strauss": Hunt refers here to "Dr. David Strauss in Weimar," *Leigh Hunt's Journal*, 22 Feb. 1851, pp. 187–90. The article is signed "J.M.," and internal evidence further indicates that it is by James Marshall, secretary of the Grand Duchess of Weimar, with whom Carlyle corresponded. Marshall acted as guide to Strauss (1808–74), author of *Das Leben Jesu* (1835–36), when he visited Weimar in Aug. 1849. Carlyle had written to his mother from Chelsea

I would fain have seen the whole article inserted just as it was sent; but Mr Smith was afraid of his Manchester or his "commercial districts"— a point upon which he was always harping.

Oh how vexed & mortified I was, on finding the condition in which you and all the other friends whose pens he had encouraged me to invite into co-operation were to be left! Not that I supposed you cared anything for such poor profits as might have accrued. Indeed it was clear you did not; and "condition" is a foolish word. The sorry condition was mine, whose only excuse left me for not paying my friends, was the having ceased to receive any payment myself, on the strange plea that the last person to be paid was the first who by agreement was to receive payment, & without whose name the journal did not exist! And to this compliment was added the violation of every other engagement, the discontinuance of even personal consultations, and finally the insult of bearding the minister in an article professing to be "Our" view of his politics, and then hindering me (by threats of not paying the printer) from disowning it in my own paper!! Such were the vagaries of the, I believe not on the whole ill intentioned, but uncouth, self-sufficient, & blunder-headed gentleman with whom I found myself suddenly & unaccountably linked, as if I had been walking arm in arm, in a dream, with a wild bull.— I have spirits enough to laugh again today, for my dear son & your friend Vincent, who has been alarmingly ill, I found yesterday mending; but for this week past I have been sore with anxiety. Nor is he well now; far from it; and has greatly wasted: but his amendment is in the right direction, & I can again think of something else. May God bless you & yours is ever the prayer of

Your affectionate friend,
Leigh Hunt.

Smith says that Ballantyne deceived him as to the amount of money necessary to set up the journal; & Ballantyne says he only spoke of money to begin it with, not to set up, & that Smith talked of a farm that he was to sell for the purpose. The opinion of men of business is, that they merely calculated on my name. They never told me what their funds were, and I, like a simpleton, took the substantiality of gesture from the "commercial districts" for granted.

---

on 19 June 1847: "We have here at present a little Irishman (or rather Ayrshire-man, for he was *bred* there), one Marshall, from Weimar; who comes down occasionally, and tells us about Goethe and old things we are interested in. An ingenious entertaining little body. He is Secretary to the Duchess of Weimar, who is here at present, one of the foreign potentates visiting our little Queen." Unpublished passage from the MS, NLS, 521.53. Marshall was Carlyle's guide when he visited Weimar in Sept. 1852. This Marshall is not to be confused with James G. Marshall of Leeds, whom Carlyle considered one of England's most enlightened and progressive industrialists.

The five letters that follow, all written in October 1852, are a unified sequence and require little comment. Perhaps the most interesting thing in them is Leigh Hunt's pride in his own ingenuousness, expressed in the second paragraph of *Letter 49*.

Letter 49. Hunt to Carlyle.[135]

2, Phillimore Terrace,
Kensington—Oct. 23 [1852].

My dear Carlyle,

I am writing, as well as illness and anxiety will let me (for Vincent is worse than he has yet been) a sort of history of Kensington; and in a book of one of its scandal-chroniclers (Lord Hervey) I meet with the word *duchtich*, upon the precise meaning of which the commentator says his German friends are not agreed, though he takes it to be "sly." Will you be kind enough to help me out with it?

I take this opportunity of picking a bit of [a] lovers' quarrel with you. In an extract from your Life of Sterling, which I met with, in a review not long after its publication, you speak of Sterling as the most "ingenuous" man you ever knew. Now I know not what *quantity* of ingenuousness you may have found in that excellent person, nor do I mean to dispute his superiority in any other point; but in regard to the *quality* of the commodity, I will venture to say, that such of it as you had from me was of the very best sort. Let me take this *superbiam* upon me, if I have a right to no other. I never deceived you in deed, word, or thought.

Your ever affectionate friend,
Leigh Hunt

Letter 50. Carlyle to Hunt.[136]

The Grange, Alresford
24 Oct[r] 1852—

Dear Hunt,

I can make nothing, or almost nothing, of Lord Hervey's *duchtich*. In the first place, it is certain, there is no such word in German; nor can his commentator ever have "consulted" any "German friend" on the subject,

135. MS, Brewer Collection, State University of Iowa. Articles on Kensington by Hunt appeared in *Household Words* for 6 Aug., 20 Aug., 3 Sept., 19 Nov., 3 Dec. 1853. His *The Old Court Suburb; or, Memorials of Kensington* was published by Hurst and Blackett in 1855. The scandal chronicler here is John Hervey, Baron Hervey of Ickworth (1696–1743), satirized as "Sporus" in Pope's "Epistle to Dr. Arbuthnot." His *Memoirs of the Reign of George II*, ed. J. W. Croker, was published by J. Murray in London, 1848.
136. MS, Brewer Collection, State University of Iowa.

but must have simply inserted his own guess upon pure chance. So much is clear enough to me: but what word his Lordship did intend, is a question difficult to answer; and without good study of the context the answer cannot well be so much as conjectured.

Drawing a bow at a venture, I have a considerable notion he may have meant the adjective *tüchtig* (which is very similar in pronunciation, especially between a Hanoverian and an Englishman, the *g* too being guttural and the *t* easily confounded with *d*): *tüchtig* signifies "effective," "solidly expert"; it is in fact fundamentally the same word as our *doughty* (from the Scotch word *dow*, "to be able"; German *taugen*); but it is not so high a word as *doughty*, nor at all exclusively applied to martial work, but it is used as a term of familiar but deliberate praise to a man of worth, who is thoroughly master of what he pretends to, in regard to work or action of any kind. *Ein tüchtiger mann*—a genuine, a sufficient man. *Tugend* (the substantive of the word) signifies *virtue* in German; but perhaps the meaning of *tüchtig* to Lord Hervey might be pretty much equivalent to "clever,"—if he used *tüchtig*, if he intended *it* when he wrote *duchtich*.

If this makes sense of the passage for you, I think you may well stand by this; such is the likelihood of the mistake in his case.

But I am coming home in about a week; and if the point is still obscure and you will then send me a copy of the passage at large, or instruct me how to find it in the London Library, I will deliberately study it, and do my best to rede the riddle for myself and you. Tuesday next, and after that *ad libitum*.

Nobody was ever more in haste than I for the present; so adieu, dear Hunt; and believe me ever (without doubt or misgiving)

Yours with sincere regard
T. Carlyle

Letter 51. Hunt to Carlyle.[137]

Kensington—Oct. 26 [1852].

My dear Carlyle,

There is plenty of context to the word in Lord Hervey, but taking it for veritable German, I would not trouble you with it. Here however it now comes. Hervey is writing to Queen Caroline:—

137. MS, Brewer Collection, State University of Iowa. In *The Old Court Suburb* (pp. 253–54) Hunt translates *dure* as "unfeeling" and *paroître* as "seem to feel what I don't." *Duchtich* he provides a not-too-helpful note for: "Disingenuous? double-meaning? I have applied to German scholars respecting this word, which is not familiar to them." German-English dictionaries today give *duchtich* in Middle Low German and Middle Dutch as meaning "capable, able" and further indicate that in later times, influenced by the Christian dogma of the virtues, it also means "virtuous" as a Middle

"Tis true, great Queen, I have your dread command
No more with ink to stain these scribbling hands;
No more in *duchtich* verse, or *teufflish* prose,
To *raccommode* my friends, or lash my foes." &c.

Upon which the editor (Croker) observes, "My German friends are not agreed as to the precise import of *duchtich*, which, however, from its use in p. 161, seems to mean *sly.*"

The passage at p. 161 is part of an imaginary conversation at court, which takes place on the supposed occasion of the writer's (Lord Hervey's) death:—

"*Princess Emily.*—I am not sorry for him.
"*Queen.* And why not?
"*Princess Em.* What, for that creature?
"*Princess Caroline.* I cannot imagine why one should not be sorry for him: I think it very *dure* not to be sorry for him. I own he used to laugh *malapropos* sometimes, but he was mightily mended; and for people that were civil to him, he was always ready to oblige them; and for my part I am sorry, I assure.
"*Princess Em.* Mama, Caroline is *duchtich*; for my part I cannot *paroître.*
"*Queen.* Ah! Ah! You can *paroître* and be *duchtich* very well sometimes; but this is no *paroître*; and I think you are [a] very great brute."—

Thanks for your long note on this point, and for your nullification of my fancy on the other.

Your affectionate
Leigh Hunt.

In an old Gazetter I read the following about Alresford:—

"An ancient borough on a little river called Alre by Camden, but Itching by the country people.— On May day, 1710, this town was burnt down by a fire which spared neither the Market House nor Church; before which disaster there was not one almsman in the parish. It has been since burnt down, but is handsomely rebuilt. Part of a Roman highway, that goes from this place to Alton, serves for the head to a great pond, or rather a little lake near this town, on which are abundance of swans."—

Low German derivative. But Carlyle must have been right in suggesting that its use in Lord Hervey's play reflecting the speech of the English Hanoverian Court and meaning "capable of feeling sincere sympathy for" was "coterie" language.

This may be old news to you, or changes may have made it curious. Being a lover of localities, especially when I take walks in imagination with friends, at all events I send it.

Letter 52. Carlyle to Hunt.[138]

The Grange, 27 Octr 1852

Dear Hunt,

There is no good sense, I fear, to be made out of *"duchtich"* on any hypothesis: *tüchtig* does not answer well in the passages you give; and I can think of only one other German word which plausibly resembles *duchtich*; this perhaps answers a little better, but this also is by no means conclusively convincing. The word *"züchtig"* (pronounce *tz* or *dz*) signifies *well-bred, polite, discreet,* also *chaste, modest,* and on the whole *comme il faut*; this, perhaps once *mis*pronounced *"duchtich"* by Hervey, *may* in "Coterie Speech" have become a common word in that circle:—at all events, *duchtich* is clearly a *coterie*-word; and need not be sought after in dictionaries; nay who knows but the English Editor himself may have misread it (*deutlich,* "evident," "clear," w^d be very like it in writing); not to say that Hervey's own MS. does not usually spell German with propriety, —*teufflish,* for example, should be *teuflisch* etc. In short, I consider it impossible to guess what the word was, from such data as we have; and advise you not to chase it farther than into the hiding-places already indicated. *"Sly"* I do not believe it to have meant; nor on the whole will *"tüchtig"* do; *"züchtig"* I give you as my likeliest guess: but with certainty (unless by Pharaoh's soothsayers, or by the writer and them) there can nothing be given.

N.B. "Coterie-Speech" is a German phrase; but I have no doubt you understand it well, and can give good account of it in an English Note. And that, I believe, will fairly help you thro' the difficulty.

Thanks for the Note on Alresford; which is yet true enough to Nature in its geographical part, tho' the *historical* (of the two burnings) has vanished from all memories that I consult. The big pond, with swans, and the bit of Roman road "to Alton" (properly from Winchester to London) are all still there; and a clean merry-looking market village as if no fire or disaster had ever been.

Adieu, dear Hunt. I remain faithfully,

Yours always
T. Carlyle

138. MS, Lilly Library, University of Indiana. The letters of both Carlyles are spiced with "Coterie-Speech," which editors and readers must become familiar with and recognize the precise flavor of if they are to understand and enjoy the letters fully.

Kensington—Oct. 30[1852]

My dear Carlyle,

I should have written yesterday to thank you for your second long and kind note, but my poor son's extreme illness prevented me, and now hinders me from saying more.— At all times and seasons, sorrowful or otherwise, believe me ever your sincere

and affectionate friend,
Leigh Hunt.

Letter 53. Hunt to Carlyle.[139]

From the time of this letter until Hunt's death on 28 August 1859, the meetings and messages between the two old friends were intermittent and infrequent. But the bond between them was never broken, and they were often in one another's thoughts when not in one another's presence. On 23 March 1853 Hunt mentioned in a letter to Dr. Southwood Smith his "beloved Chinese novel, *In-Kiao-Li,*" which he spoke of as "a work of genius, as well as curious for its national manners, and exhibiting in passages the most exquisite refinement of heart. The notes marked T.C. are by Carlyle, to whom I lent it once, and who read it with delight."[140] Old as they were getting to be, both men were still quick to see the humorous side of life. In 1854 the movement to grow beards was well under way. Lord Ashburton made Carlyle promise to grow one and when he seemed to delay pressed him. Carlyle wrote to him on 30 September 1854:

But what shall I say of the grand question, the Beard? Certainly I am, and have ever been, a fixed enemy of shaving. . . . I am mindful of my promise, and even my wife assents. . . . Really, the Beard-movement does proceed, I perceive. Leigh Hunt, I heard not long since, had produced a copious beard, white or nearly so; he complained that there were two

---

Many of the coterie phrases were, in the first instance, peculiar and often amusing expressions that the Carlyles had heard others use, such as the Hunt child's "good joy," Mazzini's "thanks God" for "thank God," and "many wits" for "much wit," and old Mrs. Carlyle's "just a fluff of feathers" for "not worth a farthing," which Jane, who did not like Browning, once applied to him.

139. MS, Brewer Collection, State University of Iowa.

140. *Correspondence of Leigh Hunt*, II, 162. *In-Kiao-Li*: apparently J. P. Abel-Remusat's *In-Kiao-Li, ou Les Deux Cousines; roman chinois,* 4 vols. (Paris, 1826); translated into English and published in two volumes in London by Hunt and Clarke, 1827. See Martha Davidson, *A List of Published Translations from Chinese into English, French and German* (Ann Arbor, Mich., 1952).

drawbacks, (1) the little boys laughed at him; (2) the beard abolished an uncommonly sweet smile he was understood to have. The latter evil will not apply to me. Nor do I think the little boys will much interfere.[141]

There was one further interchange of letters written in the kindliest spirit.

Letter 54. Hunt to Carlyle.[142]

Hammersmith—Dec. 31 [1857].

My dear Carlyle,

Mr. Moran, an American friend of mine, and great admirer of yours, and as worthy a man withal as becomes his admiration, has asked me whether I thought you would be displeased at his begging your acceptance of a number of a new American magazine, which the post will bring you with this letter. I have ventured to say I thought you would not. Emboldened by this opinion, he would fain quash a fear which he retains of the terrible dictum which you once fulminated across the Atlantic respecting certain millions of "bores," and hope that he might be permitted to deprive you of half an hour of your time some morning in Cheyne Row.

I was not venturous enough, I think, to speak with as much confidence on that point as on the other; though notwithstanding his natural Republican courage, and even his official situation (for he is Assistant Secretary to the American Minister) he says, that under all circumstances, and considering how you must have been beset by his countrymen, he "does not wonder" at the dictum. But to give your secret goodnature as many reasons as I can for according with his desire, I will add what might otherwise, or to a less Catholic man, appear irrelevant to the matter, and even extravagant; namely, that he has lately undergone a great domestic sorrow; and that any momentary diversion of it such as he values, is an addition to his stock of supports.

Whether in joys or in sorrows of my own, believe me ever, dear Carlyle,

Most sincerely yours,
Leigh Hunt.

141. MS in possession of the Marquess of Northampton. A week or two later Lord Ashburton, returning from the Highlands with a beautiful beard, swooped down upon Carlyle's Chelsea home and with Jane's cooperation carried off all of Carlyle's razors. On 13 Oct. Carlyle wrote to his brother John that he had not shaved in four days. *New Letters of Thomas Carlyle*, II, 166–67.

142. MS, NLS, 3218.127. Benjamin Moran (1820–86), diplomat and contributor to American periodicals, became James Buchanan's private secretary at the American Embassy in London in 1854. The London *Times* once praised him as the "ablest and most honest" representative the United States had ever had there. The *Atlantic Monthly* began in Nov. 1857.

P.S. You ought to have had the book some days ago; but expecting to see Forster here, and to speak to him about it, I delayed. He came the day before yesterday; and then, in our talk, which was at once brief and full of matter, I forgot.

Letter 55. Carlyle to Hunt.[143]

Chelsea, 3 Jany 1858

Dear Hunt,

I received your kind Note; which was very welcome to me,—the hand-writing on the cover was like the knock of and [*sic*] old Friend at the door. By a later post, the same day, the Magazine arrived; for which you must report me much obliged to Mr Moran.

I am crushed down with contemptible overwhelming labour this long time; scarcely able to keep alive under it at all;—at it night and day for 18 months past, cut off from the cheerful face of my fellow creatures, and almost from the light of the Sun at this season. To rummage 100 wagon-loads of contemptible *marine-stores*, and weld out of them a malleable bar of any kind: it is such a job, now in my old days, as was never laid on me before;— and, what perhaps is worst of all, I intrinsically set no value on the beggarly enterprise; and have only one wish & hope about it, that poor I had done with it, forever and a day! There is at last fair prospect that I shall be out of the First Part, *taliter qualiter*, in May coming.

Mr Moran, & any friend of yours, may have half an hour of me, when-ever he resolves to send up your Card. If he wait till May, he may find me (it is to be hoped) a much saner man than now:—but he may take his choice. I remain ever

Dear Hunt Yours sincerely
T. Carlyle

Through the years they had written some other undated notes and letters for which the dates are now difficult to establish.

Letter 56. Carlyle to Hunt.[144]

My dear Sir,

Here is an American admirer of yours, a very pleasant gentleman, who (after requesting an autograph with your signature) requests that I would

---

143. MS, Brewer Collection, State University of Iowa. *Marine-stores*: material from old ships often sold for junk. *Taliter qualiter*: "For what it may be worth."
144. MS, Brewer Collection, State University of Iowa.

take him over, and let him see you face to face. May I bring him? Or should I send him at some other time?

Yours always
T.C.

Letter 57. Hunt to Carlyle.[145]

My dear Sir,

Your note was laid so quietly on the table by the servant, that I did not see it till this moment. I am forced to add, most unwillingly, that it happens to be almost the only impossible moment for receiving a friend that has occurred during the week, for I am in the double agony of running a race with time for the printer, & with ditto for an appointment by omnibus with the Strand. May I hope that your friend will find leisure to give me a look in *any other* day before one, or after five?

Ever yours most truly,
Leigh Hunt.

Letter 58. Carlyle to Hunt.[146]

Thanks for the Books, for the promised visit, for the corrections, for all that you have done and say! The "Sybilline" [*sic*] doggerel—ah me, had all the world such a conscience as Leigh Hunt!

We are at home tomorrow night, and shall be right glad to see your face again.

T.C.

Letter 59. Carlyle to Hunt.[147]

[Before 1840]

My Dear Sir,

Your little German Annual for 1791, not uninteresting otherwise, does seem rather questionable in the part you suspect. It treats there of Father Origen's feat, in *Language* as good as Gibbons; but warns its lady-readers (as it well enough may) to "look only thro' their fans" at such a *thing*.— I fear you must not send it.

How often has your kind soliloquy an exact counterpart within my own person!— I am good for nothing at all, during these late weeks; sunk in confusion of dyspepsia, dispiritment, and the impossibility to make any

145. MS in the collection of Professor Frederick W. Hilles.

146. MS, Brewer Collection, State University of Iowa. The note is addressed to 4 Upper Cheyne Row and therefore dates before Hunt moved to Kensington in 1840.

147. MS, Brewer Collection, State University of Iowa. Addressed to 4 Upper Cheyne Row.

way in my confused work. Tonight or tomorrow night, you shall have share of my dulness since I have nothing better to impart.

God bless you!

Yours always,
T.C.

Letter 60. Hunt to Carlyle.[148]

Kensington—July 15 [after 1840].

My dear Sir,

The bearer of this, Mr. Whelpdale, is a gentleman desirous of being engaged in German tuition, and on that & other accounts, ambitious of being known to you. From the brief acquaintance I have had with him, he appears to me to be a man of no common capacity, with an ingenuous nature, & of the right aspirations; & his intercourse is very gentle & pleasing. You will therefore I trust, give him audience for his own sake, & I hope a little for mine.

Some time ago, & now again lately, I have been wishing to send you a book or two; but I have not the command over the copies which former arrangements gave me; & am thus obliged to sigh & be shabby. It is a consolation to me, that at all events you thus escape the necessity of thanks, & perhaps the perplexities of unwilling criticism.

Pray beg Mrs. Carlyle to accept, with yourself, my kindest remembrances. I have had the old struggles, & fluctuations of health, but they have been accompanied with the old consolations; & I can laugh heartily still, thank God, as well as sigh. The young visitor you had the other day, would have returned to you, had the occasion continued; but it passed away.

Ever your obliged & faithful

Leigh Hunt.

When Hunt died at the age of seventy-five Carlyle wrote to John Forster: "Poor Hunt, poor Stephen! The ranks are getting thin to one's right and to one's left:—it is an evident suggestion, 'Close, then; rank closer, and stick to one another, ye that still stand!' "[149] Carlyle would continue his battle until 1881, about twenty-two years after

---

148. MS, NLS, 2883. 306–307.
149. Of 26 Oct. 1859. *New Letters of Thomas Carlyle*, II, 204. Sir James Stephen (1789–1859), colonial undersecretary (dubbed by Charles Buller "Mr. Mother Country"), was the father of Sir James Fitzjames Stephen, J. K. Stephen, and Sir Leslie Stephen; grandfather of Virginia Woolf and Vanessa Bell. *The Memoirs of James Stephen*, ed. Merle M. Bevington (London, 1954), pp. 430–31.

Hunt's death. His comments on Hunt during these years were entirely consistent with what he had said about him while he was alive. Hunt had been one of the few people whose reading aloud he had enjoyed. His voice not only conveyed meaning effectively but was delightful to listen to in itself. Carlyle told William Allingham: "Leigh Hunt used to walk with me in the first years after I came to Chelsea. He was sweet and dignified, and his talk like the song of a nightingale."[150] Always a lover of nature, Hunt had delighted, as Keats knew, in the songs of real nightingales and had directed Carlyle to where he could hear them sing. When John Burroughs visited Carlyle in 1863, he was astonished by his knowledge of birds and his love for them. Carlyle told him that Leigh Hunt used to send him to various places to hear nightingales sing but that he did not really hear one until there came a song that he recognized by Goethe's description, a song like that of the poet, "sounding amid the din—touching and strong," words that told the story. He listened to this bird for fifteen minutes but never heard a nightingale again.[151] Some of the old differences of opinion between him and Hunt also came back into Carlyle's mind. He told William Allingham in 1873: "Leigh Hunt was saying one day, what a fine thing it would be if a subscription could be made *to abolish Hell*; but I remarked, 'Decidedly a bad investment, that would be!'— which grieved Hunt considerably."[152] In his old age he could not keep up very well with Hunt's large family, but he continued to maintain an interest in them, especially in Thornton. "I have known little of Th^n Hunt, these many years; indeed ever since his father's death," he wrote to W. D. Christie. "I used to think him an extremely ingenious quick-witted man; of loyal dispositions and intentions;— given up to *Journalism*, this long while past; and grown to I know not what in that turbid element of things. Somebody told me not long since, that he was a 'Writer in the D^y Telegraph'; it is very possible he may be *Editor* too,—at least if talent in such matters carries the prize."[153]

But the memories concerning Leigh Hunt that the old Carlyle lingered over with most delight had to do with the first years he and Jane had spent in London when Hunt was their near neighbor in

150. *Diary*, p. 204. See also Wilson, *Carlyle*, V, 455.
151. Wilson, *Carlyle*, V, 215–16.
152. *Diary*, 30 June 1873, p. 226. Allingham also records the fact that Carlyle took note of the death of Thornton Hunt at this time.
153. MS, 2 June 1863, Yale University Library.

Chelsea. They had not found him the kind of man that talk had represented him as being. He was "a fine kind of man," Carlyle told Allingham. "I used to read the *Examiner* with much interest when I was living down in Scotland. Some used to talk of him as a frivolous fellow, but when I saw him he had a face as serious as death."[154] And from his pleasant memories of the evening visits that Hunt made to the Carlyles' Chelsea home in these early years, Carlyle with a sure art drew unforgettable vignettes in which all the old shadows came into harmony with the brightness of life and the supreme beauty of friendship. In these vivid pictures, woven of the stuff of life itself, Jane Carlyle fittingly had an important part.

Still prettier were Leigh Hunt's little nights with us; figure and bearing of the man, of a perfectly graceful, spontaneously original, dignified and attractive kind. Considerable sense of humor in him; a very pretty little laugh, sincere and cordial always; many tricksy turns of witty insight, of intellect, of phrase; countenance, tone and eyes well seconding; his voice, in the finale of it, had a kind of musical warble ("chirl" we vernacularly called it) which reminded one of singing-birds. He came always rather scrupulously, though most simply and modestly, dressed. "Kind of Talking Nightingale," we privately called him—name first due to her. He enjoyed much, and with a kind of chivalrous silence and respect, her Scotch tunes on the piano, most of which he knew already, and their Burns or other accompaniment: this was commonly enough the wind-up of our evening; supper being ordered (uniformly "porridge" of Scotch oatmeal), most likely the piano, on some hint, would be opened, and continue till the "porridge" came—a tiny basin of which Hunt always took, and ate with a teaspoon, to sugar, and many praises of the excellent frugal and noble article. It seems to me, in our long, dim-lighted, perfectly neat and quaint room, these "evening parties" of three were altogether human and beautiful, perhaps the best I anywhere had before or since![155]

Again:

Leigh Hunt was in the next street, sending kind *un*practical messages; in the evenings, I think, personally coming in. . . . Huggermugger was the type of his Economics, in all respects, financial and other; but he was himself a pretty man, in clean cotton nightgown, and with the airiest kindly style of sparkling talk,—wanting only wisdom of a sound kind, and true insight into fact. A great want![156]

154. *Diary*, p. 172.
155. Froude, *Letters and Memorials*, I, 3.
156. *Reminiscences*, I, 101–102.

And again:

Leigh Hunt was here almost nightly, three or four times a week, I should reckon;—he came always neatly dressed, was thoroughly courteous, friendly of spirit, and talked—like a singing bird. Good insight, plenty of a kind of humor too;— I remember little *warbles* in the turns of his fine voice which were full of fun and charm. We gave him Scotch Porridge to supper ("nothing in nature so interesting and delightful"): she played him Scotch tunes; a man he to understand and feel them well. His talk was often enough (perhaps at first oftenest) Literary-Biographical, Autobiographical, wandering into Criticism, *Reform of Society*, Progress, etc., etc.,—on which latter points he gradually found me very shocking (I believe,—so fatal to his rose-colored visions on the subject). An innocent-hearted, but misguided, in fact, rather foolish, *un*practical, and often much-suffering man.[157]

And again:

Our commonest evening sitter, for a good while, was Leigh Hunt, who lived close by, and delighted to sit talking with us (free, cheery, *idly* melodious as bird on bough), or listening, with real feeling, to her old Scotch tunes on the Piano, and winding up with a frugal morsel of Scotch Porridge (endlessly admirable to Hunt). . . . Hunt was always accurately dressed, these evenings, and had a fine chivalrous gentlemanly carriage, polite, affectionate, respectful (especially to her) and yet so free and natural. Her brilliancy and faculty he at once recognized, none better; but there rose gradually in it, to his astonished eye, something of positive, or practically steadfast, which scared him off, a good deal; the like in my own case too, still more;—which he would call "Scotch," "Presbyterian," who knows what; and which gradually repelled him, in sorrow, not in anger, quite away from us, with rare exceptions, which, in his last years, were almost pathetic to us both. Long before this, he had gone to live in Kensington;—and we scarcely saw him except by accident. His Household, while in "4 *Upper* Cheyne Row," within few steps of us here, almost at once disclosed itself to be huggermugger, *un*thrift, and sordid collapse, once for all; and had to be associated with on cautious terms;—while he himself emerged out of it in the chivalrous figure I describe. Dark complection (a trace of the African, I believe), copious clean strong black hair, beautifully-shaped head, fine beaming serious hazel eyes; *seriousness* and intellect the main expression of the face (to our surprise at first),—he would lean on his elbow against the mantelpiece (fine clean, elastic figure too he had, five feet ten or more), and look round him nearly in

157. *Ibid.*, I, 104.

silence, before taking leave for the night: "as if I were a *Lar*," said he once, "or permanent Household God here!" (such his polite *Ariel*-like way). Another time, rising from this *Lar* attitude, he repeated (voice very fine) as if in sport of parody, yet with something of very sad perceptible: "While I to sulphurous and penal fire"—as the last thing before vanishing. Poor Hunt! No more of him. She, I remember, was almost in *tears*, during some last visit of his, and kind and pitying as a Daughter to the now weak and time-worn old man.[158]

They were so much unlike that even the gods could not have predicted the success and quality of their friendship. But they were both wonderful men in whom differences of opinion, character, and even temperament were transcended by what Carlyle called Hunt's "purest humanity" and what Hunt called Carlyle's "paramount humanity."[159] Hence, it is after reading the story of their friendship we may feel justified in quietly congratulating ourselves that we belong to the human race with its high but at times inscrutable potential of friendship.

---

158. *Ibid.*, I, 174–75. Hunt's superb manners, which Carlyle significantly noted more than once, are reflected in Hunt's epigram: "Theophrastus was known not to have been born in Attica by his too Attic nicety." Wylie, *Carlyle*, p. 227. "Sulphurous and penal fire": see the speech of the Ghost in *Hamlet*, I, v.

159. Wylie, *Carlyle*, p. 224.

CARLYLE AND TENNYSON

According to Sir Charles Tennyson, Carlyle met Tennyson at the Sterling Club as early as 1839, if not earlier. Previously, Sir Charles says, Carlyle had heard much about him from John Sterling, who had helped to found the Cambridge Apostles' Club, of which Tennyson had also been a member.[1] D. A. Wilson, however, in his multi-volumed life of Carlyle says that the two first met in Carlyle's garden at Chelsea in the autumn of 1840.[2] Sir Charles is more nearly right. Wilson's date is too late, for on 5 September 1840 Carlyle wrote to his brother: "Some weeks ago, one night, the Poet Tennison [sic] and Matthew Allen were discovered here, sitting smoking in the garden. Tennison had been here before, but was still new to Jane,—who was alone for the first hour or two of it. A fine large-featured, dim-eyed, bronze-colored, shaggy-headed man is Alfred; dusty, smoky, free-and-easy: who swims, outwardly and inwardly, with great composure in an inarticulate element as of tranquil chaos and tobacco smoke; great now and then where he does emerge: a most restful, brotherly, solid-hearted man."[3] From the very first the friendship seemed to flourish. "He seemed to take a fancy to me," Tennyson later told a visitor at Farringford in speaking of Carlyle's favorable treatment of him in the early 1840s.[4] In those years Carlyle's reputation had already been firmly established by his *French Revolution* and his lectures; but Tennyson had not published the two volumes of 1842 that were to do much to give him fame. Both had found the road to fame a long, steep, and difficult one. Both had lost manuscripts: Carlyle that of the *French Revolution*, volume one; and Tennyson that of *Poems, Chiefly Lyrical*.[5] Both had been battered much by hardships and

---

1. *Alfred Tennyson* (New York, 1949), pp. 176–77.
2. *Carlyle*, 6 vols. (London and New York, 1923–34), III, 121.
3. From the original letter, in the NLS, 523.95. The passage on Tennyson is quoted in part, without an exact date, by Froude in *Carlyle*, III, 190.
4. *Tennyson and His Friends*, ed. Hallam Lord Tennyson (London, 1911), pp. 131–32.
5. Tennyson later misplaced the manuscript of *In Memoriam*, not long before publication, and it had to be found and reclaimed for him by Coventry Patmore, with considerable difficulty. See W. F. Rawnsley, "Personal Recollections of Tennyson," *Nineteenth Century and After*, XCVII (Feb. 1925), 191.

disappointments. Carlyle, who was fourteen years older than the poet, had struggled over a much longer period before being acclaimed by the literary world. But the period of their fame would also be a long one, and in terms of rough chronology they enjoyed their fame during the same years.

The letter that Carlyle wrote Tennyson in praise of the poems in the 1842 volumes gave the poet great pleasure and encouragement. He valued this letter highly the rest of his life.

> Cheyne Road, Chelsea,
> 7th Dec. 1842

Dear Tennyson,

Wherever this find you, may it find you well, may it come as a friendly greeting to you. I have just been reading your Poems; I have read certain of them over again, and mean to read them over and over till they become my poems: this fact, with the inferences that lie in it, is of such emphasis in *me*, I cannot keep it to myself, but must needs acquaint you too with it. If you knew what my relation has been to the thing call'd English "Poetry" for many years back, you would think such fact almost surprising! Truly it is long since in any English Book, Poetry or Prose, I have felt the pulse of a real man's heart as I do in this same. A right valiant, true fighting, victorious heart; strong as a lion's, yet gentle, loving and full of music: what I call a genuine singer's heart! There are tones as of the nightingale; low murmurs as of wood-doves at summer noon; everywhere a noble sound as of the free winds and leafy woods. The sunniest glow of Life dwells in that soul, chequered duly with dark streaks from night and Hades: everywhere one feels as if all were fill'd with yellow glowing sunlight, some glorious golden Vapor; from which form after form bodies itself; naturally, *golden* forms. In one word, these seems to be a note of "The Eternal Melodies" in this man; for which let all other men be thankful and joyful! Your "Dora" reminds me of the *Book of Ruth*; in the "Two Voices," which I am told some Reviewer calls "trivial morality," I think of passages in *Job*. For truth is quite *true* in Job's time and Ruth's as now. I know you cannot read German: the more interesting is it to trace in your "Summer Oak" a beautiful kindred to something that is best in Goethe; I mean his "Müllerinn" (Miller's daughter) chiefly, with whom the very Mill-dam gets in love; tho' she proves a flirt after all and the thing ends in satirical lines! very strangely too in the "Vision of Sin" I am reminded of my friend Jean Paul. This is not babble, it is speech; true deposition of a volunteer witness. And so I say let us all rejoice somewhat. And so let us all smite rhythmically, all in concert, "the sounding furrows"; and sail forward with new cheer, "beyond the sunset," whither we are bound—

It may be that the gulfs will wash us down,
It may be we shall touch the happy Isles
And see the great Achilles whom we knew!

These lines do not make me weep, but there is in me what would fill whole Lachrymatories as I read. But do you, when you return to London, come down to me and let us smoke a pipe together. With few words, with many, or with none, it need not be an ineloquent Pipe!

Farewell, dear Tennyson; may the gods be good to you. With very great sincerity (and in great haste) I subscribe myself

Yours,
T. Carlyle[6]

Apart from its function of encouraging the poet, this letter, written in haste as it was, is an excellent piece of literary criticism. Carlyle's affinities being what they were, we are not surprised at his readiness to praise poems echoing the Bible, Goethe, and Richter, or expressing eloquently, as "Ulysses" does, his own dynamic spirit. At the same time, we should not overlook his praise of Tennyson as a "singer," as Shakespeare, Burns, and Goethe had been in their songs and lyrics. Carlyle had little patience with verse that was not melodious; for him poetry must always be an expression of "The Eternal Melodies."[7] Another aspect of Tennyson's art did not escape him, although he was always, we know, one who scorned the fine arts as such. The interweaving of glorious gold with black—with an intense darkness born out of deepest grief and the confusion of chaos itself—that all who know Tennyson will recognize as one of the most characteristic qualities of his poetry, counting for much both aesthetically and philosophically, Carlyle discovered and spoke of eloquently in this letter. His later comments show that this quality remained for him a distinguishing element in Tennyson's nature and work. Perhaps most important to Carlyle, however, was "the pulse of a real man's heart" that he found in Tennyson's poetry. What he sought for first in all art was its humanity and the invincibility of the human spirit. The

6. Hallam Tennyson, *Alfred Lord Tennyson: A Memoir by His Son* (New York and London, 1897), I, 213–14. I have not found the original of this letter. In 1869 Tennyson spoke to Frederick Locker-Lampson about it and of how much he valued Carlyle's praise in it. He thought at the time the letter had been lost. *Ibid.*, II, 73.

7. When Carlyle was told that Tennyson had no ear for music, he said, according to Edward FitzGerald, "The man must have music dormant in him, revealing itself in *verse*"; and he spoke of Tennyson's voice as being like "the sound of a pinewood." Wilson, *Carlyle*, III, 122.

distinction between what was human and what was not was always a vital one to him, whether he was judging the arts or the institutions of society. In Tennyson's poems he was delighted to find humanity in rich abundance and in virile strength.

Carlyle's sincerity is not to be questioned. His influence, which was now great, he used vigorously in Tennyson's behalf. He praised both the poems and the poet in letters to various correspondents. One of these was Jane Wilson, who with Harriet Martineau had arranged for his own London lectures several years before. To her he wrote just two days after writing to Tennyson himself:

Perhaps the cheerfulest phenomenon I have fallen in with of late is Alfred Tennyson's new book of *Poems*. It is infinitely gratifying to find one true soul more, a great melodious Poet-soul, breathing the vital air along with us. Such I discover, to my own satisfaction, is this book of Alfred's. There has no man tried *singing* for a long while in whom I found such a talent for it. Praised be Heaven!—You do not know Alfred? A massive, irregular, dusty, brown-complexioned man; a large rough-hewn face full of darkness, yet of kindness, even of good-humor; large, gloomy-kindly, Indian eyes, an immense shock of dusty black hair; and one of the best *smokers* now living! Right well do I like a pipe beside Alfred; his speech in that deep, clear metallic voice, is right pleasant to me; his very silence, amid the tobacco clouds, eloquent enough.— As you can have no hope of ever smoking with him, I will advise you at least to read his book.[8]

In dealing with Tennyson, as in dealing with all his other contemporaries, Carlyle struck off with fine economy many such intensely vivid and memorable Rembrandt portraits. To his brother Alexander he wrote on 28 December 1842: "We had a Poet here (last night), a very clever man called Alfred Tennyson; and Jack, and a friend named Darwin, both admirers of Alfred's, 'came to see.' We had a pleasant little evening. Alfred is a right hearty talker; and one of the powerfullest *smokers* I have ever worked along with in that department!"[9]

8. "Carlyle's Unpublished Letters to Miss Wilson," *Nineteenth Century*, LXXXIX (May 1921), 811. For Carlyle, Tennyson, and tobacco, see Wilson, *Carlyle*, I, 326; W. Gordon McCabe, "Personal Recollections of Alfred Lord Tennyson," *Century Magazine*, XLI (March 1902), 733–34; Anne Thackeray Ritchie, *Records of Tennyson, Ruskin, Browning* (New York, 1893), pp. 59–60. Previously Carlyle had praised Richard Monckton Milnes for his favorable review of Tennyson's two volumes: "The review of Tennyson [in the *Westminster Review*, XXXVIII] is worthy of all acceptation; that 'R.M.M.' is a truehearted man, I do think, and has eyes in his head." MS letter, 6 Oct. 1842, Trinity College, Cambridge.

9. *New Letters of Thomas Carlyle*, ed. Alexander Carlyle (London & New York, 1904), I, 279–80. "Jack" is Dr. John A. Carlyle, brother of Thomas; "Darwin" is most

During the next year or two Carlyle's praise of Tennyson was extended across the ocean to Emerson. In his letter of 17 November 1843 he wrote: "Let a man try to the uttermost to *speak* what he means, before *singing* is had recourse to. . . . Alfred Tennison, alone of our time, has proved it to be possible in some measure."[10] And on 5 August 1844 he gave Emerson a full and detailed estimate of the poet, brilliantly written and containing a pen-portrait that has been often quoted:

Alfred is one of the few British or Foreign Figures (a not increasing number I think) who are and remain beautiful to me;—a true human soul,

---

likely Erasmus Darwin, brother of Charles and great friend of both Carlyles. See Grace J. Calder, "Erasmus A. Darwin, Friend of Thomas and Jane Carlyle," *MLQ*, XX (March 1959), 36–48. On 28 Dec. Jane Welsh Carlyle wrote to Jeannie Welsh: "Last night he [John A. Carlyle] was here again to dine with—Alfred Tennyson. (Ah Babby what you have lost). . . ." MS, NLS, 1891.141. Carlyle wrote to Charles Redwood, 31 Dec. 1842: "Many thanks again for your new punctual Package of Christmas Gifts,—. . . . Alfred Tennyson the Poet, as it chanced, lent help in doing honour to the magnificent Cambrian Goose. A fowl destined to be eaten could desire no more! Do you know Alfred's Poems? If you do not, pray get the two little volumes, and read them, especially the second." MS, Sir Charles and Lady Redwood.

10. Joseph Slater, ed., *The Correspondence of Emerson and Carlyle* (New York and London, 1964), p. 353. Carlyle's willingness to help Tennyson bring out an American edition of his works is indicated by the following extract from a letter to Edward Moxon, 3 Aug. 1844:

"I am earnestly applied to out of America to know, whether Mr Tennyson received a certain Parcel of Books, addressed to him from Boston in january last, to your care, and forwarded by Monroe and Co the Booksellers there? The Books were Copies of the American Edition of Tennyson[']s Works. There was, in the Parcel, or accompanying it outwardly, a Letter from a Dr Lebaron Russell; who in fact was the sender of the Books, and I believe the Manager of that American Edition: the Letter 'related to business'; neither it nor the Parcel have ever been acknowledged;—and I now am earnestly applied to, as above stated.

"Not knowing where Tennyson is at present, I have no course but inquiring of you first of all. It is possible you may be able to resolve me without farther investigation. I am to write to America on Monday; your Note, if you at once recognize the matter, and are ready with a response, would be here in time.

"Failing that, can you be so good as let me know Tennyson's Address. I will ask you to let me, in either case, know *how he is*,—for on that also I am very vague." MS, Baker Library, Dartmouth College.

Writing from Scotland, Carlyle had sent Jane the following interesting information in a letter of 21 Aug. 1843 (NLS, 611.153): "Did I ever tell you that Alfred Tennyson has a Brother [Arthur, Edward, or Septimus, probably Arthur; see Sir Charles Tennyson, p. 199] in the Dumfries Asylum? It is quite true; but we need not speak of it. I saw the poor young man on the street, a disguised keeper walking in sight; Aird [Thomas Aird, Dumfries poet and newspaper editor] spoke to this Tennyson, naming him, that I might notice: a miniature polished edition of Alfred, like in his very voice, nay in his very turn of ideas and phraseology. He is at present perfectly sane: he told John [Dr. John A. Carlyle, Carlyle's brother] since: 'I am liable to terrible fits of drinking!' Great wits to madness are allied. We need not speak of this."

or some authentic approximation thereto, to whom your own soul can say, Brother!— However, I doubt he will not come; he often skips me, in these brief visits to Town; skips everybody indeed; being a man solitary and sad, as certain men are, dwelling in an element of gloom,—carrying a bit of Chaos about him in short, which he is manufacturing into Cosmos!

Alfred is the son of a Lincolnshire Gentleman Farmer,[11] I think; indeed, you see in his verses that he is a native of "moated granges," and green, fat pastures, not of mountains and their torrents and storms. He had his breeding at Cambridge, as if for the Law or Church; being master of a small annuity on his Father's decease, he preferred clubbing with his Mother and some Sisters, to live unpromoted and write Poems. In this way he lives still, now here, now there; the family always in reach of London, never in it; he himself making rare and brief visits, lodging in some old comrade's rooms. I think he must be under forty, not much under it. One of the finest-looking men in the world. A great shock of rough dusty-dark hair; bright-laughing hazel eyes; massive acquiline face, most massive yet most delicate; of sallow-brown complection, almost Indian-looking; clothes cynically loose, free-and-easy; smokes infinite tobacco. His voice is musical metallic,—fit for loud laughter and piercing wail, and all that may lie between; speech and speculation free and plenteous: I do not meet, in these late decades, such company over a pipe!— We shall see what he will grow to. He is often unwell; very chaotic,—his way is through Chaos and the Bottomless and Pathless; not handy for making out many miles upon.[12]

Among the friends with whom Tennyson stayed when he came to London were his fellow "Apostles" James Spedding and Richard Monckton Milnes, now also friends of Carlyle. Another old Cambridge friend, Edward FitzGerald, had also become Carlyle's friend and was providing some help as Carlyle worked on *Cromwell's Letters and Speeches*.[13] In a letter to FitzGerald of 26 October 1844 Carlyle described a recent visit from Tennyson:

One day we had Alfred Tennyson here; an unforgettable day. He stayed with us till late; forgot his stick: we dismissed him with Macpherson's Farewell. Macpherson (see Burns) was a Highland robber; he played

11. The poet's father had been Rector of Somersby Church. But Carlyle's point about the influence of Lincolnshire and Cambridge on Tennyson's poetry still holds pretty well.

12. Slater, p. 363. At the beginning of this letter Carlyle had written: "Today I get answer about Alfred Tennyson: all is right on that side. Moxon informs me that the Russell Books and Letter arrive duly, and were duly forwarded and safely received; nay farther that Tennyson is now in Town, and means to come and see me."

13. FitzGerald's father owned the site of the Battle of Naseby.

that tune, of his own composition, on the way to the gallows; asked, "If in all that crowd the Macpherson had any clansman?" holding up the fiddle he might bequeath it to some one. "Any kinsman, any soul that wished him well?" Nothing answered, nothing durst answer. He crashed the fiddle under his foot, and sprang off. The tune is rough as hemp, but strong as a lion. I never hear it but with something of emotion,—poor Macpherson; tho' the artist hates to play it. Alfred's dark face grew darker, and I saw his lip slightly quivering.[14]

Mrs. Ritchie describes Tennyson at this time as "living in poverty with his friends and his golden dreams."[15] According to Sir Charles Tennyson, during the first half of 1846 Patmore's sympathy and comradeship and Tennyson's affection for Carlyle were the chief influences that kept Alfred in London.[16] Carlyle, FitzGerald, and Tennyson were often together and sometimes dined at "The Cock" in the Strand, among other places.[17] FitzGerald reported that Carlyle "opened the gates of his Valhalla" to the poet and now kept a pipe for him in a special niche in the garden wall at Cheyne Row.[18] But Tennyson's comings and goings were such during the middle forties that even Carlyle often found it difficult to keep up with him. He wrote to FitzGerald on 22 September 1846: "From Moxon I heard the other day that Tennyson and he *had* just been in Switzerland; that T. was actually at that time in Town, his address unknown; Moxon very kindly . . . undertook to send Alfred to me if he could; but has not succeeded hitherto."[19]

An extremely valuable service that Carlyle rendered to Tennyson during the 1840s was to use all his influence in an effort to get financial aid that the poet very badly needed. Particularly after early 1843, when Tennyson lost £3,000, his whole fortune, which he had invested in a furniture-carving enterprise with the trade name "Pyroglyphs," was Carlyle active in his friend's behalf. Dr. Matthew Allen, the head of the enterprise, whom Tennyson had trusted, was Carlyle's friend as well as Tennyson's. Carlyle's correspondence with him dates back to 1820.[20] Dr. Allen maintained a home for mental patients at Fair-

14. *Some New Letters of Edward FitzGerald*, ed. F. R. Barton (London, 1923), I, 321–22.

15. P. 35.   17. Ritchie, p. 36.
16. P. 214.   18. Sir Charles Tennyson, p. 202.

19. *Some New Letters of Edward FitzGerald*, II, 131–33. The original letter is in the Yale University Library.

20. See also the quotation above from Carlyle's letter to his brother John, 5 Sept. 1840.

meed, near High Beech, where Tennyson had spent some time in the early 1840s. Although Carlyle called him "a speculative, hopeful, earnest-frothy" man,[21] he seems to have had considerable esteem for him, and not only Tennyson but other members of Tennyson's family had believed Allen to be trustworthy. The old Carlyle in 1873 told Charles Eliot Norton that when Tennyson was poorest FitzGerald had given him £300 a year.[22] At the time Carlyle seems to have heartily approved of the arrangement as a temporary one. In his letter to FitzGerald of 26 October 1844, quoted above, he added: "He [Tennyson] said of you that you were a man from whom one could accept money; which was a proud saying; which you ought to bless Heaven for." But he also added: "It has struck me as a distinctly necessary Act of Legislation that Alfred should have a Pension of £150 a year. They have £1,200 every year to give away. A hundred and fifty to Alfred, I say; *he* is worth that sum to England! It should be done and must."[23] The excellent story has been told many times of how Carlyle brought great pressure to bear upon Richard Monckton Milnes to get a pension for Tennyson, of how Milnes had said that such a thing would not be easy and might raise question in the minds of his constituents, and of how Carlyle had then told him, solemnly and emphatically: "Richard Milnes, on the Day of Judgment, when the Lord asks you why you didn't get that pension for Alfred Tennyson, it will not do to lay the blame on your constituents; it is you that will be damned." According to the story, Sir Robert Peel took steps to get the pension of £200 that Tennyson was given in 1845 after Milnes had got him to read "Ulysses."[24] About the same time Allen died. Carlyle was very much pleased by the news that Tennyson might now be able to retrieve a considerable portion of the money that had appeared to be lost in the "Pyroglyphs" venture and wrote to FitzGerald, 6 February 1845: "Alfred went away on Sunday, I think; twice I met him, the fiery Son of Gloom. There seems no doubt but he will now get hold of £2,000 by Allen's death: I wish he would straightway buy himself an annuity with it."[25] When Tennyson, however, partly because of fine scruples that made him reluctant to accept

21. Sir Charles Tennyson, pp. 185–86.
22. Wilson, *Carlyle*, VI, 279; Charles Eliot Norton, *Letters*, ed. Sara Norton and M. A. De Wolfe Howe (Boston and New York, 1913), I, 464–65.
23. See n. 14 above.
24. *Tennyson: A Memoir*, I, 225.
25. From the original letter in the NLS, 1808.121.

a pension and partly because of what Carlyle considered his characteristic lethargy, was slow to draw out his pension money, Carlyle was both concerned and disgusted. He wrote to his brother John on 3 May 1846: "Alfred looks haggard, dire, and languid: they *have* got him however to go and *draw* his Pension; that is reckoned a great achievement on the part of his friends! Surely no man has a right to be so lazy in this world;—and none that is so lazy will ever make much way in it, I think!"[26]

In spite of Carlyle's misgivings, his friendship with Tennyson during the 1840s was in the main a very happy one. During these years Mrs. Carlyle shared his high opinion of Tennyson. The contrast is marked between her enthusiastic admiration for Tennyson and her very real dislike of another poet who was her husband's friend, Robert Browning. In March 1843 she wrote to her cousin Helen Welsh:

Three of the autographs which I send you today are first-rate. A Yankee would almost give a dollar apiece for them. Entire characteristic letters from Pickwick, Lytton Bulwer and Alfred Tennyson; the last the greatest genius of the three, though the vulgar public have not as yet recognized him as such. Get his poems if you can, and read the "Ulysses," "Dora," and the "Vision of Sin," and you will find that we do not overrate him. Besides, he is a very handsome man, and a noble-hearted one, with something of the gypsy in his appearance, which for me is perfectly charming. Babbie never saw him, unfortunately, or perhaps I should say fortunately, for she must have fallen in love with him on the spot, unless she be made absolutely of ice; and then men of genius have never anything to keep wives upon.[27]

His visits to Cheyne Row, even with the clouds of tobacco smoke that came with him, were always delightful to her. During one such visit, which she gives an account of in another letter of 31 January 1845 to Helen Welsh, she and Tennyson both seem to have been at their very best:

Carlyle went to dine at Mr. Chadwick's the other day and I not being yet equal to a dinner altho' I was asked to "come in a blanket and stay all night"! had made up my mind for a nice long quiet evening of *looking into*

---

26. From the original letter in the NLS, 524.64. Carlyle had rejoiced over the news of Tennyson's pension in a letter to his wife of 8 Oct. 1845. See *New Letters of Thomas Carlyle*, II, 5–8.

27. *Tennyson: A Memoir*, I, 188. "Babbie" is another cousin of Mrs. Carlyle, Jeannie Welsh.

the fire, when I heard a carriage drive up, and men's voices asking questions, and then the carriage was sent away! and the men proved to be Alfred Tennyson of all people and his friend Mr. Moxon—Alfred lives in the country and only comes to London rarely and for a few days so that I was overwhelmed with the sense of Carlyle's misfortune in having missed the man he likes best, for stupid Chadwicks, especially as he had gone against his will at *my* earnest persuasion. Alfred is dreadfully embarassed with women alone—for he entertains at one and the same moment a feeling of almost adoration for them and an ineffable contempt! adoration I suppose for what they *might be*—contempt for what they *are!* The only chance of my getting any right good of him was to make him forget my womanness—so I did just as Carlyle would have done, had he been there; got out *pipes and tobacco*—and *brandy and water*—with a deluge of *tea* over and above.— The effect of these accessories was miraculous—he *professed* to be *ashamed* of polluting my room, "felt" he said "as if he were stealing cups and sacred vessels in the Temple"—but he smoked on all the same—for *three* mortal hours!—talking like an angel— only exactly as if he were talking with a clever *man*—which—being a thing I am not used to—men always adapting their conversation to what they *take to be* a woman's taste—strained me to a terrible pitch of intellectuality.

When Carlyle came home at twelve and found me all *alone* in an atmosphere of tobacco so thick that you might have cut it with a knife his astonishment was considerable![28]

Several months later when the Irish leader C. J. Duffy was calling at Cheyne Row, Mrs. Carlyle told him: "Alfred Tennyson does not, as you supposed, tell his own story in 'Locksley Hall'; . . . he is unmarried, and unlikely to marry, as no woman could live in the atmosphere of tobacco-smoke which he makes about him from morn till night."[29] Jane Welsh Carlyle had, as her husband very well knew, as fine a talent as any woman who ever lived for flirting with various men without for one moment overstepping the bounds of propriety. She had exercised this talent fully in her dealing with Francis Jeffrey in the old days at Craigenputtoch, much to the delight of everyone concerned, including Thomas Carlyle, who admired her performances.[30] While

28. *Jane Welsh Carlyle: Letters to Her Family, 1839–1863*, ed. Leonard Huxley (New York, 1924), pp. 228–30. Sir Charles Tennyson erroneously dates the passage 1839 or early 1840 (pp. 176–77).

29. Sir Charles G. Duffy, *Conversations and Correspondence with Carlyle* (New York, 1892), p. 5.

30. See the sketches of Jane Welsh Carlyle and Francis Jeffrey in Carlyle's *Reminiscences*. There is abundant evidence in Carlyle's contemporaneous letters to substantiate the point.

Carlyle was in Scotland in the early autumn of 1845, she had two encounters with Tennyson, the second of which failed through neither her fault nor Tennyson's to produce the excitement promised by the first. In her sprightly dramatic style she gave her husband a detailed account:

[At private theatricals got up by Dickens and John Forster] in the interval between the play and the farce I took a notion to make my way to Mrs. Macready. . . . Passing through a long dim passage, I came on a tall man leant to the wall, with his head touching the ceiling like a caryatid, to all appearance asleep, or resolutely trying it under most unfavorable circumstances. "Alfred Tennyson!" I exclaimed in joyful surprise. "Well!" said he, taking the hand I held out to him, and forgetting to let it go again. "I did not know you were in town," said I. "I should like to know who you are," said he; "I know that I know you, but I cannot tell your name." And I had actually to name myself to him. Then he woke up in good earnest, and said he had been meaning to come to Chelsea. "But Carlyle is in Scotland," I told him with due humility. "So I heard from Spedding already, but I asked Spedding, would he go with me to see Mrs. Carlyle? and he said he would." I told him if he really meant to come, he had better not wait for backing, under the present circumstances; and then pursued my way to the Macready's box. . . .
    Craik arrived next evening (Sunday), to make his compliments. . . . John was smoking in the kitchen. I was lying on the sofa, head-achey, leaving Craik to put himself to the chief expenditure of wind, when a cab drove up. Mr. Strachey? No. Alfred Tennyson alone! Actually, by a superhuman effort of volition he had put himself into a cab, nay, brought himself away from a dinner party, and was there to smoke and talk with me!—by myself—me! But no such blessedness was in store for him. Craik prosed, and John babbled for his entertainment; and I, whom he had come to see, got scarcely any speech with him. The exertion, however, of having to provide him with tea, through my own unassisted ingenuity (Helen being gone for the evening) drove away my headache; also perhaps a little feminine vanity at having inspired such a man with the energy to take a cab on his own responsibility, and to throw himself on providence for getting away again! He stayed till eleven, Craik sitting him out, as he sat out Lady H——, and would sit out the Virgin Mary should he find her here.[31]

31. Letter of 23 Sept., in *Letters and Memorials of Jane Welsh Carlyle*, ed. J. A. Froude (London, 1883), I, 339–44. "Mrs. Macready" is the wife of the well-known actor W. C. Macready. "John" is Carlyle's brother, Dr. John Aitken Carlyle. "Craik" is Professor G. L. Craik (1798–1866) nicknamed "Creek" by the Carlyles. "Mr.

To her cousin Jeannie Welsh she gave a briefer but similar account of her experience: "I saw Alfred Tennyson in the lobby—and *that* was the best of it! And better still he came to take tea, and talk, and *smoke* with me—me—by myself me—the following evening—such at least was his *intention*, not a little flattering to my vanity considering his normal state of indolence—but the result was, that he found *Creek*, and *John*, and *they* made a mess of it— 'The Devil fly away with them both!' "[32] It was while Carlyle was in Scotland on this visit that his wife was able to write him the good news that Tennyson was to get his pension. In a letter of 5 October 1845 she told him this news and added that Tennyson was looking for a wife: "Did you know that Alfred Tennyson is to have a pension of £200 a year after all? Peel has stated his intention of recommending him to Her Gracious Majesty, and that is final: 'A chaqu'un selon sa capacité!' Lady Harriet told me that he wanted to marry; 'must have a woman to live beside; *would prefer a lady*, but—cannot afford one; and so must marry a maidservant.' Mrs. Henry Taylor said she was about to write to him on behalf of their housemaid, who was quite a superior character in her way."[33] Both bits of news delighted Carlyle, and he felt gratification at the part he had played in getting the pension: "What you tell me today of Tennyson's Pension is very welcome indeed. Poor Alfred, may it do him good;—'a Wife to keep him unaisy,' will be attainable now, if his thoughts tend that way. I admire his catholicity of humor too: 'Would prefer a *lady*, but,' etc.! . . . By the bye, was it not I that first spoke of that Pension, and set it afloat in the world! In that case it may be defined as our *ukase* not less than Peel's. This world is a most singular place!"[34] Tennyson was not to marry, we know, until 1850. In the meantime, Jane Welsh Carlyle continued to enjoy his visits to Chelsea. "Your pretty teapot was not broken," she wrote Jeannie Welsh in 1848. "I made tea in it for Alfred Tennyson the other night."[35] And in 1851 she told Coventry

---

Strachey" is very probably Sir Edward Strachey, uncle of Lytton Strachey. "Lady H——" is probably Lady Harriet Baring, who in 1848 became Lady Ashburton, first wife of the second Lord.

32. 30 Sept. 1845. In Huxley, pp. 252–54.

33. *New Letters and Memorials of Jane Welsh Carlyle*, ed. Alexander Carlyle (London and New York, 1903), I, 179–81. Lady Harriet is Lady Harriet Baring.

34. 8 Oct. 1845. In *New Letters of Thomas Carlyle*, II, 6.

35. From the original letter in the NLS, 1893.161. Characteristically, Mrs. Carlyle merely dated it "Saturday."

Patmore that she very much wanted a cast of Thomas Woolner's medallion of Tennyson.[36]

Even during these early years of Tennyson's friendship with the Carlyles, however, the way was not always smooth. Both Carlyles, it will be recalled, in some of the passages already quoted refer to Tennyson's laziness. The critical attitude was not lacking on either side of this friendship. The three persons involved in it were to some degree creatures of mood, and all their meetings could not come off satisfactorily. Not all of Tennyson's later poems would please the Carlyles so well as "Ulysses" and "Dora" had done. As early as 12 October 1844 we find Carlyle writing to his brother John: "Alfred Tennyson came to us the other day about 2; staid till near 11 at night: good company; but I got an ugly headache from the jog, and still have it."[37] It cannot be assumed, furthermore, that Carlyle spared even Tennyson in his general admonition to the writers of his time to write prose, not poetry. He would at times banter Tennyson and call him "a Life-Guardsman spoiled by making poetry."[38] The utmost extreme to which Carlyle ever went in this direction was, if Margaret Fuller's statement is to be taken at face value, in what he said at a dinner that she attended in the autumn of 1846. Obviously, Carlyle was in one of his moods of wild exaggeration in which he enjoyed saying things that shocked his listeners. Miss Fuller reported to Emerson that Carlyle had said that Tennyson had written verse because the schoolmasters had taught him that it was great to do so. He had thus, unfortunately, been turned from the true path for a man; Burns and Shakespeare had made the same mistake. All three, Carlyle said, according to Miss Fuller, would have done better to write prose.[39] In the 1840s, too, Carlyle introduced Sir John Simeon to Tennyson at the Ashburtons' London residence, Bath House, by first pointing him out and then saying, "There he sits upon a dung-heap, surrounded by innumerable dead dogs." The metaphor was suggested by Tennyson's fondness for subjects taken from Greek and Roman literature. When Tennyson teased Carlyle about this intro-

---

36. Amy Woolner, *Thomas Woolner, Sculptor and Poet* (London, 1917), p. 12.
37. From the original letter in the NLS, 512.28.
38. *Tennyson and His Friends*, p. 133.
39. Wilson, *Carlyle*, III, 348; Margaret Fuller Ossoli, *Memoirs*, ed. J. F. Clarke, R. W. Emerson, and W. H. Channing (Boston, 1852), II, 186.

duction many years later, he replied, "Eh! that was not a very luminous description of you."[40]

There were also important differences of opinion between the two friends, particularly on the subject of immortality. Tennyson, we know, was favorably disposed toward Anglicanism and considered its doctrine of affirmation the very keystone of Christian belief. Carlyle was highly skeptical about both the Church of England and the doctrine of immortality. FitzGerald reports that on 3 May 1846 he found Carlyle and Tennyson together at Tennyson's London lodgings arguing vehemently about immortality: "They two discussed the merits of this world and the next till I wished myself out of this, at any rate. Carlyle gets more wild, savage and unreasonable every day; and I do believe will turn mad. 'What is the use of ever so many rows of stupid, fetid animals in cauliflower wigs—and clean lawn sleeves—calling themselves Bishops—Bishops I say of the Devil—not of God—obscene creatures, parading between men's eyes and the eternal light of Heaven,' etc., etc., etc. This, with much abstruser nonconformity for two whole hours!" Tennyson may not have had the worst of the argument. Tennyson told Thackeray's daughter, later Mrs. Ritchie, that during a heated argument on immortality with Carlyle, possibly on the same occasion, for FitzGerald was there, Carlyle turned to him and said: "Eh! Old Jewish rags! Ye must clear your mind of all that! Why should we expect a hereafter? Your traveller comes to an inn and he takes his bed. It's only for one night, and another takes it after him." This time Tennyson turned the metaphor, always a tricky and risky device in debates, against him: "Your traveller comes to his inn and lies down in his bed almost with the certainty that he will go on his journey rejoicing next morning." Carlyle merely grunted and smoked in silence, but after he left FitzGerald told Tennyson, "You had him there." But FitzGerald later, in the *Rubáiyát*, stanza three, uses the tavern figure in Carlyle's sense.[41]

During the late 1840s Carlyle continued to consider Tennyson and his work with mixed feeling. On 26 December 1847 he wrote Lady Harriet Baring, later Lady Ashburton, that he was sending her "The Princess," newly published, "very gorgeous, fervid, luxuriant, but in-

---

40. Arthur Waugh, *Alfred Lord Tennyson: A Study of His Life and Work* (London, 1892), p. 100; Ritchie, p. 35; *Tennyson: A Memoir*, I, 340.
41. *Tennyson and His Friends*, p. 379; Wilson, *Carlyle*, III, 325–27.

dolent, somnolent, almost imbecile."[42] Four days later he commented on Tennyson in a letter to Emerson: "A truly interesting Son of Earth, and Son of Heaven,—who has almost lost his way among the will-o-wisps, I doubt; and may flounder ever deeper, over neck and nose at last, among the quagmires that abound! I like him well; but can do next to nothing for him. . . . He wants a *task*."[43] As for *The Princess*, Carlyle told Francis Espinasse curtly at its first appearance that it had "everything but common-sense."[44] On 9 February 1848 Carlyle wrote in his journal: "Alfred Tennyson here sometimes lately. Gone out of town with a certain Aubrey de Vere to Curragh Chase, Limerick. His 'Princess' a gorgeous piece of writing, but to me new melancholy proof of the futility of what they call 'Art.' Alas! Alfred too, I fear will prove one of the *sacrificed*, and in very deed it is a pity."[45] Despite his misgivings, however, Carlyle maintained at this time and later the lively interest in Tennyson and his possibilities that he had had from the beginning. Late in 1848 he wrote to Lady Ashburton: "Alfred Tennyson is to Italy; actually carried off, by some friendly brother of his, to execute what he has long been meditating, and might have forever meditated."[46] In a letter to Aubrey de Vere of early 1849 Carlyle described a glimpse of Tennyson walking in Regent Street in terms suggesting Sir Bedivere striding along the ridge: "Tennyson it seems, has returned to Town: a glimpse of him was got, the other day, 'walking with large strides into Regent Street,'— in a northerly direction; and then he went over the horizon again, and has not reemerged since."[47] It is clear that in these years Tennyson did not seek out Carlyle as often as he could have. Significance can be attached to what he is reported to have said of Carlyle in 1848 to Elizabeth Rundle, afterward Mrs. Rundle Charles: "You would like

42. Lawrence and Elisabeth Hanson, *Necessary Evil: The Life of Jane Welsh Carlyle* (London, 1952), p. 361. The original letter is in the possession of the Marquess of Northampton.

43. Slater, pp. 436–37.

44. Francis Espinasse, *Literary Recollections and Sketches* (London, 1893), pp. 213–14.

45. Froude, *Carlyle*, III, 422.

46. Wilson, *Carlyle*, V, 11–12. The brother was Frederick, and the subject being meditated upon was King Arthur. But the two brothers did not actually go to Italy at this time. They started but were back in London in two days. Sir Charles Tennyson, p. 232.

47. From the original letter, dated 17 Jan., in the NLS, 546.43. Yet Tennyson seems to have visited Carlyle just a little later. Carlyle wrote to John Forster, 21 March 1849: "Alfred, I think, has left his umbrella here; tell the oblivious Son of Apollo that comfortable truth." MS, Victoria and Albert Museum.

him for one day, but then get tired of him; so vehement and destructive."[48]

The year 1850, the "Golden" one of Tennyson's life, was also important in the history of his friendship with Carlyle. On 1 June *In Memoriam* was published. On 13 June Tennyson married Emily Sellwood. On 5 November he was offered the Laureateship, which he accepted the next day. For some mysterious reason almost none of Carlyle's comments on *In Memoriam* and on Tennyson's appointment to the Laureateship, which must have been interesting enough, have yet come to light;[49] but unquestionably Tennyson's marriage and Carlyle's liking for Tennyson's wife, a liking that was spontaneous and immediate and that continued through the years, did much to strengthen the friendship. He first met Mrs. Tennyson while the Tennysons were at Tent Lodge, Coniston, where they were the guests of Mr. and Mrs. James G. Marshall, who were also Carlyle's friends and hosts. Carlyle appears to have known in advance that the Tennysons would be at Coniston, for on 29 September, from Keswick, on the way there, he included Tennyson's name in a list of the guests who would be there in a letter to his brother John.[50] His first view of Mrs. Tennyson is well described by Hallam Tennyson: "Here for the first time my mother saw Carlyle, who was staying with the Marshalls. The meeting was characteristic; he slowly scanned her from head to foot, then gave her a hearty shake of the hand. Next day he called at Tent Lodge; and, hearing her cough, 'with his invariable kindness,' stole round, while the others were talking, and shut the window which was open behind her."[51] On 1 October he wrote to his wife, "Alfred Tennyson and Mrs. Alfred . . . are here;"[52] and then on 3 October he gave her a detailed account of the newlyweds:

48. Sir Charles Tennyson, p. 231. Carlyle gives a very unfavorable description of Tennyson just before his marriage, in a letter to Dr. John Carlyle, 29 April 1850: "Alfred Tennyson came down with Fitzgerald one evening: very mouldery and dilapidated A. looks;—does nothing but travel in railways and dine; his 'work-arm' seemingly as good as broken." NLS, 524.88.

49. We may wonder whether what Brookfield's diary, 7 Dec. 1853, tells us about Lady Ashburton's manner of reading *In Memoriam* reflects to any degree Carlyle's opinion of the poem: "Lady Ashburton read part of a French Play well, and a bit of *In Memoriam* hurriedly, and rather as if it bored her." The Carlyles were at the Grange at the time of the reading. Wilson, *Carlyle*, V, 66.

50. The original is in the NLS, 513.52. Mrs. Marshall was the sister of Stephen Spring Rice, Tennyson's friend at Cambridge.

51. *Tennyson: A Memoir*, I, 334.

52. Trudy Bliss, *Thomas Carlyle: Letters to His Wife* (Cambridge, Mass., 1953), p. 270.

The Tennysons are lodged in what they call "the Cottage," a plan [place?] similar to a Factor's House or Minister's Manse as I judged; one of the several little Properties which Marshall has bought as they fell in, "to keep them out of bad hands." There Alfred lives with his new better half, for the present; does not mean to stay "a couple of weeks" more: indeed I should judge it much more charming for the Marshalls than for him: "Sir, we keep a Poet!" Softest of soft sowder *plus* a vacant Cottage and to dinner as often as you like *"magna est pecunia prevalebit."* For the rest, Alfred looks really improved, I should say; cheerful in what he talks, and looking forward to a future less "detached" than the past has been. Poor fellow, a *good* soul, find him where or how situated you may! Mrs. T. also pleased me; the first glance of her is the least favorable. A freckly *round*-faced woman, rather tallish and without shape, a slight lisp too: something very *kleinstadlisch* ["small-townish"] and unpromising at the first glance; but she lights up bright glittering blue eyes when you speak to her; has wit, has sense, and, were it not that she seems to be very delicate in health, "sick *without* disorder," I should augur really well of Tennyson's adventure.53

Mrs. Tennyson seems to have had spunk too during these days when Carlyle first knew her. Hallam Tennyson says that Carlyle took a fancy to her partly because, in answer to one of his wild grumbles, she said, "That is not sane, Mr. Carlyle."54

On 5 October Carlyle, now back at Chelsea, wrote a letter to Tennyson, who was still at Coniston, in which he again paid his respects to Mrs. Tennyson and also gave him an account of a horrible misfortune that had befallen a skillful physician of Leamington, a great admirer of both Tennyson and Carlyle. A friend of Carlyle's brother, Dr. John A. Carlyle, he was sensible and brave but ill-starred. He had lost the greater part of his face by a disease known as caries of the bone. After being terribly disfigured he had at last been cured. Carlyle wrote that he had fled to Keswick and that "there he now resides, not idle still, nor forsaken of friends, or hope, or domestic joy—a monument of human courtesy, and really a worthy and rather interesting man. Such is your admirer and mine. Heaven be good to him and us."55 Such a story may have produced another quivering of Tennyson's lip like that caused by Carlyle's tale about Macpherson and his fiddle.

53. *Ibid.*, pp. 271–72; Wilson, *Carlyle*, IV, 318.
54. *Tennyson and His Friends*, p. 133.
55. *Ibid.*, p. 134. Two fragments of the original letter are at Yale University.

Pleasant as Carlyle's meeting with the Tennysons at Coniston had been and as much as Carlyle now liked Mrs. Tennyson, he would not have been Carlyle if his critical faculty had not continued to exercise itself even in his relationship to these friends. His comments on Tennyson continued to be of a rather mixed nature. On 21 December 1850 he wrote to his brother John: "Tennyson appears to be continually hovering about this scene of things; looking out for a house and unable to find one: I have never actually seen him since the evening at Coniston,—nor in fact in my present mood and his do I much wish it."[56] He was very much concerned over the news that all was not well with the child that the Tennysons were expecting, and on 26 April 1851 he wrote to Lady Ashburton: "Finally Mrs. Alfred Tennyson has not prospered, poor soul: they say she is herself doing well."[57] On 25 August following he wrote to Emerson: "Alfred Tennyson, perhaps you heard, is gone to Italy with his wife: their baby died or was dead-born; they found England wearisome: Alfred has been taken up on the top of the wave and a good deal jumbled about since you were here."[58]

Early in 1852 the Carlyles seem to have been with the Tennysons and the Alan Kers one evening at a house in Cheltenham. Mrs. Ker was Tennyson's sister Mary. The Kers were soon to leave for Jamaica, where Mr. Ker had been appointed judge. The following letter of Mrs. Carlyle to Mrs. Tennyson written on the day after their evening refers to the fact that the Kers would soon be leaving England and also, rather touchingly, to a "black cross of jet" that Mrs. Carlyle's mother, who had died in 1842, had given to her:

> 5 Cheyne Row
> Monday [1852]

Dear Mrs. Tennyson,

In the flutter of coming away last night, after a day so unusually *white*; I left, on the toilet of Mrs. Ker's room, a great black cross of jet—important to me enough to have a special message about it; for it was given to me once at parting, by my Mother—who is dead. If it be given into *your* hands, will you take good care of it, till we meet, or till some perfectly safe op-

56. MS, NLS, 513.66.
57. Lawrence and Elisabeth Hanson, p. 405.
58. Slater, p. 474. Emerson had delivered lectures in England in 1848. Occasionally Carlyle could strike a sour note even in reference to Mrs. Tennyson. See Charles and Frances Brookfield, *Mrs. Brookfield and Her Circle* (London, 1906), II, 383 ff.; Wilson, *Carlyle*, IV, 463.

portunity offer of sending it. I would rather be without it a long while, than run any risk of having it lost or broken in any public transit.

Thank you much for being so good to me yesterday, and thanks to your husband for letting me *smoke* with him, and talking to me "all to myself" (as the children say). I hope to hear you do not find the Gloucestershire house feasible, and that you have made peace with the one you are in. Mrs. Ker, I suppose is off by this time. God prosper them, poor souls— uprooting at that time of life is a sorrowful business.

Most truly yours,
Jane Carlyle[59]

Tennyson's "Ode on the Death of the Duke of Wellington" was published on the day of Wellington's funeral, 19 November 1852. Carlyle, who had refused Dean Milman's invitation to be present at St. Paul's for the occasion but who had watched the funeral procession from Lady Ashburton's London home, Bath House, wrote at the time: "Tennyson's verses are naught. Silence alone is respectable on such an occasion."[60] Yet Carlyle had learned through the years to have an admiration for Wellington equal to Tennyson's, and he admired Wellington for the very qualities praised in Tennyson's ode.[61]

59. From the original letter at Yale University. I have normalized the punctuation in this and other letters hitherto unpublished. The dating of this letter is uncertain. A long letter to Carlyle from Alan Ker in the West Indies, 10 May 1856, in the NLS, discussed the Tennysons.

60. Carlyle's letter of regret to Milman, dated 16 Nov. 1852, is in the NLS, 1796.86. In it he says: "On Thursday I am elsewhere engaged for that affair; and indeed could not, in any case, have ventured on St. Paul's, for such a length of time as they predict, and thro' such deluges of hard-elbowed human Stupidity and Irreverance as I see too well there will certainly be." Wilson, *Carlyle*, IV, 449–50; Froude, *Carlyle*, IV, 125–26.

61. Carlyle had written to his mother on 1 Dec. 1834: "In Wellington's shoes I would not willingly be: he thinks to rule Britain like a drill-sergeant; but will find it not answer. As bonny a man I have seen before now lose his head in such a business." *Letters of Thomas Carlyle, 1826–1836*, ed. C. E. Norton (London and New York, 1889), pp. 469 ff. On 19 July 1835 he wrote to his mother after seeing Wellington at a grand review in Hyde Park: "I felt kindly drawn towards the old man. He is honest, I do think, in his fashion; he had fought his way round half the terrestrial Globe, and was got *that* length; at no great distance (from him and me) lay—Eternity too!" *Ibid.*, pp. 534 ff. After seeing Wellington at a grand ball at Bath House, Carlyle wrote in his journal, 25 June 1850: "I had never seen till now how beautiful, and what an expression of graceful simplicity, veracity, and nobleness there is about the old hero when you see him close at hand. His very size had hitherto deceived me. . . . He glided slowly along, slightly saluting this and that other, clear, clean, fresh as this June evening itself, till the silver buckle of his stock vanished into the door of the next room, and I saw him no more. Except Dr. Chalmers, I have not for many years seen so beautiful an old man." Froude, *Carlyle*, IV, 46. Carlyle heard of Wellington's death when he was in Germany doing research on Frederick II, and he wrote from there to Lady Ashburton on 17 Sept. 1852: "Poor old Wellington, I had heard that evening [on the day before] he was dead! . . . In all the world there is not left now, that we know

It was not the feeling that he objected to; it was the ceremony. In him even more than in John Milton there was a Puritan distrust of the ceremonious in both life and literary art as incompatible with sincerity and depth of feeling. The pageantry and bad taste of the funeral procession disgusted him even more than Tennyson's poem;[62] but both were to him a form of mockery. Neither seemed to him in keeping with the death of the leader whom Carlyle had praised as "the only Englishman in the Aristocracy who will have nothing to do with any manner of lie."[63]

Possibly related is an undated story about Carlyle that Espinasse tells, apparently belonging to the period of the early 1850s:

I found him one forenoon deep in the *Acta Sanctorum*, and full of the story of the dealings of an early Christian missionary with some Scandinavian and heathen potentate. "Alfred," he declared, "would be much better employed in making such an episode interesting and beautiful than in cobbling his odes," the occupation in which, when visiting him sometime before, Carlyle had found him engaged, and with the futility of which he had then and there reproached him. I asked Carlyle if the late Laureate did not "stand up" for his literary procedure. "No! he lay down for it," Carlyle replied, doubtless with a reference to Alfred's careless, indolent ways. At that time Tennyson was not so averse, as he became in later years, from being looked at, and positively enjoyed, Carlyle averred, the abundant lionizing bestowed on him during his occasional visits to London.[64]

There was no dislike of Greek literary forms as such in Carlyle's criticism of Tennyson for "cobbling his odes." To Carlyle there were Greeks and Greeks. Plato was to him "high, and radiant, and classically graceful always," "a rare and opulent human genius, and most

---

of, such a man. . . . Farewell to him, the farewell due to heroes." From the original letter in possession of the Marquess of Northampton. When Carlyle attended the funeral of Lady Augusta Stanley in Westminster Abbey in 1876 he was annoyed because the congregation were "kept processioning and antheming and chanting hither, thither, through all the parts of the sublime edifice for about two hours long." He had been told that Queen Victoria herself had planned the ceremony. From the original letter to Lady Ashburton, 21 March 1876, in the possession of the Marquess of Northampton. See also Froude, *Carlyle*, II, 295.

62. See Froude, *Carlyle*, IV, 125–26.
63. Wilson, *Carlyle*, III, 399.
64. Pp. 213–14. No doubt Carlyle wished that Tennyson's visits to him were more frequent. He wrote to John Forster, 1 June [?1855]: "If Alfred do come to you, remind him that there is an old inhabitant living here, whom he ought not to have been so long without seeing." MS, Victoria and Albert Museum.

lofty Athenian Gentleman"; but "very unsubstantial; a beautiful *zodiacal* light," and a person dreadfully "*at his ease* in Zion." On the other hand, he read with pleasure and was always ready to praise Herodotus, Sophocles, Aeschylus, and Homer. He was very much interested in the Greek translations and textual studies of his day, and, according to one report tried vainly to get Tennyson to undertake a translation of Sophocles.[65] In his later years he was to be more successful in getting Browning to translate the *Agamemnon* of Aeschylus. But pomp and ceremony in an ode fared no better with him than the lush, "gorgeous" style of "The Princess" had done.

When "Maud," one of Tennyson's own favorites that he was fond of reading aloud, was published in 1855, it pleased Carlyle no better. He told FitzGerald that it was a "cobweb."[66] On 26 September 1855 he wrote to his brother John: "Tennyson's *Maud* I have never yet read; I tried while at Farlingay, Fitz having it; but wanted heart to persist. A very *mixed* grumble seems to be rising from the general Critical Pig's trough over it,—such as I have seen *you* excite by kicking on the door, at Scotsbrig, in old times!"[67] It was not merely the gorgeous style that Carlyle disliked this time; there was probably very little in the story of "Maud" that would move him, and he did not share Tennyson's sympathetic attitude toward the Crimean War. In the spring of 1854 he had written in his notebook: "A lazy, ugly, sensual, dark fanatic, that Turk, whom we have now had for 400 years. . . . One perceives clearly the ministers [of the British government] go forward in it [war with Russia] against their will. Indeed, I have seen no rational person who is not privately very much inclined to be of my opinion; all fools and loose-spoken inexperienced persons being of the other."[68] Mrs. Brookfield says that on 2 January 1856, when there was great excitement among Lady Ashburton's guests at the Grange over the news that Tennyson was going to read "Maud" aloud to the assembled group, Carlyle refused to listen but took a walk instead, with Mr. Brookfield and Goldwin Smith as his companions.[69] Mrs. Carlyle had to listen, much to her disgust. Despite

65. See Carlyle's letter of 27 April 1852 to J. Llewelyn Davies congratulating him on the translation of Plato's *Republic* that he and D. J. Vaughan had made. In *From a Victorian Post-Bag: Being Letters Addressed to the Rev. J. Llewellyn Davies* (London, 1926), pp. 10–11.

66. Wilson, *Carlyle*, V, 146.

67. From the original letter in the NLS, 525.10.

68. Wilson, *Carlyle*, V, 93.

69. *Mrs. Brookfield and Her Circle*, II, 428–29.

her general fondness for Tennyson, she did not like "Maud" and Tennyson's sensitive feelings about the poem. He had read it to her in manuscript at least three times before, at Chelsea. When he had read it the first time and then asked how she liked it, she had replied, "I think it is perfect *stuff*!" When, discouraged, he insisted on reading it again, she conceded, "It sounds better this time." And after he had read it the third time, she felt compelled to say that she liked it very much. But now, at the Grange in the midst of all the noise and stir of fashionable society, Tennyson's fourth reading was too much for her.[70] She wrote to her uncle's widow, Mrs. George Welsh: "God help me! what a number of '*distinguished*' men have passed through this house since I came into it! . . . Then there have been Poets; Alfred Tennyson among them, going about asking everybody if they like his *Maud*—and reading *Maud* aloud—and talking Maud, Maud, Maud, till I wished myself far away among people who only read and wrote prose or who neither read nor wrote at all.— Oh Heavens! Yes! I am getting to the same conclusion as George Sand, that the only pleasant people to associate with are the idiots!"[71] To the young poet William Allingham she wrote in very much the same vein at this time, but also added some advice concerning the proper behavior of poets: "Alfred Tennyson read *Maud* and other poems aloud to us, and was much made of by all the large party assembled there. He seemed strangely excited about *Maud*—as sensitive to criticisms as if they were imputations on his honor: and all his friends are excited about *Maud* for him! . . . Dear Mr. Allingham, be a poet by all means, for you have a *real gift* that way; but for God's sake beware of becoming too caring about whether your gift is *appreciated* by the million of Jackasses. The nightingale doesn't trouble itself about *appreciation*, and sings none the worse for that."[72]

We are not to infer, however, from what the Carlyles said about "Maud" that their personal relationship with Tennyson even at this time was not a pleasant one. On the very day when Tennyson read "Maud" aloud at the Grange, 2 January 1856, we find Carlyle writing from there to John Forster: "The agreeablest phenomenon at present is Alfred Tennyson, who came two days ago and is still to hold out

70. William Howie Wylie, *Thomas Carlyle: The Man and His Books* (London, 1881, p. 282.
71. Leonard Huxley, ed., "Letters from Jane Welsh Carlyle," *Cornhill Magazine*, N.S. LXI (Nov. 1926), 633–35.
72. Wilson, *Carlyle*, V, 201–202.

a little while. He has a big moustache carefully cultivated, and, with his new wide-awake, looks flourishing. Good company to smoke with in the Conservatory of the place,—tho' he often loses his pipe:—more power to him!"[73] Lieutenant-Colonel David Davidson, an old friend of Mrs. Carlyle's who had grown up in her home town of Haddington, gives an account of an evening spent with the Carlyles and Tennyson at Chelsea, probably in very late 1855 just before the Carlyles went to the Grange, at which the talk could even touch not too unpleasantly upon the Crimean War. When Tennyson suggested that Peter the Great would have been a better subject than Frederick II for Carlyle's writing at the time, Carlyle agreed with him and added, "And it would have been *better for me.*" When the question came up as to whether titles should be accepted when they were offered, Tennyson said that he was disposed to decline such honors for himself and that no title could equal the simple name of "Thomas Carlyle."[74]

As the years passed, the Tennysons sent invitations to the Carlyles to visit them at their beautiful home Farringford, Freshwater, Isle of Wight, invariably, it appears, without success. Mrs. Carlyle was almost never well when the invitation came; and Carlyle was deeply and unhappily involved in writing *Frederick the Great.* Here is part of Mrs. Carlyle's reply to Mrs. Tennyson of 21 January 1857:

You *are* a darling woman to have gone and written to me on the "voluntary principle" such a kind little note! *You* to have been at the trouble to know that *I* was ill! *You* to express regret at *my* illness! I feel both surprised and gratified as if I were an *obsolete* word that some great Poet (Alfred Tennyson for example) had taken a notion to look up in the Dictionary. . . . Wouldn't I like to go and visit you if that man would leave his eternal *Frederick* and come along! nay wouldn't I like to go on my own small basis if only I had the *nerve* for it, which I have not yet! He goes nowhere, sees nobody, only for two hours a day he rides like the wild German hunter on a horse he has bought, and which seems to like that sort of thing. Such a horse![75]

73. From the original letter in the Victoria and Albert Museum.
74. David Davidson, *Memories of a Long Life* (Edinburgh, 1890), 299–309; Wilson, *Carlyle*, V, 151. When Carlyle's *Frederick II* was published, Tennyson attempted to read it but did not enjoy it. For one thing he found it too long. For another, he told Allingham that he had read in it until he found Carlyle saying, "*They* did not strive to build the lofty rhyme," whereupon he flung the book into a corner. Wilson, *Carlyle*, V, 582. See also *Tennyson and His Friends*, pp. 378–79; and Ritchie, pp. 56, 59.
75. Lawrence and Elisabeth Hanson, p. 456.

Another invitation to Farringford is reflected in Mrs. Carlyle's letter of June 1858 to the sculptor Thomas Woolner, a great favorite of the Tennysons:

As to Farringford I need no *representations* to make me feel its desirableness! The idea of being *in the country with the Tennysons* is quite tempting enough; independent of "beauty of scenery" etc. etc.! But till Mr. C is gone to Scotland, and has settled *his* further plans, it is no use, I know, entertaining a plan of my own. There is talk of my meeting him in Yorkshire and in various parts of Great Britain! I must just wait till I know if I am *wanted*, before I think about what I wish. If I am allowed "to wander at my own sweet will," however, and Mrs. Tennyson's angelic invitation be still open then, I should really, I think, be able to muster *faith* and *hope* and even physical *strength* enough to go to her for a few days.[76]

An invitation to Farringford in the autumn of 1862 likewise had to be tactfully refused. Mrs. Carlyle wrote to Mrs. Tennyson from Dover, where she was the guest of Miss Davenport Bromley:

> Dover
> 4th October [1862]

My dear Mrs. Tennyson,

Your kind note has reached me here, this morning; forwarded, unopened by Mr. C., and undevined [*sic*]!

I will not put off answering it, till I shall have talked it over with *him*. I shall not see him till Monday; and cannot reach him by letter any sooner —tomorrow being Sunday. So I will answer at once, what I *know* he would bid me answer, were I beside him. That it is very beautiful and tempting what you propose! but—*impossible*, at this time!— He has a great pressure of work on him, he would throw over the visit to the Grange; only that he had promised it, and put it off—and promised again—and cannot *hither and thither* any more about it this time; as the Ashburtons are going away to spend the winter at Nice. It will be a very short visit however and having performed his engagement, he must rush back home to his work—and not dream of prolonging his holyday [*sic*], by going on to Freshwater *just now*. He hopes another time, in happier circumstances, that "the Destinies" (his particular friends) will permit him &c &c. I know as well that I should be bid say all that, as if he were there saying it!

I return on Monday, and shall then give him your note without telling him what I have written. And if by possibility—or rather by *impossibility*, I have put wrong words in his mouth, I shall be only to [*sic*] happy (I who am not writing Frederick) to unsay them, dear Mrs. Tennyson.

76. *Thomas Woolner*, p. 150.

What a beautiful photograph of your Husband, that new one! And there is as good a one of *my* Husband by the same artist.

Yours very truly,
Jane Carlyle[77]

But in the years just before Mrs. Carlyle's death in April 1866, there were meetings of the Carlyles and Tennysons at Chelsea and at various other places in London. On Tuesday, 5 December 1865, Carlyle wrote to his brother John: "On Sunday Alfred Tennyson was here; had a dilapidated kind of look, but in talk was cheerful of tone."[78] Sir Charles Tennyson says that the Tennysons saw much of the Carlyles early in 1866, "Mrs. Carlyle for the last time on March 22nd, when Lionel played with the little black dog which was to be the cause of her death just a month later." After Mrs. Carlyle's death Tennyson spoke with horror to Mrs. Warre Cornish of the letters of condolence that Carlyle had received. He said that such letters were intolerable. "When my wife dies," he declared, "I want no letters."[79]

The American Civil War, according to Hallam Tennyson, was a dreadful thing to the poet. He had always wanted to see slavery abolished but had hoped to see it done gradually and peacefully. Yet he enjoyed singing "The Battle Hymn of the Republic."[80] His liberalism was always of a very moderate kind. Carlyle was even more conservative, and he refused to be shocked by the institution of slavery or to be moved by reforming zeal toward it. The lot of the black man needed to be improved, he said, but so did that of the white workers in Great Britain. The greatest political fallacy, he believed, was that which assumed that all men were equal and denied that some men were born to command and others to obey. And he simply detested Harriet Beecher Stowe and her "Yankee-Governess Romance," and he never grew tired of scoffing at what he called "Uncle Tomism."

Tennyson was an active member of the Committee that Carlyle helped to organize in 1866 to defend General Eyre, who was being accused of using dictatorial, cruel, and barbarous methods in putting

77. From the original letter in the Yale University Library. I cannot identify the photographs or photographer mentioned by Mrs. Carlyle. The photograph of Tennyson is possibly the benign one, dated April 1861, used as a frontispiece in T. J. Wise, *A Bibliography of the Writings of Alfred Lord Tennyson*, II (London, 1908).

78. From the original letter in the NLS, 518.18.

79. "Personal Memories of Tennyson," *Living Age*, CCCXIII (1922), 477.

80. *Tennyson: A Memoir*, I, 490.

down a rebellion in Jamaica. To Carlyle and Tennyson, as to Ruskin, Kingsley, and other members of the Committee, Eyre had simply done what was necessary in order to reestablish and maintain authority, law, and order. Tennyson, furthermore, felt a certain personal attachment to Eyre because he hailed from Lincolnshire and had attended Louth Grammar School, though after Alfred and the other Tennysons had left it. His defense of Eyre was fully as spirited as that of Carlyle himself. Tennyson wrote to the Committee: "I send my small subscription as a tribute to the nobleness of the man, and as a protest against the spirit in which a servant of the State, who has saved to us one of the islands of the Empire, and many English lives, seems to be hunted down."[81]

Many of Carlyle's letters show his willingness to use his influence to help people who had undertaken worthwhile tasks. Such were the letters that he wrote to help Professor F. J. Child, when he was editing the ballads, to get access to the papers left by Sir Walter Scott; and such were the letters he wrote on behalf of Emerson and others who were trying to collect the papers and gather information concerning Margaret Fuller's life in Europe. Such also is the following letter. Mrs. Oliphant was interceding in behalf of her friend Sir John Frederick Bridge, one-time organist of Westminster Abbey, who wished to compose part-music to some of the lines of *In Memoriam*. She had been informed that Tennyson did not wish any part of this poem set to music. But we know that in this instance he yielded and that the music was composed.

Chelsea,
8 Oct^r, 1869

Dear Tennyson,

Mrs. Oliphant, whose Note this accompanies, is an old and esteemed Friend in this house; distinguished in literature (*Life of Edwd Irving*, etc. etc.), and, what is best of all, a highly amiable, rational, and worthy Lady. Be pleased to answer her needful little Inquiry, and oblige withal,

Y^{rs} ever truly,
T. Carlyle[82]

---

81. Wilson, *Carlyle*, VI, 102; Waugh, pp. 199–200.

82. From the original letter in the Yale University Library, published in incomplete form in *Tennyson: A Memoir*, II, 237. Hallam Tennyson says he found the letter in the bottom of a tobacco box that Carlyle had given to his father as a pledge of eternal brotherhood. See also Wilson, *Carlyle*, VI, 195–96.

As the two old friends continued to meet from time to time, sometimes with and sometimes without other members of their families,
Carlyle recorded his impressions of Tennyson with a technique occasionally suggesting the brilliance of his earlier pen portraits. On
2 April 1870 he wrote to his brother John: "I had a *second* night of
insomnia, and a weary walk yesterday seeking out Alfred Tennyson's
London Lodgings,—upon whom I felt bound to 'leave a card'; he
having called here last Sunday on very good-natured terms, and
borne me ditto company on my walk. Good-natured, almost kind; but
rather dull to me! He looks healthy yet, and hopeful; a stout man of
60,—with only one deep wrinkle, *crow* wrinkle, just under the cheek
bones.— I was lucky enough (for my then mood, lucky) to find nobody; nothing required but a *card*."[83] In the autumn of 1873 he wrote
to the same brother: "Tennyson was distinctly rather wearisome [at
John Forster's]; nothing coming from him that did not smack of utter
indolence, what one might almost call torpid sleepiness and stupor;
all still enlivened, however, by the tone of boylike naivete and total
want of malice except against his *Quarterly* and other unfavorable
Reviewers."[84] Toward the end of this year Mrs. Tennyson wrote in
her journal: "The boys walked with him [Tennyson] to call on Mr.
Carlyle, who thought that we were to be ruined by a 'government of
party, headed by a gentleman Jew who sits at the top of chaos.' However he preferred Disraeli to Gladstone. Mr. Carlyle called upon me,
and was very interesting and touching about old days, and was afraid
of tiring me by overtalking."[85] About the same time Carlyle wrote
again to his brother John: "Have seen Tennyson, with his two boys,
this week; and, day before yesterday, Mrs. Tennyson called, who is
very weak and old looking but full of innocent eagerness and I believe ardor in smoothing down all asperities from her Alfred's sublime career; writes all his letters for him, etc. etc. I ought to call there
this very day, and will, never having done it before; & they go, it
seems, on Monday morning. Poor souls after all."[86]

To Carlyle, as to FitzGerald, Tennyson's later poems were dis-
appointing and fell far short of what earlier poems like "Ulysses" had
led him to expect. Although Carlyle never completely lost his faith

83. *New Letters of Thomas Carlyle*, II, 265–66.
84. *Ibid.*, 300–301.
85. *Tennyson: A Memoir*, II, 152.
86. From the original letter, dated 20 Dec. 1873, in the NLS, 527.104.

in Tennyson as a poet, his comments on his later work and career are highly critical. *The Idylls of the King*, for instance, he could praise only with the greatest reservations. On 27 January 1867 he wrote to Emerson: "We read, at first, Tennyson's *Idyls*, with profound recognition of the finely elaborated execution, and also of the inward perfection of *vacancy*,—and, to say truth, with considerable impatience at being treated so very like infants, though the lollipops were so superlative."[87] In talking with Leslie Stephen in March 1874, he agreed that Tennyson had been too timid in expressing doubts. But he again praised "Ulysses" and contrasted it with Tennyson's later poems "tender to the happy views of secluded ladies." Stephen quotes Carlyle as saying: "The old poem has the true heroic ring. Tennyson has declined into a comparatively sentimental and effeminate line of writing, mere aestheticisms, instead of inspiring a courageous spirit to confront the spiritual crisis. *The Idylls of the King* could not be the epic of the future, but at best a melodious version of conventional and superficial solutions of the last problem. King Arthur has too much of the 'Gigman' to be a great leader of modern man."[88]

Sir Charles Tennyson believes that the work of Carlyle, Green, and Froude, which was making historical studies more realistic and human, had much to do with Tennyson's turning to the historical drama about 1874. But Tennyson's first effort in this field, *Queen Mary*, did not please Carlyle, who wrote to John Forster on 17 September 1875: "Alfred Tennyson's so-called Shakespearean tragedy I had read before leaving home with little *disappointment*, but with a dismal inclination to exclaim Scene after Scene, "Did you ever?' "[89] And he wrote to his brother John on 26 October following: "Have you seen Alfred Tennyson's sublime Tragedy?— Mary says you read it while here and will not long to know more of it; but will have to read the newspaper comments on the acting of it, I suppose. To me it seems no more stone-dead, ineffectual 'Tragedy' had ever come across my experience—at all events for me it shall fight its own battle & do me neither ill n'a gude from this date."[90]

To this brother, likewise, in a letter of 30 January 1875, Carlyle

---

87. Slater, pp. 552–53.
88. Wilson, *Carlyle*, VI, 323–24. By "Gigman" Carlyle usually meant a prosperous, conventional-minded, middle-class conformist who was chiefly concerned about respectability.
89. From the original letter in the Victoria and Albert Museum.
90. From the original letter in the NLS, 528.41.

ridiculed what he had heard was Tennyson's manner of refusing a baronetcy offered to him by Disraeli: "Tennyson too, it appears, had refused; and in a way much less clear than mine in respect of courtesy & otherwise: Gladstone, he rather proudly intimated, had already offered him this 'Baronetcy'; which Alfred had declined for his own person, but accepted for his eldest Son & Successor when himself should have disappeared; to which it had to be answered that if Gladstone or any other friendly potentate were in office on the Poet Laureate's decease *he* c^d certainly make his Son a Baronet; but otherwise the British Constitution c^d not at this stage effect such a thing!"[91]

C. E. Norton records in his journal on 13 January 1873 that he had recently heard Carlyle talk at one of John Forster's dinners and that among the topics touched on were "Browning's spoiling; Tennyson's decline, and the exaggerations of his admirers, his maltreatment and perversion of the old Round Table Romance."[92] Generally speaking, however, Carlyle believed that Browning's later work was worse than Tennyson's. He told Allingham in 1871: "Browning has far more ideas than Tennyson, but is not so truthful. Tennyson means what he says, poor fellow! Browning has a meaning in his twisted sentences, but he does not really go into anything, or believe much about it. He accepts conventional values."[93] And in 1876 he told Allingham: "Tennyson's later things are better than Browning's. But Browning is a man of great abilities."[94] Even later, in the summer of 1879, he surprised Mrs. Richard Greville by ranking Browning after Tennyson and declaring: "Alfred from the beginning took a grip at the right side of every question."[95] As for Swinburne and his followers, with whom Carlyle could feel almost no sympathy, Carlyle naturally considered Tennyson's work infinitely superior. According to William Black, the old Carlyle in talk with him showed great esteem for Ten-

91. From an unpublished part of the original letter in the NLS, 528.28. Disraeli offered Carlyle the title of Grand Cross of the Bath in a letter of 27 Dec. 1874, and in a letter of 29 Dec. Carlyle turned it down. Wilson, *Carlyle*, VI, 342–47.

92. *Letters*, I, 457.

93. William Allingham, *A Diary*, ed. H. Allingham and D. Radford (London, 1907), p. 205.

94. *Ibid.*, p. 244.

95. Wilson, *Carlyle*, VI, 452. Tennyson enjoyed Browning's playful verses on the Carlyles. See *Tennyson: A Memoir*, II, 230. For a companion study to this article, see my "The Carlyle-Browning Correspondence and Relationship," *Bulletin of the John Rylands University Library of Manchester*, LVII (Autumn 1974, Spring 1975), 213–46, 430–62.

nyson and some uneasiness lest the "Banjo Byrons" might displace him.[96]

Carlyle's various references to his delight in smoking a pipe with Tennyson is obviously, in considerable part, praise of Tennyson as a listener and talker. If we may believe Edward FitzGerald and others, Tennyson's talk was excellent.[97] In conversation with Carlyle, he was almost never merely passive. He often followed Carlyle's lead but usually made substantial contributions of his own to the subject under discussion, and occasionally, as FitzGerald's account of the argument over immortality testified, would flash out in vigorous disagreement with Carlyle. The samples of their talk preserved by Hallam Tennyson in *Tennyson: A Memoir* (II, 233–37) show further that Carlyle often but by no means always brought the conversation to a point. When the two visited the British Museum together, for instance, and examined the Greek and Roman statues, it was Carlyle who exclaimed characteristically, "Neither man nor god can get on without a decent jaw-bone, and not one of them has a decent jawbone." Once when Tennyson had been recalling an experience with Macaulay, Carlyle said, "Alfred, Macaulay was afraid of you, you are such a black man." In a discussion of death Tennyson said that he would like to get away from the tumult of civilization and see the splendors of the Brazilian forests before he died. Carlyle said that he too would like to get away from it all. Tennyson said that if he were young he would head a colony out somewhere. And the old Carlyle replied: "O, ay, so would I, to India or somewhere: but the scraggiest bit of heath in Scotland is more to me than all the forests of Brazil. I am just twinkling away, and I wish I had had my Dimitis long ago." At times Carlyle praised Tennyson's poetry. He told him that "The May Queen" was "tender and true" and that his niece sometimes said it to him. He expressed great admiration for Tennyson's historical play *Harold* and said that it was "full of wild pathos" and that it was founded on the Bayeux tapestry, which was "a very blessed work indeed." What he said when Tennyson read him "The Revenge" has

96. Wilson, *Carlyle*, VI, 357–58.
97. Sir Charles Tennyson says that on a visit to Holland in the summer of 1841 the poet spent some time with an American, Dr. Shepherd, from whom he concealed his name. Shepherd for a time thought that he must be Carlyle "because of his unconventionality and the brilliance of his conversation" until on one occasion Tennyson mentioned Carlyle (p. 189).

often been quoted: "Eh! Alfred, you have got the grip of it." Once when they were talking about Goldsmith, both made delightful comments:

Carlyle. Goldie was just an Irish blackguard, with a fine brain and sun-like eyes, and a great fund of goosery.
Tennyson. And of tender-heartedness: I love Goldie.

Both were fond of jokes, which certainly at times were broadly based, roughly masculine, and hardly suited for the tender ears of shy maidens. G. S. Venables believed that a joke about a corpse at a Scotch drinking party that Carlyle was very fond of repeating had been told him by Tennyson.[98] Neither squeamishness nor fear of Carlyle but rather the Tennyson of the Lincolnshire dialect poems is in the story that the elder Henry James told about the two. Carlyle, he said, had been defending one of his heroes, William the Conqueror, for cutting off the legs of 1,200 men in Cambridgeshire and expressing the wish that such a leader would again appear in England, when Tennyson burst out: "Let me tell your returning hero one thing, then, and that is that he had better steer clear of my precincts, or he will feel my knife in his guts very soon."[99]

After Carlyle's death in early 1881 and the publication of Froude's works on the Carlyles that soon followed, Tennyson, we know, was one of those most shocked. Moncure D. Conway records an experience that reflects Tennyson's great concern about the matter:

When the excitement about Froude's publications was at its height, I was one day at the London Library, and soon after Lord Tennyson's son entered and told me his father wished to speak to me. He was in his carriage at the door, and said, "I saw you go into the door there, and wished to tell you an incident of some interest. When Carlyle's appointment of his literary executor was announced, I asked him why he had chosen Froude. He answered, 'Because of his reticence'!"

I should certainly have equally ascribed that character to Froude, and said so to Tennyson, whose distress at the publications was extreme. But I could not give any theory of the astounding affair. Tennyson's main trouble seemed to be that the bones of Carlyle should be flung about, and one evening he repeated to my wife and myself a quatrain he had composed about the delight of apes in seeing a man dragged down to their own apehood. The lines impressed me as mistaken. The people generally were as much troubled as Tennyson at the lowering of Carlyle.[100]

When the Virginia schoolmaster Gordon McCabe visited the old Tennyson and asked whether he would appoint a Boswell, Tennyson "boomed out" his negative reply: "I don't want to be ripped up like a hog when I'm dead." He also told McCabe that he did not believe "all that stuff about Mrs. Carlyle's being so unhappy and Carlyle's being such a selfish tyrant. I was constantly there during those years that Froude writes of, and I never saw anything but the greatest affection between them."[101] And Hallam Tennyson says that his father would say to the family: "Mr. and Mrs. Carlyle on the whole enjoyed life together, else they would not have chaffed one another so heartily."[102]

Wilfrid Ward reports that in his conversations with Tennyson a few years after Carlyle's death Tennyson spoke of Mrs. Carlyle as "a most charming, witty converser, but often sarcastic." He added that she never spoke before her husband, who absorbed the conversation. Ward asked Tennyson, "Did he not listen to *you* when you talked?" "In a way," Tennyson replied, "but he hardly took in what one said." Tennyson's talk with Ward touched on Carlyle in various other ways. At one point he said, paradoxically, that Carlyle "was at once the most reverent and the most irreverent" man he had known. At another he said, "I admire his estimate of Boswell and hate Macaulay's." When the conversation came round to the first Lady Ashburton, he told Ward: "Carlyle was at his best *rollicking* at the Ashburton's house— the Grange. He and Lady Ashburton were the life of the party. Those parties were very interesting, and Lady Ashburton was a woman of great brilliancy. She liked Carlyle, but I think at that time, if she had

100. *Autobiography: Memories and Experiences* (Boston and New York, 1904), II, 212.
101. "Personal Recollections," pp. 723, 730–31. See also A. C. Gordon, *Memories and Memorials of William Gordon McCabe*, 2 vols. (Richmond, Va., 1925), *passim*.
102. *Tennyson: A Memoir*, II, 233. Tennyson was himself very curious about an earlier man-and-wife relationship that in the public mind was mysterious and controversial, that of Byron and his wife. He told McCabe that he had once said to Thomas Campbell, "I am told that you are, perhaps, the only man in England who really knows why Lord and Lady Byron separated," and that Campbell did not affirm or deny but replied significantly, after a pause, "You may be sure, Tennyson, of one thing —that Lord Byron *was a very bad man*." "Personal Recollections," p. 727.

a favorite, it was George Venables." When the subject of heroes and hero-worship was discussed, Tennyson, despite what he had once said to Carlyle in protest against the methods of William the Conqueror, was generally inclined to agree with Carlyle. He spoke of Carlyle's persistent feeling that nineteenth-century England needed a strong man and of how he would say at times, "Our Cromwell is being born somewhere." Tennyson agreed with Carlyle that none of the British statesmen of the second half of the century were really great rulers. When one eminent statesman, probably Gladstone, was mentioned, he told Ward: "You cannot rule, as he thinks he can, with a silk glove. You must have an iron gauntlet; though you need not always make people feel the iron."[103]

A delightful visit that Tennyson made to the Queen at Osborne, probably that of 7 August 1883, suggests the meeting that Carlyle had had with her at the Westminster Deanery in 1869. She had found Carlyle very "singular," partly because he had told her that he was an old man and had begged her permission to sit down. Now, some years later, the Queen motioned Tennyson to a chair, saying, "You and I, Mr. Tennyson, are old people, and we like to sit down." And so they sat and talked.[104]

The full impact of Carlyle's mind on Tennyson's poetry can merely be suggested here. It is important and should be investigated fully. It is concerned with such matters as common sense and practicality in Carlyle's Abbot Samson and Cromwell and in Tennyson's first Northern Farmer, the Duke of Wellington, and King Arthur; with a protest against all kinds of shams and a holding up of veracity and sincerity as high ideals; with a literary art making extensive use of materials handed down by the past but also vitally interested in contemporaneous economic, social, political, and religious problems; with a praise of honest doubt but also with faith in the imagination and a conception of reality that emphasizes the part mystery has in the nature of things; with a persistent protest against materialism and a fresh interpretation of the Christian religion; with the protection of individualism against mass pressures and many kinds of conformity; and of a style that at times makes much of suggestion, silence, simplicity, and brevity and at other times unfolds itself in forms that are colorful, complex, irregular, richly ornamented, rough-

---

103. "Talks with Tennyson," New Review, XV (July 1896), 80–81.
104. Rawnsley, p. 194. See also Sir Charles Tennyson, pp. 467–68.

grained, expansive, or baroque. In the background of almost all that they wrote is shadow; and in the heart of almost every subject they were able to find music, each in his own way.

A short, undated letter of Carlyle to Tennyson, which seems to belong to the 1840s or early 1850s when their lives and their friendship were in full vigor, may serve here as an appropriate ending. Still intensely alive, it has a spirit of invincibility that faces and yet scarcely admits the possibility of death. Hence, it may be read both literally and symbolically with pleasure:

Chelsea, Friday Morng

Dear Tennyson,

With the rising sun we discover Venable's stick, safe, leaned ag^t the wall of the garden, where you and I first went to smoke. I leave it at Moxon's for you; it is already there while you read this.

Thanks for your visit of yesterday. Luck on your journey; and all your journies in this world, and in the next; and come and hail me, now and then, while there is possibility of doing it! Courage!—

Yours ever truly,
T. Carlyle[105]

105. From the original letter in the Yale University Library.

THE CARLYLES AND THACKERAY

The relation of Carlyle to Thackeray, like that of Carlyle to most of his other major contemporaries, is complex. Temperamentally and in many matters concerning art and literary taste extremely different, Carlyle was an untamed, almost savage Thor among writers, working in the tradition of biblical, seventeenth-century, and German models, while Thackeray with supreme aplomb sought for and to a considerable degree achieved the urbanity and surface brilliance of a Horace or a Pope. Both had highly social natures, but Carlyle's friendships were based in the main on the picturesqueness and even the rough edges of a rugged and pronounced individualism, whereas Thackeray's ways were the accepted ways of the world, which usually kept the paths smooth for those who would come to him as friends. Despite important differences and philosophies of life, however, Carlyle and Thackeray found much to admire in one another and a considerable amount of common ground to stand on.[1]

As early as August 1831, in a letter to Ottilie von Goethe, the poet's daughter-in-law, Thackeray asked for the identity of the person who had written Carlyle's song beginning "Now yarely soft my boys," which he understood had appeared in Frau von Goethe's magazine *Chaos* but which he had found in *Fraser's Magazine*.[2] On 25 January 1832 he wrote again to her to say, "The bearer of this letter [Henry Reeve] comes recommended to your father-in-law by Mr. Carlyle."[3] Although Carlyle, like Thackeray, was still an obscure writer at this

---

1. For a helpful summary of the relationship, see Gordon N. Ray's Introduction to his edition of *The Letters and Private Papers of William Makepeace Thackeray* (Cambridge, Mass., 1946), I, cvi–cix (hereinafter refered to as Ray, *Letters*); and his *Thackeray: The Uses of Adversity* (1811–1846), (New York, Toronto, London, 1955), pp. 215, 382.

2. *Chaos* ran from 28 Aug. 1829 to the middle of February 1832. Carlyle's poem mentioned by Thackeray was "The Sower's Song," which appeared in the thirty-seventh number of the journal, 25 April 1830, and in *Fraser's Magazine*, III (April 1831), 390. He later altered the first line of the poem to read "Now hands to seedsheet, boys." See his *Works*, Centenary Edition (London, 1896–99), XXVI, 472–73. Carlyle made other contributions to *Chaos*, namely, "What Is Hope," "Faust's Curse," "Tragedy of the Night-Moth," and "All Mute." Thackeray, who became an intimate friend of Ottilie von Goethe, also made contributions to *Chaos*, beginning in 1830. See Trevor D. Jones, "English Contributors to Ottilie von Goethe's 'Chaos, X,'" *Publications of the English Goethe Society*, N.S., IX (1931–33; reprinted 1966), 68–91.

3. Ray, *Letters*, I, 184.

time, quite clearly Thackeray knew of him and even of his correspondence with Goethe. Furthermore, one of Thackeray's best
friends, Charles Buller, whom he had known at Cambridge, had been
tutored many years before by Carlyle and was still Carlyle's intimate
friend. Buller had always admired Carlyle greatly, and it appears that
Thackeray too had come to share this admiration. He wrote in his
diary for 29 and 30 April, 1832, "I wish to God, I could take advantage
of my time & opportunities as C Buller has done— It is very well to
possess talents but using them is better still. . . . To be sure as to
advancement & society & talent he has had greater than most men,
not the least of them that Carlyle was his tutor."[4]

Just when Carlyle and Thackeray first met has not been precisely
determined. Both wrote for *Fraser's Magazine* in the early years of
its existence, and their pictures appear in Maclise's well-known picture "The Fraserians," published in the magazine for January 1835.
Carlyle contributed to the very first issue, February 1830; and
Thackeray may have contributed to the magazine as early as February 1831, certainly as early as May 1834. Furthermore, another of
Thackeray's old Cambridge friends, John Sterling, was a friend of
Carlyle, and Carlyle himself states that he had seen Thackeray at
both the Bullers' home and the Sterlings' before he finished *The
French Revolution* and went to Scotland for a vacation in late June
1837.[5]

That Jane Carlyle, later to establish for herself a high reputation
not merely as a letter writer but as a reader of novels and an authority
on their merits, also knew Thackeray and had won his confidence by
this time is attested by the following passage from an undated letter
to her husband of late July or early August 1837. It deals, scarcely
justly, with Thackeray's review of Carlyle's *The French Revolution,*
which would appear in the *Times* on 3 August and which she had
read in proof.

Apropos of the *French Revolution*; I have read Thacker[a]y's article in
proof—, and as Tommy Burns said of Eliza Stodart's leg—"it's nae great
ting"! so small a *ting* indeed that *one* barrel of the Inevitable-Gun may be
decidedly said to have missed fire— He cannot boast of having, in any
good sense, "*served Thacker[a]y*" however he may have "*served Carlyle.*"
When you consider that this is Thacker[a]y's *coup d'essai*, in his new part

4. *Ibid.*, I, 196.
5. Ray says that Thackeray first met Carlyle soon after leaving Paris and settling in
London in March 1837 (*ibid.*, I, cvi).

of political renegade, you will however, make some allowance for the strange mixture of bluster and platitude which you will find in his two Columns, and rather pity the poor white man, wishing with Mrs Sterling so often as his name comes up that "he would but stick to his sketchings."[6]

Carlyle, however, was at least moderately pleased with Thackeray's review, a copy of which Jane sent to him in Scotland. To his brother John he wrote on 12 August: "I understand there have been many reviews of a very mixed character. I got one in the 'Times' last week. The writer is one Thackeray, a half-monstrous Cornish giant, kind of painter, Cambridge man, and Paris newspaper correspondent, who is now writing for his life in London. I have seen him at the Bullers' and at Sterling's. His article is rather like him, and I suppose calculated to do the book good."[7] On 18 August he wrote to Jane with less restraint and gave in full detail an account of how much he and two of his other brothers enjoyed reading Thackeray's review together:

He [John Stuart Mill in a recent letter] says in reference to Thackeray's Article, which he attributes to Sterling, it will get me many new readers: *esto*! By the by this Article did us all some good here. It was a sunny monday morning; Alick had been up here, Jamie and I were escorting him homewards: daily for above a week had the little messenger flown to the Post Office without any effect at all; what was Goody about, why was there no tidings or token? Lo, on the top of Potter's Knowe (the height immediately behind Middlebie), Betty Smeal unfastening her luggage; presenting two Newspapers with their strokes in Goody's hand; one of which was this *Times*! They made me take place under the shade of the head [hill] and beech-trees; and read it all over to them, amid considerable laughter and applause. One is obliged to men in these circumstances who say even with bluster and platitude greater than Thackeray's, Behold this man is not an ass.[8]

Many years later, after Jane's death in 1866, Carlyle touched on the subject of Thackeray's review once more, this time with mixed

6. From the MS letter in the Pierpont Morgan Library. "Pity the poor white man" is coterie speech deriving from Mungo Park's *Travels in the Interior Districts of Africa* (London, 1799). Cf. *The Collected Letters of Thomas and Jane Welsh Carlyle*, Duke-Edinburgh Edition (Durham, N.C., 1970), III, 390.

7. MS, NLS, 523.51.

8. MS, NLS, 610.34. Edward FitzGerald's comment in a letter to Thackeray of 1 September was not so favorable: "As to Carlyle's book [*The French Revolution*] I looked into it, but I did not desire to read it—I do not admire the German school of English." Ray, *Letters*, I, 347.

feelings intensified by his memory of the great encouragement his
wife had given him at the time and by his deep sense of loss now
that she was gone:

Thackeray's laudation, in the *Times*, I also recollect the arrival of (how
pathetic now *Her* mirth over it to me!)—but neither did Thackeray inspire
me with any emotion [any more than the hostile review in the *Athenaeum*],
still less with any ray of exultation: "One other poor judge voting," I said
to myself; "but what is he, or such as he? The fate of that thing is *fixed!*
I *have* written it; that is all my result." Nothing now strikes me as affecting
in all this, but *Her* noble attempt to cheer me on my return home to her,
still sick and sad; and how she poured out on me her melodious joy, and
all her bits of confirmatory anecdotes and narratives; "Oh, it has had a
great success, Dear!"—and not even she could irradiate my darkness, beautifully as she tried for a long time, as I sat at her feet again by our own
parlor-fire. "Ah, you are an unbelieving creature!" said she at last, starting
up, probably to give me some tea. There was, and is, in all this something
heavenly;—the rest is all of it smoke, and has gone up the chimney, inferior
in benefit and quality to what my pipe yielded me. I was rich once, had
I known it, very rich; and now I am become poor to the end.[9]

In spite of Jane's satirical comments on it, Thackeray's long review,
coming at a time when it could be extremely helpful in furthering
Carlyle's career, was well calculated to produce the feeling of jubila-
tion that Carlyle and his two brothers felt when they read it at Potter's
Knowe near Dumfries. It was a friendly, well-intentioned, but at the
same time well-balanced piece of criticism. In the main, it defends
Carlyle and calls attention to his great merits as a writer and historian.
"Never did a book sin so grievously from outward appearance,"
Thackeray wrote, "or a man's style so mar his subject and dim his
genius. It is stiff, short, and rugged, it abounds with Germanisms and
Latinisms, strange epithets, and choking double words, astonishing
to the admirers of simple Addisonian English, to those who love history as it gracefully runs in Hume, or struts pompously in Gibbon—no
such style is Mr. Carlyle's." But the reader, Thackeray said, "speedily
learns to admire and sympathize; just as he would admire a Gothic
cathedral in spite of the quaint carvings and hideous images on door
and buttress." Carlyle's nonpartisan point of view is highly praised:
"He is not a party historian like Scott, who could not, in his benevolent
respect for rank and royalty, see duly the faults of either: he is im-

9. *Reminiscences*, ed. C. E. Norton (London and New York, 1887), II, 288.

partial as Thiers, but with a far loftier and nobler impartiality. . . . It is better to view it [history] loftily from afar, like our mystic poetic Mr. Carlyle, than too nearly with sharp-sighted and prosaic Thiers. Thiers is the *valet de chambre* of this history, he is too familiar with its dishabille and off-scourings: it can never be a hero to him." Lazy readers, repelled by Carlyle's strange style or merely amused by his grotesqueness, would never be able to understand or appreciate Carlyle's philosophy or his remarkable power of description. Thackeray quoted with admiration Carlyle's account of the charge upon the Bastille, which, he said, is given "with an uncouth Orson-like shout," and passages dealing with Mirabeau and Charlotte Corday. He added: "The reader, we think, will not fail to observe the real beauty which lurks among all these odd words and twisted sentences, living, as it were, in spite of the weeds; but we repeat, that no mere extracts can do justice to the book; it requires time and study." Finally, after giving long extracts from Carlyle's account of the deaths of Danton and Robespierre, Thackeray concluded in a vein that permitted his own philosophy and his own penchant for satire to creep in (here at the expense of Carlyle's critics):

The reader will see in the above extracts most of the faults, and a few of the merits, of this book. He need not be told that it is written in an eccentric prose, here and there disfigured by grotesque conceits and images; but, for all this, it betrays most extraordinary powers—learning, observation, and humour. Above all, it has no CANT. It teems with sound, hearty philosophy (besides certain transcendentalisms which we do not pretend to understand), it possesses genius, if any book ever did. It wanted no more for keen critics to cry fie upon it! Clever critics who have such an eye for genius, that when Mr. Bulwer published his forgotten book concerning Athens, they discovered that no historian was like to him; that he, on his Athenian hobby, had quite out-trotted stately Mr. Gibbon; and with the same creditable unanimity they cried down Mr. Carlyle's history, opening upon it a hundred little piddling sluices of small wit, destined to wash the book sheer away; and lo! the book remains, it is only the poor wit which has run dry. . . . The hottest Radical in England may learn by it that there is something more necessary for him even than his mad liberty—the authority, namely, by which he retains his head on his shoulders and his money in his pocket.[10]

Early in 1838 some papers entitled "Old England" done in imitation of Carlyle, which he believed were written by Thackeray, ap-

10. Thackeray's review was reprinted in his *Sultan Stork and Other Stories and Sketches*, ed. R. H. Shepherd (London, 1887).

peared in the *Times*. On 10 January he wrote to his brother Alexander: "By the bye, a man in the *Times* Newspaper, for the last ten days, is writing diligently a series of Papers called 'Old England' extravagantly in my manner; so that several friends actually thought it was I! I did not see them till last night; and had a loud laugh over them then. It is that dog Thackeray (my Reviewer in the Times); you remember the Potter Knowe; he, I am persuaded, and no other: I take it as a help and compliment in these circumstances; and bid it welcome so far as it will go." The papers, however, signed "Coeur de Lion," were written not by Thackeray but by Disraeli.[11]

From 27 April to 11 June 1838 Carlyle gave his second series of lectures, *On the History of Literature*. It is highly probable that Thackeray attended some of these and that two of the reviews of them in the *Times* are by him. In the review of 1 May the reporter states that he was struck by "the look of strong and ardent individual character" in the lecturer, "such as fashion and outward advantages never can form, and sometimes tend to stifle. And in harmony with this was the whole discourse which he delivered—often rough, broken, wavering, and sometimes almost weak and abortive; but full throughout of earnest purpose, abundant knowledge, and a half-suppressed struggling fire of zeal and conviction, which gave a flash of headlong impulse to faltering sentences, and lighted up and clothed in dignity, meanings half obscure, and undeveloped images." Unquestionably, the speaker was motivated by "an insatiable thirst for truth" and had attained "a devout faith in reason and conscience, . . . a large and pure humanity, . . . [and] a comprehensive and guiding knowledge as to the whole progress and all the achievements of man's nature." The forthcoming lectures promised much, especially to those who were already familiar with Carlyle's "generous, imaginative, and soul-fraught writings."

The second review, that of 22 May, covered three of Carlyle's lectures and dealt delightfully with Carlyle's comments on the German race in the Middle Ages, on Dante, and on Cervantes:

The three last lectures have presented to us in bold forms and startling light the great spectacle of the Middle Ages. We have seen the grey and huge ruins of the Roman world as their background, with the energetic masses of the German race swelling up and bursting across these, while

11. For Carlyle's letter and evidence of Disraeli's authorship, see Edwin W. Marrs, *The Letters of Thomas Carlyle to His Brother Alexander* (Cambridge, Mass., 1968), pp. 434–35.

hymns and shrines have been noticed as arising slowly above the tumult, and Gothic life and Christian faith have been painted in all their grave depth and rich variety of aspect. In the midst of this noble and stirring world, the lecturer evoked for us with a hand of quiet power the great singer of old Christian Europe, "that deep voice from the innermost heart of man"—Dante, the exiled Florentine. His three visionary kingdoms, the Inferno, Purgatorio, and Paradiso, were laid open as embodying on the mysterious stage of an extra-mundane eternity the three essential conditions of man's existence, such as we know it here on earth—its penal agonies, its hopeful progress, and its assured and peaceful triumph. The lecture which followed on the disclosure of this gigantic scenery, and which is the last delivered, transferred us into superstitious, chivalrous, and loyal Spain, and after a description, to which we can only allude, of the various elements of race and faith which entered into the formation of the old Castilian mind, it introduced us to the presence of the maimed and destitute soldier, "Naked Adam," as he called himself, of "Spanish posts" [poets?]—the genial and heroic Cervantes, author of *Don Quixote*. This man has never, we are persuaded, been made so thoroughly and delightfully intelligible to Englishmen as by Mr. Carlyle's description, which presented him as completely realizing both the old Teutonic courage and daring, and the purely Christian element, unknown to the Pagan world, of meek generosity and affectionate self-sacrifice. This lofty and idealizing character, united with a profound sense of the hindrances which it must needs meet with in practical life, and which through all his days entangled Cervantes, was animated and brightened by the truest, kindliest humour, which was the proper genius of the man, and stamped itself for all ages and nations in the imperishable and exquisite creation of *Don Quixote*. The few words we have here set down can at best give no conception of the inimitable earnestness and humane glowing sincerity of the lecturer's discourse, which perpetually break out in touches of high eloquence and the deepest pathos, and would, in our estimate, amply excuse far more than his imperfections in the purely technical part of oratory.[12]

On 20 August 1836 Thackeray had married Miss Isabella Shawe in Paris. After the Thackerays settled in London in 1837 the social relationship soon established with the Carlyles was made more felicitous not merely by common friends like Sterling and Buller but also by the honest criticism and words of encouragement for Carlyle con-

12. For evidence of Thackeray's authorship and a full text of the two reviews, see Harold Strong Gulliver, *Thackeray's Literary Apprenticeship* (Valdosta, Ga., 1934), pp. 92, 198–200.

tained in Thackeray's reviews in the *Times*. The pleasant nature of the situation is reflected in a letter from Mrs. Thackeray to Mrs. Carmichael-Smyth, 15 May 1839, in which she wrote: "Besides there was a report that Charles Buller was to be a cabinet minister. . . . We met Charles Buller at Mr. Carlyle's yesterday he laughed and joked about it but of course neither said yea or nay."[13] In late December of the same year Thackeray wrote to his mother: "We were to have gone to Carlyle's tonight, but 4 good dinners last week were too much for my poor dear insides and I was compelled last night to dosify."[14] Thackeray wrote to his mother on 18 January 1840 that he had recently paid a visit to Chelsea "to see Carlyle and Mrs. C.—pleasanter more high-minded people I don't know."[15] Carlyle, on his side, encouraged Thackeray in his efforts to write fiction. After the last numbers of *Catherine*, Thackeray's novel to show what criminals really are, appeared in *Fraser's Magazine* in early 1840, Thackeray proudly wrote to his mother: "The judges stand [up] for me: Carlyle says Catherine is wonderful, and many more laud it highly, but it is a disgusting subject & no mistake."[16] Clearly by the middle of 1840 Carlyle had for Thackeray become an extremely important part of the London scene. On 29 June of that year he proposed writing for *Blackwood's* a light humorous sketch of London life that would include such things as "the London Library, Tom Carlyle and the 'Times,' as well as other matters."[17]

The tremendous admiration Thackeray had for Carlyle in this period is reflected particularly in the generous and even striking praise he gave to his *Miscellanies* in four volumes (1838–39), first appearing like *Sartor Resartus* in an American edition. In the late 1839 Thackeray wrote to his mother: "I wish you could get Carlyle's Miscellaneous Criticisms, now just published in America. I have read a little in the book, a nobler one does not live in our language, I am sure, and one that will have such an effect on our ways of thought and prejudices. Criticism has been a party matter with us till now, and literature a poor political lacquey—please God we shall begin ere

13. Ray, *Letters*, I, 382. The State University of Iowa possesses a very friendly letter from Thackeray to Mrs. Carlyle, undated, but since it was written from 13 Great Coram Street, Brunswick Square, it belongs to the period from May 1838 to April 1843, when Thackeray lived there.
14. Ray, *Letters*, I, 404.
15. *Ibid.*, I, 413.
16. From a letter dated 11–15 Feb., *ibid.*, I, 421.
17. *Ibid.*, I, 451.

long to love art for art's sake. It is Carlyle who has worked more than any other to give it its independence."[18] Twentieth-century scholars and critics may be astonished to find the phrase "art for art's sake" in such an early English context, though Gautier, who would become Thackeray's friend and visit him in England some years later, had used it earlier; but they may be even more astonished to find Thackeray applying the phrase with considerable emphasis to the writings of Thomas Carlyle. If Carlyle himself had been called on to defend Thackeray's application of the phrase to his writings, however, he probably would have made some remark about what he owed to old Samuel Johnson and Johnson's great respect for the dignity and independence of the man of letters.

Thackeray's confidence in Carlyle's scholarship and faith in his authenticity as a historian as evidenced by *The French Revolution* caused him to come to his defense when Carlyle was attacked by some newspapers in 1839–40 in what came to be known as the *Vengeur* controversy, a controversy in which the press of both Great Britain and France engaged. In giving an account of a naval battle near Brest between the British and the French that took place on 1 June 1794, Carlyle in the first edition of *The French Revolution* had described in glowing colors and with dramatic vividness the heroism displayed by many members of the crew of the French ship *Vengeur*, who even when the ship was sinking stayed with it, firing from the upper deck when the lower one was under water, refusing to strike but keeping the tricolor proudly aloft, and shouting *Vive la République* until the ship completely disappeared under water. Some months after his book was published Carlyle discovered evidence that convinced him that virtually the whole story of the heroism of some members of the crew of the *Vengeur* was a fabrication put in circulation soon after the battle by a French journalist and historian named Barère[19] for purposes of patriotism and propaganda, and soon was accepted as truth and handed down through the years as traditional by both the French and British press. Particularly telling as evidence against the accepted story was a letter printed in the *Sun* in November 1838 from Rear-Admiral A. J. Griffiths, who had been on board the British ship *Culloden* during the battle, had seen the whole action, and had helped to rescue and receive as prisoners on

18. *Ibid.*, I, 396.
19. Bertrand Barère de Vieuzac (1755–1841).

the *Culloden* many members of the *Vengeur's* crew, including its captain Renaudin. Griffiths refuted practically every article of the story that would exemplify French *gloire* and said that the crew of the sinking *Vengeur* acted as members of a sinking ship usually do act: they took to their boats and did what they could to save their lives. In *Fraser's Magazine* for July 1839 Carlyle published an article on the sinking of the *Vengeur* in which he examined the evidence provided by Griffiths and others and concluded that the heroic version which he and others had accepted was based on a hoax perpetrated by Barère. In addition in the second edition of *The French Revolution* (1839), after retaining his stirring account of the glorious behavior of the French crew when the *Vengeur* sank, he followed it by a paragraph that emphatically denied it all and compared Barère with other tellers of tall tales, "Mendez Pinto, Munchhausen, Cagliostro, Psalmanäzar," and declared that this story "may be regarded as Barrère's [sic] masterpiece; the largest, most inspiring piece of *blague* manufactured, for some centuries, by any man or nation."[20]

The controversy continued to rage in the press, however, even though new evidence appeared to support Carlyle's conclusions. Thackeray more and more took an interest in the question, entirely convinced that Carlyle was right. In an undated letter of probably late 1839 Carlyle wrote to his friend Mrs. Mary Rich, eldest daughter of Sir James Mackintosh: "It appears, a certain official man has discovered in the French Naval Archives the original dispatch of Rénaudin [sic] the *Vengeur* Captain, entirely confirming our old Admiral's account; and moreover has been so honest as publish it in the *Revue Britanique* some months ago;—of which publication the *National* Newspaper has *not* taken any notice! I am inquiring for the thing, but have not yet got it. Thackeray talks of making some trumpet-blast about it. As the *Vengeur* article is to go into this new *Miscellanies* edition, I must see it myself."[21] Thackeray did make his "trumpet-blast" in defense of Carlyle in a twelve-page article in *Fraser's Magazine* for March 1840, in which he examined all the evidence. The article is entitled "On French Criticism of the English, and Notably in the Affair of the Vengeur" and is printed under the amusing pseudonym "Nelson Tattersall Lee Scupper." It incorporates a second

---

20. See Carlyle's *Works*, IV, 241–42; I. W. Dyer, *A Bibliography of Thomas Carlyle's Writings and Ana* (Portland, Me., 1928), p. 253.
21. MS, Professor Frederick W. Hilles.

and even more convincing letter from Admiral Griffiths, who quotes from a letter he had received from Captain Renaudin of the *Vengeur* in confirmation of his testimony. Speaking to one Labédollière, to whom the whole article as one of *Fraser's* "Epistles to the Literati" is addressed, Thackeray insists: "Sir, your country needs no such lies to support its reputation for valour; and if it finds a sham jewel among those ten thousand real stones that ornament its crown of glory, character demands that the paste should be flung away." He quotes and then translates from the French a poem by the "celebrated and sublime Jules Baget" attacking Carlyle as a calumniator, but then adds a spoofing last stanza ending in "Aid me, ye Muses nine— 'Cockdoodledoodledoo!'" He also quotes a long letter signed by Captain Renaudin "and seven others" giving a detailed account of how the ship went down. Finally, Thackeray concludes in terms of realistic common sense: "That certain men did cry out ['*Vive la République*'] we believe, although Admiral Griffiths did not hear them; that all did their duty most gallantly, none will deny; that they hung their colours *en berne* (in token of distress), implored succour, and all rushed for the boats which were sent to relieve them, we know from Renaudin's own testimony;—but guns firing, colours flying, crew refusing to surrender, and shouting *Vive la République!*—all this is what Mr. Carlyle calls a windbag, which Admiral Griffiths and Captain Renaudin have flapped out. And this made the point of the story, and formed the theme of Barrère's declamation." Carlyle naturally found gratification and satisfaction in Thackeray's article. "Thackeray's article is well enough," he wrote to his brother John on 2 March 1840; "I am glad that I did not write any further on the subject."[22] Possibly the whole episode caused Carlyle to intensify and clarify his thinking on the exact nature of heroism: his lectures for the spring of this year were to be entitled "On Heroes, Hero-Worship and the Heroic in History." Perhaps too it may be a small, shadowy part of the background of a work called *Vanity Fair: A Novel without a Hero*.

In July 1840 Thackeray brought out his first book, *The Paris Sketch Book*. Carlyle took due note of it in a letter to his brother John: "Thackeray has brought out a book; kind of picture-book about Paris."[23] But the year was not a good one for Thackeray. Since his marriage in 1836 his wife had borne him three daughters: Anne Is-

22. MS, NLS, 523.77.
23. MS, NLS, 523.90.

abella, later Lady Ritchie, born 9 June 1837; Jane, born 9 July 1838, who died the following year; and Harriet Marian ("Minny"), later Mrs. Leslie Stephen, born 27 May 1840. In September 1840 on the way from London to Cork Mrs. Thackeray attempted to drown herself, and the first symptoms of what was to be her lifelong insanity revealed themselves. After spending a few weeks in Cork, Thackeray took his wife to London and from there to Paris, where for a brief period he placed her in an institution for the insane. In May 1841 he placed her in the care of a nurse. Later that year he took her to a sanatorium near Boppard on the Rhine; and in February 1842 he left her with Dr. Puzin at Chaillot. Eventually, in 1845, he brought his wife back to England and placed her in the hands of Mrs. Bakewell in Camberwell. Mrs. Thackeray lived on insane until 1894, long after Thackeray's own death. During the early years of Mrs. Thackeray's illness Carlyle learned of it and wrote about it with compassion to his mother in a letter of 16 June 1841: "Alas, here is a poor man, by name Thackeray, just come in from Paris; where his poor Wife is left, having fallen *insane* on his hands some six or eight months ago! I believe he is not well off for cash either, poor Thackeray (tho' born a rich man); he is very clever, with pen and pencil; an honest man, in no inconsiderable distress! He seems as if he had no better place, of all the great places he once knew, than our poor house to take shelter in! — Welcome the coming guest, especially him that is in misfortune! I must go down to poor Thackeray, and bid my Mother farewell."[24]

Another old Cambridge friend of Thackeray's, Edward FitzGerald, had heard with admiration Carlyle's lectures on *Heroes* in 1840 and later described the lecturer as "very handsome then, with his black hair, fine Eyes, *and a sort of crucified expression.*"[25] In September of 1842 the painter Samuel Laurence brought FitzGerald to meet Carlyle at Chelsea.[26] FitzGerald proved to be an extremely helpful friend, not only then, when Carlyle was deeply involved in his book on Cromwell, but seven years later, when he toured Ireland. FitzGerald's father owned the battlefield of Naseby, which Carlyle had walked over in company with Dr. Arnold of Rugby. Carlyle wrote to his brother John on 29 September 1842: "A certain Mr Fitzgerald,

    24. MS, NLS, 520.106. There is a letter from Thackeray in Paris to Jane Carlyle, 25 Feb. [1841], in which in considerable distress he writes of his great need of money to keep his ill wife in a *pension* (MS, NLS, 665.45).
    25. David A. Wilson, *Carlyle* (London and New York, 1923–34), III, 88.
    26. *Ibid.*, 184.

an acquaintance of Thackeray's, who had been here before, called one night about a week ago; told me he had just come from Naseby; *he*, or his Father, was now proprietor of Naseby Battle-field!"[27] Through later meetings with FitzGerald and correspondence with him Carlyle was able to achieve a considerable degree of accuracy and fullness of detail in writing his description of the famous battle. For many years the future translator of *The Rubáiyát of Omar Khayyám* (1859) was known to Carlyle chiefly as the heir to Naseby, the relative of wealthy landowners in Ireland, and the friend of Thackeray. And even some years after the famous translation was published, Carlyle told Charles Eliot Norton: "I've read that little book which you sent to me, and I think my old friend FitzGerald might have spent his time to much better purpose than in busying himself with the verses of that old Mohammedan blackguard."[28]

Thackeray's tour of Ireland, which he recorded delightfully in his *The Irish Sketch Book* (1843), took place from 4 July to 1 November 1842. Many of the places he visited and people he saw were the same as those that Carlyle would see and write about after his tour of Ireland in the late summer of 1849. FitzGerald's uncle, Peter Fitz-Gerald, and his family seat Halverstown, near Kildare, figure largely in both narratives. Thackeray wrote in his brilliant conversational style, Carlyle in a somewhat vivid, choppy, emphatic way. Thackeray was more interested in manners, Carlyle in Ireland's horrible economic plight after two years of potato famine. But both were sharp observers and keen critics of Irish institutions, both were very much interested in many individual Irishmen, particularly those who stood out because of either personal oddity or strength of character, and both gave minimum attention to descriptions of places as such.

The Carlyles saw Thackeray soon after his return from Ireland. On 11 November 1842 Carlyle wrote to his brother John: "We had Thackeray here, two nights ago; fresh from Ireland, and full of quizzical rather honest kind of talk: he is now off to Paris; has a Book on Ireland with caricatures nearly ready: I cannot but wish poor Thackeray

27. MS, NLS, 524.37. See Thomas A. Kirby, "Carlyle, FitzGerald, and the Naseby Project," *Modern Language Quarterly*, VIII (Sept. 1947), 364–66. See also Wilson, *Carlyle*, III, 184.

28. Charles Eliot Norton, *Letters* (Boston and New York, 1913), I, 425–27; see also 471.

well. Nobody in this region has as much stuff to make a man out of, —could he but *make* him."[29]

During the years immediately following, the Carlyles saw much of Thackeray, sometimes with feelings that were happy, sometimes with feelings that were unpleasant if not unhappy, and sometimes with feelings that were mixed. Thackeray, for his part, maintained his feeling of admiration and affection for the Carlyles consistently. Frequently FitzGerald or others came to Chelsea with Thackeray. On 23 March 1843 Jane Carlyle wrote to her cousin Jeannie Welsh:

Today my head is specially bad and I am not up to a decent letter—in compensation I send you a document from Thackeray, which has wit enough in it to make up for any sort of scrap. To understand it aright I must tell you that he and FitzGerald came here that evening we were at the musical lecture, the *only* evening in which they *could* have failed to find at least one of us at home— Ever since I have been thinking occasionally that I should write him a note of regrets and fix an evening—but my intention like too many others during the last week had gone to the paving of *the bad place!*— To sharpen my sense of hospitality there arrived this letter from Fitzboodle two days ago which would have made even old Pitrucci [*sic*] "in the Character of Heraclytus" laugh. Pray return it to be present among my genuine treasures.[30]

A few days later she again wrote to her cousin:

Thack[era]y and FitzGerald were to dine with us that day (Friday)—I baked a mutton pie and a raspberry tart in a state of great suffering—got through the dinner—hoped to get through the tea—and then promised myself to go to bed—but just before the men came up stairs, my affairs reached a consummation—I fainted—and had to be carried to bed—and lay for three hours alternating between fainting and retching—Helen blubbering over

29. MS, NLS, 524.39. Among the caricatures made about this time, according to John Sterling, was a "first-rate pen sketch of Carlyle sitting on a tub and smoking— only to be paralleled by the Prophets of Angelo—I never laughed more heartily at anything." See Lionel Stevenson, *The Showman of Vanity Fair* (New York, 1947), p. 105. Thackeray undoubtedly felt very kindly toward Carlyle in this period. In a letter to Jane dated 30 March [1842] he expressed his appreciation for the praise that he said Carlyle had bestowed upon *The Great Hoggarty Diamond*, which had begun to appear in *Fraser's Magazine* for Sept. 1841 (MS, NLS, 665.46).

30. MS, NLS, 1891.224. Heraclitus of Ephesus (fl. 500 B.C.) was known as "the weeping philosopher." Scipione Petrucci, whom Jane knew as a member of Mazzini's circle, had because of his melancholy disposition acquired the nickname of Heraclitus. See *Jane Welsh Carlyle: Letters to Her Family, 1839–1863*, ed. Leonard Huxley (New York, 1924), pp. 22 and 31.

me—and the men, increased by the arrival of Spedding and Robertson, raging and laughing in the adjoining room— Oh I assure you I have not passed such an evening for a good while.[31]

There were many joyous occasions, however. One of these was the birthday party of Nina Macready, daughter of the actor, who was absent from home at the time. In a letter to Jeannie Welsh of 23 December 1843 Jane Carlyle gave full details. Thackeray, Dickens, John Forster, Daniel Maclise, and others were all there. "It was the *very* most agreeable party that ever I was at in London—everybody there seemed animated with one purpose to make up to Mrs Macready and her children for the absence of 'the Tragic Actor' and so amiable a purpose produced the most joyous results. . . . Only think of that excellent Dickens playing the *conjuror* for one whole hour—the *best* conjuror I ever saw—(and I have paid money to see several)—and Forster acting as his servant. . . . Then the dancing—old Major Burns with his one eye—old Jerdan of the Literary Gazette, . . . the gigantic Thackeray &c &c all capering like *Maenades*!! Dickens did all but go down on his knees to make *me*—waltz with him!" After supper there was champagne and the making of speeches.

A universal country Dance was proposed—and Forster *seizing me round the waist*, whirled me into the thick of it, and *made* me dance!! . . . In fact the thing was rising into something not unlike the *rape of the Sabines* . . . when somebody looked [at] her watch and exclaimed "twelve o'clock!" . . . Dickens took home Thack[era]y and Forster with him and his wife '*to finish the night there*' and a *royal* night they would have of it I fancy! . . . After all—the pleasantest company, as Burns thought, *are* the *black-guards*!— . . . I question if there was as much witty speech uttered in all the aristocratic, conventional drawing rooms th[r]o'out London that night as among us little knot of blackguardist literary people who felt ourselves above all rules, and independent of the universe![32]

In another letter to her cousin (15 February 1844), Jane mentioned an amusing note from Dickens commenting on "an absurd mistake of Thackeray's who put five shillings into Robertson's hand one night in the idea he was reduced to the last 'extremity of fate'!! and then (what was much more inexcusable) told Dickens and myself of the transaction before witnesses in Mrs. Macready's drawing room!"[33]

31. MS, NLS, 1891.247. The letter is undated but was probably written on 8 April.
32. MS, NLS, 1892.95.
33. MS, NLS, 1892.146. Carlyle identifies Robertson as "the blusterous John Robert-

On the more serious side, we find during these years Thackeray proposing to no avail in a letter to Bradbury and Evans of 26 February 1844 that they put him at the head of a new "slashing brilliant, gentlemanlike, sixpenny, aristocratic, literary paper," a weekly that would carry signed reviews and articles "by good men, Buller, Carlyle, Forster, Milnes, [Fitz]Gerald, and a University man or two."[34] Not until he became editor of the *Cornhill Magazine* in 1859 was this dream to be in any part fulfilled. His loyalty to Carlyle continued. "I got angry," he wrote in a letter to Richard Bedington, 13 May 1844, "on reading 'The Miser's Son' at some reflections on Thomas Carlyle made by a young author."[35] Yet it was quite possible even during these years when the friendship was at its best for Thackeray to catch Carlyle in one of his dour moods. On 30 July 1845 Carlyle wrote to Jane, who was visiting in Liverpool, that on the day before he had had "a grand ride" but that "after that, while at tea—Thackeray: no work farther done. Weary, weary."[36]

The most disagreeable episode in the relation of Carlyle to Thackeray arose, however, in January 1846; it stemmed from a comment made by Carlyle to Charles Buller on the trip to the Mediterranean that Thackeray made from August 1844 to February 1845 as the guest of the Peninsular and Oriental Steam Navigation Company, a trip that he recorded in his *Notes of a Journey from Cornhill to Grand Cairo* (1846). Carlyle told Buller that for Thackeray to accept a free berth for this voyage was like "a blind fiddler going to and fro on a penny ferry-boat in Scotland, and playing tunes to the passengers for half-pence." Buller very indiscretely repeated the remark to Thackeray. Thackeray, hurt and indignant, confronted Carlyle, only to be told by him frankly: "It is undoubtedly my opinion that, out of respect for yourself and your profession, a man like you ought not to have gone fiddling for halfpence or otherwise in any steamboat under the sky."[37] A year or two later, according to Francis Espinasse,

---

son, whom Mill had at that time as Sub-editor, or Subaltern generally in the Westminster Review; and who took absurdish airs on that dignity." See *New Letters and Memorials of Jane Welsh Carlyle, ed. Alexander Carlyle,* (London and New York, 1903), I, 124.

34. Ray, *Letters,* II, 163.

35. *Ibid.,* II, 167. The author of *The Miser's Son* has not been identified, but William Harrison Ainsworth published a novel called *The Miser's Daughter,* illustrated by Cruikshank, in 1842. Ainsworth was thirty-eight years old at that time.

36. MS, NLS, 611.191.

37. See Wilson, *Carlyle,* III, 354–57; Ray, *Letters,* I, cvii–cviii; Stevenson, pp. 139,

Carlyle spoke of the sagacity and knowledge of his own uneducated father, even though "he could not tell you of the bitter ale consumed in the City of Prophets," a comment interpreted as a thrust at Thackeray's *Cornhill to Cairo*.[38] Thackeray became increasingly critical of Carlyle and showed his resentment in various ways. In a letter to FitzGerald of early 1846 he touched upon the ugly incident and in so doing employed an uglified spelling of Carlyle's name: "Gurlyle has called twice upon me and I've returned the visit once in rather a haughty & patronizing way"; and FitzGerald in a later letter refers to the "Gurlyles."[39] Carlyle, never a great admirer of the novel as a literary genre, in a letter to Browning on 23 June 1847 wrote critically of both Thackeray and Dickens: "Dickens writes a *Dombey and Son*, Thackeray a *Vanity Fair*; not *reapers* they, either of them. In fact, the business of rope-dancing goes to a great height."[40] On his side, Thackeray kept up the fight. In the spring of 1848 he wrote to Fitz-Gerald: "My dear old Yedward It is not true what Gurlyle has written to you about my having become a tremenjuous lion. . . . Gurlyle is immensely grand and savage now. He has a Cromwellian letter against the Irish in this weeks Examiner. I declare it seems like insanity almost his contempt for all mankind, and the way in which he shirks from the argument when called upon to préciser his own remedies for the state of things."[41] And yet the amenities and the sense of fair play were in considerable part preserved. On 4 August 1848 Thackeray wrote to his mother: "Tom Carlyle lives in perfect dignity in a little house at Chelsea, with a snuffy Scotch maid to open the door, and the best company in England ringing at it. It is

---

159. Stevenson says that Carlyle's comment goaded Thackeray to make a sarcastic retort in *Punch*. Yet Moncure D. Conway says that Carlyle told him that while Thackeray was writing *Cornhill to Cairo* and "with urgent work on hand, [he] escaped from invitations, callers, and letters, and went off from his house without leaving any address," a messenger came to him one night from a public house nearby "with a request from Thackeray for the loan of a Bible." *Autobiography* (London, Paris, etc., 1904), II, 4. See also Stevenson, p. 135.

38. Francis Espinasse, *Literary Recollections and Sketches* (New York, 1893), p. 151.

39. Ray, *Letters*, II, 227, 265. Yet there does not seem to have been an open breach, certainly not between Thackeray and Jane Carlyle at least. In an effort to help Thackeray find a proper governess for his daughters, Jane had told her German friend Amely Bölte of the position. Thackeray wrote to Jane on 25 July 1846 (?): "For God's sake stop Mme. Bölte. . . . I don't want a Gerwoman." *Ibid.*, II, 242–43.

40. Wilson, *Carlyle*, III, 384.

41. Ray, *Letters*, II, 365–66.

only the second and third chop great folks who care about Show."[42]
On 24 August the Carlyles and John Forster took Jeannie Welsh to
hear a concert by Jenny Lind that Thackeray also attended.[43] Perhaps there was some friendly talk with Thackeray there, for just four
days later Carlyle wrote to his brother John: "We are next to go and
dine with Thackeray, who has been at Spa and back again; not a
lovely outlook either."[44] In December 1848 Thackeray wrote rather
cryptically in a letter to Mrs. Brookfield: "As I was writing to Carlyle
last night (I haven't sent the letter as usual and shall not most likely)
Saint Stephen was pelted to death by Old Testaments; & Our Lord
was killed like a felon by the law which he came to repeal."[45]

The friendship continued to progress on its uneasy, uncertain, irregular course, with a great deal of nip and tuck on both sides. But
it did not die, and neither man quite lost his deep, underlying respect
and even affection for the other. On 5 January 1849, Carlyle wrote to
James Marshall, secretary of the Duchess of Weimar: "Thackeray,
Dickens and the others carry on their affairs; Thackeray has risen
quite into fashion since you were here. Nothing can convince me that
the like of all that is a noble employment under this Sun; or that it is
in fact any employment at all, different from what we see at Astley's
Amphitheatre, or what the black Bayaderes perform, in Oriental
Countries, for some big surfeited rajah, who pays them surprisingly."[46] As Gordon Ray points out, however, "The coolness that had
developed between Thackeray and Carlyle did not prevent Mrs. Carlyle from inviting Anny and Minny to her little haven at Chelsea,"
and he quotes Lady Ritchie's charming account of how Jane served
the two little girls hot chocolate on cold winter days.[47] Just the same,
Jane wrote to Jeannie Welsh on 27 February 1849: "I must make an
end for the present—and try to walk off the headache I got at a dinner
at Thackeray's last night where *you* were not."[48] When Jane was

42. *Ibid.*, II, 418. About this time Jane wrote to Carlyle: "I brought away the last
four numbers of *Vanity Fair* and read one of them during the night. Very good indeed,
beats Dickens out of the world." Stevenson, p. 166. On 14 July 1848 (her birthday)
Thackeray had written to her apologetically, "Our dear little party of pleasure is put
off." MS, NLS, 665.65. Very probably they were planning to celebrate the completion
of *Vanity Fair*, finished on 29 June.
43. Wilson, *Carlyle*, IV, 56.   45. Ray, *Letters*, II, 472–73.
44. MS, NLS, 512.89.   46. MS, British Museum, 3032, f.5.
47. *Thackeray: The Age of Wisdom (1847–63)* (New York, Toronto, London, 1958),
pp. 20–21.
48. MS, NLS, 1893.174.

away on a visit, Carlyle wrote to her on 5 April 1849: "I have got *Nowvigisch Näturchen* for you; *Pendennis* too (not by myself yet read): hope the tea will be agreeable!"[49] On 12 May following we find the Carlyles, Samuel Rogers, Thackeray, and others at a dinner party given by Dickens.[50] Just five days later Jane wrote to Jeannie Welsh to complain about a rather horrible practical joke perpetrated upon her by Thackeray. "Thackeray is returned from Paris; he was here with FitzGerald the other evening. I was upstairs when they came in, and on coming into the room went to Thackeray first, to shake hands *in enthusiasm*—as one does after a journey to Paris—but I gave a loud scream on finding a small, cold, hard hand, as of a dead fairy—laid in mine. It was *your* hand which he had fastened at the end of his sleeve! I declared the joke to be a heartless one, which seemed to vex him greatly. He repeated a dozen times during the evening that he wished he had not done it."[51] On 8 June Thackeray wrote to Mrs. Brookfield: "And now concerning Monday. You must please remember that you are engaged to this house at 7—I have written to remind the Scotts—to ask the Pollocks, and the Carlyles are coming."[52]

Early in his tour of Ireland during July and August of 1849 Carlyle visited Edward FitzGerald's relatives Peter FitzGerald and Mrs. Purcell at their home Halverstown near Kildare, as Thackeray had done seven years before. In his letters written at the time and in his *Reminiscences of My Irish Journey in 1849* he gave an account of his experience there. More interesting, however, was a comparison of Thackeray with Dickens that he made in conversation with Charles Gavan Duffy, who acted as his guide during a considerable part of the Irish tour. Duffy's account follows:

I suggested that the difference between his [Dickens'] men and women and Thackeray's seemed to me like the difference between Sinbad the Sailor and Robinson Crusoe.

Yes, he said, Thackeray had more reality in him and would cut up into a dozen Dickenses. They were altogether different at bottom. Dickens was doing the best in him, and went on smiling in perennial good humour; but Thackeray despised himself for his work, and on that account could

49. MS, NLS, 613.292.
50. Wilson, *Carlyle*, IV, 88–90.
51. MS, NLS, 1893.187. Just what the "hand" was and in what sense it belonged to Jeannie Welsh has not been determined.
52. Ray, *Letters*, II, 548.

not always do it even moderately well. He was essentially a man of grim, silent, stern nature, but lately he had circulated among fashionable people, dining out every day, and he covered this native disposition with a varnish of smooth, smiling complacency, not at all pleasant to contemplate. The course he had got into since he had taken to cultivate dinner-eating in fashionable houses was not salutary discipline for work of any sort, one might surmise.

When Duffy asked Carlyle whether he saw much of Thackeray, Carlyle gave him a detailed account of his comment on Thackeray's Mediterranean tour and the ill-feeling that grew out of it. But he also told Duffy that, as to criticism, Thackeray, John Sterling, and John Mill had written of his work in various quarters with appreciation and more than sufficient applause, but that criticism in general on books, men, and things had become the idlest babble.[53]

In spite of this comment on Thackeray, Carlyle knew very well that there could never be any agreement between Thackeray and himself on the subject of the hero. George Venables, who knew both men well, wrote: "He [Carlyle] had naturally but little sympathy with Thackeray's instinctive dislike of greatness, as it is exemplified in his antipathy to Marlborough and to Swift. I think it was after a conversation between them on the character of Swift that I heard Carlyle say, 'I wish I could persuade Thackeray that the test of greatness in a man is not whether he (Thackeray) would like to meet him at a tea-party.' He liked Thackeray himself, and I think he never spoke of him with the contempt which, before he became comparatively intimate with Dickens, he expressed for 'the infinitely small Schnüspel, the distinguished novelist.' "[54]

Back at Chelsea, Carlyle wrote to his brother John on 6 October:

Thackeray has been dangerously ill, still lies close in bed: "slow inflammation," that to be produced by too diligent a course of dinners,—poor Thackeray! He has had formally to suspend his Pendennis nonsense; and everybody says he had better give it up, the total, and even, tiresome inanity of it being palpable to all creatures. Dickens again is said to be flourishing beyond example with his present series of funambulisms [David Copperfield!]:— I read one No of it (I am quite fallen behind) last

53. *Conversations with Carlyle* (London, Paris, and Melbourne, 1896), 75–77, 91; Wilson, *Carlyle*, IV,112; V, 304.
54. Ray, *Letters*, I, cix.

night; innocent waterest of twaddle with a *suspicion* of geniality,—very fit for the purpose in view, which Th's is not.[55]

On 10 November he again wrote to his brother: "Thackeray is still utterly weak, but is reported out of danger."[56] Thackeray's illness was a long one and recovery was slow, but by late November he was pretty well back on his feet again. Henry Reeve reports in his diary that on 19 December he had dinner at Bryan Waller Procter's with Kinglake, Harriet Martineau, the Carlyles, and Thackeray.[57] Thackeray wrote to Mrs. Procter on 3 January 1850: "I will come with much pleasure on Sunday and I should like to have Carlyle and Reeve over again only I know it's wrong and impossible."[58] Just why it was impossible for Carlyle and Reeve to come is explained in a letter that Thackeray wrote to James Spedding on 5 January: "The fun goes out of a man at 40: where are the jokes that came in such plenty? Ah me as Tom Carlyle says he was here the other day and very kind. I wish you could have heard him though, in a different mood, at Procter's. He fell foul of Reeve who had a stiff white neckcloth, which probably offended the Seer. He tossed Reeve and gored yea as a bull he chased him and horned him: for an hour or more he pitched him about ripping open his bowels and plunging his muzzle into Reeves smoking entrails. Reeves had to appear perfectly goodhumoured all the time of the operation, and indeed bore it with wonderful face & patience."[59] According to an account of the incident that Dickens gave to Yates, Carlyle became furious when Reeve smugly and suavely tried to dismiss a subject, perhaps Ireland, that Carlyle considered important.[60]

Just a few days later at a dinner given by Misses Agnes and Mary Berry, Thackeray was even more severe in his judgment upon Carlyle. Miss Kate Perry gives this account of the conversation: "Carlyle was discussed, and Miss Berry asking what his conversation was like, Kinglake said Ezekiel which we all thought a happy illustration of the denouncing style with which he cries out woe and desolation to all existing ordinances, men, and habits of the world. Thackeray said that he was a bully—attack him with persiflage and he was silenced,

55. MS, NLS, 513.23. In a letter to Jane of October, probably written some days later, Thackeray reports, "I am getting better." Ray, *Letters*, II, 597.
56. MS, NLS, 513.27.
57. Wilson, *Carlyle*, IV, 235.
58. Ray, *Letters*, II, 626.
59. *Ibid.*, II, 628.
60. Wilson, *Carlyle*, IV, 235–36.

in fact Carlyle is no longer the Prophet he used to be considered—I remember his palmy days when his words were manna to the Israelites."[61] Thackeray's friend FitzGerald, however, was much more tolerant when Carlyle's *Latter-Day Pamphlets*, written in an extremely angry tone, began to appear in February. He wrote to Tennyson: "Do you see Carlyle's *Latter-Day Pamphlets*? They make the world laugh, and his friends rather sorry for him. But that is because people will still look for practical measures from him. One must be content with him as a great satirist who can make us feel when we are wrong, though he cannot set us right. There is a bottom of truth in Carlyle's wildest rhapsodies."[62]

Whatever their comments on the side and their true feelings toward one another may have been, Carlyle and Thackeray continued to meet and maintain the social amenities from time to time. Often they met with other members of the Ashburton circle, which from about 1848 until the death of Lady Ashburton in 1857 was one of the most brilliant groups in the history of British literature and culture. Needless to say, however, things did not always go off well even at Lady Ashburton's parties. In early March 1850 Thackeray wrote to Mrs. Brookfield: "We had a dull dinner at Lady Ashburton's, a party of Barings chiefly. . . . Carlyle glowered in the evening."[63] But on 12 June Carlyle attended a dinner given by Thackeray for Charlotte Brontë.[64] We find both Carlyle and Thackeray at Addiscombe, one of the Ashburton country houses, on 30 June, when word came that Peel had been thrown from his horse the day before, an accident from which he soon died.[65] Thackeray and Mrs. Carlyle were among Lady Ashburton's guests at The Grange in early October. Jane wrote to Carlyle on 6 October: "Thackeray is here—arrived yesterday—greatly to the discomfort of Henry Taylor evidently who 'had the gang all to himself' so long. First he (Thackeray) wrote he was coming; then Lady A. put him off on account of some *Punch*-offence to the Taylors. Then Thackeray wrote an apology to Taylor!! Then Lady A. wrote that he

61. Ray, *Letters*, I, cviii. For an anecdote concerning Thackeray's own use of persiflage to choke off a Unitarian minister's serious theological discussion, see Stevenson, p. 193.
62. *Tennyson and His Friends*, ed. Hallam Tennyson (London, 1911), p. 132.
63. Ray, *Letters*, II, 647.
64. *Ibid.*, II, 674 n.
65. Wilson, *Carlyle*, IV, 288–89. Jane wrote to Helen Welsh on Thursday, 4 July: "Mr. C. and Thackeray came to dinner on Sunday but had to return at night every room being taken up." MS, NLS, 1893.231.

was to come after all, and went to Winchester to meet him, and Taylor sulked all yester evening and today is solemn to death. In fact he had been making a sort of superior *agapemone* here in which *he* was the Mr. Price, *The Spirit of Love*—and no wonder he dislikes the turn that has been given to things by the arrival of the *Spirit of Punch*."[66] Soon Carlyle himself came down, as was duly noted by Thackeray in a letter to Mrs. Brookfield.[67] On 10 October Carlyle wrote from The Grange to his brother John: "We are a shifting party, Thackeray and Rawlinson (Bagdad) went today; a nice little French-woman (Mrs Craven) remains; and here are the *wheels of newcomers* while I write: a shifting party; with whom I have not much to do beyond looking at them."[68]

One of the most delightful records in the story of the relation between the Carlyles and Thackeray is that which Jane Carlyle made concerning her dealings in early 1851 with Theresa Reviss, adopted daughter of Charles Buller's mother and generally assumed to be one of the most important prototypes of Becky Sharp, although Mrs. Carlyle identifies her with Blanche Amory in *Pendennis*. Thackeray had been in and out of the Buller home many times throughout the years when Theresa was growing up and had always found her to be a detestable brat. Mrs. Carlyle's record is to be found in two letters of early 1851 to John Welsh, her mother's brother in Liverpool. The first is dated 2 January:

And now I must simply *promise* you a long letter for today is most unfavorable for *writing* one— There arrived on us yesterday a young Heroine of Romance with a quantity of trunks and a Lady's maid—who is for the moment keeping this poor house and my poor self in a state of utter disquiet. I had invited her to dine one day and, if it suited her better, to stay *over the night*— And she has so arranged her affairs that if she leave here today it must be to live till next week in a Hotel—(at nineteen!). What can one do then but let her remain—with *protest* against the Lady's—maid— She is *Mrs* Buller[']s adopted daughter whom you may have heard of, and has just been playing the Sultana in India for a year, and———. Oh dear, here

66. MS, NLS, 604.344. Two days later Jane wrote to Carlyle: "Henry Taylor and Thackeray have fraternized finally, *not* 'like the carriage horses and railway steam engine' as might have been supposed but like *men* and *Brothers!*" MS, NLS, 604.335. An Agapemone is a communistic, free-love institution like that found about 1849 at Spaxton, England.

67. Ray, *Letters*, II, 699.

68. MS, NLS, 515.53.

is her *lover* come to see her and in a quarter of an hour a Prison Inspector is coming to take Mr C and me thro Pentonville prison. I am bothered to death, my blessed Uncle.[69]

Her second letter to her uncle was written on 7 January:

Have you been reading Thackeray[']s *Pendennis?* if so, you have made acquaintance with *Blanche Amory,* and when I tell you that my young lady of last week, is the original of that portrait, you will give me joy that she, Lady's maid, and infinite baggage is all gone! Not that poor little 'Tizzy' (Theresa Revis[s]) is *quite* such a little devil as Thackeray, who has detested her from a child has here represented—but the looks, the manners, the wiles, the *Larmes,* "and all that sort of thing["] are a perfect likeness—the blame, however, is chiefly on those who placed her in a position so *false,* that it required extraordinary virtue not to become false along with it— She was the only *legitimate* child of a beautiful young 'improper female' who was for a number of years Arthur Buller[']s mistress. She had *had* a husband, a swindler—his [Buller's] Mother took the freak of patronizing this mistress, saw the child and behold it was very pretty and clever. Poor Mrs Buller had tired of parties, of Politics, of most things in Heaven and earth; "a sudden thought struck her," she would *adopt* this child; give herself the excitement of *making a scandal* and *braving public opinion,* and of educating a flesh and blood girl into the Heroine of the three volume novel which she had for years been trying to *write*; but wanted perseverance to elaborate!—The child was made the idol of the whole house—even Charles did whatever she pleased—her showy education was fitting her more for her own Mother[']s profession than for any honest one—and when she was seventeen and the *novel* was just rising into the interest of *love-affairs*—a rich young man having been refused—or rather *jilted* by her—Mrs Buller died—her husband and son [Charles] being already dead and poor Tizzy was left without any earthly stay and with only 250£ a year to support her in the extravagantly luxurious habits she had been brought up in— She has a splendid voice and wished to get trained for the Opera— Mrs Buller's fine Lady friends screamed at the idea—but offered her nothing instead—not even their countenance—her two-male guardians, to wash their hands of her resolved to send her to India to Sir Arthur Buller, whose wife hated her—naturally—being the child of her husbands ci-devant mistress— To India she had to go however; vowing that if their object was to marry her off—she would disappoint them, and return "to prosecute the Artist Life"— She produced the most extraordinary *furor* at Calcutta, had offers of Sudor Judges and what not,

69. MS, NLS, 604.341.

every week—refused them point blank, terrified Sir Arthur by her extravagance, tormented Lady Buller by her caprices, "fell into *consump-
tion*"—for the nonce—was ordered by the Doctors back to England! and to
the dismay of her two cowardly guardians arrived here six months ago—
with her health perfectly restored! But her Indian reputation had preceded
her and the fine Ladies who turned their backs on her in her extreme need
now invite a girl who has refused Sudor Judges by the dozen— She had
been going about from one house to another, while no *home* could be
found for her! The guardians had a brilliant idea—"Would *we* take her?"
—not for her weight in gold I said—but I asked her to spend *a day* with
me that I might see what she was grown to, and whether I could do anything in placing her with some proper person— The result of this invitation
was that alarming arrival, bag and baggage on newyears day! She has
saved me all further speculation about her however by engaging herself
to a Capt. Neale (from Ayrshire) who came home in the ship with her
and seems a most devoted Lover—SHE "does not love *him* a bit" she told
me—"had been hesitating some time betwixt accepting him, or going on
the stage, or drowning herself—" I told her, her decision was good, as
marrying did not preclude either 'going on the stage' at a subsequent
period, or 'drowning herself'—whereas had she decided on *the drowning*;
there could have been no more of it."— I have my own notion that she will
throw him over yet; meanwhile it was a *blessed calm* after the *Fly* rolled
her away from here on Saturday— "Oh my Dear!" Mr C said "we cannot
be sufficiently thankful!!"—indeed you can have no notion how the whole
routine of this quiet house was tumbled heels over head— It had been for
these three days and three nights *not* Jonah in the Whale's belly—but the
Whale in Jonah's belly!—that little creature seemed to have absorbed this
whole establishment into *her*self—[70]

From 22 May to 3 July Thackeray delivered his lectures on "The
English Humourists of the Eighteenth Century." Thackeray's friends,
including the Carlyles, attended them. Thackeray had his misgivings
concerning the merits of lecturing but was grateful for the brilliant
circle of friends who came to hear him. On 23 May he wrote to Abraham Hayward: "But the truth is that lectures won't do. They were all
friends, and a packed house; though, to be sure, it goes to a man's
heart to find amongst his friends such men as you and Kinglake and
Venables, Higgins, Rawlinson, Carlyle, Ashburton and Hallam, Milman, Macaulay, Wilberforce looking on kindly."[71] The Carlyles, however, were not uncritical. Jane wrote to her cousin Helen Welsh in

70. MS, NLS, 604.343.
71. Ray, *Letters*, II, 777. For a note to the Carlyles that, according to Ray, may

early June: "Thursday is Thackeray's Lecture day, and I have a ticket waiting for you. The Lectures between you and me are no great things—as *Lectures*—but it is the fashion to find them 'so amusing'! and the *audience* is the most brilliant I ever saw in one room—unless in Bath House drawing-rooms."[72] After the last lecture Carlyle wrote to his brother John: "On Thursday I went to hear Thackeray *end*; Jane and I. The audience inferior to what I had heard; *item* the performance. Comic *acting* good in it; also a certain gentility of style notable: but of *insight* (worth calling by the name) none; nay a good deal of *pretended* insight (morality &c with an ugly 'do' at the bottom of it) which was worse than none. The air grew bad; I had only one wish, to be out again, out, out!— Thackeray has not found his feet yet; but he may perhaps do so in that element, and get (as Darwin expresses it) into some kind of 'Thackeray at Home,' in which he might excel all people for delighting an empty fashionable audience."[73] Gordon Ray makes clear one reason why Carlyle did not greatly enjoy Thackeray's lectures: "With regard to doctrine Thackeray intended his lectures to be pointedly anti-Carlylean. He made 'The Humorist as a Man of Letters' almost the antithesis of 'The Hero as a Man of Letters' as Carlyle had described him. . . . He reserved his warmest praise for such completely unheroic figures as Dick Steele and Noll Goldsmith. This aspect of Thackeray's lectures did not escape Carlyle, who was a faithful member of his audience."[74]

Nevertheless, the Carlyles continued to maintain a friendly interest in Thackeray and his activities, and Thackeray continued to visit them. On 18 October 1851 Carlyle wrote to his brother John: "Thackeray was here last night; he is going to Edinr to lecture in December,

have been written on the day after Thackeray's first lecture and in which he says "you are both very kind to me: and always have been my kind old friends and I am yours in return," see *ibid.*, II, 775. The note is accompanied by an amusing sketch of a tightrope walker.

72. MS, NLS, 1893.249. Bath House in Piccadilly was the town house of the Ashburtons.

73. MS, NLS, 513.86. See also Stevenson, p. 238.

74. *Thackeray: The Age of Wisdom*, pp. 144–45. Carlyle wrote to Emerson on 25 Aug.: "Item Thackeray; who is coming over to lecture to you: a mad world, my Masters!" Joseph Slater, ed., *The Correspondence of Emerson and Carlyle* (New York and London, 1964), p. 474. Slater quotes as follows from a letter of 25 Feb. 1852 by Harriet Martineau to Emerson: "I saw the Carlyles a few months since;—just saw them, & O! dear! felt them too. They put me between them, at Thackeray's last lecture; & both got the fidgets. After the first half hour, C. looked at his watch, & held it across me, about once in two minutes; & he filled up the intervals with shaking himself, & drumming his elbow into my side." *Ibid.*

then to America ('to send round the hat'), is meanwhile writing an illustrious Novel [*Henry Esmond*]:—'poor fellow, after all!' "[75] On 24 October he wrote again to the same brother: "Thackeray was here the other night, 'just waiting for his dinner hour' somewhere: perhaps I told you?"[76] And to Lady Ashburton Carlyle wrote on 27 October: "Thackeray was here one night; going to Edinburgh with his Lectures in December; then to Yankeeland with do: having first published a Novel in 3 volumes; and so smitten heartily on the big drum."[77]

Carlyle's *The Life of John Sterling* was published during the second week in October. Late in the same month Thackeray wrote to Lady Stanley of Alderley: "Carlyle's Life of Sterling is delightful have you read it?" It is hard to reconcile this praise with his savage attack on the book and Carlyle that appeared in more than three long columns in the *Times* for 1 November.[78] Of course there had been rumblings under the surface of Thackeray's mind before in such things as his account of Carlyle's goring of Henry Reeve and his speaking of Carlyle as a bully. It should also be noted that two of Carlyle's chief admirers, John Sterling and Charles Buller, both of whom could have acted as restraining influences on Thackeray, were now dead. Whatever the explanation and however great the inconsistency may be, Thackeray's review was something far removed from the persiflage with which he had said the bully could be silenced; it was veritably the explosion of a volcano. Brief excerpts from it follow:

Weak minds will be sorely distressed by the last production of the redoubtable Thomas. That angry gentleman is more indignant than ever. His wrath has got to its height. . . . We doubt whether the life would have been written at all but for the matchless opportunity it affords for the pugilistic efforts of the author. . . . We may doubt the prudence of the undertaking, but who shall question the valour of the man who, single-handed, takes upon himself to thrash the whole world! A memoir of John Sterling has already been written. The reading public, which did not call for that, hardly required another almost upon its heels. . . . The great object of the author of the *Latter Day Pamphlets* in this his last work seems

75. MS, NLS, 514.29. "Poor fellow, after all!" is coterie speech, a favorite expression of Carlyle's brother John.
76. MS, NLS, 514.30.
77. MS, Marquess of Northampton.
78. Ray, Letters, II, 808. Thackeray's review is included in his *Centenary Works* (London, 1910–11), XXV, 373–86.

to be—as far as we can gather it—to prove the utter impossibility of an honest man's making way in life, and the absolute rottenness of all existing things. The world, according to Mr. Carlyle, has never been so bad as it is. . . . : There is throughout this book no cessation of abuse; but we have searched through it in vain, though most carefully and anxiously, for a single line of wholesome counsel. Mr. Carlyle keeps a school in which scolding goes on from morning till night, but certainly no teaching. . . . Nothing but fighting suits Mr. Carlyle or lies within his scope to recommend. But, if we are to fight, let us at least know against whom and what for. . . . But we altogether deny the wild and incoherent yet very grave accusations which Mr. Carlyle brings against society—accusations which he finds much easier to make than to justify. The age in which we live is *not* the very worst since the fall of man. Would Mr. Carlyle, who asserts that it is, willingly exchange it for any age that has preceded it? . . . It is not always easy, as our readers may have discovered, to have the full benefit of Mr. Carlyle's thoughts, so strangely are they garbed in that gentleman's most peculiar diction. . . . The world, bad as it is, will be grateful to Mr. Carlyle if he will put his shoulder to the wheel and help it to repair a crying evil. But putting a shoulder or even a finger to the wheel is just what this writer will not do. . . . Coleridge is presented to us in glowing colours, sitting "on the brow of Highgate-hill, looking down on London and its smoke tumult, like a sage escaped from the inanity of life's battle." This is a "good man"; the only "good" man of whom especial mention is made in the volume. . . . But Coleridge, coolly leaving Robert Southey to take care of his children, retires to a snug retreat opened for him by his friends at Highgate—a refuge which he had not the chivalry and manly courage to decline; and he, in that very epoch of his life, assumes in Carlyle's eye the form of perfect human grandeur. . . . The moment the philosopher creeps to his chamber, and there humbly falls on his knees as a Christian, he is scornfully left to his own devices. . . . Poor Coleridge, in spite of all his metaphysical entanglements, took shelter in his latter days from his many bodily and mental troubles under cover of those simple truths which give peace to the tempest-tossed, hope to the despairing, resignation to the sorely-afflicted; and, for this obvious outrage to philosophy, Carlyle deserts him. . . . It suits the humour of Mr. Carlyle to mock every faith but his own, and to render his own wholly unintelligible even to his disciples.

Finally, Thackeray criticizes Carlyle for publishing in the *Sterling* some private correspondence between Edward Sterling, editor of the *Times* and John Sterling's father, and Sir Robert Peel. Thackeray's comment today sounds strangely ironical in view of the controversy

later over Froude's revelation of intimate details in his biography of
Carlyle. Thackeray wrote: "From the reckless way in which he [Car-
lyle] had made use of this private communication we cannot refrain
from expressing a hope that Mr. Carlyle himself may never be placed
in the same position, with regard to any public journal, as that so
ably filled by Edward Sterling with regard to *The Times*. Should he
be so situated we cannot undertake to say how soon such private communications as that to which we have called attention would become
common property." It is strikingly ironical that Thackeray's most
blistering attack on Carlyle, written just three years after the publication of his own *novel* without a hero, concerned itself with a book in
which Carlyle, following the example of Dr. Samuel Johnson's *The
Life of Richard Savage*, proved that he could write a truly excellent
biography without a hero.

One would be hard pressed to draw a nice distinction between
Carlyle's pessimism, as Thackeray conceived it, and what Carlyle
thought of as Thackeray's "terrible cynicism." Did Carlyle know that
Thackeray was the author of the hostile review in the *Times*? Pre-
sumably he did. There were other unfavorable reviews of Carlyle's
Sterling, however, and he dismissed them all with a disdainful shrug
of his shoulders. On 4 November he wrote to the Rev. Henry Brookfield, who had known Sterling well and who appears to have defended
Carlyle's biography:

Thanks for your candid little Testimony on my behalf; which is a real
pleasure to me; and was a glad surprise withal, for I thought you had
already sailed. That small Sterling affair,—a poor little job incumbent on
me in this world, and now hurtled off me and finished,—will do very well;
in spite of the roaring of the Bulls of Bashan, who, in various regions as
I understand, are busy enough,—more power to their elbow! I adopt, in
late years, a simple precaution, not to read any of that balderdash how
loud soever: sense is worth reading, even tho' abusive of you; but nonsense
is not, nor should one read it when there is a remedy,—not if it were proclaimed with a "10,000 jackass power," would I read it, for one!—79

The book sold extremely well and soon went into a second edition.
Carlyle gave some of the credit for its success to the hostile reviews
such as that which had appeared in the *Times*. On 20 November he
wrote to his brother John: "Robson is at the 2d edition of Sterling,

79. MS, Pierpoint Morgan Library.

as you know; I have sent him 3 or 4 corrections, and take no farther charge at all. The foolish people talk of this Book, as if it were a great *new* thing! And possibly *the Times* Balderdash has shoved it faster abroad. For example, the other night a French able editor (he of the *Revue des 2 Mondes*) applies to me for a copy; also for a Portrait of myself, and even for some touches of authentic 'Autobiography': Ach Gott!"[80]

As formerly, ripples continued to appear in the friendship from time to time, but in the main it proceeded rather pleasantly along its course down to Thackeray's death on 24 December 1863. The Carlyles, Thackeray, and his two little girls spent late December of 1851 and the New Year's season with the Ashburtons at the Grange. On 27 December Jane wrote Helen Welsh from the Grange that Thackeray was coming that day and that she was remaining to help take care of his two girls.[81] On 29 December Carlyle wrote to his brother John from the same place: "Thackeray is just returned from lecturing and lionizing in Edinburgh; he is not of great profit to talk with, but he is easy and agreeable, and his presence, taking away the burden of talk from others, is so far very welcome."[82] Back at Chelsea on 3 January, Carlyle wrote again to the same brother: "Thackeray and his two girls were with us. . . . I have never seen him so well before. There is a great deal of talent in him, a great deal of sensibility,—irritability, sensuality, vanity without limit; and nothing, or little, but sentimentalism and playactorism to guide it all with: not a good or well-found ship in such water on such a voyage."[83]

On 23 February Carlyle wrote to this brother: "We were at dinner on Friday night with one Ellice in Arlington Street (a wide-flowing old Canadian Scotchman, Politician, Negociator &c &c, called 'Bear

---

80. MS, NLS, 514.30. Robson was the chief printer of Carlyle's publishers, Chapman and Hall. Carlyle's reply to François Buloz (1803–77), editor of *Revue des Deux Mondes*, an excellent letter dated 17 Nov., is in the Charlotte and Norman H. Strouse Collection, University of California, Santa Cruz.

81. MS, NLS, 1893.266. In an undated letter written perhaps several days later Jane told Kate Sterling, daughter of John Sterling, "Well! I write to-day to tell you that we go home on Friday next—having staid a week longer than bargain[ed] on account of the—Misses Thackeray!— 'As they knew *me* and did not know *her*'; Lady A begged me to stay over their visit in case of their 'being shy'! a needless apprehension on her part!— Besides these little girls and their Father there are no other visitors at present except Miss Farrer [Farrar]—much better humoured and every way more compatible with children than I am." MS, Carlyle's House, Chelsea.

82. MS, NLS, 514.42.

83. MS, NLS, 514.47.

Ellice' in society here, but rather for his *oiliness* than any trace of ferocity ever seen in him): Thiers, the Ashburtons, Thackeray &c &c were there; and much confused talk, in bad French and otherwise."[84] On 5 April he wrote to him: "Anthony Sterling has finished his Zinc House, and holds *tabagies* (or smoking parties in it, Spedding, Ford, Thackeray &c) in it, to none of which do I go."[85] A very amusing account of two robberies, one of them at the expense of Thackeray, is to be found in a letter that Jane Carlyle wrote to Carlyle in Scotland on 12 August 1852. Carlyle repeated it in a letter to Lady Airlie:

> Jane added a rumour of two robberies: robbery first, the pocket of Thackeray picked of a £100 Note in foreign parts (may it burn the thief's fingers!)—robbery second, Mrs Ruskin's jewels (pretty Mrs Ruskin, one of the daintiest Scotch women married to *a Prince* "of Criticism," and I doubt not valuable jewels, for they are rich and she is bright and gay) all stolen, in Italy, by some English-Austrian spy and swindler; and, what makes it worse, the Newspaper narrative of the affair, is headed 'Stones of Venice,' which is the title of her husband's last Book. How mischievous are mankind one to another, with object and without![86]

Thackeray's old dislike of heroes is reflected in a letter to Dr. John Brown of 6 October: "Carlyle is away in Germany looking after *Frederick the Great*. I don't know what Literature is about."[87] Back at the Grange, Carlyle wrote to his mother on 23 October: "Thackeray is coming, for whom I care nothing, though he is a clever and friendly man; he comes today with a nobleman and a Portrait-Painter; comes, but is soon to go:—'Di tha naither ill na' guid!' "[88] A day or so later

---

84. MS, NLS, 514.56. "Bear" Ellice is Edward Ellice, who appeared frequently in the Ashburton circle.

85. MS, NLS, 514.61. Anthony Sterling, who was to become a captain and fight in the Crimean War, was John Sterling's brother.

86. MS, NLS, Acc. 2427.

87. Ray, *Letters*, III, 91.

88. MS, NLS, 514.89. Jane wrote Kate Sterling on the same day: "I hear the carriage come back with Laurence who is to paint Thackeray here in these days—for the world—" MS, Berg Collection, New York Public Library. Laurence is Samuel Laurence (1812–84). Carlyle's dialectal phrase "Di tha etc." is coterie speech, the saying of an Annandale cattle dealer. See the *Letters and Memorials of Jane Welsh Carlyle*, ed. J. A. Froude (London, 1883), I, 278–79. Thackeray wrote to George Bancroft on 18 Nov. 1853: "My friend Mr. S. Lawrence [*sic*] is the bearer of this note: and I recommend him to your good offices during his stay in New York. You have a specimen of his handy-work in the portrait of the undersigned. I think Lawrence is the best drawer of heads since Van Dyke. . . . Lawrence has done all the philosophers and literary men here Carlyle Dickens F. Maurice Kingsley Ashburton, Monteagle que scais je?" Ray, *Letters*, III, 317.

he wrote to Joseph Neuberg: "We have agreeable enough people, Thackeray among them."[89]

Henry Esmond, published in October 1852, was soon read by both Carlyles. Carlyle gave their estimate of it in a letter to Lady Ashburton of 10 November:

We have gone thro' Thackeray's Novel; my Wife first, with great admiration "for the fine delineations of women"; I next, with aversion and contempt mainly for his feline phantasms of "women," with many reflexions on his singular fineness of sense and singular want of do—and on the whole with fairly more esteem for this Book than seemed likely at the Grange. I find the "style," both of painting and writing, worthy of peculiar recognition, in general quite excellt for clearness, simplicity and grace,—and here and there with a fine *adagio* of affectionate sentimentality, which is almost beautiful, almost pious. Poor Thackeray, God help him, and us, after all![90]

But Thackeray's comment on Carlyle in a letter to Mrs. Procter of 25 November is not so charitable: "I wish you had seen it [the Duke of Wellington's funeral on 18 November]. . . . You can imagine the whole of this large City, but with one idea (except Carlyle who is entirely without sympathy and thinks all enthusiasm wrong, except what is felt for himself), I thought."[91] From Philadelphia in a letter to Lady Stanley of 21 January 1853 he made a lighter and somewhat amusing thrust at Carlyle: "They [his American audiences] are great about pronunciation especially, and take down at my lectures the words which this present Arbiter of English pronounces differently to them. If Carlyle comes I wonder if they'll take *him* as an exemplar."[92]

Thackeray returned to England in early May but aftei a few weeks went abroad to Paris, Germany, and Switzerland. In a letter of 9 September Carlyle gave Emerson what has become his most quoted pen portrait of Thackeray: "Thackeray has very rarely come athwart me since his return [from America]: he is a big fellow, soul and body; of many gifts and qualities (particularly in the Hogarth line, with a

89. Wilson, *Carlyle*, IV, 445.
90. MS, Marquess of Northampton.
91. Ray, *Letters*, III, 126. Carlyle admired the Duke of Wellington, but as he watched the funeral procession from the second-floor windows of Bath House he saw nothing in it "of the least dignity" except the four thousand soldiers and was disgusted with much in it that seemed to him ugly and inappropriate. See Wilson, *Carlyle*, IV, 449–50.
92. Ray, *Letters*, III, 179.

dash of Sterne superadded), of enormous *appetite* withal, and very uncertain and chaotic in all points, except his *outer breeding*, which is fixed enough, and *perfect* according to the modern English style. I rather dread explosions in his history. A *big*, fierce, weeping, hungry man; not a strong one."[93]

In 1854 Carlyle saw very little of Thackeray, who was abroad a good part of the time. But on 4 November he wrote to Lady Ashburton: "Thackeray came over to see us one night; was very gentle and friendly-looking; ingenious too here and there; but extremly difficult to talk with, somehow—his talk lying all in flashes, little detached pools, you nowhere got upon a well or vein."[94] On 18 November he again wrote to her: "Thackeray, I hear, has fled the country somewhither, not being well in these weeks: poor soul, busy to[o] and I suppose not in high spirits always—as the like of me. God help us all."[95] Thackeray's one comment on Carlyle for this year comes late and does not amount to much. On 4 December he wrote to Lady Stanley: "Ashburton has grown a beard I hear & Tom Carlyle has a scrubby one."[96]

On 13 October 1855 Thackeray sailed from Liverpool to Boston in order to begin his lecture tour on *The Four Georges*. Two days earlier Carlyle had written to Lady Ashburton: "Thackeray, I suppose, is gone to America? A fortnight ago I saw him once for a moment; poor Thackeray: what a life poor mortals have in this world at present—with all loadstars gone out, locker emptyish, and the sea running high!"[97] Thackeray's American tour lasted all winter and ran into the early spring. A curious bit of confusion involving pronunciation and spelling got him in trouble and at the same time reflected the popularity of Carlyle in the United States, especially the South, at this time. On 15 March Thackeray wrote to Mrs. Procter from New Orleans: "I am whipped for a malignant attack on Carlyle in my lectures—the fact being that I mentioned in the very most courteous and kindly terms, Lord Carlisle, G. Selwyn's correspondent in the early reign of George III. Only a malignant blundering Paddy-

93. Slater, p. 496.
94. MS, Marquess of Northampton.
95. *Ibid.*
96. Ray, *Letters*, III, 404. Carlyle stopped shaving on 9 Oct. when Lord Ashburton, who had already grown a beautiful beard, came to Chelsea and took away his razors to compel him to keep his promise to stop.
97. MS, Marquess of Northampton.

whack could write in this way."[98] It seems inconceivable, as Thackeray suggests, but careless American journalists had misconstrued two points in Thackeray's discussion of Lord Carlisle that offended an American public thinking of Thomas Carlyle: one was a close association with George III, and the other was Thackeray's statement that "Lord Carlisle was one of those English fine gentlemen who was well-nigh ruined by the awful debauchery and extravagance which prevailed in the great English society of those days."[99]

On 4 May 1857 Lady Ashburton died at Paris, and an era ended for both Carlyle and Thackeray. Jane Carlyle gave an account of her death to her friend in a letter written several days after the funeral, which took place on 12 May: "I have been long in answering your dear Letter. If you saw Lady Ashburton's death in the Newspapers you would partly guess why; that I was shocked, and dispirited, and feeling *silence* best. . . . I never heard of so easy a death. She was dressing about four o'clock; felt faint, and called for Dr. Rous (her private Doctor); he told her, in answer to her question, 'what is this?' 'you are going to faint, it is nothing; you mustn't mind these faintnesses!' He put his arm round her to support; she clasped her hands over his other arm, leant her forehead on his shoulder, gave a sigh, and was dead!" In the same letter Jane commented on the funeral, which Carlyle, Thackeray, Henry Taylor, George Venables, and other members of Lady Ashburton's circle attended: "On Tuesday Mr C. went to the Grange to be present at her funeral. It was conducted with a kind of royal state; and all the men, who used to compose a sort of *Court* for her, were there, *in tears!* I never heard of a gloomier funeral."[100]

In July following Thackeray ran for a seat in Parliament to represent Oxford. His opponent was Edward Cardwell (1813–86), a politician, statesman, and military reformer of considerable note who had held the seat earlier. Carlyle commented in a letter to his wife of 16 July: "Thackeray is candidate for Oxford: Thackeray *versus* Cardwell! It seems to be extremely foolish; but perhaps not *more* so than the rest. Cardwell, at any rate, I suppose, will prevail."[101] Cardwell did prevail, and on 26 July Carlyle again wrote to his wife:

98. Ray, *Letters*, III, 585.
99. See the ninth and tenth paragraphs of Thackeray's lecture "George III."
100. *New Letters and Memorials*, II, 135–36.
101. MS, NLS, 614.443.

"Thackeray has lost his Election, as you see; what a big form of the species Dingle-dousie that is!"[102] According to Gordon Ray, Thackeray did not willingly face so formidable an opponent and afterward confessed that he was "himself a Cardwellite."[103]

In the middle of May 1858 Thackeray was guest at a dinner in London at which the historian John Lothrop Motley was also present. Motley gave an account of the dinner in a letter to his wife: "Something was said of Carlyle the author. Thackeray said, 'Carlyle hates everybody who has arrived—if they are on the road, he may perhaps treat them civilly.' Mackintosh praised the description in the 'French Revolution' of the flight of the King and Queen (which is certainly one of the most living pictures ever painted with ink), and Thackeray agreed with him, and spoke of the passages very heartily."[104]

When the Reverend Alexander Scott was planning a trip to America in 1858, Carlyle wrote to him on 30 June: "Have you applied to Thackeray on the matter? . . . He is of course the Cortez and Columbus of that element;—he is a very kind obliging soul too."[105]

Throughout his life Carlyle had grappled with what was to him the formidable problem of finding good pens to write with and good paper to write on. This had been something of a problem to Thackeray too, and between the years 1856 and 1859 they discussed the matter from time to time and even corresponded about it. When in 1856 Thackeray found a steel pen that he liked, he sent one to Carlyle with the following note, dated 3 August: "Perhaps this small present may be useful to you— It is the only steel-pen with w*h* I could ever write comfortably, and if it suits your hand as it does mine, why it will save you much pen-knife work and may make your life easier."[106] In a similar vein of helpfulness we find Carlyle writing to Thackeray on 9 April 1859: "Thanks for your merry little Note and the two Pens. It is like a little pearl of human cheerfulness and friendliness, turning up for one in the dreary wash of commonplace and botheration, wh*h*

102. MS, NLS, 614.448. A "dingle-dousie" is Scottish for a stick ignited at one end and swung about for the entertainment of children.

103. *Thackeray: The Age of Wisdom*, pp. 269–70.

104. Ray, *Letters*, IV, 82 n.

105. MS, Berg Collection, New York Public Library.

106. Ray, *Letters*, IV, 147. There is some question about the date of this letter, which Ray dates 1859. I am dating it 1856 because on 7 Aug. of that year Carlyle wrote to Lady Ashburton: "Thackeray sent me a steel Pen which he had found answer; 'just going away somewhither,' he says" (MS, Marquess of Northampton); and Thackeray's note to Carlyle ends: "Yours ever (just on the point of starting somewhither)."

is one's common lot!— I have been true as Mitchell's own steel to his Pens and him these many years. . . . And observe farther, *here* is a kind of Paper wh*h* I find the best of many for suiting Mitchell. Try that too: It is made partly of *straw*; smooth enough; and bites at the ink with an appetite one likes. 'Parkins & Gotto' Stationers;—and I will send you a ream of it whenever you hold up your finger."[107]

In the late summer of 1859 Thackeray accepted the editorship of the *Cornhill Magazine*, the first issue of which was to appear the following January. Carlyle was among those whom he invited to contribute to the periodical. In a letter to Thackeray of 20 October 1859 Carlyle wrote that "crushed to death amid Prussian rubbish," he could not make a contribution then but that if and when he ever got *Frederick the Great* finished he would be glad to write for Thackeray's magazine.[108] On 23 October he wrote to his brother: "Thackeray *is* to do a new Magazine; has applied to me; one of my climbings upstairs was to say handsomely, 'No, can't at all.'"[109] On 30 November he wrote to Edward FitzGerald: "Thackeray *fell* lately in a dark fog and lamed a leg, I am told, which still keeps him prisoner: no doubt he is busy exceedingly with his *Magazine*, with his &c &c. I cannot get to see him yet."[110] In a letter to Thackeray of 26 May 1860 Carlyle spoke of a French subject on which he had considered writing for the *Cornhill* but which he could not use because he could not get permission to include some of the basic material that he needed. Yet he wished Thackeray and his magazine well: "If I ever in the end of this book have life left, you shall have plenty of things. . . . Fair wind and full sea to you in this hitherto so successful voyage, for which the omens certainly are on all sides good."[111] And although Carlyle never did write anything for the *Cornhill Magazine*, he was delighted when Thackeray published in it four instalments of Ruskin's *Unto This Last*, which because of public outcry had to be stopped with the issue of November 1860. Unquestionably he wished Thackeray well and was on the most friendly terms with him during the first year of the enterprise, as the tone of the following letter, dated 24 May 1860, indicates: "Alas, dear Thackeray, I durst as soon undertake to dance a hornpipe on the top of Bond Steeple, as to eat a white-bait dinner

107. MS, NLS, Acc. 2517. For an anecdote of 1858 concerning Thackeray's daughters told by Jane to Mrs. Russell, see Lawrence and Elisabeth Hanson, *Necessary Evil* (London, 1952), p. 471.

108. Ray, *Letters*, IV, 157–58.   110. MS, Trinity College, Cambridge.
109. MS, NLS, 516.96.   111. Ray, *Letters*, IV, 188.

in my present low and lost state! Never in my life was I at such a pass. You are a good brother man; and I am grateful. Pray for me, and still hope for me if you can."[112]

In these last years of Thackeray's life it is clear that the two Carlyles continued to read him. On one occasion, possibly in 1860, Carlyle sent his helper Henry Larkin a note reading: "W*d* you now demand *Thackeray's* Chatham at Londn Library, for me," probably a reference to the many passages on the two William Pitts in *The Four Georges*, published as a book that year.[113] Jane wrote to her friend Mrs. Russell on 14 April 1862: "The two numbers of the Story [probably Thackeray's *Philip*, then appearing in the *Cornhill*] I sent you the other day will be followed up to the end; and I am sure you will like it, and even the Doctor [Mrs. Russell's husband] may read it with satisfaction. The Author is one of the best Novelists of the day."[114] One of the most amusing stories concerning Carlyle and Thackeray in these last years is quoted by D. A. Wilson from Martin Tupper. "Thackeray mentioned to somebody that, were he not himself, he would like to be Martin Tupper. I repeated this to Carlyle. He evidently thought Thackeray presumptuous in hinting at such a thing, for he at once exclaimed,—'Save us frae a guid conceit of ourselves!' " The wits who were listening to Tupper tell the story, Wilson says, "dissolved in inextinguishable laughter," and Tupper laughed along with them, supposing it was Thackeray who was conceited.[115]

On 29 December 1863, five days after Thackeray's death, Carlyle wrote in a letter to Richard Monckton Milnes what may be taken as his obituary, certainly a very moving one:

Poor Thackeray! I saw him not ten days ago. I was riding in the dusk, heavy at heart, along by the Serpentine and Hyde Park, when some human brother from a chariot, with a young lady in it, threw me a shower of salutations. I looked up—it was Thackeray with his daughter: the last time I was to see him in this world. He had many fine qualities, no guile or malice against any mortal; a big mass of a soul, but not strong in proportion; a beautiful vein of genius lay struggling about in him. Nobody in our

---

112. *Ibid.*, IV, 187. A letter from Thackeray to Carlyle of 16 Oct. [?1860] that I have not seen is in the NLS, 666.82. It may shed further light on Thackeray's relation to both Carlyle and Ruskin at this time. See also Wilson, *Carlyle*, V, 406–407.
113. From an undated fragment of a note in the Huntington (Chatham) Library.
114. MS, NLS, 607.587B.
115. Wilson, *Carlyle*, V, 449.

day wrote, I should say, with such perfection of style. I predict of his books very much as you do. Poor Thackeray!—adieu! adieu![116]

In the period of about seventeen years in Carlyle's life that remained after Thackeray's death, his experiences and comments relating to Thackeray were of the same mixed nature as those when Thackeray was alive. The Carlyles continued to see and take an interest in Thackeray's daughters. On 24 October 1864 Anne Thackeray wrote in a letter to a friend: "Minny is going out for a drive with Mrs. Carlyle this afternoon,—we met old Thomas the other day on his horse & he suddenly began to cry. I shall always love him in future, for I used to fancy he did not care about Papa."[117] Minny Thackeray wrote to Carlyle on 15 December 1866 to announce her coming marriage to Leslie Stephen, which took place the following 19 June.[118] In a letter of 1871 to a friend Anne made a rather curious reference to her father's review of Carlyle's *Sterling*, considering the hostile nature of that review: "The other day I met dear old Mr. Carlyle walking along, and I rushed after him to talk about his *Life of Sterling*. . . . I wonder have you ever come across my father's review of it in the *Times*?"[119] It would indeed be interesting to know just what Carlyle said to Anne on this occasion.

On 2 January 1872 William Allingham wrote in his *Diary*:

C[arlyle] said Thackeray's *Irish Ballads* were the best things he ever wrote, and quoted (as he often did) with great gusto and a strong brogue—
> 'Twould binifit your sowls
> To see the butther'd rowls,
laughing heartily afterwards.

For Thackeray's novels, except *Esmond*, he had little praise. The fact is he had not read most of them.[120]

On 27 December 1872 Carlyle wrote to his brother John: "A knock at the door and word that 'Miss Thackeray,' a very rare individual here, is waiting in the dining room below."[121] The old Carlyle could not always be tolerant and good-natured in commenting on Thackeray's daughters. To his brother John he wrote again on 9 December 1873: "Alas, alas, here has been a flight of Thackeray ladies and others;

116. T. Wemyss Reid, *Richard Monckton Milnes* (London, 1890), II, 113.
117. Ray, *Letters*, IV, 304.
118. MS, NLS, 1768.204.
119. Ray, *Letters*, II, 808 n.
120. (London, 1907), p. 208.
121. MS, NLS, 527.78.

beyond expression *unfurthersome* to me. I will end[,] I will end."[122]
William Black's notes of July 1875 indicate that Carlyle was critical of
Thackeray's conception of Goethe: "He regretted he had never seen
Goethe face to face, and added: 'Thackeray's recollection of Goethe
was vague and inaccurate. Thackeray had a confused memory of
Goethe being a dark man."[123] Yet on 1 December 1875, just three
days after Minny had died, he spoke with deep compassion to Leslie
Stephen when he met him on a walk on Cromwell Road. "I am very
sorry for you, sir," he said. "My own loss did not come in so grievous
a way."[124]

Duffy, who had acted as a guide to Carlyle during his tour of Ire-
land in 1849, had a very distinguished career afterward and became
Sir Charles Gavan Duffy. In 1856 he emigrated to Australia, where
he was very active in reform movements, as he had been in Ireland.
At one time he was Prime Minister of that country and at another
Speaker of the House. From time to time he returned on visits to Great
Britain, always making it a point to see and talk with his old friend
Carlyle and to record what Carlyle said. Some of the talk concerned
Thackeray. In his diary Duffy states that about 1866 or 1867 Carlyle
told him: "The huge edifice called the New Palace of Westminster
was not insignificant or grotesque, but it wanted the unity of design
which is apt to impress one in a work which is a single birth from one
competent mind. When Thackeray saw the river front he declared he
saw no reason why it stopped: it ended nowhere, and might just as
well have gone on to Chelsea."[125] On one of the long walks that Duffy
took with Carlyle some years later, Carlyle reverted to a subject they
had discussed years before on the Irish tour, the characteristic qualities and relative merits of Dickens and Thackeray. Duffy reports:

Speaking of both after they were dead, Carlyle said of Dickens that
his chief faculty was that of a comic actor. He would have made a successful one if he had taken to that sort of life. His public readings, which were
a pitiful pursuit after all, were in fact acting, and very good acting too.
He had a remarkable faculty for business; he managed his periodical skil-
fully, and made good bargains with his booksellers. Set him to do any
work, and if he undertook it, it was altogether certain that it would be done
effectually. Thackeray had far more literary ability, but one could not
fail to perceive that he had no convictions, after all, except that a man

122. MS, NLS, 527.103.   124. *Ibid.*, VI, 379.
123. Wilson, *Carlyle*, VI, 358.   125. *Conversations*, pp. 228–29.

ought to be a gentleman, and ought not to be a snob. This was about the sum of the belief that was in him. The chief skill he possessed was making wonderful likenesses with pen and ink, struck off without premeditation, and which it was found he could not afterwards improve. Jane had some of these in letters from him, where the illustrations were produced, apparently as spontaneously as the letter.

I said I was struck with a criticism which I heard Richard Doyle make on Thackeray, that he had a certain contempt for even the best of his own creations, and looked down not only on Dobbin, but even on Colonel Newcome. He was a good-natured man, however. It was notable that he had written over and over again with enthusiasm about Dickens, but I could not recall any reference to Thackeray in Dickens' writings during his lifetime, and only a lukewarm "In Memoriam" after his death.

I asked him, was it as a practical joke, or to win a bet, that Thackeray named the heroine of "Pendennis" after a famous courtesan then in London? He said he did not know anything of this, but it could scarcely be an accident with a man about town like Thackeray.[126]

From time to time through the years Carlyle had also discussed Thackeray and Dickens with Francis Espinasse, who recorded much of the conversation:

Of Thackeray's earlier performances Carlyle said that they showed 'something Hogarthian' to be in him, but that his books were 'wretched.' Of course this was before the appearance of *Vanity Fair*, the immense talent displayed in which Carlyle fully recognized, pronouncing Thackeray 'a man of much more judgment than Dickens.' Yet, when *Vanity Fair* in its yellow cover was being issued contemporaneously with *Dombey and Son* in its green one, Carlyle spoke of the relief which he found on turning from Thackeray's terrible cynicism to the cheerful geniality of Dickens. The highest praise bestowed by him on Thackeray's lectures was that they were 'ingenious.' Personally Carlyle preferred Dickens, who always treated him with deference, to Thackeray, who often opposed to his inopportune denunciations of men and things at miscellaneous dinner-parties some of that persiflage which was more disconcerting to Carlyle than direct contradiction. It was a startling parallel between two surely most dissimilar men which was drawn by Carlyle, when he once said to me, 'Thackeray is like Wilson of Edinburgh (Christopher North), he has no convictions.' Possibly this was said after Carlyle had been more than usually irritated by Thackeray's persiflage.[127]

126. *Ibid.*, pp. 77–78.
127. *Literary Recollections and Sketches*, pp. 215–16.

The same preference is indicated in what Carlyle said to Mrs. James Anstruther in 1874, to whom he spoke of Thackeray as an unsatisfactory and dissatisfied man for whose books he did not care. On the other hand, he did not like the comparisons of Dickens with Shakespeare, such as he had heard recently.[128]

With these comparisons that Carlyle made between his two old friends we may appropriately end this record of his relation to Thackeray. To attempt to arrive at general conclusions or to speak in terms of broad generalizations in dealing with the subject would be unwise and perhaps even misleading. Both Carlyle and Thackeray were far too complex in themselves and the relationship between them was too complex for such an attempt to be very convincing or profitable. We must take human nature in its individual manifestations and human relationships as they are and not mold them into the forms of logic unless they flow into them naturally. Thackeray and Carlyle were two very different human beings, different in taste and different in temperament, neither of which has much to do with logic or its processes. Thackeray could never have been or quite understood the earnest mystic that Carlyle was; Carlyle could never have been or quite understood the urbane and sophisticated artist and man of the world that Thackeray was. Yet both in their own way were artists, reformers, and haters of sham; and they found sufficient common ground to stand on for their friendship, critical as they were of one another, to be significant and in some of its most revealing incidents dramatically moving. Most important, the thundering, untamed Thor and the urbane, sophisticated London club member at their best were comrades in arms in fighting against the Philistines and against the venders of cheap tinsel wares in the glittering booths of Vanity Fair.

128. Wilson, *Carlyle*, VI, 333.

RETRACING CARLYLE'S JOURNEY
OF 1849 THROUGH IRELAND*

It was Sunday, July 31, 1960, and the London air was drenched with warm sunshine. The big Viscount plane that was to carry us to Dublin took off promptly at 6:20 P.M. As it rapidly gained altitude, England became a fairy land of green forests, yellow fields of ripening grain, and silver lakes and rivers, with the golden light raining down upon it all. It was easy to identify Windsor Castle with its spacious grounds as we flew over the River Thames toward Wales. But soon rifts of clouds appeared, and as we rose above them they shut off from time to time the view below. By the time we crossed the River Severn and were over Wales, we were able to get only occasional glimpses of the world beneath us; and by that time we were so high that the mountains of that country appeared to have flattened down to nothing. The sky opened for ten minutes over the Irish Sea, with its million wrinkles and one or two white splinters of ships breaking the uniformity of its surface. Then a really formidable cloud came between us and Dublin. It was an angry black in color, and it was high, wide, and deep. The pilot of the plane could not get above it and finally had to go around it on the right side. Even so, it could not be avoided entirely, and as we approached the Dublin airport it gave us a backlash with its tail. The heavy rain washed us down onto the landing strip with soggy grass on each side of it. The hour and a half that had passed since we left London, though eventful enough, had seemed very short.

Carlyle's journey to Ireland in July 1849 was very different. About eight o'clock one morning he got in a small boat on the Thames near his home at Chelsea, was rowed down the river a considerable distance to where a ship called the *Athlone* was waiting, and was pulled on board just before the ship sailed at ten. The small ship moved slowly down to the mouth of the Thames and then all the way along

---

* Although some of the statements and comments in this article, written in 1960, now appear dated, I am letting the article stand as first written because of the basis of comparison and contrast it provides both with the Ireland Carlyle saw in 1849 and with the Ireland of 1977 and the years to come.

the southern coast of England before it rounded Land's End and could turn northwestward across the Irish Sea. The trip from London to Dublin required four days. Carlyle could have taken a shorter route, but he chose this one in order to see the southern coast of England. In spite of its leisureliness, the journey was not without difficulties and even terrifying incidents. A drunken passenger was lost overboard one night, and all sorts of complicated situations developed among the heterogenous passengers and the crew. Carlyle considerately did not write his wife about the passenger who was drowned but waited to tell her about it after he was once more safe at home.

During the month that Carlyle was to spend in Ireland he was not to see the country at its best. Much of the misery that the Great Famine of 1846–48 had brought to it still remained. But to Carlyle the wretched conditions he saw there did not differ in kind but only in degree from similar conditions in England and other parts of the world. Ireland was to him simply the place where one could see in its worst form what was wrong with the world. He believed that such evils, wherever they occurred, were always the result of mismanagement. A Joseph, he felt sure, would never have allowed himself to become the slave of a single crop such as the potato or to be daunted by several successive years of crop failure. Mere laissez-faire, mere drifting, with an unthinking acceptance of whatever time might bring, lay at the root of most of Ireland's troubles, and England's. These came as the result of neglecting or violating basic laws and truths. One of Carlyle's chief wishes was to be able to stand on the top of Croagh Patrick on the west coast of Ireland where, symbolically emulating the example of the Saint, he could "gather all the serpents, devils, and *malefici* thither again, and rolling them up into one big mass, fling the whole safely into Clew Bay again!"

Always an admirer of Carlyle's courage, of his unwavering devotion to justice and truth, and of his unwillingness to accept excuses from those from whom the world had a right to expect deeds, I had set out to retrace his footsteps through Ireland 111 years after his journey with a suspicion in my mind that he had oversimplified his problem and its solution but also with a conviction that much might be learned from comparing what he saw and heard with what I might be able to see and hear. I had with me not only the highly interesting *Reminiscences of My Irish Journey in 1849* that he wrote out in de-

tail soon after his return but also about twenty-five letters, many of
them unpublished, collected from all over the world, with which I
had briefed myself and which would serve as basis of comparison.
Carlyle had been writing his *Cromwell* just before he went to Ireland
and was far too much inclined to see Ireland through Cromwell's eyes.
But he also saw Ireland through other eyes. For many years he had
been reading and rereading Swift, always a major influence on him.
He knew and loved Goldsmith. Among his friends, furthermore, were
some highly enlightened and competent Irishmen, Charles Gavan
Duffy, Edward Twistleton, Edward FitzGerald, and Aubrey de Vere,
who were determined that he should get the whole truth about Ireland. They had armed him with far more letters of introduction than
he was able to use, and during much of the journey Duffy served as
a guide and tour manager. With friends like these and with his own
remarkable gifts of sight and insight, Carlyle was placed in a position
to observe Ireland with unusual fullness and accuracy and to arrive
at conclusions concerning it that are well worth looking into. On the
other hand, I was aware that I possessed one or two advantages that
Carlyle had lacked. I was very fortunate in being able to read two
books by Irish friends of Carlyle who had known both Carlyle and
Ireland thoroughly and intimately, Duffy's *Conversations with Carlyle* (1892) and William Allingham's *Diary* (1907). I knew what
had happened in Ireland after Carlyle's death in 1881. I knew about
the movement that brought independence to Ireland, and about the
great cultural movement called the Irish Renaissance. To some extent I could see Ireland through the eyes of Shaw, Joyce, and Yeats.
And I had lived through two monstrous World Wars arising partly
from the assumption that it is possible to stand like Saint Patrick
upon the top of Croagh Patrick and hurl all devils at once into Clew
Bay. I had begun to doubt the soundness of the Big Splash method
of ridding the world of its evils. Yet I was by no means ready to echo
several Irishmen who told me, "Carlyle did not like Ireland," and
wanted to dismiss the subject with that. Here, too, was an over-
simplification. I was far readier to agree with Carlyle himself in
assuming that to understand Ireland was to go a long way in understanding the world.

Carlyle remained in Dublin five days, July 3–8, where he met
various Irish notabilities, including the landscape painter and anti-
quary George Petrie, was entertained at meals, and was shown the

sights. He had visited Dublin once before very briefly, in September 1846, when Duffy had taken him in hand, had introduced him to friends who were active with him in the Young Ireland movement, and had shown him Daniel O'Connell, whom Carlyle from first to last detested, speaking in Conciliation Hall. He would not have been pleased if he had known that Sackville Street, Dublin's principal thoroughfare on which his hotel, the Imperial, was situated, would have its name changed to O'Connell Street. Although he declared himself "half killed with attentions" on his 1849 visit, he seems to have had a reasonably good time. He visited the learned societies, the libraries, and the museums, at one of which he almost wept at the sight of Stella's skull, which for some reason had been dug up from its resting place beside the grave of Swift and soon was to be buried there again. At Howth he enjoyed sea bathing, a pastime in which he always took great delight. He was annoyed, however, by the way the talk had of drifting into the everlasting subject of England *versus* Ireland and by the class hatred that gave heat to most conversations. And he concluded that Dublin was not truly the capital of Ireland as London was the capital of England. Ireland, with its marked tendencies toward disintegration, lacked controlling forces that moved toward a center.

In Dublin today (1960) the subject of England against Ireland is still a live subject but one that can be discussed with much less vehemence by liberated Irishmen than in the middle of the nineteenth century. Class hatred still exists but in a much milder form. The glorification of the peasant by Synge and Yeats and of aristocrats by Yeats has helped to tear down the old distinctions. The peasant is no longer the starving underdog, and the aristocrat, whether English or Irish, is no longer the landowning robber. The aristocrats, like the aristocrats of medieval Ireland and all true aristocrats, have their horses, and very fine horses they are, symbolic of the breed of human beings to whom they belong. These, too, are rightly celebrated in Yeats's poetry. All true Irishmen love horses. When I arrived in Dublin on July 31, the Dublin Horse Show was about to begin, and for a week afterward there was almost nothing else in the newspapers. Nothing else really seemed to matter much, whether you loved horses for their intrinsic qualities or placed money on them in the races. An Irishman becomes fully alive only when his blood is galloping at a horse race. Dublin too has come into its own as a capital city since

1849. Its universities, its hotels, its Abbey Theater, and its places of amusement all pulsate with the national life and reflect a consciousness of the nation's culture.

On Sunday, July 8, Carlyle left Dublin and began his tour around the island. Moving clockwise, he spent almost a month as he moved southward through Kildare, Kilkenny, and Waterford; then westward through Lismore, Cork, and Killarney; then northeastward and north to Mallow, Limerick, Gort, Tuam, Westport, Sligo, Ballyshannon, Donegal, Letterkenny, Rathmelton, Gweedore; then eastward to Derry, where he took a steamer for Glasgow. He traveled by railway, by horse-drawn coach, and by gig, with the assistance of his various hosts and guides. In attempting to follow his route, I found that I could do so by shifting back and forth from trains to buses, very easily and conveniently done in Ireland where both services use the same stations. Occasionally, I had to rent a taxi in order to reach an out-of-the-way place.

Carlyle's first stop was at Kildare and nearby Kilcullen. His host here was Peter FitzGerald, brother of his old friend Edward Fitz-Gerald, not yet famous as the translator of *The Rubáiyát of Omar Khayyám* (1859) but known to Carlyle through Tennyson and Thackeray and through the generous help that he gave Carlyle in his work on *Cromwell*. The FitzGeralds' father owned the site of the Battle of Naseby. Peter FitzGerald, an enormously fat man, entertained Carlyle at his country house Halverstown, near Kilcullen, and took him through the Wicklow Gap to see Glendalough, in the Middle Ages St. Kevin's lovely City of the Seven Churchs in the Glen of the Two Lakes, with its lakeside cave called "St. Kevin's Bed." Here Carlyle did some not too sympathetic speculating upon the nature of medieval Catholicism and of the Roman Catholic Church in all ages. At Kildare he saw the ancient Round Tower and the ruins of St. Bridget's cathedral. He was impressed by the Curragh Race Track near Kildare, with its "5,000 acres of the richest land in Ireland," and was shown the army barracks nearby. And he saw at Kildare swarms of beggars, the worst that he saw anywhere in Ireland," "a harpy-swarm of clamorous mendicants, men, women, and children" in "a village *winged*, as if a flight of harpies had alighted in it."

Nowhere in Ireland did I find the contrast between the country in 1849 and Ireland over a century later more apparent. The Fitz-Geralds, I was told, have pretty well vanished from this region, though some of them living in England still own land here. The land upon which Halverstown stood, however, has been bought by a Scottish jam company that has built a factory near the site of the house. The old house itself has been pulled down almost entirely, only part of the drawingroom, packed with hay, remaining to suggest the elegance that was there in Carlyle's time. The rich fields around it, rather ragged and poorly cultivated when Carlyle saw them, are now producing berries in abundance for the jam factory. The Curragh Race Track, perhaps even more famous now than in 1849, still has its lovely green expansiveness, with sheep grazing everywhere. The army barracks at Curragh, which once housed hated British troops, are now being used by Irish soldiers. Some of them have gone out to help police the Congo for the United Nations. The newspapers reflect the pride that the whole nation has in them. It is very pleasant to the people of Ireland, for a change, to be helping to solve problems elsewhere in the world instead of being a problem. The ruins of the Seven Churches at Glendalough are now in the summer visited by many busloads of tourists. There is some slight and perhaps unavoidable suggestion of commercialization in the accommodations for tourists provided close by, but the two lakes and the site of the ruins must be pretty much as they were when Carlyle saw them. Probably few visitors there today would feel the Calvinistic Protestant antipathy and yet fascination for medieval Catholicism that Carlyle felt. As a matter of fact, I was told all over southern Ireland that throughout the country Protestants and Catholics live peaceably side by side, practicing mutual tolerance, and that only in Ulster did intensified ill-feeling between the two break out from time to time. A religion that does not have to fight for its life constantly may mellow and become benign. In Kildare, however, the Protestants seem to have had the better lot: they have rebuilt St. Bridget's old cathedral, which Carlyle saw in ruins, and the Catholics have had to build a new church on another site.

There are no beggars in Kildare today and very few in all Ireland. A small percentage of people are "on relief," as in the United States, and there are a few professional bums, who in all countries and economic conditions beg from choice, but Ireland has no true beggars who are the result of poverty. The Irish people are very proud of their government, which is to a considerable extent a welfare government, and have complete confidence in it. At Kildare a fairly large factory for printing wallpaper pays wages of about eleven pounds a week. Agricultural labor in the surrounding country gets almost eight pounds a week. Although these wages seem low to Americans, the balance of the economy there is such, I was told, as to make them reasonably satisfactory to the workers receiving them. Workhouses, many of which Carlyle visited in Ireland, always with disgust, have like the abject poverty that produced them all disappeared.

Carlyle was one of the great picture writers of all time, whether he was dealing with people or places. His gifts here served him well while he was in Ireland. The letters he wrote at the time and the narrative he wrote a little later are well worth reading for the brilliant pen portraits and landscape sketches that they contain. Instead of continuing to follow Carlyle step by step on his journey, a procedure that could become tedious, let us look at some of these pictures made in various places at various times. We may then examine his ideas about Ireland in the same way.

Even on board the *Athlone* as it sailed along the southern coast of England he "made out some five or six type-physiognomies" that he recognized as "specimens of Irish *classes* of faces." Three of these were particularly vivid to him: the face of "a lean withered show of a creature with hanging brows, droop nose, mouth corners drooping, chin narrow, eyes full of sorrow and rage"; the face of a mixed breed, "a blond big tiger-face," a north country face; and the face of an Irish sailor at the helm "in wig and storm hat," bulky, aquiline, and with closed mouth and a "wild cunning little eye." Then there was the face of Isaac Butt, to whom Duffy introduced him in Dublin: "a terrible black burly son of earth: talent visible in him, but still more animalism; big bison-head, black, not *quite* unbrutal: glad when he went off 'to the Galway Circuit' or whithersoever." He describes thus one of the guests at a dinner party in Dublin: "In white neck cloth, opposite side, a lean figure of sixty; wrinkly, like a washed black-smith in face, yet like a gentleman too,—elaborately washed and dressed, yet still dirty-looking." In Dublin too he met a Mrs. Hutton with "big black eyes *struggling* to be in earnest." In Kilkenny his host and hostess were the Mayor and his wife, Dr. and Mrs. Cane. Cane, "really a person of superior worth," was a "tall, straight, heavy man, with grey eyes and small globular black head; deep bass voice, with which he speaks slowly, solemnly, as if he were preaching,"—an "Irish (moral) Grandison—touch of that in him." He was greatly struck by the "strange dialect" of Mrs. Cane, who came from Scottish people. Her voice, he said, "rings with such a *lilt* in speaking as is unexampled hitherto; all is *i's, oi's*, etc;—excellent mother and wife, so far as heart goes, 'sure-ly.'" At Cork he met a "fine brown Irish figure," Denny Lane, "distiller, ex-repealer; frank, hearty, honest air; like Alfred Tennyson a little." At Cork also he found Father O'Shea, who, Carlyle always said, with Emerson had been the only two readers to recognize the merits of *Sartor Resartus* when it first appeared in *Fraser's Magazine*. Before this visit to Cork Carlyle had assumed that Father O'Shea was dead. He suddenly appeared one day at Carlyle's hotel and, much to Carlyle's astonishment, introduced himself. Carlyle described him as "a little greyhaired, intelligent-and-bred looking man, with much gesticulation, boundless loyal welcome, *red* with dinner and some wine." At Killarney he saw Shea Lawlor, "tallow-complectioned, big, erect man, with sharp-croaking Irish voice, small cock-nose, stereotype glitter of smile, and small, hard blue eyes." At King William's Town, not far from Killarney, he met a highly efficient and productive farm manager by the name of Boyne whom he greatly admired: "Remarkable Triptolemus, this Boyne.— Heavy broad man, fat big cheeks, grey beard well shaven; clean enough; smallish but honest kindly intelligent hazel-eyes and nice brows to his big round head, which he flings slightly back in speaking and rather droops his eyelids; Irish accent, copious *bubbling* speech in querulous-genial tone, wholly *narrative* in character. Simplicity, energy, eupepticity; a right healthy thicksided Irish soul; would one knew of a thousand such."

At Ballygiblin House, near Mallow, Carlyle was the guest of Sir William and Lady Beecher. Lady Beecher had been the famous actress Peggy O'Neill. He found it very difficult to like her and wrote to his wife that she was now "a most strict religious Lady, of very high poses indeed, with a sumptuous well-ordered House, and the stamp of her own rigorous correct character impressed on all her people and possessions"—that she was a woman "worth seeing once and away." He told Duffy that she had a striking figure but that she had cold cruel eyes and a silent reserved air that was altogether disagreeable.

North of Limerick he saw a sight that both amused and disgusted him: "Two drunk block-heads, stagger into a cross road to be alone; are seen *kissing* one another as we pass,— Just Heaven, what a kiss, with the drowned bog, and gaping full of ditches on each hand!"

Probably the most charming person in all Ireland to Carlyle was Lord George Hill, his host at Ballyarr House near Rathmelton. It was not merely that Lord George was giving much money and time to his efforts to improve the lot of the poor people on the coast of Donegal at Gweedore and to make their land more productive; in his appearance and personality he won Carlyle's admiration and even affection almost immediately. "Handsome grave-smiling man of 50 or more; thick grizzled hair, *elegant* club nose, low cooing voice, military composure and absence of loquacity; a man you love at first sight." He was agile, earnest, truthful, and courteous, with a long head and an "intellectually protrusive" mouth.

Through these and scores of other pen portraits Carlyle has given us a representative cross-section of the people of Ireland as he observed them on various social levels and in various activities. As I traveled around Ireland in the summer of 1960, studying faces and engaging in conversation with many people in various walks of life as I knew he had done, I more and more admired the art with which, like Chaucer in his time, he had filled his canvas with individuals who adequately represented a whole people, a whole age, and who at the same time had qualities suggesting the universal and the timeless.

In dealing with places he was not so successful, partly because he usually kept his pen reined in when treating them out of a fine scorn for what he called "the picturesque." Self-conscious followers of Wordsworth and seekers of romantic scenes and vistas had gone far in spoiling for Carlyle the pleasure he naturally and spontaneously took in such sights. It was with landscapes as it was with the fine arts in his thinking. Too much gush spoiled the effect. At Killarney, in certainly one of the most beautiful regions in the world, now sought out each summer by thousands of tourists, he wrote: "Lake clear, blue,—almost black; slaty precipitous islets rise frequent; rocky dark hills, somewhat fringed with native arbutus (very frequent all about Killarney), mount skyward on every hand. Well enough;—but don't bother me with *audibly* admiring it: Oh! if you but wouldn't!" And this is the way he wrote about the Giant's Causeway, which he saw as he was sailing from Derry to Glasgow: "Giant's Causeway, tourists dabbling up and down about in boats; Heaven be their comforter! We seem to be quite near it here, and it isn't worth a mile to travel to see." In Ireland, of all places, with its hundreds of almost unbelievably

beautiful places appealing to the romantic and the picturesque sides
of our imagination, a writer with such an attitude is handicapped, to
say the least.

A few of his descriptions of Irish places, however, do something
to make amends. Many of the details in his picture of Sligo, for instance, must have made pleasant reading for Yeats himself, who loved
the town and the surrounding country with all the passion of a great
poet and who is buried nearby at Drumcliff Church under the brow
of high Ben Bulben:

Sligo at last; beautiful descent into it, beautiful town and region altogether. Down, down, to the river bank. . . . Up, some three miles; then on
a pleasant shelf of the big hill or mountain 'Knocknarea' dividing Sligo
from the other bay, a trim fertile little estate, beautifully screened and
ornamented (or soon about to be so), a neat little country house, and
elegant welcome: thanks, thanks!

[Next day]: Fine morning, fine outlook over Sligo, bay, city, mountain
[Ben Bulben, which on the other side of the bay faces Knocknarea where
Carlyle was]; around us pretty walks and garden, with farm improvements fast progressing, behind us the mountain rises trim and green, on
the top of it an ancient *cairn*, conspicuous from afar,—which Petrie asserts
gravely to be the 'Grave of Queen Mab,'—some real old Irish 'queen' who
had grown in the popular fancy to be this! Good Petrie, he is much loved
here. . . .

Beauties of 'Hazelwood' . . . are very considerable; really fine lake (the
Lough Gill itself [which contains Yeats's Lake Isle of Innesfree]), wide
undulating park, umbrageous green-sworded, silent big house, pleasure
boats on lower *arm* of Lough, and queer windmill pump; very good indeed. . . . Part of Sligo belonged to Lord Palmerston; I didn't learn, or ask,
which part.

Yeats more than once expressed a strong dislike of Carlyle, and
such poems as his "The Curse of Cromwell" suggest the reasons. It
was natural that he should have found distasteful Carlyle's heavy-
handed Puritan emphasis upon morality and Carlyle's generally un-
sympathetic attitude toward Ireland in her relation to England. Yet
the two men had much in common. Both had faith in the peasant and
the aristocrat and suspected the shopkeeper. Both looked on the new
science as both shallow and arrogant. Both were mystics who were
also at times down-to-earth realists. And both were highly unorthodox
in religion, though deeply interested in the things of the spirit. Yeats

was wrong in implying that Carlyle had a conventional mind that accepted the platitudes and clichés of Christianity. Quite by coincidence I met at Yeats's grave a Scotchman from Ecclefechan, Carlyle's birthplace and burial place, who proceeded to tell me that in his native village Carlyle, because he had lacked an adequate religious faith, had never been well thought of by the people of the village, very few of whom attended his funeral. They had neglected to take care of his grave, the Scotchman said, and considered it unimportant. Carlyle would have understood very well, I thought, the inscription, deceptive in its simplicity, that Yeats wrote for his own tomb:

> Cast a cold eye
> On life, on death.
> Horseman, pass by!

But there was a practical side to Carlyle's mind that Yeats did not possess. Carlyle had a marked sympathy with Swift's King of the Brobdingnags, who told Gulliver that "whoever could make two ears of corn or two blades of grass to grow upon a spot of ground where only one grew before, would deserve better of mankind, and do more essential service to his country than the whole race of politicians put together." On the morning when I left Sligo and traveled by bus to Donegal, on the highway as it passed Drumcliff Church and for ten miles or so farther along to the north I was struck by numerous donkey carts, trucks, and even tractor-drawn trailors all bringing milk to a large creamery. Such evidence of economic productivity under the very shadow of towering Ben Bulben would have meant much to Carlyle, who also had not been blind to the wild grandeur that to Yeats was the glory of this country. Yeats's mind would have found gratification in the economic fact, but it would not have intensified his imagination as the sight of romantic beauty did. Carlyle's imagination responded vigorously to both. But what he looked for mainly as he toured Ireland was some evidence that the natural resources of that country were being made productive in terms of human welfare by the application of human wisdom and the work of the human hand.

Wisdom implied education and the diffusion of light. Carlyle wrote in his account of his Irish tour: "If the devil were passing through my country and he applied to me for instruction on any truth or fact of this universe, I should wish to give it to him. He is *less* a devil, know-

ing that 3 and 3 are 6, than if he didn't know it; a light-spark tho' of
the faintest is in this fact; if he knew *facts enough*, continuous light
would dawn on him, he would (to his amazement) understand what
this universe *is*, on what principles it conducts itself, and *cease* to be
a devil!" In Ireland there were abundant opportunities for enlightened intelligence and leadership to rid the country of the evils from
which it had long suffered and to make the earth more productive.
"How a man 'prints his image' here on the face of the earth," Carlyle
wrote; "and you have beauty alternating with sordid disordered ugliness, abrupt as squares in a chess-board! So all over Ireland." After
visiting Galway on the west coast, he exclaimed: "Stones, stones,—
with greenest islets here and there. Oh for men, pickmen, spademen,
and masters to guide them!" Such work was needed to mend the many
bad fences in the country: "Alas, I found the universal rule in Ireland,
not one fence in 500 that will turn." It was needed, he said, to drain
the bogs and to put lime, found in abundance all over Ireland, on
them to counteract their acid and make them agriculturally productive. It was necessary to put the rich Cevigna mines near Sligo into
operation: "Talk of the 'Cevigna mines' rich in coal and iron, say
richest; not worked, company once, 1st manager,—shot; second manager sent to Chancery; mines sleep till 'Government' make some canal
or do something."

On the positive side, Carlyle praised such work wherever he found
it already producing useful results. At Dublin he was very favorably
impressed by the Glasnevin agriculture school and model-farm producing "*anti*chaos missionaries," "practical missionaries of good order
and wise husbandry." He wished that there were a thousand such
establishments in Ireland. At Mount Melleray Monastery, near Cap-
poquin in southern Ireland, he was able to observe how monks had
been able to make their industry count in very much the same way
as had the twelfth-century English monks about whom he had written in *Past and Present*: "Banished from Mount Meilleraye in France
about 1830 for quasi-political reasons; the first of these Irishmen arrive penniless at Cork, know not what to do: a Protestant Sir Something gives them 'waste land,' wild craggy moor on this upland of
the Knockmeildowns, charitable Catholics intervene, with other help:
they struggle, prosper, and are now as we see. Good bit of ground
cleared, drained, and productive; more in clear progress thereto."
He was delighted with the work of Boyne at King William's Town:

"Boyne has now been 17 years there: a most solid, eupeptic, energetic, useful-looking man; whose *mark* stands indelible on this bog.
'Couldn't stand without sinking here, when I first came'—excellent
rye and oats growing now, hedges of thorn, bright copious green of
grass, 100 head of 'specimen cattle' (among others), clean cottage-
farms; a country beautiful to eye and mind as we drove through it
in the bright fresh evening." Similar work at Castlebar done by Lord
Lucan pleased him greatly. In Carlyle's words, Lord Lucan had said,
"Abominable bog, thou *shalt* cease to be abominable, and become
subject to man!"

The most interesting project he saw of this kind, however, was that
of Lord George Hill at Gweedore, near Bunbeg, just north of the
Rosses on the Donegal coast. Many were the social and economic
evils and great was the suffering among people in this part of Donegal
before Lord George bought about 25,000 acres there in 1838. The
land was poorly distributed and property rights were confused. There
was frequent quarreling and litigation as to trespass. The roads were
bad, and there were almost no bridges. There were no plows or carts.
There was no doctor, no store, no post office, no market for produce.
The mill was a very primitive one. There was no inn. There was no
dock where ships might tie up. There was not even hay for the cattle
and sheep. In the years just before Carlyle's visit to Gweedore Lord
George had proceeded to try to cure these evils one by one. Carlyle
saw the new mill, the dock, and the big store that he had built, and
observed the new system that he was using for distributing and im-
proving the land. He met the doctor who had been brought into the
community, and he was charmed, as we have seen, with Lord George
himself, who acted as his guide, as they traveled around over the new
roads.

But Carlyle was not completely convinced at Gweedore and kept
his fingers crossed about the ultimate success of the project. For one
thing, it was then unfinished, and he doubted whether it ever could
be finished. " 'Improvements' all are swallowed in the chaos, chaos
remains chaotic still." It was, furthermore, too quixotic, too utopian,
too softly idealistic: "On the whole, I had to repeat often to Lord
G. what I said yesterday; to which he could not refuse essential consent. His is the largest attempt at benevolence and beneficence on
the modern system (the emancipation, all-for-liberty, abolition of
capital punishment, roast-goose-at-Christmas system) ever seen by

me, or like to be seen; alas, how can it prosper; except to the soul of
the noble man himself who earnestly tries it, and works at it, making
himself a 'slave' to it these 17 years!?" The sporadic efforts of Lord
Lucan, of Boyne, and of Lord George Hill, even if each was completely successful, could come to what in the end? Not to very much,
Carlyle believed, and they could never be a substitute for what he
called "organic government," government that was vital and in its
salutary functions permeated the whole country as blood circulates
through a living body. England lacked an organic government, Carlyle declared, but he hoped that in the very near future Robert Peel
might produce one. Poor Ireland suffered from the same lack, to a
much greater extent. Peel was thrown from his horse and killed the
next year after Carlyle's journey through Ireland. Gladstone, Disraeli,
and other British prime ministers in the second half of the nineteenth
century did not for Carlyle produce an organic government, for England or for Ireland.

When I visited Gweedore in the summer of 1960, I was shown the
farms that had come into being when Lord George Hill redistributed
the land. I was shown the mill, the big store, the docks that he built.
I was shown the big house that he built to stay overnight in himself
when he would make his rather long journey from his home near
Rathmelton to Gweedore. I was also shown the church that he had
built and in which a plate commemorates him and pays tribute to
him for his great service to this community. The signs of his work
were still there, and the people still remembered him and were grateful to him.

On the other hand, I also saw signs of what Carlyle called organic
government. Much is being done to promote education in this part
of Ireland, one of the several areas in the country where the Gaelic
language and cultural traditions have lingered and have a chance to
survive. The government is also putting money into comfortable small
cottages, many of which I saw. And an electric power project has been
developed by bringing water from one river to the channel of a lower
river and releasing it near the big store built by Lord George Hill. The
countryside at Gweedore is thickly populated, and I was told that no
one who had ever lived there wanted to live anywhere else. Many of
the young men and women went to England or Scotland to work for a
while, but as soon as possible they returned to Gweedore with what

they had saved to live out their lives. Some of the great black bogs that Carlyle saw at Gweedore are still there too.

I have no doubt that if Carlyle could repeat his tour of Ireland today he would be greatly struck by the way nearly everything has changed for the better. He would be astonished and, I think, gratified that Ireland, the problem child, has produced a president of the United Nations. He would not be sure that Ireland, even today, had entirely solved its population problem. In his old age he came to look with favor on birth control. But the contentment he would find at Gweedore and the social and economic health he would find throughout most of Ireland would certainly reassure him. And though he would approve of Ireland's government as organic, I believe that he also would be a little more ready than he was in 1849 to praise the philanthropic enterprises of men like Lord George Hill. Their work is not wasted. A principle of balance, of complementary function, operates in the body politic when the relation between the government and the private citizen is at its best. Carlyle had not seen, as we have, what too much authority in the hands of someone at the head even of an organic government may lead to. But he did learn. With all his passion for heroes and things Prussian, just before his death he began to doubt the greatness of Bismarck.

Whether we can accept Carlyle's conclusions or not, we shall always find his *Reminiscences of My Irish Journey* (not in his collected works and hard to find in second-hand book catalogues and shops) and the letters that he wrote about Ireland good reading. For he wrote in the tradition of the philosophical-minded traveler, of Sir Thomas More's Raphael Hythloday, of Swift's Gulliver, and of de Tocqueville's *Democracy in America*, of those who sought for ways to improve human society. Furthermore, behind his displays of impatience and contempt there was a basic optimism: he believed that human beings could make the world much better if they would only will to do so, have courage, and use their heads. He was also, almost in spite of himself, a very great literary artist.

THE LETTERS OF JOHN STUART MILL*

The scholarship of our century excels in good editions, if in nothing else. Here is another excellent edition of letters by an important nineteenth-century writer to add to Earl Leslie Griggs's edition of Coleridge's letters, Gordon N. Ray's edition of Thackeray's letters, Gordon Haight's edition of George Eliot's letters, Cecil Lang's edition of Swinburne's letters, and others that have appeared during the past twenty-five years. Mineka and Lindley are trustworthy and enlightened editors, and there is almost nothing to complain about in these six attractive volumes. The task of collecting the letters has been done as thoroughly as possible; the authentic texts are presented on attractive pages; the notes are brief but adequate, genuinely elucidative, never ostentatious or pedantic; and the index is full and accurate. Perhaps, considering the shortcomings of our age and the inadequate command of foreign languages that otherwise competent scholars have today, all quotations not yet naturalized from foreign languages, and not just some, should have been translated for the reader. Nevertheless, with these volumes one of the most significant undertakings in the literary scholarship of the nineteenth century has been brought to a successful conclusion. Many of the approximately 2,350 letters in the six volumes have never been published before.

How much new light do these letters throw on Mill? Certainly we need as much light as we can get concerning him, for despite his lucid style, the orderly structure of his writings, and his seeming simplicity of character, he was a highly complex human being, and his mind was one of many facets and of a surprisingly large number of paradoxes. He was sophisticated intellectually, unusually complicated in his social relationships, and yet emotionally and in many respects psychologically naïve. Socially he was involved with his father James Mill, with his mother, and with a large family of brothers and sisters; with Mrs. Harriet Taylor (with whom he was in love and whom he eventually married) and her husband and children; with the Uni-

* *The Earlier Letters of John Stuart Mill, 1812–1848*, ed. Francis E. Mineka, 2 vols.; *The Later Letters of John Stuart Mill, 1849–1873*, ed. Francis E. Mineka and Dwight N. Lindley, 4 vols. (Toronto: University of Toronto Press; London: Routledge & Kegan Paul, 1963, 1972). Vols. XII–XVII of *The Collected Works of John Stuart Mill*.

tarian-Radical group headed by W. J. Fox, which included the Flower sisters, the Gillies sisters, and Mrs. Sarah Austin; with the Carlyles, John Sterling, G. H. Lewes, Robert Browning, Charles Buller, and Mr. and Mrs. Henry Fawcett. His intellectual orientation included important points of reference with Bentham, James Mill, Bacon, Aristotle, Comte, the Saint-Simonians, Coleridge, Carlyle, Tocqueville, and Wordsworth. He was not content to be merely a thinker who had established logic and economics on more rational and more valid grounds, but he also associated himself with many active enterprises and movements, such as the repeal of the Corn Laws, giving the vote and higher education to women, and through the Durham Report establishing dominion status for Canada. He was not religious, but he was fully as eager as Blake had been to see the New Jerusalem established on earth.

Gladstone dubbed him "the Saint of Rationalism," and Disraeli sneered when he first saw him in the House of Commons and called him a "finishing governess." Both missed the mark rather widely. Mill was actually in many respects a very remarkable and admirable human being, neither a saint nor an effeminate man. He openly courted another man's wife in defiance of conventions in the Victorian age; and the word *damn*, naturally and effectively employed, appears from time to time in the letters. He was a master of the scathing denunciation and did not always spare women, as some fine passages on Harriet Martineau show. His shortcomings, too, are reflected in the letters, which are not spontaneous enough and which do not glow intensely enough with the fire of humanity to be among the best literary letters. Carlyle complained to Mill that his letters were not "hearty" enough and complained to others that Mill seemed incapable of real laughter. Yet his integrity and courage were of the purest ray serene, and they proved practical even in a political campaign. When in running for a seat in the House of Commons in 1865, Mill was confronted by a sign reading, "The Lower Classes, Though Mostly Habitual Liars, Are Ashamed of Lying," at a meeting attended by many working men and was asked whether he had written the words on the sign. "I did," he replied. Another sign, soon raised near the political headquarters in Westminster, read: "If such a being can sentence me to Hell, to Hell I will go." Mill won the election. Other admirable qualities that Mill had as a human being are also clear in the letters. Two that should be mentioned are the delight he

took in studying nature and discovering views as a true disciple of
Wordsworth, and the zeal with which he collected unusual specimens
of plants for his scientific friends on his long walks in England and
France.

But perhaps the chief question that we wish to ask about Mill today is, "What kind of liberal was he?" We know that his intellectual
leanings were, in the main, toward France and away from Germany,
though he could admire Goethe and the Humboldt brothers. His mind
was truly remarkable in that it continued to grow and change through
the years without losing its central stability, assimilating important
ideas from schools of thought opposite to those that were essentially
its own. For instance, though basically a Benthamite Utilitarian, Mill
learned much from Coleridge's transcendental philosophy and liberalism, from Carlyle, and despite the secular, unreligious cast of his
mind, from F. D. Maurice's profound and subtle studies in Christian
theology and the other religions of the world. Mill's liberalism was
highly complex and not entirely in line with our current definitions
of liberalism. The word has become so slippery that scarcely any two
liberals today can agree on its meaning. Much of Mill's liberalism
would prove shocking to many so-called liberals today who assume
that liberals can flock together like sheep and in an atmosphere of
sweetness and light enjoy the peace of uniformity as they graze upon
the green grass of prosperity. The key to Mill's liberalism lies in his
emphasis upon the independent mind and unconventional conduct.
"No society," he wrote, "in which eccentricity is a matter of reproach
can be in a wholesome state." Following de Tocqueville, he warned
against "the tyranny of the majority." He was never once tempted to
believe in equality and advocated a plural system of voting based
upon education and ability. Though the word *niggers* appears from
time to time in the letters, he agreed with his friend Gustave
d'Eichthal that Western culture needed enrichment from Oriental
sources and from blacks much more than the Orient and Africa needed
missionaries. He was against the national debt (tremendous heresy
in our day) and quoted Jefferson to the effect that no generation is
entitled to mortgage the fruits of the labors of posterity. He would
not tax savings and would encourage thrift, not spending. He did not
have complete faith in free discussion: "I have not any great notion
of the advantage of what the 'free discussion' men called the 'colli-
sion of opinions,' it being my creed that Truth is *sown* and germinates

in the mind itself, and is not to be struck *out* suddenly like fire from a flint by knocking another hard body against it." He did not believe in soup kitchens. And, most shocking to those of us who like to award numerous university scholarships and fellowships, he did not approve of making the path easy for young persons of merit. "The more the path to any meritorious attainment," he wrote, "is made smooth to an individual or a class, the less chance there is of their realizing it. Never to have had any difficulties to overcome seems fatal to mental vigor." What sort of liberalism is this? Certainly not softheaded or that of a finishing governess. What sort is ours? Mill's letters are very profitable to read with such questions in mind.

Although Mill does not rank among the great letter writers of English literature, the high quality of his letters is attested to in part by the names of his correspondents: John Morley, Frederick J. Furnival, Sir William Molesworth, John Elliot Cairnes, Charles Eliot Norton, Louis Blanc, Herbert Spencer, Florence Nightingale, Edwin Chadwick, Charles Gavan Duffy, Henry and Millicent Fawcett, George Grote, Harriet Martineau, Gustave d'Eichthal, John L. Motley, and many other distinguished contemporaries. His letters to Harriet Mill (formerly Mrs. Taylor), which bulk rather large in the third volume, do not reflect what he often says about the highly intellectual quality of her mind: long as they are, they are mainly accounts of his travels, descriptions of sights seen, details concerning his botanical collections, and an abundant flow of lush sentiment. His letters to her daughter, Helen Taylor, are far more intellectual.

In general the letters show that although Mill was a very great man who had dedicated his unusual talents to making the world better, his faculties were not always harmoniously, comfortably, and effectively integrated. His emotions and his mind, for instance, were not always at peace with one another. He was not always a good judge of character: people tended to be all good or all bad in his thinking. Macaulay was to him an almost empty entity, while Cairnes, Thomas Hare, George Grote, and Chadwick were the incarnation of pure good. The letters that Mill wrote to some of his brothers and sisters soon after his marriage are shockingly harsh, angry, and severe. His tone is frequently dogmatic; though he advocates the liberal's multiple approach to truth and the free mind, once he has reached a conclusion those who disagree with him are not merely wrong but ignorantly and stupidly wrong. His condemnation of the

South during the American Civil War was completely one-sided; and his one great fear at the end of that war was that the victors would exercise too much clemency in dealing with those who had been defeated. Even St. Paul gets treated rather roughly by Mill: "I hold him to have been the first great corrupter of Xtianity. He never saw Christ, never was under his personal influence, hardly ever alludes to any of his deeds or sayings, seems to have kept aloof from all who had known him & in short, made up a religion which is Paulism but not, *me judice*, Xtianity."

Yet we must not let any personal faults that Mill's letters manifest or any disagreement that we may feel with his opinions blind us to the rich and varied substance of these letters both in terms of the wide range of topics they touch upon and the multiplicity of important ideas in them with a power to stimulate and vitalize the mind. He had a truly international outlook, and his comments on Greece, France, India, China, and Russia, not to mention the United States, are very much worth reading. He was the patron saint and chief instigator of the movement to give women equal rights with men. His contributions to the subjects of logic and political economy in his published books are well known, and the letters throw fresh light on these subjects. His proposals concerning the reform of representative government are well worth reading today. He not only enjoyed walking and view-hunting, but he was a modern ecologist as early as 1866, when he wrote: "I have all my life been strongly impressed with the importance of preserving as much as possible of such free space for healthful exercise, & for the enjoyment of natural beauty as the growth of population and cultivation has still left to us. The desire to engross the whole surface of the earth in the mere production of the greatest possible quantity of food & the materials of manufacture, I consider to be founded on a mischievously narrow conception of the requirements of human nature." And he sounds almost uncannily modern in opposing corrupt spending in elections and in government. "When a government is continually requiring its functionaries to commit rascalities for its sake, they will go on committing rascalities for their own: & there can be no publicity & no effectual system for the detection of abuse when the government itself has an interest in concealment, the funds intended for the service of the State find their way into private pockets & all who want to get rid of onerous public obligations are able to buy them off."

TENNYSON AND THE HUMAN HAND

Willa Cather, in one of her most delightful stories, "Neighbor Rosicky," gives considerable attention to farmer Rosicky's hands. His was a "warm, broad, flexible brown hand," with perhaps a touch of the Gypsy in it, "alive and quick and light in its communications." There was cleverness in it and a great deal of curiosity. But most important of all there was love in it. It expressed Rosicky's special gift for loving people, "something that was like an ear for music or an eye for color." It was quiet, unobtrusive, and always there.

Such a treatment of the human hand is by no means typical of modern literature. Miss Cather, we say, was a traditionalist among modern writers of prose fiction, somewhat inclined to deal in the sugary beautiful and the almost unbelievably admirable and good. We turn away from her to a writer who, we believe, is one of us, living in our world in our way. And the hands we find in Hemingway are likely to be either rapacious hands, hotly clutching a woman's body, or the hands of soldiers, huntsmen, and fishermen, hands that have learned to adjust themselves to the contours of guns and the barbs of giant fishhooks. Or perhaps we may prefer the marvellously skillful, dexterously mechanical, dehumanized hands grasping the test tubes in science fiction or, even more horribly, in documentary scientific pictures. But if we wish to consider some hands that will be completely adequate in representing our age, we may turn to those that T. S. Eliot's J. Alfred Prufrock speaks of wishfully:

> I should have been a pair of ragged claws
> Scuttling across the floors of silent seas.

Borrowing from the New Critics the techniques of explication that are almost guaranteed to draw rich clusters of meanings from certain poetic contexts, let us briefly interpret these lines from Eliot in terms of what is characteristic of our age. First, Prufrock thinks he should have been an animal that has become all hands, with no soul, no mind, and almost no body except for hands. He lives in a dynamic age of mighty events, when much is done and little is understood, when, as Einstein has said, the means have been perfected but the ends are confused. Second, the claws of the animal are extremely ugly and a striking symbol of what is inhuman. Third, the claws "scuttle," that is, they rush about hither and thither. Being the claws of a crab or lobster, furthermore, they dart backward more often and in a greater hurry than they move forward; and, whatever the direction, they are guided only by uncertainties and the improvised decisions of the moment as they proceed by zigzag paths. And fourth, they live in darkness on the floors of seas that permit their existence but tell them nothing.

Now Eliot himself, we know, is in considerable part a traditionalist fully aware of what human life and literature have been in past centuries. If he considers ragged claws the best symbol for Prufrock and for us, we must, I fear, assume that he has chosen the symbol knowingly and deliberately. The human hand has always been a mighty instrument and a powerful symbol, lending itself to many various situations, purposes, and needs. Chaucer's references to it are numerous and highly interesting to study. Shakespeare's plays have many references to hands. Lady Macbeth grieves because all the perfumes of Arabia will not sweeten her little hand. Hamlet, borrowing a phrase from the Church Catechism, speaks of his hands as pickers and stealers. He also tells the players not to saw the air too much with their hands but to use all gently. Emilia in *Othello* would

> Put in every honest hand a whip
> To lash the rascals naked through the world.

Othello declares Desdemona's hand "a good one, a frank one"; and she replies prettily:

> You may, indeed, say so;
> For 't was that hand that gave away my heart.

And Othello does not wish to be

> The fixed figure for the time of scorn
> To point his slow and moving finger at.

Gloucester begs to kiss King Lear's hand, and the old King replies: "Let me wipe it first; it smells of mortality." When King Lear finally wakes from his long, confused, and troubled sleep, he will not swear that his hands are his own and pricks them with a pin to make sure. In Milton there are comparatively few references to hands, and these tend to be rather general. In Sonnet 22, for instance, he will not argue against Heaven's hand or will; and at the end of *Paradise Lost*, Adam and Eve

> Hand in hand, with wandering steps and slow,
> Through Eden took their solitary way.

Boswell tells us that Dr. Johnson, even though he lived in the age of Garrick and Siddons, detested gesticulation in ordinary talk and once actually reached out, caught, and firmly held the hands of a man who would not keep them still. Keats, with a somewhat different idea in mind, tells us to imprison the soft hand of our beauty and let her rave. The references to hands in Wordsworth are rich and various.[1] Coleridge's Ancient Mariner grips the wedding guest with a skinny hand. Rossetti places three lilies in the hand of the Blessed Damozel. A minor poet of the nineteenth century declares that

> Nature's own Nobleman, friendly and frank,
> Is a man with his heart in his hand.[2]

Another minor poet of that century is equally sure that "The hand that rocks the cradle is the hand that rules the world."[3] Walter Savage Landor, who was not a minor poet or a restrained one, warmed both hands before the fire of life.

Among the greatest English poets, Chaucer, Shakespeare, and Wordsworth have given most attention to hands. And the hands in their poetry are not like the ragged claws in Eliot's poem. In their writings the hands, even when covered with blood or smelling of mortality, reflect the broad, deep, and warm humanity of the poets themselves. These were poets who had faith in human nature and even some critical affection for it. To their tradition belongs the poetry of Tennyson, whose treatment of the hand is possibly the most ingenious and delightfully various of any poet in our language. A brief examination of selected passages from his works may reflect

---

1. Wordsworth gives us, for instance, "A sleepy hand of negligence," the "kindly warmth from touch of fostering hand," and a careful hand, wilful hand, eager hand, lavish hand, venturous hand, dutiful and tender hand, practiced hand, dying hand, sparing hand, industrious hand, slack hand, unknown hand, magical hand, tremulous hand, and a withered hand. In Tennyson, as in Wordsworth, this eye for the human hand is related to an ear for the "still sad music of humanity."

2. Martin Tupper, "Nature's Nobleman."

3. William R. Wallace, "The Hand That Rules the World."

credit on the art of a poet who today is too often associated with rose-water and sugar.

Let us omit the hundreds of lines in which Tennyson uses the word *hands* idiomatically, as he does when he tells Lady Clara Vere de Vere that if time be heavy on her hands she might do something about the beggars at her gates and the poor on her lands. Yet these lines are not unimportant, for a poet's command of idiom is not unimportant. It is more interesting, however, in the work of a poet famous for his verbal pictures to study Tennyson's use of the hand for the purposes of description.

In "The Princess" we see King Gama "Airing a snowy hand and signet gem." In the same poem we have in an amusing context the Amazon bodyguard of Princess Ida:

> Those eight mighty daughters of the plow . . .
> On my shoulders hung their heavy hands,
> The weight of destiny.

In "The Princess" we also find this picture:

> Then took the king
> His three broad sons; with now a wandering hand
> And now a pointed finger, told them all.

After the battle in "The Princess" the wounded are taken care of in a place where

> Low voices with the ministering hand
> Hung round the sick.

When we go from this poem to "The Eagle," a bird that "clasps the crag with crooked hands," we are struck by the contrast between Eliot's Prufrock and Tennyson's eagle. In the one a man feels that he should be claws; in the other even an eagle has hands. Perhaps we had better close our eyes to the grim implications of the contrast. In "Maud" Tennyson speaks of the "mattock-harden'd hand" of the laborer. In "Merlin and Vivien" Merlin makes the big mistake of teaching Vivien his mighty charm "Of woven paces and of waving hands." Then there is the last wish that Elaine, in "Lancelot and Elaine," expresses to her brothers:

> Lay the letter in my hand
> A little ere I die, and close the hand
> Upon it; I shall guard it even in death.

In "Guinevere" King Arthur's hands play a part in expressing the forgiveness that he bestows upon the contrite Queen:

> And while she grovell'd at his feet
> She felt the King's breath wander o'er her neck,
> And in the darkness o'er her fallen head,
> Perceived the waving of his hands that blest.

In "Queen Mary" Cranmer remembers the dying King Edward with

> His frail transparent hand,
> Damp with the sweat of death, and gripping mine.

Frequently, however, the hands in Tennyson's poetry are not merely pictorial but are primarily intended to communicate or suggest emotion, either lyric or dramatic. It is here, to be blunt, that we may encounter Tennyson at his worst. We may find pretty-pretty verses that are nothing if not silly, as in the early "Lilian":

> Airy, fairy Lilian,
> Flitting, fairy Lilian,
> When I ask her if she love me,
> Claps her tiny hands above me,
> Laughing all she can;
> She'll not tell me if she love me,
> Cruel little Lilian.

Not much better than the hand-clapping of airy, fairy Lilian is the unmitigated bathos in another early poem, "My Life Is Full of Weary Days":

> And now shake hands across the brink
> Of that deep grave to which I go;
> Shake hands once more; I cannot sink
> So far—far down, but I shall know
> Thy voice, and answer from below. . . .
> Then let wise Nature work her will,
> And on my clay her darnel grow;
> Come only when the days are still,
> And at my headstone whisper low,
> And tell me if the woodbines blow.

We are more inclined to laugh than to weep when we encounter the sentimentalism in the following passage from "The May Queen":

> But sit beside my bed, mother, and put your hand in mine,
> And Effie on the other side, and I will tell the sign.

Nevertheless, when the lady proprietor of "The Palace of Art" claps her hands with delight as she gazes upon the glories of the place, cultured people can share her feelings. In many contexts the feeling may be Tennyson's own, as it is in "The Bridesmaid" (1872), recording his experience when he attended Emily Sellwood at the wedding of her sister to his brother in 1836. She was her sister's bridesmaid.

> And all at once a pleasant truth I learn'd,
> For while the tender service made thee weep,
> I loved thee for the tear thou couldst not hide,
> And prest thy hand, and knew the press return'd,
> And thought, "My life is sick of single sleep:
> O happy bridesmaid, make a happy bride!"[4]

Many of the references to hands in "In Memoriam" are, as we shall see, intensely personal ones based on actual experiences with Arthur Hallam. But the emotions conveyed or suggested by the hands in Tennyson's poetry are often dramatic and are highly various in the wide range they cover. In "Hands All Round," a drinking song, the hands upon the wine glasses pledge their loyalty to the Queen and their belief in Imperialism. In "Dora" when William refuses to marry Dora, his old father is "wroth" and doubles up his hands. Another old man, the fierce one in "Aylmer's Fields" in uncontrolled anger

> Under his own lintel stood
> Storming with lifted hands.

The cynical old man in "The Vision of Sin" thinks of the time of his youth:

> When thy nerves could understand
> What there is in loving tears,
> And the warmth of hand in hand.

In "Edwin Morris" a lover is confronted with "hands of wild rejection." And after the lover in "Maud" has struck down Maud's brother, he gazes down with remorse at his "guilty hand." One of the most

---

4. Compare these lines from "The Sisters": "Till that dead bridesmaid, meant to be my bride, / Put forth cold hands between us."

effectively dramatic scenes in Tennyson is that where Guinevere, jealous because she fears that Lancelot has found a new mistress in Elaine, flings herself down upon the king's great couch,

> And clench'd her fingers till they bit the palm,
> And shriek'd out "Traitor" to the unhearing wall.

Particularly interesting is the use of hands to express various emotions in "Enoch Arden." When Enoch leaves his home for the long voyage, he does not linger or draw out the farewell but

> hastily caught
> His bundle, waved his hand, and went his way.

He fails to return after a long time, and his old rival Philip generously offers to put Annie's boy and girl in school.

> She rose, and fixt her swimming eyes upon him,
> And dwelt a moment on his kindly face,
> Then calling down a blessing on his head
> Caught at his hand, and wrung it passionately.

Convinced that Enoch will never return, she finally marries Philip. But she is not happy and cannot throw off her uneasiness and misgivings:

> But never merrily beat Annie's heart.
> A footstep seem'd to fall beside her path,
> She knew not whence; a whisper on her ear,
> She knew not what; nor loved she to be left
> Alone at home, nor ventured out alone.
> What ail'd her then, that ere she enter'd, often
> Her hand dwelt lingeringly on the latch,
> Fearing to enter.

The hands in Tennyson's poetry may also indicate character. The idle, frustrated, unsuccessful poet in "Will Waterproof" sits with his

> empty glass revers'd,
> And thrumming on the table.

In "Edwin Morris" we have these lines:

> I call'd him Crichton, for he seem'd
> All-perfect, finish'd to the finger-nail.

And here is how Tennyson deals with a boring, self-satisfied orator whom he had known in the Cambridge Union:

> With a sweeping of the arm,
> And a lack-luster dead-blue eye,
> Devolved his rounded periods.[5]

He gives similar treatment to a fanatical preacher in "Sea Dreams":

> A heated pulpiteer,
> Not preaching simple Christ to simple men,
> Announced the coming doom, and fulminated
> Against the scarlet woman and her creed;
> For sideways up he swung his arms, and shriek'd.

Then there is the horrible new doctor of "In the Children's Hospital":

> Fresh from the surgery-schools of France and of other lands—
> Harsh red hair, big voice, big chest, big merciless hands!
> Wonderful cures he had done, O yes, but they said too of him
> He was happier using the knife than in trying to save the limb.[6]

We may remember, too, that the "grim Earl," husband of Tennyson's Godiva, has a heart "as rough as Esau's hand." Tennyson's Isolt of the White Hands is quiet, lovely, and submissive, very much as he had found her in medieval romance. But his treatment of some of the other characters in *The Idylls of the King* shows a real talent for characterization in which his interest in the human hand may play its part. There is a delightful passage, for instance, in which Lancelot rebukes Sir Kay, who has been mistreating Gareth, for not knowing how to tell a good man when he sees one:

> A horse thou knowest, a man thou dost not know:
> Broad brows and fair, a fluent hair and fine,
> High nose, a nostril large and fine, and hands
> Large, fair and fine.

And certainly we all remember how the dying King Arthur, his strength almost spent, says to Bedivere after he had twice failed to throw Excalibur back into the lake that if he fails again, "I will arise and slay thee with my hands." The style here has something of the

---

5. From "A Character."
6. The lines suggest Henley's "In Hospital" and his good luck in being saved by Dr. Lister from the hands of such a doctor as Tennyson describes. They also suggest that Henley's diction is not one whit firmer or more realistic than Tennyson's here.

biblical in it, something of an epic ring, and something that echoes King Lear's invincible "I kill'd the slave that was a-hanging thee."

To our age, however, with its delight in the metaphysical poetry of Donne, Hopkins, Eliot, and Yeats, probably the most interesting use to which Tennyson puts the human hand is as an image to express concepts, ideas, and abstract entities that may appear to be inexpressible. And here is precisely where Tennyson's chief strength lies. He had his metaphysic, not an original one perhaps but one that has proved itself to be of universal significance throughout many centuries and that has always had a marked affinity for new facts, problems, and ideas. Complimenting this metaphysic in Tennyson is a marked instinct and respect for the concrete, the physical, the intimate, and the human. He is, like Wordsworth's skylark, true to the kindred points of heaven and home. The hand image, therefore, serves him well here. In his well-known early poem "The Poet," he tells us, for instance, as he echoes Shelley:

> No sword
> Of wrath her right arm whirl'd,
> But one poor poet's scroll, and with *his* word
> She shook the world.

In "A Dream of Fair Women," the poem that gave us the phrase "The spacious times of great Elizabeth," we have these lovely lines:

> In every land
> I saw, wherever light illumineth
> Beauty and anguish walking hand in hand
> The downward slope to death.

Princess Ida tells women students under her, as women students should be told by their deans today, that she does not want them to be

> Laughing-stocks of Time
> Whose brains are in their hands and in their heels.

And there is a more general philosophy in "The Princess":

> This fine old world of ours is but a child
> Yet in the go-cart. Patience! give it time
> To learn its limbs: there is a hand that guides.[7]

7. A figurative application of the concept of "What does little birdie say?" that much maligned poem that has been derided as serious poetry intended for adults, although Tennyson introduces it as a cradle song in "Sea Dreams."

In "The Lover's Tale" folded hands become an ironic symbol of the futile advice that the smugly successful are ready to give to those who have met bitter failure:

> Like a vain rich man,
> That, having always prosper'd in the world
> Folding his hands, deals comfortable words
> To hearts wounded forever.

In "Lucretius," in which the philosopher had thought there would be

> Nothing to mar the sober majesties
> Of settled, sweet, Epicurean life,

the hand image is one of great power:

> But now it seems some unseen monster lays
> His vast and filthy hands upon my will
> Wrenching it backward into his; and spoils
> My bliss in being.

In the lines "To the Queen" at the end of *The Idylls of the King* we have this well-known passage:

> Or him
> Of Geoffrey's book, or him of Malleor's, one
> Touch'd by the adulterous finger of a time
> That hover'd between war and wantonness,
> And crownings and dethronements.

In "The Higher Pantheism," a poem almost ruined by Swinburne's parody, we have this perfect line:

> Closer is He than breathing, and nearer than hands and feet.

Tennyson's skill in using the human hand for the purposes of poetry cannot, however, be adequately demonstrated by references to lines from many widely scattered contexts. To see how variously, extensively, and ingeniously Tennyson uses the human hand for the purposes of achieving continuity, development, artistic unity, and accumulated power, let us therefore make a rapid examination of two of his most substantial poems, "In Memoriam" and "The Passing of Arthur."

In a sense the whole of "In Memoriam" is an expansion and development of the fine lines in "Break, Break, Break":

> But O for the touch of a vanish'd hand,
> And the sound of a voice that is still.

Behind both of these poems dealing with the death of Arthur Hallam were a real hand and voice, specific and individual, and actual experiences associated with these, remembered and cherished.[8] Tennyson could not forget, and did not want to forget, the qualities of Hallam's handclasp—quick, direct, masuline, vigorous, firm, affectionate, warm and human, the clasp of a man who was in every respect manly and who had been touched by no ascetic gloom. The man whom Tennyson admired and loved most was no Galahad. Yet "In Memoriam" is not merely a personal poem but one that, though always consistently human, has universal elements and metaphysical ideas. The hand thus may serve well here to express the personal and particular and to embody ideas that require an appropriate image for their expression. It may also bind all these component elements into one whole. As we work rapidly through the poem we find:

> But who shall so forecast the years
> And find in loss a gain to match?
> Or reach a hand thro' time to catch
> The far-off interest of tears?

The reaching hand provided Tennyson with one of his favorite images, as it did his contemporary who wrote:

> Ah, but a man's reach should exceed his grasp,
> Or what's a heaven for?

Early in Tennyson's poem, also, Sorrow, a priestess in the vaults of death, is represented as a hollow form with empty hands. A little farther along we find these lines:

> Dark house, by which once more I stand
> Here in the long unlovely street,
> Doors, where my heart was used to beat
> So quickly, waiting for a hand,
>
> A hand that can be clasped no more.

8. Note these fragmentary lines from Tennyson's notebook, winter, 1833–34, concerning Hallam: "Where is the voice I loved? ah where / Is that dear hand that I would press?" Tennyson could be almost theatrical in the significance that he attached to the handshake: "I would pluck my hand from a man even if he were my greatest hero, or dearest friend, if he wronged a woman or told her a lie." Hallam Tennyson, *Alfred Lord Tennyson: A Memoir by His Son* (London and New York, 1897), I, 107, 250.

In lyric 10 the poet's morbid and grotesque imagination places Hallam's corpse at the bottom of the sea:

> And hands so often clasp'd in mine
> Should toss with tangle and with shells.

In lyric 13 the bereaved one finds

> Where warm hands have prest and clos'd,
>   Silence, till I be silent too.

A little later he conceives an idea that, though impossible, has a gleam of cheerfulness in it:

> And if along with these should come
> The man I held as half-divine;
>   Should strike a sudden hand in mine,
> And ask a thousand things of home; . . .
>
> I should not feel it to be strange.

In lyric 21 we have some familiar lines on science:

> When Science reaches forth her arms
> To feel from world to world, and charms
>   Her secret from the latest moon.

In number 33 we have praise for what embodies the ideal in human form:

> Her faith thro' form is pure as thine,
>   Her hands are quicker unto good:
>   Oh, sacred be the flesh and blood
> To which she links a truth divine!

In number 40:

> But thou and I have shaken hands,
>   Till growing winters lay me low.

In lyric 55 Tennyson's desperate search for spiritual strength is near its nadir:

> I falter where I firmly trod,
>   And falling with my weight of cares
>   Upon the great world's altar-stairs
> That slope thro' darkness up to God,

> I stretch lame hands of faith, and grope,
>> And gather dust and chaff, and call
>> To what I feel is Lord of all,
> And faintly trust the larger hope.

In lyric 69, after the poet questions whether the springtime of his soul will ever return, an angel of the night "reach'd the glory of a hand" that seemed to touch his nature "into leaf."

In number 70, full of ghostly details, a mysterious "hand that points" directs the poet's eyes to where, beyond a confused jumble of spectral faces, they come to rest upon the fair face of Hallam. Grim also is lyric 72:

> When the dark hand struck down thro' time,
> And cancell'd nature's best.

In number 75 more than a spark of faith and courage appears:

> But somewhere, out of human view
> Whate'er thy hands are set to do
> Is wrought with tumult of acclaim.

In lyric 80:

> Unused example from the grave
> Reach out dead hands to comfort me.

Number 84:

> And He that died in Holy Land
> Would reach us out the shining hand
> And take us as a single soul.

Number 85 has the familiar lines on Hallam's death:

> In Vienna's fatal walls
> God's finger touch'd him, and he slept.

The same lyric touches upon the difficult problem of uniting the ideal with the practical:

> Yet none could better know than I,
>> How much of act at human hands
>> The sense of human will demands
> By which we dare to live or die.

In lyric 87 Tennyson revisits Hallam's old room at Cambridge, where the joyful noises of young students strike upon his ears with a pathetic irony:

> Another name was on the door;
>   I linger'd; all within was noise
>   Of songs, and clapping hands, and boys
> That crash'd the glass and beat the floor.

And in the great New Year lyric the poet prays:

> Ring in the valiant man and free,
>   The larger heart, the kindlier hand.

Hallam is praised thus in lyric 109:

> And manhood fused with female grace
>   In such a sort, the child would twine
>   A trustful hand, unask'd in thine,
> And find his comfort in thy face.

In lyric 119 the memory expressed is one that emphasizes the warm intimacy of Hallam's handclasp:

> Thy lips are bland,
>   And bright the friendship of thine eye;
>   And in my thoughts with scarce a sigh
> I take the pressure of thine hand.

In 124 we have these famous lines:

> And out of darkness came the hands
> That reach thro' nature, molding man.

And finally in lyric 129 we find these lines reassuring:

> Known and unknown; human, divine;
>   Sweet human hand and lips and eye;
>   Dear heavenly friend that canst not die,
> Mine, mine, for ever, ever mine.

Much of the essential thought of "In Memoriam" is gathered into these lines and finds its fitting sign and token in a hand that is known and unknown, human and divine, lost and found, dead and immortal.

Even more memorable and vividly, hauntingly imaginative is the use of hands in "The Passing of Arthur" (1869), which, we know, incorporates most of the lines of the "Morte D'Arthur" (1842). Tennyson owes something, of course, to his sources here; but his images far surpass anything to be found in any source. This idyll begins with King Arthur's last great battle in the west in which he slays Mordred but receives from him the wound from which he later dies. The battle had taken place beside the sea, and many of the slain are in the surf up and down the beach. Atmosphere counts for much:

> Only the wan wave
> Brake in among dead faces, to and fro
> Swaying the helpless hands.

King Arthur, attended by Sir Bedivere, thinks of his good sword Excalibur and recalls the way in which the sword came to him in happier days:

> For thou rememberest how
> In those old days, one summer noon, an arm
> Rose up from out the bosom of the lake,
> Clothed in white samite, mystic, wonderful,
> Holding the sword.

Then follows the familiar scene in which Bedivere has to be commanded three times to throw the sword back into the lake. When he fails the first time and lies about what he has done and seen, the King is disappointed and suspicious:

> For surer sign had follow'd, either hand,
> Or voice, or else a motion of the mere.

After the command is given the second time, the intensity of the debate in Bedivere's mind over whether he should obey it is indicated in part by the behavior of his hands:

> But when he saw the wonder of the hilt,
> How curiously and strangely chased, he smote
> His palms together, and he cried aloud:
>
> . . . .
>
> "The King is sick, and knows not what he does."

After Bedivere's second failure, the King threatens, as we have already seen, to rise and slay him with his hands if he fails again. All of this, of course, is excellent dramatic build-up for the third try, which is successful; and Tennyson meets the dramatic expectation of the reader with a picture that is completely adequate and satisfying. Bedivere, running and leaping lightly down the ridges, plunges into the bulrush beds. He clutches the sword; he gets a strong grip on it with both hands; he wheels like an Olympic champion throwing the hammer;[9] and he flings the sword out into the space over the lake. As Sir Bedivere says, "Then with both hands I flung him, wheeling him." And the mysterious hand clothed in white samite receives the sword just before it descends into the water:

> So flash'd and fell the brand Excalibur:
> But ere he dipt the surface, rose an arm
> Clothed in white samite, mystic, wonderful,
> And caught him by the hilt, and brandish'd him
> Three times, and drew him under in the mere.

But this is by no means the last we hear of hands in the poem. Bedivere lifts the wounded, dying King to carry him through the place of tombs:

> Kneeling on one knee,
> O'er both his shoulders drew the languid hands.

When the two reach the sea, they find a black funeral barge and on it three Queens dressed in black waiting for the King:

> There those three Queens
> Put forth their hands, and took the King, and wept.
> But she that rose the tallest of them all
> And fairest, laid his head upon her lap,
> And loosed the shatter'd casque, and chafed his hands,
> And called him by his name, complaining loud,
> And dropping bitter tears against his brow
> Striped with dark blood.

In his famous farewell words, Arthur admonishes human beings to pray:

> For what are men better than sheep or goats
> That nourish a blind life within the brain,
> If, knowing God, they lift not hands of prayer
> Both for themselves and those who call them friend.

He also suggests that he is going a long way to the island valley of Avilion where he hopes to be healed of his grievous wound. As the

9. There are two wheelings here: Bedivere wheels his whole body as he throws the sword, and the sword wheels through the air after it leaves his hands.

barge moves farther and farther out to sea until it is merely a "black dot against the verge of dawn," the poem nears its conclusion with Sir Bedivere gazing intently upon it from the highest point along the beach. As he grieves for the departing King and longs for his return, the position of his hand here helps to provide a perfect ending for the poem:

> And saw,
> Straining his eyes beneath an arch of hand,
> Or thought he saw, the speck that bare the King.

The implications of this evidence from many poems are so clear that few comments are needed, and these may be brief. We should certainly not assume that Tennyson had an obsession for the human hand. There is plenty of evidence, even in the quotations above, that he does not neglect the other parts of the body—the tongue, the lips, the eyes, the ears, the hair, the knees, the feet, and so on. A study could be written to show that the connotation of *voice* in "The sound of a voice that is still" is almost as rich and significant as that of *hand* in "But O for the touch of a vanish'd hand." Tennyson works in the humanistic tradition that gives the whole human body due respect and adequate attention.[10] On the other hand, we must not dismiss the many references to the human hand in his poetry as merely casual or as details introduced incidentally as he concentrates his talent upon other matters. The abundance and nature of the evidence will not permit such a conclusion. Tennyson was an artist, conscious of his craftsmanship, much greater and more deserving of serious study than Swinburne, or the art-for-art's-sake school at the end of the nineteenth century, or the Edwardians at the beginning of this, or even than some critics of our own day have been willing to allow. He was capable of writing passages and poems of such haunting power and beauty that, once we have read them, they remain with us the rest of our lives. He was, moreover, a master spirit, if not a respectable

10. To Tennyson, as to Browning, the ideal was not spirit discarding body but spirit and body *joined*. Hence, Tennyson's praise of Hallam as "High nature amorous of the good, / But touch'd with no ascetic gloom." The character of Galahad, therefore, confronted him with a formidable artistic problem. Galahad, the ideal knight of medieval asceticism, never really won Tennyson's sympathy; and he should be studied in conjunction with "St. Simeon Stylites," in which the poet condemns an arrogant, snobbish asceticism. The Round Table is destroyed by corruption of the flesh on one hand, and by an impractical, inhuman, impossible ascetic idealism on the other. See Hallam Tennyson, *Alfred Lord Tennyson*, I, 265.

philosopher. Certainly we should not reject him entirely because he liked sweet melody or even because he occasionally lapsed into sentimentalism. But the point is that we are giving too little consideration to the remarkable quality of Tennyson's imagination and to the artistic gifts and the insight into life that are related to it. Only when we learn again to do this will we be able to judge such an important work as *The Idylls of the King* with some degree of validity, or even read it with pleasure. Our brief examination of the human hand in Tennyson's poetry has provided us with a simple device by which we may get glimpses into the workings of that imagination, assay some of its products, discover some of the springs from which life flows into Tennyson's poetry, realize more fully the extensive range of experience, thought, and feeling from which he wrote, and reconsider an idealism that whether embodied in the laboring hand, the friendly hand, the praying hand, or the Divine Hand reaching downward, may still give comfort to the human body and strength to its spirit. Perhaps we also may have been led into a clearer apprehension of the brooding sense of humanity, with all its tangibilities and all its mysteries, that gives a peculiar value to his poetry.[11]

11. Tennyson's friend Dakyns, we are told, always stressed "the width of his humanity." *Tennyson and His Friends*, ed. Hallam Tennyson (London, 1911), p. 202. And Sir Charles Tennyson wisely concludes his biography of his grandfather with the opinion of "an acute young critic" of our time that Tennyson is "the most human of the great poets." *Alfred Tennyson* (New York, 1949), p. 541. This sense of humanity, which we too often think of merely in its emotional manifestations, is one of the chief bonds connecting such major Victorian writers as Dickens, Carlyle, Tennyson, Thackeray, Trollope, George Eliot, Ruskin, Arnold, and Hardy.

TWO KINDS OF POETRY

Let us begin with the assumption that every good poem has a center, expressed or implied—something that unifies it—the core of reality underneath its forms, its communicative processes, and its outer layers of substance. All the parts of the poem should be related to this center, connected with it, as it were, by radii. In the best poetry the center is like a ball of molten fire heating the whole poem to a semi-transparent incandescence, and is thus revealed as the fiery nucleus in the middle of the mass. The intensity of the conception or intuition making up this center determines the degree of concentration in the phrases of the poem, the relative strength and vividness of its images, the pitch of its sounds, and the power in the surge of its rhythm. It does not determine, at least directly, the kind of rhythm or the tempo.

The center reveals itself through a harmonious activity of the parts, in which lines of energy, force, and movement appear. These lines, surging with life, constitute the essence of the poem. Each line, which should coincide with a radius, has its own identity and autonomy but is connected by the center with all the other lines. One of the problems and opportunities of the poet is to give the parts their freedom and yet manage to preserve their essential unity: to preserve what is unique in each part—whatever distinguishes one part from all the other parts—so that the parts do not run together and lose themselves in the unity, and even to give to parts of particular energy and significance so much freedom and independence that they may delight the reader by threatening at times to break away from their proper radii —and yet never allow them to break completely away. To escape from its center would mean disaster for a part, for even its freedom would lose its significance if the relation of the part to the unity were destroyed.

The force within the lines, however, may move outward from the center or inward toward the center. Hence, it is possible to classify poems according to whether their movement is outward or inward. The distinction between the two kinds of poetry thus conceived is important since it is based, not on superficial considerations concerning the form and mechanics of the poem, but on a difference in the directions that the vital flow of the poem proper may take.

Both kinds of poetry actually exist in great abundance, and are clearly recognizable. The one kind is centrifugal; the other centripetal. The one is masculine; the other, feminine. The dominant process of the one is assimilation; of the other, radiation and communication. Both may be charming. The one is aggressive, masterful, and impressive; the other is alluring, captivating, seductive. The poet of the outmoving poem says to the reader: "Wait a moment. I want to walk along with you and talk." The poet of the inmoving poem whispers: "There is great meaning here. Come closer or you will miss my explanation." The outmoving poem produces the impression of letters raised upon marble; the inmoving poem produces that of lichen-filled letters deeply inscribed in the stone. The degree of intensity in the conception of the poem and of the activity involved in composing or reading it may be as great for the one kind as for the other. The degree of pleasure, likewise, may be as great in reading the one kind as in reading the other. Neither kind, therefore, is as such better than the other.

A given poet will usually be inclined to write chiefly either the one kind of poem or the other. Some poets who, in the main, have written outflowing poetry are Chaucer, Shakespeare, Ben Jonson, Gray, Coleridge, Byron, Keats, Scott, Poe, Macaulay, Tennyson, Swinburne, and Kipling. Some poets who have written inflowing poetry are Spenser, Donne, Blake, Wordsworth, Shelley, and Robert Frost. Matthew Arnold wrote both kinds: "The Forsaken Merman" and "Sohrab and Rustum" move outward; but "Resignation," "Dover Beach," and parts of "Tristram" move inward. Women may write either kind. Emily Brontë's poems move inward; but Christina Rossetti's move outward.

The inflowing poem delights us by drawing us nearer and nearer to its center: the best meanings, the most exciting activities, the most enchanting music are to be discovered as we are drawn farther and farther inward. As the radii come closer and closer together, they more and more illuminate and intensify each other. Because the dominant forces of such a poem pull inward and contract, in it the parts are likely to be more closely related, the texture of the phrases finer, and the meanings more subtle than in an outflowing poem. To read this kind of poem with full enjoyment and understanding usually requires a more alert intelligence and more penetrating perceptions than are required by the other kind.

The poet who writes outflowing poetry delights us by arousing and stimulating our receptive faculties. He meets us more than half way. To enjoy him fully we need only to respond to him willingly, sensitively, and vigorously. At its best outflowing poetry contains impulses originating in the center that are still so strong as they enter the reader's mind that he at no time senses any diminishing of vigor or activity, but rather discovers in these impulses the beginning of a whole series of processes taking place in his own mind and growing more and more delightful as he takes successive steps farther and farther away from the center of the poem, and yet enjoys a constant and secure grasp on a chain of living and interrelated processes that can carry him back to the center at any moment with swiftness and certainty.

At his worst the writer of inflowing poetry degenerates into a pure introvert or egocentric who, having allowed self to become the center of his poem, gets lost in the caverns of his own personality; or he becomes a confused guide who, forgetting his center, whatever it may be, loses both himself and his reader in his enigmas and overdelicate shades of thought, feeling, and sound. His confusion may result from an unsuccessful attempt to bring the whole world into focus through the art of the microcosm, or from his failure to provide sufficient clues to guide himself and his reader through the maze, or from his lack of the intellectual and imaginative force and perspicacity necessary to conduct the reader to a tightly crowded center.

At his worst the poet who writes outflowing poetry displays the fault of doing too much for us and of conveying to us impulses that, having reached us, lie dead, like a hard baseball caught in a mitt. His rhythms and sounds become too obvious, blatant, loud. His meanings become more and more magnified out of proportion to their importance as he gets farther and farther from the center. An overdiffuseness weakens his power; the reader becomes more and more aware of the empty space between his radii, which are themselves thin and feeble. Scott, Macaulay, Poe, and Kipling illustrate in their poorest poems the dangers to which this sort of poetry is susceptible. Most mediocre poets, including "popular" poets like Edgar Guest, Longfellow at his worst, and R. W. Service, write such verse.

Poets with little energy are more likely to succeed by writing centripetal verse, in which their power can be concentrated. Only poets of robust genius and unusual energy can write great masculine poetry such as Homer's, Vergil's, Shakespeare's, and Milton's. Interesting enough, some of the great masters of masculine poetry have so far vitalized their lines that in them two currents of unequal strength seem to be flowing in opposite directions at the same time. In Shakespeare's best passages, for instance, the great breakers of almost unlimited poetic energy move ever outward from the center of the sea and clearly dominate the verse, but beneath these one senses almost constantly the powerful pull of the undertow.

An introvert may not necessarily write poetry that flows inward. Byron was an introvert and egoist; yet the flow within his lines is ever outward, even when he himself, as is so often the case, is at the center of his poem or passage. Pope, another introvert, almost consistently wrote masculine poetry. An extrovert, however, usually writes outmoving poetry. Scott and Macaulay could write no other kind. Coleridge, in whom there was a great abundance of strong, outgiving impulses, could occasionally write verse that seems to weave inward, as do "Kubla Khan" and parts of "Christabel." But Coleridge was himself at times an introvert. Perhaps one reason why he never was able to finish "Kubla Kahn" and "Christabel" was that they ran counter to the dominant and essential currents of his life and genius, which moved outward, and he could not at will recapture the abnormal state of mind that had produced them as far as they go.

Hence, too, one explanation of the felicity of Coleridge's relation to Wordsworth. Wordsworth's was primarily a genius for assimilating the cosmos, for recollecting it in tranquility. Coleridge was for him a great stimulus, a vitalizing, awakening force, one who could energize his mind and help to bring about in it the "spontaneous overflow of powerful feelings." On the other hand, Coleridge found opportunity and stimulus in the vast, latently energetic receptivity of Wordsworth. In their relationship at its best almost unlimited abundance met almost unlimited capacity.

No better example of inmoving poetry could be given than a familiar passage from "Tintern Abbey."

> Those beauteous forms,
> Through a long absence, have not been to me

As is a landscape to a blind man's eye;
But oft, in lonely rooms, and 'mid the din
Of towns and cities, I have owed to them
In hours of weariness, sensations sweet,
Felt in the blood, and felt along the heart;
And passing into my purer mind,
With tranquil restoration: feelings, too,
Of unremembered pleasure; such, perhaps,
As have no slight or trivial influence
On that best portion of a good man's life,
His little, nameless, unremembered acts
Of kindness and of love. Nor less, I trust,
To them I may have owed another gift,
Of aspect more sublime; that blessed mood,
In which the burthen of the mystery,
In which the heavy and the weary weight
Of all this unintelligible world,
Is lightened—that serene and blessed mood,
In which the affections gently lead us on—
Until, the breath of this corporeal frame
And even the motion of our human blood
Almost suspended, we are laid asleep
In body, and become a living soul;
While with an eye made quiet by the power
Of harmony, and the deep power of joy,
We see into the life of things.

Now contrast this with Shakespeare's 116th sonnet:

Let me not to the marriage of true minds
Admit impediments. Love is not love
Which alters when it alteration finds,
Or bends with the remover to remove.
O no! it is an ever-fixed mark
That looks on tempests, and is never shaken;
It is the star to every wandering bark,
Whose worth's unknown, although his height be taken.
Love's not Time's fool, though rosy lips and cheeks
Within his bending sickle's compass come;
Love alters not with his brief hours and weeks,
But bears it out even to the edge of doom.
If this be error and upon me proved,
I never writ, nor no man ever loved.

Clearly, both poets are here concerned with the concrete expression of abstract ideas. Shakespeare, however, like his own poet whose eye

> Doth glance from heaven to earth, from earth to heaven;
> And as imagination bodies forth
> The forms of things unknown, the poet's pen
> Turns them to shapes and gives to airy nothing
> A local habitation and a name,

proceeds from the abstraction "Let me not to the marriage of true minds admit impediments," which is the center and essence of his poem, to tangible representations of the idea. First, the word *impediments* is particularized in the two concepts: (1) alteration or change and (2) complete removal of the love. Then follow a succession of images, each a kind of radius out from the central idea: the ever-fixed mark in the tempest; the pilot's trustworthy star; the rejected concept of Time's fool with its vivid related details—the rosy lips and cheeks and the bending sickle; the unavailing pressure of brief hours and weeks, and the sure persistence of true love to the very edge of doom. All of these move out from the abstract center to find a local habitation and a name for the idea, which, like love itself, does not change. The concluding couplet confirms the idea rather than adds to it, or, we may say, it neatly touches upon the end of each radius and supplies the poem with a circumference. Keats proceeds in the same manner in his sonnet on the grasshopper and the cricket, in which the first line "The poetry of earth is never dead" provides him with a center from which he works outward. Shakespeare's use of this method sometimes assumes mighty proportions, as it does in the spreading of fear, distrust, cruelty, and antisocial attitudes from a small beginning to something colossal in *King Lear*; and as it does in *Othello*, where Iago's terse statements of evil intentions develop into a veritable mountain of hideous tangibilities.

Wordsworth, on the other hand, begins with "the beauteous forms" —the lovely landscape at Tintern Abbey, or with his daffodils, or with his "meanest flower that grows," or with his highland reaper— and habitually progresses from the image to the abstraction, from the form to the idea, from the particular to the universal, from the clear tangibility to the obscure mystery, from the meanest flower to thoughts too deep for tears. He nearly always glances from earth to heaven. Observe how he goes from the scene at Tintern Abbey, first to physical "sensations sweet" made possible by memory, sensations that are felt in the blood and along the heart; then to a tranquil restoration of his "purer" mind; then to feelings of "unremembered" pleasure that help produce "nameless, unremembered" moral acts; then to the "gift, of aspect more sublime" that makes it possible, while the body sleeps, for the spirit to awaken and the power of insight to function and "see into the life of things."

Perhaps the most remarkable fact about this passage, and about all of Wordsworth's great passages of inmoving poetry, is that the writer, however far he may proceed toward the abstruse, never loses his firm grip on the good solid image with which he started. Even in heaven he never forgets earth. As a result, he is at ease even there, for he knows that he will not get lost. He is like his own skylark:

> Type of the wise who soar, but never roam;
> True to the kindred points of Heaven and home!

Blake's poetry, which, like Wordsworth's, moves farther and farther inward, sometimes illustrates what may happen to even a writer of brilliant imagination who, approaching his center, jumps from radius to radius. The image of his "Tyger! Tyger! burning bright" is, to be sure, as intensely vivid in the center of the poem as it is at the circumference; his Sunflower, likewise, is *everywhere* in the poem. But in "The Fly," after experiencing a sense of comfortable security as we journey toward what seems to be the center, we suddenly discover in the last lines that we have been unknowingly upon a radius with an entirely different center.

Finally, we may ask what value the distinction between inmoving and outmoving poetry can have for us. The distinction does, of course, deal with only one aspect of poetry and provides only one approach to the understanding and experiencing of poems. But it should be repeated that this aspect and this approach have to do with the vital element of poetry, not with its mechanism or its outline, but with the movement and life of its very substance. We cannot know a stretch of seacoast unless we know how the tides behave there. We cannot learn too much about them. But we should remember, too, that though we may learn much about tides, and profit from the knowledge, tides are mysterious things, variable and frequently unpredictable. The tides of poetry are very much like those of the sea. It is no wonder that poets are fascinated by the moon.

THE ANCIENT MARINER AND COLERIDGE'S THEORY OF POETIC ART

It has been generally assumed that if ever a volume of verse grew out of a matrix of conscious literary theory the *Lyrical Ballads* of Wordsworth and Coleridge, first published in 1798, did so. The long walks and talks among the Quantock Hills in which the two young poets delighted when they were composing the poems, the testimony they both give in letters written during this period, the statements Wordsworth made in his Preface to the second edition of the volume, and the long critique on Wordsworth and his theories of poetic art that Coleridge wrote later for the *Biographia Literaria*, all testify to the fact. That they agreed in accepting some principles and disagreed in dealing with others, as Coleridge was careful to make clear in the *Biographia*, merely reflects the stimulus that each received from their discussions, the intensity of their thought about what was to them an extremely exciting subject, and the seriousness with which each attempted to develop, clarify, and validate conceptions through his own individual thinking and writing of verse. The recognition that each of them displayed of differences of temperament, character, and cast of mind in the other did little if anything to diminish at the time the pleasure they found in one another's company and the gratification they experienced in being able to discuss, on what both considered a very high level, a subject so dear to the hearts of both of them.

Certainly it was in such an atmosphere that *The Ancient Mariner* was written. Coleridge the poet had been a theorist and experimenter for some years before he met Wordsworth, and he continued to theorize and experiment with verse as long as he lived, long after the best years of his friendship with Wordsworth; but his close association with Wordsworth at the time he was writing *The Ancient Mariner* intensified his thinking about the true nature of poetry and encouraged him to test his theories in the poem he was writing, a poem markedly different from any of its type that had been written before. Unfortunately, Coleridge did not at the time draw up a systematic statement of his ideas about poetry as Wordsworth soon did in his famous Preface of 1800; but Coleridge did say as early as the autumn of 1800, "The Preface contains our joint opinions on Poetry."[1] A little later, July 1802, he wrote, "It is most certain that that P[reface arose from] the heads of our mutual Conversations &c—& the f[irst pass]ages were indeed partly taken from notes of mine / for it was at first intended, that the Preface should be written by me."[2] During the same month he wrote Southey that the Preface was "half a child of my own Brain."[3] And although at this time, as well as years later in the *Biographia*, Coleridge took exception to some of the things Wordsworth said about the nature of poetry, it is easy to recognize in the Preface much that is clearly Coleridgean.

The point is that the basis of poetic theory which Coleridge had in mind when he wrote *The Ancient Mariner* was much broader and more complex than that indicated in his well-known statement in the *Biographia*: "My endeavours should be to persons and characters supernatural, or at least romantic; yet so as to transfer from our inward nature a human interest and a semblance of truth sufficient to procure for these shadows of imagination that willing suspension of disbelief for the moment, which constitutes poetic faith."[4] This is, of course, a wonderful statement that fits the poem perfectly; but it is very general and falls far short of being an adequate summary of all the ideas about the true nature of poetry with which Coleridge experimented in this poem.

The question naturally arises, How do we know what ideas belonging to Coleridge's theory of poetic art as explicitly stated later in his lectures, the *Biographia*, his other published writings, his notebooks, and his marginalia were already in his mind when he wrote *The Ancient Mariner*? The answer is not simple, but most assuredly, once we are thoroughly and clearly familiar with his favorite ideas about poetry, repeated many times in his later works and not difficult to grasp or remember, we are in a position to recognize them in writings roughly contemporaneous with *The Ancient Mariner*: Words-

1. *Collected Letters of Samuel Taylor Coleridge*, ed. E. L. Griggs (Oxford, 1956, 1959), I, 627. Hereinafter referred to as *Letters*.
2. *Ibid.*, II, 811.
3. *Ibid.*, II, 830.
4. *Biographia Literaria*, ed. J. Shawcross (Oxford, 1907), II, 6.

worth's Preface, his other poems, significantly including *The Prelude*
written about this time, and Coleridge's own poems belonging to this
period. Then, too, nothing is more Coleridgean than his belief that
ideas, both philosophical and aesthetic, were often prefigured in his
mind long before he found them expressed by others or rendered
them articulate himself. The letters, too, provide much help. But the
best evidence is provided by Coleridge's practice in *The Ancient Mariner* itself, a poem that, though revised from time to time, never underwent radical revision in terms of artistic principles. It may therefore be valid to set up as a working hypothesis the assumption that
most of the ideas about poetic art which Coleridge made articulate
later were in his mind (or in his instincts as an artist) when he wrote
the poem, to summarize these as clearly and briefly as possible, and
then to ascertain the extent to which Coleridge was governed by
them in writing the poem. If the ideas fit, they may be said to belong
to the poem as surely as Cinderella's slipper belonged to her. So far
as this method succeeds it may complement Lowes[5] in a modest but
useful way, since he worked forward from Coleridge's sources to the
fusion they underwent in the artistic unity of the poem, while the
present method, by concentrating on Coleridge's artistic principles,
may throw new light on just how that fusion took place.

Fundamental to Coleridge's thinking is his definition of a poem
in a well-known passage in the *Biographia Literaria*: "A poem is that
species of composition, which is opposed to works of science, by
proposing for its *immediate* object pleasure, not truth; and from all
other species (having *this* object in common with it) it is discrim-
inated by proposing to itself such delight from the *whole*, as is compatible with a distinct gratification from each component *part*. . . .
The reader should be carried forward, not merely or chiefly by the
mechanical impulse of curiosity, or by a restless desire to arrive at the
final solution; but by the pleasurable activity of mind excited by the
attractions of the journey itself."[6] Further, the poet "diffuses a tone
and spirit of unity that blends, and (as it were) *fuses*, each into each,
by that synthetic and magical power, to which we have exclusively

---

5. J. L. Lowes, *The Road to Xanadu* (Boston and New York, 1927).
6. II, 10–11. Cf. Humphry House, *Coleridge* (London, 1953), p. 149, quoting from
Notebook 18: poetry is "the Art of representing Objects in relation to the *excitability*
of the human mind . . . for the purpose of immediate pleasure, the most pleasure from
each part that is compatible with the largest sum of pleasure from the whole."

appropriated the name of imagination," a power revealing itself through many functions, among which two of the most important are the balancing or reconciling of opposite or discordant qualities and of sameness with difference.[7] Poetry is among the imitative arts, and "imitation, as opposed to copying, consists either in the interfusion of the SAME throughout the radically DIFFERENT, or of the different throughout a base radically the same."[8] In this last function, as in some of the others, poetic art may reflect the workings of Nature herself: "The requisite and only serviceable fiction, therefore, is the representation of CHAOS as one vast homogeneous drop! In this sense it may be even justified, as an appropriate symbol of the great fundamental truth that all things spring from, and subsist in, the endless strife between indifference and difference. . . . The symbol only is fictitious: the thing signified is not only grounded in truth—it is the law and actuating principle of all other truths, whether physical or intellectual."[9] Coleridge insists further: "Perhaps the most important of our intellectual operations are those of detecting the difference in similar, and the identity in dissimilar, things. Out of the latter operation it is that wit arises. . . . The true comic is the blossom of the nettle."[10]

Coleridge feels that as a poet, critic, and philosopher he is working in the tradition of Pythagoras and Plato. He asserts that his "Dynamic Philosophy scientifically arranged" will be when completed "no other than the system of Pythagoras and of Plato revived and purified from impure mixtures."[11] He accepts Pythagoras' definition of the Beautiful as "multeity in unity." "The safest definition, then, of Beauty, as well as the oldest, is that of Pythagoras: THE REDUCTION OF MANY TO ONE. . . . *The sense of beauty subsists in simultaneous intuition of the relation of parts, each to each, and of all to a whole: exciting an immediate and absolute complacency, without intervenence, therefore, of any interest, sensual or intellectual.*"[12] "To perceive and feel

7. *Biographia Literaria*, II, 12.

8. *Ibid.*, II, 56.

9. Roberta Florence Brinkley, *Coleridge and the Seventeenth Century* (Durham, N.C., 1955), p. 589. The word *homogeneity* was to Coleridge particularly applicable to Wordsworth. See *Letters*, II, 811.

10. Brinkley, p. 615.

11. *Biographia Literaria*, I, 180.

12. "On the Principles of Genial Criticism concerning the Fine Arts," printed with the *Biographia Literaria*, II, 238. Coleridge also writes in this essay: "Thus the Phi-

the Beautiful, the Pathetic, and the Sublime in Nature, in Thought,
or in Action—this combined with the power of conveying such Perceptions and Feelings to the minds and hearts of others under the
most pleasurable Forms of Eye and Ear—this is poetic Genius. . . .
To counteract this Disease [the loss of poetic power and perception]
of long-civilized Societies, and to establish not only the identity
of the Essence under the greatest variety of Forms, but the congruity
and even the necessity of that variety" is one of Coleridge's own principal aims.[13] He disagrees with John Locke's assertion that simple
ideas are adequate: "A simple Idea, as a simple Idea, cannot refer to
any external Substance, representatively: for as Pythagoras said,
nothing *exists* but in complexity."[14] Fond of the words *homogeneous*
and *heterogeneous*, he draws a distinction between the poetry of
Greek drama and that of his day in terms of them: the great rule of
Greek drama was the "separation, or the removal, of the Heterogeneous—even as the Spirit of the Romantic Poetry, is modification, or
the blending of the Heterogeneous into an Whole by the Unity of
the Effect."[15]

But fully as important, Pythagoras and Plato discovered ways to
free the mind from the dominance of the senses and to make possible
a mode of thought upon a high level of abstraction, which becomes
one of the glories of human experience. Coleridge declares:

To emancipate the mind from the despotism of the eye is the first step
towards its emancipation from the influences and intrusions of the senses,
sensations and passions generally. Thus most effectually is the power of
abstraction to be called forth, strengthened and familiarized, and it is
this power of abstraction that chiefly distinguishes the human understanding from that of the higher animals—and in the different degrees in
which this power is developed, the superiority of man over man mainly

losopher of the later Platonic, or Alexandrine school, named the triangle the first-born
of beauty, it being the first and simplest symbol of *multeity in unity*" (p. 230; see also
p. 232). Using a grotesque figure of which he was fond, he says on one occasion: "I
envy dear Southey's power of saying one thing at a time, in short and close sentences,
whereas my thoughts bustle along like a Surinam toad, with little toads sprouting out of
back, side, and belly, vegetating while it crawls." From R. W. Armour and R. F.
Howes, *Coleridge the Talker* (Ithaca, N.Y., and London, 1940), p. 32.

   13. *Inquiring Spirit: A Coleridge Reader*, ed. Kathleen Coburn (New York, 1951),
pp. 151–52.
   14. *Letters*, II, 691. This is from a letter dated 24 Feb. 1801.
   15. *Inquiring Spirit*, p. 152. See also p. 106 and *Coleridge the Talker*, p. 134. Lowes,
passim, makes much of the aurora borealis as a useful symbol to Coleridge.

consists. Hence we are to account for the preference which the divine Plato gives to expressions taken from the objects of the ear, as terms of Music and Harmony, and in part at least for the numerical symbols, in which Pythagoras clothed his philosophy.[16]

Pythagoras, he also says, included music and rhythm as a preparatory discipline "to the study and contents of mathematics," through which his pupils were to pass "on their road to wisdom or the knowledge of the immediate."[17] And he links up this principle with the understanding and appreciation of poetry. "Some persons have contended that mathematics ought to be taught by making the illustrations obvious to the senses. Nothing can be more absurd or injurious: it ought to be our never-ceasing effort to make people think, not feel; and it is very much owing to this mistake that, to those who do not think, and have not been made to think, Shakespeare has been found so difficult of comprehension."[18] Aristotle likewise affirms this principle, Coleridge says in a highly illuminating passage:

I adopt with full faith the principle of Aristotle, that poetry as poetry is essentially *ideal*, that it avoids and excludes all *accident*. [Coleridge then adds this note quoted from *The Friend*:] Paradoxical as it may sound, one of the essential properties of Geometry is not less essential to dramatic excellence; and Aristotle has accordingly required of the poet an involution of the universal in the individual. The chief differences are, that in Geometry it is the universal truth which is uppermost in the consciousness; in poetry the individual form, in which the truth is clothed. . . . [The ancients were not mere realists copying what they perceived through their physical senses.] Their tragic scenes were meant to *affect* us indeed; but yet within the bounds of pleasure, and in union with the activity both of our understanding and imagination. They wished to transport the mind to a sense of its possible greatness, and to implant the germs of that greatness, during the temporary oblivion of the worthless "thing we are," and

16. Alice D. Snyder, *Coleridge on Logic and Learning* (New Haven and London, 1929), pp. 126–27. In quoting, as we like to do, Coleridge's "I love Plato—his dear *gorgeous* Nonsense!" we should note that the letter in which he says it is very early, 31 Dec. 1796 (*Letters*, I, 295).

17. Snyder, pp. 107–108.

18. From Lecture II, 1811–12, quoted in *Samuel Taylor Coleridge: Selected Poetry and Prose*, ed. Elisabeth Schneider (New York and London, 1951), p. 393. Sir John Taylor Coleridge heard Coleridge say that he wished some portion of mathematics was more essential to a degree at Oxford, as he thought a gentleman's education incomplete without it, and had himself found the necessity of getting up a little, when he could ill spare the time (*Coleridge the Talker*, p. 157). For Coleridge's delight in playing with the number three, see *ibid.*, pp. 173–74.

of the peculiar state in which each man happens to be, suspending our individual recollections and lulling them to sleep amid the music of nobler thoughts.[19]

It follows that the writing of great poetry is a very exacting art. In a frequently quoted passage from the *Biographia*, Coleridge expresses his gratitude to his old schoolmaster James Bowyer for teaching him this lesson: "I learnt from him that Poetry, even that of the loftiest and, seemingly, that of the wildest odes, had a logic of its own, as severe as that of science; and more difficult, because more subtle, more complex, and dependent on more, and more fugitive causes."[20] Possibly Bowyer pushed his point too hard for the tender young Coleridge in his formative period. Throughout life he expresses some doubts about his own qualifications as a poet;[21] and, even though he was proud of *The Ancient Mariner*, he did not consider it a perfect poem. The perfect balance between philosopher and creative artist is very difficult to achieve. "There is no profession on earth," he says, "which requires an attention so early, so long, or so unintermitting as that of poetry; and indeed as that of literary composition in general, if it be such as at all satisfies the demands both of taste and of sound logic."[22] And he also says: "No man was ever yet a great poet, without being at the same time a profound philosopher. For poetry is the blossom and fragrancy of all human knowledge, human thoughts, human passions, emotions, language. In Shakespeare's *poems* the creative power and the intellectual energy wrestle as in a war embrace. Each in its excess of strength seems to threaten the extinction of the other."[23] John Frere reports that he heard Coleridge say: "The depravity of the spirit of the times is marked by the absence of poetry. For it is a great mistake to suppose that thought is not necessary for poetry; true, at the time of composition there is that starlight, a dim and holy twilight; but is not light necessary before? Poetry is the highest effort of the mind; all the powers are in a state of equilibrium and equally energetic, the knowledge of individual existence is forgotten, the man is out of himself and exists in all things. . . ."[24]

19. *Biographia Literaria*, II, 33.
20. *Ibid.*, I, 4.
21. See W. J. Bate, *Coleridge* (New York and London, 1965), pp. 41–42, 46.
22. *Biographia Literaria*, I, 32. Coleridge writes of Southey in 1796: "I think that an admirable Poet might be made by *amalgamating him & me. I think* too much for a Poet; he too little for a *great* Poet" (*Letters*, I, 294).
23. *Biographia Literaria*, II, 19.
24. *Coleridge the Talker*, pp. 213–14.

De Quincey, who we know was not always generous in his comments on Coleridge, testifies: "I can assert, upon my long and intimate knowledge of Coleridge's mind, that logic the most severe was as inalienable from his modes of thinking as grammar from his language."[25] Yet Coleridge always remembers Bowyer's teaching that poetry has a logic "of its own," distinct from ordinary logic; and he insists that it must use both kinds: "Poetry must be *more* than good sense, or it is not poetry; but it dare not be less, or discrepant. Good sense is not, indeed, the superstructure; but it is the rock, not only on which the edifice is raised, but likewise the rock-quarry *from* which all its stones have been, by patient toil, dug out."[26] Finally, however profound the thought of the poem may be, its tone must not be dogmatic. The tone of a poem should be dictated by the ways of the imagination, which "hovers between images" and, remaining on the wing, refuses to commit itself to "fixities and definites" as the mere fancy does, but manifests its life in its power to suggest multiple and at times ambiguous entities vital to the unity of the poem.[27] This is what Coleridge had in mind in replying to Mrs. Barbauld's objection that *The Ancient Mariner* had no moral by saying that the moral sentiment of the poem obtruded too openly on the reader for "a work of such pure imagination."[28]

Most if not all of these principles are followed in the composition of *The Ancient Mariner*. They do much to determine the quality of its artistic texture and aesthetic dynamics. In their operations they are interwoven with amazing dexterity in order to give to the reader both maximum pleasure and a deep and unforgettable sense of the theme or "truth" of the poem. This theme is not a mere "notion" of Coleridge's but a lifelong conviction that had roots deep in his own nature. It is a sense of the mysterious unity that binds together creation in all its vastness and complexity and of the infinite power that love has to vitalize and make healthy all relationships. To Coleridge this is a universal law with which the human will may place itself in

25. *Ibid.*, p. 193.
26. *Letters*, III, 470.
27. Lecture VII, 1811–12, in Schneider, *Selected Poetry and Prose*, pp. 419–20. "The deeply shaken Mariner is no philosopher, no prophet, no leader of men. He has learned a profound and simple truth. But he is not able—he is not even pretending—to explicate the entire mystery of what he has encountered. That continues to elude him. . . . It is left for the reader as well to infer or guess at them [meanings] from the greatest and certainly the most dramatic of Coleridge's poems" (Bate, p. 65).
28. From *Table-Talk*, quoted in Schneider, p. 462.

harmony and thereby work toward good; but fundamentally it is independent of the human will. In the poem neither the shooting of the
albatross nor the blessing of the water snakes is an act of will. There is
no more forethought in the shooting of the albatross than there is in
the act of a trigger-happy twelve-year-old boy who shoots a friendly
robin; but there is cruelty in it just the same, as Coleridge says in his
prose gloss, and the Mariner has violated a fundamental relation
among God's creatures that cannot, regardless of motive, be violated
with impunity. Likewise he blesses the water snakes "unaware" rather
than through conscious act of will; yet the dead albatross falls from
his neck just the same. Furthermore, Coleridge provides as the motto
of the poem a Latin quotation from T. Burnet's *Archaeologiae Phi-
losophiae* (1692), which has been translated as follows:

> I readily believe that there are more invisible beings in the universe
> than visible. But who shall explain to us the nature, the rank and kinship,
> the distinguishing marks and graces of each? What do they do? Where
> do they dwell? The human mind has circled round this knowledge, but
> never attained to it. Yet there is profit, I do not doubt, in sometimes con-
> templating in the mind, as in a picture, the image of a greater and better
> world: lest the intellect, habituated to the petty details of daily life, should
> be contracted within too narrow limits and settle down wholly on trifles.
> But, meanwhile, a watchful eye must be kept on truth, and proportion
> observed, that we may distinguish the certain from the uncertain, day
> from night.[29]

Hence, in the poem most of the action is controlled by the "Storm-
Blast," "the good south wind," "the lonesome Spirit from the south-
pole," "guardian saints," "angelic spirits" that enter the bodies of the
dead crew, the gambling of Death with Life-in-Death, and the mysterious influence and potencies of the sun and moon. All these operate
in accordance with the universal law.

And to Coleridge, although this law is fixed, it is also benign. God
was to him essentially and primarily a God of Love, not a God of
wrath and punishment.[30] The power of love and the need for it, as
many passages in his writings attest, were among the things most

---

29. The translation is from G. B. Woods, *English Poetry and Prose of the Romantic
Movement* (Chicago and New York, 1916, 1929), p. 1236.
30. See C. R. Sanders, *Coleridge and the Broad Church Movement* (Durham, N.C.,
1942), pp. 78, 184.

deeply rooted in his own nature.[31] His nature was social, and there were times when he suffered, almost as much as the Ancient Mariner on the wide, wide sea, from loneliness, whether it derived from incompatibility with his wife, misunderstandings with his friends Charles Lloyd and Wordsworth, or from many other incidents involving his relationships with other people.

Coleridge's extension of the principle of love to the lower animals was not a mere passing fancy, limited to the albatross and the water snakes in this poem. The jackass, which he hails as a brother in his much derided poem of 1794—even though the poem is amusing in its ineptness, has its place in Coleridge's affections near that of the albatross of *The Ancient Mariner.* Also in 1794, in a passage that is jocular only in part, Coleridge writes to Francis Wrangham: "I call even my Cat Sister in the Fraternity of universal Nature. Owls I respect & Jack Asses I love: for Aldermen & Hogs, Bishops & Royston Crows I have not particular partiality."[32] In 1796 he writes in another letter: "I mean to raise vegetables & corn enough for myself & Wife, and feed a couple of snouted & grunting Cousins from the refuse."[33] In *This Lime-Tree Bower My Prison* (1797), he addresses Lamb significantly:

> My gentle-hearted Charles! when the last rook
> Beat its straight path along the dusky air
> Homewards, I blest it! deeming its black wing
> (Now a dim speck, now vanishing in light)
> Had cross'd the mighty Orb's dilated glory,
> While thou stood'st gazing; or, when all was still,
> Flew creeking o'er thy head, and had a charm
> For thee, my gentle-hearted Charles, to whom
> No sound is dissonant which tells of Life.
>
> (ll. 70–78)

His delight in real nightingales, which sing joyful songs and not the sad ones of the traditional Philomela, is expressed in a poem of April 1798.[34] Coleridge read and admired William Cowper; no doubt he

---

31. "To be beloved is all I need, / And whom I love, I love indeed." From *The Pains of Sleep*, ll. 51–52. Cf. Coleridge's letter to Southey, 10 [11] Sept. 1803, in *Letters*, II, 982–84.

32. *Ibid.,* I, 121.

33. *Ibid.,* I, 277.

34. The emphasis on joy appears very early in Coleridge. "When a man is unhappy,

shared his affection for the lower animals and feeling of intimacy with them. His albatross is not a mere symbol; Coleridge belongs to the tradition of St. Francis of Assisi and Androcles.[35]

Given, then, this theme that to Coleridge relates to "truth," that is, to the way in which the universe actually does operate, and given also an albatross that Wordsworth had found in his reading, together with a dream about a specter ship that a Somerset neighbor, John Cruikshank, had related to him,[36] Coleridge proceeds to draw upon the riches of his own mind and compose a poem that will intensify the activity of the imagination by uniting the "real" with the supernatural. His problem at the beginning is to elicit from the reader "that willing suspension of disbelief for the moment" that he calls "poetic faith." This he does skillfully by starting with the usual (though highly interesting and joyful), a wedding feast; proceeding to the unusual, as the guest, who is next of kin, is stopped at the door; going then to the strange, as the mysterious-looking Mariner holds the guest first with his skinny hand and then with his glittering eye; and then to the improbable and the supernatural as the Mariner gets into his tale, which more and more as he goes along carries the listener away from the world of ordinary reality. At the end of the poem the transition back to this world uses abnormal psychology similarly in the behavior of the Hermit, the Pilot, and the Pilot's Boy as they observe the Mariner.[37] Other details in the poem also appeal to "our inward nature" and help produce that "semblance of truth" that Coleridge believes is necessary. He not only exploits the paradoxical truth that

---

he writes damn bad poetry, I find." To Southey, 21 Oct. 1794, in *Letters*, I, 116. The delight in "happy living things" is vitally related to the joy theme in all of Coleridge's poetry, coming out with great strength in *Dejection: An Ode*, lines 69–75. See House, pp. 102, 138. His insistence that nightingales sing joyful songs, we know, influenced Keats, whose nightingale is not a sad Philomela but a happy bird. It may even be possible to leap forward and link Coleridge and Keats with another great Romantic, Yeats, in whom the gaiety theme is a vital part of his philosophy of life and whose golden bird of Byzantium singing in ecstasy becomes the symbol of highest value in the art of living. For Coleridge and nightingales, see not only his two poems on the subject but *Coleridge the Talker*, pp. 283–84, and *Letters*, II, 797, and IV, 942.

35. With all his love for the lower animals, Coleridge cannot stomach Swift's reasoning horses, which to him are highly abnormal and inconsistent in their behavior. He writes: "Critics in general complain of the Yahoos; I complain of the Houyhnhnms" (*Coleridge's Miscellaneous Criticism*, ed. T. M. Raysor [Cambridge, Mass., 1936], pp. 128–30).

36. See Lowes, pp. 222–24.

37. For Coleridge on animal magnetism or hypnotism, see *Inquiring Spirit*, pp. 45–51. Cf. also his use of hypnotism in *Christabel*.

we may find our humanity in our affection for the lower animals (here
a friendly, playful albatross and water snakes beautifully alive), but
he also comforts and delights us with other details in which human
beings and their institutions are represented in a favorable light: the
wedding guest, who is thoroughly human in all his responses to the
Mariner's amazing story; the benign, sweet-natured old Hermit; the
merry minstrelsy of the wedding feast, with the bride and her brides-
maids singing together in the garden-bower (very appropriate in a
poem that has much to teach us about broadening the basis of love);
and the "goodly company" of "Old men, and babes, and loving friends
/ And youths and maidens gay" (ll. 608–609) joyfully walking together to the church, each blessed by the great Father as He bends
over them. There is much that is deeply Coleridgean in the human
side of *The Ancient Mariner*, clearly related to the thought that he
gives later to the high potentialities of man's nature, of his institutions, and of social relationships.

But the immediate object of a poem, Coleridge insists, is pleasure,
not truth; and in this respect it is one of the fine arts. It differs from
the other fine arts in that it seeks to derive as much pleasure from the
parts as the central purpose of producing maximum pleasure from
the whole will permit. The imagination is the vitalizing as well as the
unifying power, and in *The Ancient Mariner* every detail, every
image, every motion, every sound has a life of its own, whether it is
the painted ship upon the painted ocean, the death fires dancing at
night, slimy things crawling with legs upon a slimy sea, the grotesque
Nightmare LIFE-IN-DEATH, the souls of the other mariners, now dead,
whizzing like arrows from a crossbow past the Ancient Mariner, the
serenely beautiful moon softly going up the sky, the pyrotechnics in
the nighttime sky as it bursts into life and a hundred shining fire flags
hurry about, while "to and fro, and in and out / The wan stars danced
between" (ll. 316–17), or the home port with the lighthouse top, the
kirk with its steady weathercock, or the bay, clear as glass, white
with the silent light of the moon. Images often move forward, become intensely vivid, and for the moment perform the function of
musical instruments in a symphony as, one by one, they emerge from
the writhing mass of sound, play their solo parts, and then recede. An
excellent example of this is the passage beginning with line 352
("Sweet sounds rose slowly through their mouths") and ending with
line 372 ("Singeth a quiet tune") that, describing all sorts of sounds

in lovely music, contains what might almost be called a nature lyric of the first water, with a skylark, "all little birds that are" filling the sea and air with "their sweet jargoning," and "A noise like of a hidden brook / In the leafy month of June, / That to the sleeping woods all night / Singeth a quiet tune." The principle, which Coleridge knows very well must not violate Horace's dictum and merely provide a sequence of "purple patches," is not a new one but is as old as epic poetry, in which the Homeric or extended simile behaves very much the same way and performs the double function of delighting the reader with its own life and injecting new life into the poem as a whole. Coleridge uses it in many of his other poems, the best-known example being "The one red leaf, the last of its clan, / That dances as often as dance it can" in *Christabel* (ll. 49–50). Other examples are "the thin blue flame" called a "*stranger*" fluttering on the grate in *Frost at Midnight* (ll. 13 ff.) and the "tiny cone of sand" with "its soundless dance, / Which at the bottom, like a Fairy's Page, / As merry and no taller, dances still" in *Inscription for a Fountain on a Heath* (ll. 9–11).

The aesthetic dynamics of the poem are further intensified and the unity further strengthened by the full use of the principle achieving the reconciliation of opposites, which Coleridge believes is one of the most important functions of the imagination. The poem literally swarms with dichotomies, most of which could be classified as polarities: joy and sadness, solitude and sociality, the old and the young, the archaic and the modern (in language particularly), the wet and the dry, darkness and light, stillness and motion, the right and the left, the south and the north, the fast and the slow, the serenely beautiful and the grotesque, the natural and the supernatural, the living and the dead, the rotting and the vital, growing, healthy, the high heavens and the deep ocean, the fiery, hostile masculine sun and the cool, kindly feminine moon, the far and the near, diffusion and concentration,[38] vastness with its long vistas and intimacy with its sharp focus and concern for details, silence and sound, simplicity and complexity, the cold and the hot, cruelty and kindness, the human and the inhuman, the perpendicular and the horizontal. These are interwoven in a complex but unified pattern in which they are related to two other principles that Coleridge delights in theorizing about,

38. For Coleridge's marked power of compression, which suggests comparison with Yeats, see *Letters*, I, 351, and *Coleridge the Talker*, p. 134.

multeity in unity, and sameness in difference. Lowes's *The Road to Xanadu* is really a massive and monumental study of how Coleridge brings together odds and ends of raw materials gathered through his reading from the four corners of the earth in accordance with the principle of multeity in unity.[39] Combined with polarity and with what Wordsworth calls the perception of "similitude in dissimilitude, and dissimilitude in similitude," this principle produces amazing results. Often one of the entities will fan out like a peacock's tail and as a multeity display itself in various forms. Darkness tends to be homogeneous, but light assumes many shades and appearances as the sun, the moon, and the stars manifest themselves under various circumstances. Against the vast whiteness of the Antarctic ice, Coleridge gives us what is almost a complete spectrum of colors, appearing in all sorts of unexpected places throughout the poem. The dryness is intensified and is very dry indeed, while the wet assumes many forms, whether it is the thousands of acres of ice, the salt water of the sea, the pleasant dew, the blood the Mariner sucks from his arm, or the refreshing rain falling in great abundance. When the ship is becalmed, the stillness is almost unbearable and provides us with an unforgettable image of a painted ship upon a painted ocean; but against this we have an almost infinite number of expressions suggesting motion in great variety. The Storm-Blast chases the ship southward; the south wind springs up behind; the white foam flies; the furrow follows free; in reel and rout the death fires dance at night; the specter ship in the distance dodges a water sprite as it plunges and tacks and veers; its strange shape drives suddenly between the mariners and the sun; "The Sun's rim dips; the stars rush

39. In a letter of 1818 Coleridge clarifies this principle in terms of his reading of Kant, whose chief merit, he says, was that he proved, as Leibnitz and Plato were unable to, that Space and Time are "the pure a priori forms of the intuitive faculty . . . the Acts of the perceptive Power." Time, he adds, equals "unity, the point, resistance"; Space equals "Multeity, area, absence of resistance." "In the circle all possible Truths are symbolized" (*Letters*, IV, 852). In *The Ancient Mariner* the almost unlimited space does much to make possible the free movement and multeity of the poem. Coleridge preserves the time sense by references to darkness and light, day and night, and thus helps to achieve point and focus. But he does not subject Time to measurement by indicating the length of the whole or the parts of the story. Thus, he draws the parts of the poem together in a closer unity by ignoring duration in a sense and suggesting timelessness in time just as he suggests space concepts in infinite space. The Mariner also, like the Wandering Jew, suggests the same thing. One of the functions of the imagination, Coleridge says, is to reduce "succession to an instant" (*Biographia Literaria*, II, 16). Thus, he makes use of space and time without being confined by them. Cf. Shakespeare's similar use of space and time in *Othello* and *King Lear*.

out: / At one stride comes the dark" (ll. 199–200); and the specter ship shoots off over the sea; the water snakes flash their colors and coil as they swim; the upper air bursts into life, and the stars dance among the shining fire flags; in lines 324–26, "Like waters shot from some high crag, / The lightning fell with never a jag, / A River steep and wide" (a delightful polarity in which the perpendicular lighting bisects not merely a horizontal line but a whole plane); the spirit slides under the boat, and the ship for a time moves backward and forward in "a short uneasy motion" and then "like a pawing horse let go, / She made a sudden bound" (ll. 389–90) and begins to move swiftly toward the home country; it spins round and round before it sinks; and the Pilot shrieks and falls down in a fit. The differentiation of sounds is even more multifarious and ranges all the way from the cacophonous cracking, growling, roaring, and howling of the ice to the music of the wedding feast and the divine sounds of the angelic spirits that animate the bodies of the dead mariners. In its heterogeneous appeal to the ear, the poem deserves its reputation as one of the most musical poems in the English language, reflecting Coleridge's own profound love of music.[40]

There are other very important ways in which similitude in dissimilitude appears. The combination of the verse narrative with a prose gloss is an application of the principle. The poem is primarily a ballad, but it is also a travel tale and a tall tale. All three have definite conventions well established throughout the centuries. These Coleridge retains as his norms or dominants. But *The Ancient Mariner* is certainly a ballad with a difference. Not only is it much longer than most ballads, but underneath its ostensible simplicity appropriate to the ballad form is an astonishing richness and complexity. It keeps the ballad stanza as its dominant, but from time to time provides many ingenious variations in its length and pattern. It makes much of dramatic situations, as the ballad does, but not just a few as is usual with the ballad; instead it develops its story through a long, heter-

---

40. Like Tennyson and Yeats, Coleridge had no ear for music proper. Yet he enjoyed it very much, delighted in Mozart and the "dithyrambic movement of Beethoven." See *Coleridge the Talker*, pp. 434–35. Late in life (6 July 1833) he wrote: "I could write as good verses now as ever I did, if I were perfectly free from vexations, and were in the *ad libitum* hearing of fine music, which has a sensible effect in harmonising my thoughts, and in animating and, as it were, lubricating my inventive faculty" (*Miscellaneous Criticism*, p. 424).

ogeneous sequence of them. It reflects the taste of its age and imposes elements of Gothic terror on the ballad form. Most daring of all, perhaps, it imposes philosophy on it. Although like many other travel tales it manifests an affinity for the tall tale, there is not another travel tale just like it. To compare it with the *Odyssey*, More's *Utopia*, *Gulliver's Travels*, or Goldsmith's *The Traveller* is immediately to sense its difference. In its compactness, which always seems unlabored, relaxed, and easy, in the magic that runs through it, and in the spell that it weaves round a succession of unforgettable images, it stands by itself. No other poem has used repetition more variously or ingeniously, and repetition is a sameness. Not merely the conventional repetitions of prosody, such as rhyme, alliteration, assonance, and so on, which are used with countless variations of form and pattern, but words, phrases, clauses, and whole lines and sentences appear and reappear without losing their identity, in fresh attire, in a new light, with a change of context, accent, or rhythm. Here again Coleridge's method is very much like that by which great music is composed. In sharing the delight in variety characteristic of Romanticism, he generously provides many of the "tiny breezelets of surprise" that he maintains poetry should have.[41]

Although at first glance a comparison of *The Ancient Mariner* with *King Lear* may seem farfetched, in certain important respects Coleridge's poem suggests Shakespeare's great tragedy in miniature. His admiration for the play was practically unlimited. "Lear is the most tremendous effort of Shakespeare as a poet," he writes; "Hamlet as a philosopher or meditator; and Othello is the union of the two." Despite the fact that the fables with which the two work are radically different, the themes have much in common, and we discover many striking similarities of method as we go from the play to the poem. Both works deal with the compelling power of love, the necessity for broadening its basis, the contrast between compassion and inhuman cruelty, the penalty that must be paid when the great, universal law of love is violated, and the possibilities of redemption through the operation of the same law. Lear discovers that he has thought too little of this and in the midst of the storm feels deep compassion for

---

41. See Schneider, *Selected Poetry and Prose*, p. 476; and *Biographia Literaria*, II, 5. Cf. Wordsworth's delight in the sudden scene or vision and Keats's praise of "fine suddenness" in poetic art.

poor naked wretches, wherever they may be; the Ancient Mariner blesses the water snakes. Both works use animal symbolism in developing the theme, though in different ways.

It is significant that Coleridge chooses the ballad, one of the most dramatic forms of narrative poetry, for his work. He writes: "There is the epic imagination, the perfection of which is Milton; and the dramatic, of which Shakespeare is the absolute master. The first gives unity by throwing back into the distance. . . . The dramatic imagination does not throw back, but brings close; it stamps all nature with one, and that its own, meaning, as in *Lear* throughout."[42] For such a tremendous theme as these two works have, a colossal stage is required; and both works use concepts that seem to reach out into almost infinite space. But even though in them the imagination provides immeasurable vistas and the possibility of apprehending the abstract and the ideal which Coleridge says that Plato and Pythagoras attempted to achieve, they do so in accordance with the dramatic method as Coleridge describes it. Nothing could be more intimate than many of the scenes in *King Lear*, the most wonderfully intimate being that of the King's awakening and reunion with Cordelia. And the Ancient Mariner, whether he is talking to the Wedding Guest, or in the region of Antarctic ice, or in the Atlantic, or in the Pacific, is always near to the reader of a poem that never loses the sharp focus of things close to the observer.

Both works have major problems concerning probability to deal with. We have already taken note of the way in which Coleridge deals with improbability related to the extensive use of the supernatural in his poem. But he also has to deal with another improbability which, on a greatly reduced scale, reminds us of that in *King Lear* when the King, with a curse in the first act, violently disowns Cordelia, the one daughter who loved him deeply; and the whole later development of the play is made to hinge on this. Coleridge discusses this improbability in a passage beginning: "It is well worthy notice, that *Lear* is the only serious performance of Shakespeare the interest and situations of which are derived from the assumption of a gross improbability"; and he proceeds to show the soundness of

---

42. *Miscellaneous Criticism*, p. 436. Lionel Stevenson has been able to show that the poem may be classified as a dramatic monologue. See " 'The Ancient Mariner' as a Dramatic Monologue," *The Personalist*, XXX (Winter 1948), 34–44.

Shakespeare's methods in dealing with the problem.[43] The foolish action of Coleridge's Mariner in shooting the Albatross, a creature that loves him, is analogous, as is the fact that the whole later development of the tale derives from this. It is a minor point but an interesting one that both works make use of the curse as a literary device, *King Lear* very extensively; but Coleridge instead of using the violent language of Shakespeare's King places the curse in the eyes of the protagonist's fellow mariners.

It is not difficult to find examples of similitude in dissimilitude in *King Lear*. It is woven into the texture of the language; it appears in the various forms that evil assumes in Goneril, Regan, Cornwall, and Edmund, and the various forms that love and loyalty assume in Cordelia, Edgar, and Kent; and it also appears in the various ways in which the King and Gloucester are alike but different. Perhaps the most striking use of it is in the relation of the main plot to the subplot, each basically the same story dealing with the same questions as the other, but stated in different dimensions and terms.

King Lear also makes extensive use of the principle which assumes that it is one of the chief functions of the imagination to reconcile opposites. In it the central conflict, both internally and externally, is vitalized, intensified, and diversified by numerous closely related polarities: the old and the young, the human and the bestial, loyalty and treachery, the natural and the unnatural, the selfish and the unselfish, fate and free will, the healthy and the diseased, the civilized and the primitive, blunt, brief, honest speech and florid, insincere speech, the calm and the stormy, the near and the far, physical suffering and suffering in the mind and spirit, unity and disintegration, order and chaos, fear and suspicion and trust, rashness and slow deliberation, cruelty and kindness, patience and impatience, the dreadful "pudder" of a horrible storm and the healing power of sweet music and soft, kind human speech.

King Lear is a classic example of multeity in unity. Coleridge describes it as such, with "its soul-scorching flashes, its ear-cleaving thunder-claps, its meteoric splendors, . . . the contagion and fearful sympathies of nature, the Fates, the Furies, the frenzied elements dancing in and out, now breaking thro' and scattering, now hand in

---

43. *Coleridge's Shakespearean Criticism*, ed. T. M. Raysor (Cambridge, Mass., 1930), I, 59–60.

hand with, the fierce or fantastic group of human passions, crimes, and anguishes, reeling on the unsteady ground in a wild harmony to the swell and sink of the earthquake."[44] And he describes Act III, Scene IV, thus: "What a world's *convention* of agonies! Surely, never was such a scene conceived before or since. Take it but as a picture for the eye only, it is more terrific than any a Michael Angelo inspired by a Dante could have conceived, and which none but a Michael Angelo could have executed. Or let it have been uttered to the blind, the howlings of convulsed nature would seem converted into the voice of conscious humanity."[45] The dynamic action of *The Ancient Mariner* is strongly suggested in both these descriptions, emphasizing both heterogeneity and the important role that nature, the weather, the heavens, and other things beyond the control of the human will may play in the action.

This kinship with Shakespeare's great work, his most tremendous effort "as a poet," if we are willing to accept Coleridge's opinion, may, when we relate it to the fact that in *The Ancient Mariner* Coleridge embodies most of the principles that he associates with what he calls "ideal" poetry, lead us to accept the high praise Leigh Hunt bestowed upon Coleridge, almost in Hunt's own terms: "Of pure poetry, strictly so called, that is to say, consisting of nothing but its essential self, without conventional and perishable helps, he was the greatest master of his time. If you could see it in a phial, like a distillation of roses, . . . it would be found without a speck."[46] The phial is an appropriate symbol with which to represent the poet Coleridge, suggesting as it does his marked power of condensation. Equally appropriate, however, is the ocean symbol; and Coleridge's ocean in *The Ancient Mariner* is one in which the bright waters on the surface as they sparkle like champagne are delightful to behold but in which also there are almost immeasurable depths where swim the shadowy, elusive fish of meaning, for which Mr. Warren[47] and others like to cast their lures.

44. *Ibid.*, I, 109.
45. *Ibid.*, I, 66.
46. From *Imagination and Fancy* (1844), quoted by George Watson in *Coleridge the Poet* (London, 1966), p. 132.
47. R. P. Warren, "A Poem of Pure Imagination: An Experiment in Reading," in *Selected Essays* (New York, 1945–46, 1958), pp. 198–305.

INDEX

Titles of literary works are usually listed under authors.